Paranormal States

PARANORMAL STATES

Psychic Abilities in Buddhist Convert Communities

D. E. OSTO

COLUMBIA UNIVERSITY PRESS *NEW YORK*

Columbia University Press
Publishers Since 1893
New York   Chichester, West Sussex
cup.columbia.edu
Copyright © 2024 Columbia University Press
All rights reserved

Library of Congress Cataloging-in-Publication Data
Names: Osto, Douglas, 1967– author.
Title: Paranormal states : psychic abilities in Buddhist convert communities / D. E. Osto.
Description: New York : Columbia University Press, 2024. |
Includes bibliographical references and index.
Identifiers: LCCN 2024012063 (print) | LCCN 2024012064 (ebook) |
ISBN 9780231216548 (hardback) | ISBN 9780231216555 (trade paperback) |
ISBN 9780231561334 (ebook)
Subjects: LCSH: Parapsychology—Religious aspects—Buddhism. | Occultism—
Religious aspects—Buddhism. | Buddhist converts—Psychology.
Classification: LCC BQ4570.P75 O84 2024 (print) | LCC BQ4570.P75 (ebook) |
DDC 294.3/36133—dc23/eng/20240402
LC record available at https://lccn.loc.gov/2024012063
LC ebook record available at https://lccn.loc.gov/2024012064

Cover design: Noah Arlow
Cover images: Shutterstock

To Marie Marotto
(January 12, 1939, to September 13, 2021)
Artist, poet, mother

eṣaṃ pustakaṃ dvāram asti

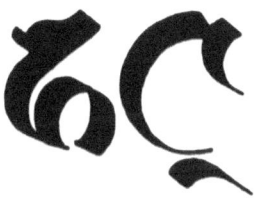

Contents

Preface xi
Acknowledgments xix

Introduction 1

ONE   The Paranormal in the Indian Buddhist Tradition   14

TWO   The Enchanted West:
The Contemporary Scientific Study of the Paranormal   42

THREE   Tales of Psychic Phenomena   70

FOUR   Tales of OBEs, NDEs, and Close Encounters   125

FIVE   The Yogin   159

SIX   The Gift   193

SEVEN   Toward a Phenomenology of the Paranormal   240

EIGHT   Autobiographical Postscript   250

Notes 279
Bibliography 303
Index 313

Preface

When I was sixteen years old, I found a little book in the basement of our house in Redding, Connecticut, about self-hypnosis, called *Scientific Autosuggestion for Personality Adjustment and Development*.[1] According to this book, hypnosis is based on the principle that when a suggestion or idea enters the mind unconsciously or consciously under favorable conditions of susceptibility or suggestibility, the person given the suggestion will carry it out automatically, as if by compulsion, as long as the suggestion does not run contrary to that person's ethical code or deep-rooted convictions. Self-hypnosis or autosuggestion occurs when someone creates a favorable condition in their own mind and plants a suggestion. Johns, the author of *Scientific Autosuggestion*, begins by emphasizing the power of imagination over the body (a power that tantric practitioners have exploited for centuries). According to the principles of suggestion, the body reacts to whatever the unconscious mind imagines or truly believes, regardless of what the conscious person may will. For instance, just about anyone could walk across a foot-wide beam placed on the ground, but place that beam a thousand feet in the air, and it is a different story altogether. Why? Most people couldn't walk across a beam that high up because they *imagine* themselves falling. First comes the image, then the body begins to tremble and shake with fear. Tightrope walkers and high-rise construction workers overcome this imaginative scenario through experience and therefore don't fear falling in the same way.

PREFACE

After reading *Scientific Autosuggestion*, I decided to conduct some of the experiments in the book with my best friend, Bob. The first was simply to place a small but heavy object on the end of a string at least eight inches long, hold it out in front of you at arm's length with your eyes closed and imagine that it is swinging back and forth. To test this, I tied some string to a pocket watch and gave it a go. After about fifteen seconds of imagining, I opened my eyes and sure enough—there was the watch swaying back and forth as if by its own power. The muscles in my hand had responded to my mental image without my conscious effort to move the watch. Next, Bob tried it and got the same result. We had found the key to a strange new reality. After this initial experiment, Bob and I took turns hypnotizing each other until we could make the other think their hands were stuck together or to the surface of a table. Although these little experiments were exciting, they were only warm-up exercises for my lifelong journey into different dimensions of consciousness.

One Sunday night after conducting our experiments for hours, after Bob left, I stayed awake late into the night sitting completely still and staring at various objects around my room. By the time I finally fell asleep, I had entered the deepest level of trance I had yet reached. The next morning when I awoke, I felt incredibly relaxed and stress free, as if a giant weight had been lifted off me. Also, everything looked different to me, as if I were in a dream. Objects appeared brighter and their edges more distinct, yet at the same time they appeared less real. Just as in a lucid dream, the objects around me seemed to lack substantiality outside of my own consciousness. This strange feeling of relaxation and heightened awareness lasted three days.

After two days of this altered state, I began to worry that I would never return to my "ordinary" state of consciousness. You might wonder why I would want to leave this new state, since it was so relaxing. I can only conclude that as prisoners of our own minds, we grow accustomed to our prison cells and find it frightening to leave. Moreover, I had no teacher or guide to lead me through this strange new psychic terrain. The magical wonderland I had entered was so different from the experience of the people around me that I began to feel alienated. The students and teachers around me at school appeared to me as if hypnotized in some kind of collective trance. So enchanted as they were by their own thoughts and concerns, they did not notice the wondrousness of the things around them. I wondered why they couldn't perceive the illusory nature of everything they took to be so real.

PREFACE

Once I "came down" from my experience, I have to admit that I was somewhat relieved to be back in the "ordinary world," although I remained extremely curious about the world beyond the mundane, and having been to that place, I held on to the memory.

Following this experience, again one evening late at night, I decided to conduct an autohypnosis experiment. I had heard stories of people who were able to relive childhood and past-life experiences through hypnosis. Fascinated by these stories, I decided to conduct one of these "regression" experiments on myself. To do this, I lay down on my bed and closed my eyes, breathing calmly and deeply. Then I began to recall the past year of my life, moving backward in time as if playing a videotape in reverse. Scenes of the past year passed before my mind's eye as I relived some of the emotions and thoughts attached to these mental images. Once I reviewed the past year, the sixteenth of my life, I went back to my fifteenth year repeating to myself, "I am fifteen, I am fifteen, I am fifteen," until scenes from the year would come to me. Of course, there were gaps in my memory—I couldn't remember everything that had happened to me when I was fifteen, only the most significant things, although trivial memories would also spring to my mind for no discernable reason.

I continued this process of moving backward in time, one year at a time, for several hours. Each time I felt that I could probe no further for a year, I would go back another one. Although part of my mind knew that I was really sixteen and lying in my bed, another part of my mind was reliving my life as the age I was remembering. Each year I went back, there were more and more gray or completely blank areas with no memories at all. Nevertheless, I kept going back to find out what would happen, thinking, "I am six," then five, four, three, and two. When I got to one year old, my hands and feet started moving about like I was a baby in my crib. While this was happening, part of mind still knew I was sixteen years old, lying in my bed, but another part of me felt exactly like a baby. I was reliving some type of muscle memory. Suddenly, a little blue ducky toy popped into my head. BAM! It was just there—a purely visual image that lasted only a fraction of a second and was gone. The image was so vivid that it shocked me out of my trance.

It had been several hours since I had started the regression, and it was about midnight. I had to work the next day, so I went to bed resolved to ask my mother about it. The next morning, I left early to work at the local grocery store. When I got home in the afternoon, I asked my mom if I'd ever had a little blue duck toy as a child. She considered it for a while and then said, "Come to think of it, you had a little blue rubber ducky bath toy you used to play with in the tub when you were about one year old." There were no pictures of this toy, and it had never been mentioned before this conversation.

After my experiments in hypnosis, I went on to learn transcendental meditation (TM) and began studying Buddhism, Zen meditation, and Isshin-ryu karate under Professor Ed Brown. An ex-Marine, Prof. Brown was a seventh-degree black belt with several world records in brick breaking. At a tournament in 1986, I watched him break sixteen chimney bricks (no spacers) with a single ox-jaw strike and set a world's record. The story I heard at the time was that physicists had constructed a brick-breaking machine that broke after eight bricks and that according to the current (scientific) knowledge of human physiology, it would be impossible for a human to accomplish such a task. This was my first experience of witnessing the "impossible" being made possible. And it left a definite impression.

The following year, I began my studies at Grinnell College in Iowa and enrolled in a course called Introduction to Psychology. During our first lecture on cognitive psychology, the professor asked if anyone in the lecture hall of about two hundred students had any childhood memories from younger than the age of three years old. Since the professor followed schema theory, which maintains memories cannot form until a schema, or mental map, develops with which to interpret them, and this was not believed to take place before the age of three, the professor was expecting no one to raise their hand. I did and then explained to him in front of the other two hundred students my experience of recalling my blue duck through autohypnosis. My story was met with deafening silence (cue the sound of crickets), the kind of polite silence that happens in an academic arena, which speaks louder than a medieval crowd shouting, "Heretic! Burn him!" Following this silent dismissal, the professor simply continued with the lecture on schema formation and conveniently ignored this piece of anomalous data.

A few weeks after this experience, I was reading Edward Conze's *Buddhist Scriptures* (1959) for my "Eastern Religions" course when I came across this passage:

> A monk who is still a beginner, and who wants to learn to remember his previous lives, should in the afternoon, after he has finished his meal, go to a solitary

and secluded spot, and enter successively into the four trances. He should then emerge from the fourth trance, which is the basis of the Superknowledges, and think of the last thing he did before his meditation, which was the act of sitting down. After that, in reverse order, think of everything he did during the day and night, i.e., how he spread the seat on which he sat down, how he entered his lodging, got ready his robe and alms bowl, the time when he ate, when he came back from the village.... In this way these things should be clear to him as if lit up by a lamp. He should furthermore think back in reverse order on what he did two days ago, three, four, and five days ago, ten days ago, half a month ago, one month ago, up to a year ago. In this manner he goes on for ten years, twenty years, and so on, until he comes to the time of his birth in this becoming, and then he should also direct his mind on the mental and physical processes which took place at the moment of his decease in his immediately preceding existence.[2]

This was the exact same regression technique I had used when I saw my blue duck!

I learned some valuable lessons from these early college experiences. First, I learned to think twice about publicly questioning the conventional (scientific) dogma or favorite theory of my academic betters based on my own experience. Second, I learned that there are things that scientists don't understand that the ancient Buddhist masters likely did. For my cognitive psychology professor, my experience of the blue duck could not be veridical because people *simply do not have* purely visual memories free of a cognitive schematic context. This is the exact same response of those skeptics who dismiss the paranormal as impossible because they believe that a priori such things *cannot* happen, therefore they *do not* happen. Thus, for the skeptic, any evidence of the paranormal must be *explained away* rather than explained. The blue duck incident was my first experience of "scientism," the dogmatic adherence to science, as opposed to true (empirically based) unbiased scientific inquiry.

While in college, my interest in Asian philosophies and meditation quickly evolved into a passion for Buddhism. I went on to major in religious studies at Grinnell, focusing on Buddhism and practicing Zen. After a Fulbright year in Sri Lanka studying Buddhism and practicing vipassana, I went on to do a master's degree in theological studies at Harvard Divinity School (1995), a master's degree in Asian languages and literature at the University of Washington (1999), and a PhD in the study of religions at the School of Oriental

PREFACE

and African Studies (SOAS), University of London (2004). During these years, I continued to practice Buddhism, explore altered states of consciousness, and along the way occasionally encounter the liminal world of the paranormal (see my autobiographical postscript for details). After a year as a teaching fellow at SOAS, I began full-time employment as a lecturer at Massey University in Palmerston North, New Zealand, where I work to this day.

In 2016, my interest in Buddhism, altered states, and psychedelic spirituality culminated in the publication of my book *Altered States: Buddhism and Psychedelic Spirituality in America*. During my research for this book, I was particularly struck by the number of people I met who described paranormal experiences they had undergone in the context of Buddhist practices entirely unrelated to psychedelic use. In one of these stories, the Bodhisattva Mañjuśrī appeared to a woman during a high fever; in another, the Buddhist goddess Tārā appeared to a man practicing tantric *sadhana* and accurately foretold major life events of the man's future; and in a third, a woman related how she'd had a full-blown spontaneous vision of the Buddha Padmasambhava (Guru Rinpoche), the legendary founder of the Tibetan Nyingma School, who imparted special teachings to her.[3] These people are successful academics and businesspeople, and their stories seemed to be sincere accounts describing profound and life-changing events in their lives. These stories and others like them, along with my own personal experiences, convinced me that there exists only the thinnest of veils between our "ordinary world" and much more mysterious realities.

Then in 2018, I read the book *Mind Beyond Brain: Buddhism, Science, and the Paranormal*, about the research conducted by the University of Virginia's Division of Perceptual Studies (DOPS), founded by Ian Stevenson in 1967.[4] Since the 1960s, DOPS has scientifically studied paranormal phenomena such as near-death experiences, past-life memories, apparitions, and psychic activity. *Mind Beyond Brain* evolved out of a daylong symposium in 2010 at Serenity Ridge Retreat Center of the Ligmincha Institute in Virginia, sponsored by Geshe Tenzin Wangyal Rinpoche, a Tibetan Bön master. Tenzin Wangyal, who moved to the United States in 1991 and founded Ligmincha in 1992, was inspired to organize this event after having learned about the unique research being conducted by DOPS. I found *Mind Beyond Brain* fascinating and was excited to learn about the current state of the art of scientific research into paranormal phenomena. However, as a Buddhist studies scholar, I was disappointed by the lack of Buddhism in the book. Missing from it were a

PREFACE

nuanced understanding of traditional Buddhist views of the paranormal and contemporary accounts of modern Buddhists and their experiences and understandings of the paranormal. Nevertheless, the book is a valuable contribution to the field for its overview of the scientific study of the paranormal and its challenge to physicalism's reduction of the mind to the brain. Moreover, it inspired me to write the current book before you, which attempts to bridge the gap between the current science of the paranormal and a more nuanced understanding of Buddhist views concerning the paranormal grounded in history, philology, and contemporary fieldwork. Thus, this book is not a scientific study but falls squarely within the realm of the humanities. The central research question driving this study is: What do contemporary Buddhists have to say about their experiences of the paranormal, and how do these narratives relate to canonical Buddhist accounts and modern scientific understandings? My hope is that this book advances the ongoing dialogue between Buddhism and science concerning the paranormal so that we may gain a deeper understanding of these profoundly transformative anomalous phenomena.

Acknowledgments

Thank you everyone who participated in the survey and agreed to be interviewed for this study. Special thanks to Rick and Kat, who really helped make this book something special, and to Jayarava of Visible Mantra (visiblemantra.org) for permission to reproduce the Siddham characters for the epigraph. Deepest gratitude and love to my wife, Trinity, and five children, Alex, Ben, Leo, Ayya, and Millie, for their undying love and support.

Introduction

THIS BOOK EXPLORES contemporary tales of paranormal experiences as narrated by convert Buddhists from around the world. To place these stories in some historical, social, and cultural contexts, I first look at two prominent approaches to the paranormal: traditional religious views found in Indian Buddhism and some contemporary (Western) scientific views. Having outlined these two different approaches, I dive into a narrative exploration of psychic abilities, out-of-body experiences, near-death experiences, and encounters with other beings, which I collected through an online survey and interviews. Following this, I focus in detail on the life stories of two of my interviewees and the important role the paranormal has played in their lives. Based on my analysis of Indian Buddhism, contemporary science, and these Buddhist stories, I suggest that future researchers of the paranormal should employ the same phenomenological approach I use here. This approach avoids both the religious dogmatism that accepts the paranormal based on faith in scripture and the scientific physicalism that dogmatically denies the reality of the paranormal. In part, this book is an argument for the phenomenological study of the paranormal ("paranormal" is a provisional term, which will be discussed in detail subsequently). My aim here is not "to prove the reality of the paranormal" but rather to demonstrate that sometimes deeply mysterious and extraordinary experiences take place for contemporary convert Buddhists that exceed our current understandings (scientific or otherwise) and that these events can productively be interpreted within the context of living Buddhist folklore.

While "proof" works quite well in mathematics and deductive logic, the "real world" appears to me much too messy for proving anything. A good empiricist can only assume that certain events or phenomena are more or less likely to happen. While some events are much more probable than others—the chance of the sun rising tomorrow morning I imagine is significantly greater than someone's chances of winning the lottery—this does not mean, however, that no one ever wins the lottery! Likewise, people do occasionally get struck by lightning or experience paranormal phenomena.[1] While anomalous phenomena such as psi, apparitions, precognition, and past-life memories are indeed rather rare, stories about them likely have been a part of the human experience since we uttered our first words. In the following pages, I investigate numerous contemporary convert Buddhist accounts of such events. These are "Buddhist" in the sense that they have been (or came to be) interpreted through a Buddhist lens and find their meanings and significance within a Buddhist universe.

What Is "Paranormal"?

The *Oxford English Dictionary* defines "paranormal" as "designating supposed psychical events and phenomena such as clairvoyance or telekinesis whose operation is outside the scope of the known laws of nature or of normal scientific understanding; of or relating to such phenomena."[2] The *OED* then attributes an early use of the word to L. I. Finch in his translation (1905) of J. Maxwell et al.'s *Metapsychical Phenomena*.[3] Thus, the term "paranormal" has only been in common usage in the English language for little more than a century. Before this time, a cluster of other English terms for anomalous phenomena were employed, such as "supernatural," "psychic" (as in "psychic phenomena"), "spiritual" (in spiritualism or mediumship), "demonic" (Catholic demonology), "angelic" (Catholic angelology), "magical," and "miraculous," among other terms. In premodern Europe, these phenomena tended to be divided into magic or witchcraft, which was demonically inspired or empowered, and divine "gifts" or "charisms" from God or the saints.

INTRODUCTION

Alongside this dichotomy existed the rich lexicons of hermetic and alchemical traditions typified by figures like John Dee (1527–1609), famous for his mathematical ability, astronomical observations, alchemical and astrological knowledge, and skill at conjuring spirits. In the premodern South Asian context, terms such as Sanskrit *ṛddhi* (Pāli: *iddhi*) and *siddhi* were commonly employed for certain psychic powers and abilities attained through the practice of yoga. Alongside these were numerous magical abilities and powers, which were referred to by many names. In premodern societies throughout the world, human encounters with nonhuman spirits, ghosts, demons, gods, and countless other creatures were often an integral ("normal") part of societies' cosmologies and worldviews, and therefore these encounters do not map easily onto contemporary English terms such as "paranormal," "supernatural," or "spiritual" encounters.

While recognizing that words have genealogies and are not value neutral, as an expedience I use "paranormal" as a generally recognized and commonly used English term for a host of phenomena that occur and have occurred throughout the world and human history. In the current study, I primarily use "paranormal" in the *OED*'s sense and focus on accounts of psi (psychic) phenomena, such as clairvoyance, telepathy, precognition, retrocognition (remembrance of past lives), out-of-body experiences (OBEs), and near-death experiences (NDEs), as well as for human encounters with other beings such as spirits, ghosts, demons, divinities, and Buddhist holy beings. By using this term, I do not mean to "whitewash" important differences in religious and cultural interpretations of such phenomena. Where closer linguistic and contextual analysis is required, I endeavor to employ whatever philological, anthropological, and textual skills I possess to provide the necessary nuance. This said, however, I do believe that, for example, whether we call the power to discern another's thoughts "telepathy" or something else does not change the fact that very similar abilities have been reported transhistorically and transculturally since humans began telling stories.[4] The current study aims to illuminate the continuities and discontinuities of these kinds of narratives primarily for contemporary convert Buddhists and their ancient Indian forebears. Through such an endeavor I seek greater understanding of these phenomena and the role stories about such events play within the Buddhist traditions, both ancient and modern.

INTRODUCTION

A Buddhist Phenomenological Approach

In the following pages, I attempt neither to prove nor disprove scientifically the reality of the paranormal stories narrated herein, nor do I employ constructivism to reduce these anomalous phenomena to mere storytelling and fantasy. For all its dazzling successes, modern science is too restrictive a lens with which to study these accounts; likewise, constructivist approaches that attempt to reduce them to a social *imaginaire* are too domesticating of their weirdness. To steer a middle path between the objective "scientific" study of the paranormal and the social-constructivist accounts, I draw on the phenomenology of Maurice Merleau-Ponty and Mahāyāna Buddhism. In *The Phenomenology of Perception*, Merleau-Ponty asserts that both the "objective world" and the "subjective world" are abstractions from a more immediate embodied lifeworld wherein meaning, interpretation, and things are inextricably intertwined.[5] And as Jeffrey Kripal has shown, nowhere is this entanglement more clearly witnessed than in experiences of the paranormal.[6] Thus, by phenomenologically investigating some extraordinary experiences of contemporary Buddhists, we can capture some of the richness and deep significance of these events for their experiencers and situate them within the larger contexts of modern religious life and traditional Buddhist understandings.

According to Merleau-Ponty, our lived bodies are characterized as "being in the world," and therefore we exist "in and toward the world," which can be neither abstracted as the objective world of a materialist science nor viewed idealistically as a product of some type of transcendental consciousness. In the preface to *The Phenomenology of Perception*, Merleau-Ponty writes:

> Phenomenology's most important accomplishment is, it would seem, to have joined an extreme subjectivism with an extreme objectivism through its concept of the world or of rationality. Rationality fits precisely to the experiences in which it is revealed. There is rationality—that is, perspectives intersect, perceptions confirm each other, and a sense appears. But this sense must not be separated, transformed into an absolute Spirit, or transformed into a world in the realist sense. The phenomenological world is not pure being, but rather the sense that shines forth at the intersection of my experiences and at the intersection of my experiences with those of others through a sort of gearing into each other. The phenomenological world is thus inseparable from subjectivity and

intersubjectivity, which establish their unity through the taking up [*la reprise*] of my past experiences into my present experiences, or of the other person's experience into my own.[7]

Here we see the emphasis is clearly on experience—rationality or "the world" arises intersubjectively from our shared experiences "gearing into each other" and a kind of merging of past experiences with present ones. For Merleau-Ponty, this world "is not what I think, but what I live [*ce que je vis*]; I am open to the world, I unquestionably communicate with it, but I do not possess it, it is inexhaustible."[8] From this inexhaustible well springs forth experience, meaning, rationality, objects, bodies, consciousness, and intentionality, which are all inextricably woven into one another. As lived bodies existing in and toward the world, we can never completely extricate the objective from the subjective, the subjective from the intersubjective, facts from interpretations, or observations from theory. In Merleau-Ponty's words, "Because we are in the world, we are *condemned to sense*, and there is nothing we can do or say that does not acquire a name in history."[9]

This world we live in is not some objectively real world "out there," naively assumed or abstracted from positivistic or materialistic science, but the "lifeworld" of our everyday lives fully enmeshed with our hopes, dreams, values, communities, histories, and physical environments. Our consciousnesses, our subjectivities, our bodies, and our agencies are fully immersed in this lifeworld, so there is no "place from nowhere" we can stand to see how "things really are" apart from the "flesh" of the lifeworld. There is no foreclosure to this process of entanglement, no discernible end to this drama, so that the undertaking of phenomenology is never complete or final but a continuous analysis of our existential condition. Thus, phenomenology brackets metaphysics while investigating experience to develop its ontology (theory of "being"). However, phenomenologically based ontology is always provisional and perspectival and therefore subject to revision.

A phenomenological approach drawing on Merleau-Ponty's thought is also consonant with basic Buddhist philosophical principles and thus can bridge the gap between emic (insider) and etic (outsider) approaches to the study of the Buddhist paranormal. In short, I argue that when dealing with the paranormal, a phenomenological approach is not only consonant with Buddhism but is to be preferred to adopting a metaphysics, which ignores our subjective situatedness within our lifeworld and forecloses the horizons of our hermeneutical frames.

Buddhism from its earliest days possessed a strong phenomenological and antimetaphysical orientation. We see from the early sources in Pāli and Chinese that the Buddha was primarily concerned with the analysis of first-person experience. He maintained that by successful analysis of the phenomena that constitute experience one would be able to realize the truths of impermanence, no-self, and suffering. The ubiquitous nature of suffering (the First Noble Truth) would lead to the realization that it is caused by craving (the Second Noble Truth), that this craving may be ended (the Third Noble Truth), and that there is a path to the cessation of this suffering (the Fourth Noble Truth). From the Buddha's analysis of the person as constituted by five categories of psychophysical aggregates (forms, sensations, conceptions, latent formations, and consciousnesses), we see no distinction between objective and subjective reality, no assumption of naïve realism or recourse to a metaphysical self or soul. In fact, Buddha analyzed experience to demonstrate that such a metaphysical self was incoherent and therefore taught no-self (*anātman*). Moreover, the early Buddhists understood consciousness in entirely experiential terms and avoided any recourse to postulating consciousness as a metaphysical principle. Consciousness was stated to be of six types, depending on which sense organ (the five senses and the mind) was in contact with their particular sense object. Thus, when the eye contacted visual objects, visual consciousness would arise, etc. In this way (as in phenomenology), consciousness is always viewed as *intentional*. In other words, consciousness is always *consciousness of* something in particular. Once again, Buddhism shows its phenomenological sensitivities by recognizing the first-person and subjective contribution to the lifeworld without collapsing experience into pure subjectivity or objectivity.

The Buddha's concern with the lived experience of the lifeworld is also evident in his avoidance of the ten "unanswerable questions" such as found in the *Cula-Malunkyovada Sutta*, each one of which assumed some metaphysical position must be asserted or denied.[10] His focus on the lived body is also clear from his famous statement in the *Rohitassa Sutta*, "Yet it is just within this fathom-long body, with its perception & intellect, that I declare that there is the cosmos, the origination of the cosmos, the cessation of the cosmos, and the path of practice leading to the cessation of the cosmos."[11] For Buddha, "the cosmos" was the lifeworld as experienced by the lived body, not some objectified external reality made of matter. Moreover, the dependent arising formula propounded by the Buddha describes the experiential links between physical and psychological phenomena leading to the repeated death and rebirth of the lived body.

It is unclear whether early Buddhists considered nirvana to be a metaphysical concept or simply as the cessation of craving. The later Theravāda maintains that nirvana possesses its own nature distinct from the cycle of rebirth (*saṃsāra*), and therefore I think it can rightly be seen as a form of metaphysical dualism. However, even from its earliest formulations nirvana was put forth as completely beyond language and conception. Nevertheless, from its earliest formulations, the Buddhist path maintained a strong empirical and pragmatic orientation through its focus on attaining liberation by means of a clear insight into the true nature of phenomena. The term used for this true nature, for things as they really are, from the earliest strata of Buddhism up through the Mahāyāna, was "suchness" (*tathātā*), a reality that can only be pointed to and directly intuited but not adequately expressed in words.

The later Abhidharma Buddhist philosophies with their obsessive concern with the own-nature (*svabhāva*) of the elements (*dharma*) of experience moved away from the Buddha's strict phenomenological analysis of what is given in experience and his avoidance of metaphysics. However, with the emergence of the Mahāyāna *Perfection of Wisdom* literature in the first century BCE, we see a reorientation of Buddhist philosophy with the doctrine of emptiness (*śūnyatā*), the notion that all psychophysical entities lack inherent existence, own-nature, or essence. We may view this emphasis on emptiness as an extension of the Buddha's no-self doctrine to encompass all phenomena. No doubt the early Mahāyānists believed this was the true intent of the Buddha's teachings and that later Buddhist philosophers had gone astray. This view of emptiness was later systematized by Nāgārjuna, the founder of the Madhyamaka school. By equating emptiness with the Buddha's "dependent arising," Nāgārjuna declared that all truths and all entities are contingent and arise in dependence on other things. This was a radical denial of metaphysics and an assertion that the only ultimate truth is that all truth is only relatively and pragmatically true. The pragmatic value of truth is understood in this view based on how efficacious teachings are to lead one to the realization of emptiness, the direct apprehension of their dependently arisen nature. Thus, the true suchness of all phenomena is their very emptiness of inherent existence. Just as in phenomenology, the world as it empirically appears is the *real world* when seen correctly as perspectival, lacking metaphysical foundation, and forever subject to revision.

Even the Yogācāra school of Mahāyāna Buddhism, which many modern scholars have interpreted as a form of metaphysical idealism, can be interpreted in the light of phenomenology. In his *Buddhist Phenomenology* (2002), Dan Lusthaus argues that Yogācāra is best understood not as a form of metaphysical idealism but as a distinctively Buddhist approach to phenomenology. After detailing some of the main principles of Husserl's and Merleau-Ponty's phenomenological approaches, Lusthaus asserts that although these are similar to Yogācāra in several ways, Yogācāra differs from them in its deployment of a "karmic reduction."[12] Lusthaus writes:

> Consequent on the preeminent function already assigned at Buddhism's inception, to consciousness in the Buddhist analysis of karma, Yogācāra's emphasis on "nothing but cognition" (*vijñapti-mātra*) serves to highlight a reductive description and analysis of the human condition to a moral sphere of advantageous (*kuśula*) and disadvantageous (*akuśala*) actions and attitudes (*kāya-vāc-manas karma*). Further, while causality is conspicuously absent from Husserl's reductions, it lies at the core of Yogācāra phenomenology. Yogācāra put forth the notion of psychosophic closure (*vijñapti-mātra*) as a way of making us aware that our karmic dilemma only occurs in that sphere; that positing a sense of externality to things is only the most basic of the self-blinding moves that keeps us enmeshed in the appropriational web we conceive of as a world.[13]

Thus, Lusthaus argues that "consciousness only" for the Yogācāra is not the valorization of consciousness as a form of metaphysical idealism but a warning not to cling to phenomena as real entities external to consciousness. According to Lusthaus, unique to Yogācāra is its "epistemo-ethics," a form of liberational ethics based on an epistemology grounded not in ontology or metaphysics but in radical experience. In this manner, rather than asserting a metaphysical idealism as the basis for their ethics, Yogācāra grounds its ethics "in the very necessity of bracketing metaphysics."[14] This antimetaphysical position is also consonant with the view of emptiness (*śūnyatā*) found in the Mahāyāna *Perfection of Wisdom* (*prajñāpāramitā*) literature and systematized in the Madhyamaka of Nāgārjuna in the second century CE. The phenomenological orientation in early Buddhism, the *Perfection*

INTRODUCTION

of Wisdom literature, Madhyamaka, and Yogācāra are synthesized and harmonized in what I refer to as the Mature Standard Model of the Mahāyāna (MSMM) as best exemplified by *The Supreme Array Scripture* (*Gaṇḍavyūha-sūtra*) some time around the fourth century CE in ancient India (see chapter 1).

We see that Merleau-Ponty, Buddha, and Nāgārjuna each eschewed metaphysics and focused on an analysis of lived experience. Likewise, by bracketing metaphysics, we can sidestep the entrenched debates about the "reality" of the paranormal and provide thick descriptions of some fascinating anomalous phenomena experienced by contemporary Buddhists. We are also able to compare these to traditional accounts and do this in a way that acknowledges the enmeshed nature of experience, interpretation, rationalities, events, subjectivities, etc. Thus, I am proposing a Buddhist phenomenology as a contemporary Buddhist approach to the paranormal. I emphasize here the use of the indefinite article—what I propose is only *a* contemporary Buddhist approach because from the vast array of Buddhist traditions any number of approaches to the paranormal *could* be developed. Moreover, the approach I propose here, while drawing on traditional Buddhist sources and concepts, is meant to address our particular contemporary context. Specifically, it is proposed as an alternative to dogmatic religious belief and dogmatic scientific physicalism.

By using this "emic" but critical approach, I fully acknowledge and reflect upon my Buddhist interpretations of these experiences and events by other contemporary and past Buddhists. This is motivated by my commitment to a Buddhist ethical framework and my belief that all conventional, conceptual knowledge is situational and perspectival. To this I would add my conviction that our understandings of the world arise to a significant degree through our co-creation of narratives about ourselves and our relation to the world. The stories told in our cultural histories, the stories we tell ourselves and relate to our audiences, the current stories circulated through countless media in our contemporary global consumer capitalist societies, and so on all structure our experiences and our interpretations of our experiences. No experience is free from this continuous process of interpretation. Stories of the paranormal by contemporary convert Buddhists take place within these larger historical and social narrative contexts. By recounting these stories and locating them within these larger contexts, I aim to add to our understanding of contemporary Buddhist folklore of the paranormal.

INTRODUCTION

Chapter Outline

Chapter 1 surveys some of the primary canonical and scholastic literature addressing the paranormal in Indian Buddhist literature. In traditional Buddhist cosmologies, the multiverse is teeming with various nonhuman intelligent beings of all sorts according to the inexorable law of karma. Also, from its earliest formation, through the Mahāyāna and up to the late tantric phase of Indian Buddhism, supernormal powers, psychic abilities, and magical powers have always been present. These phenomena would continue to play an important role in the Buddhist traditions as Buddhism spread from India to Southeast, Central, and East Asia. Everywhere Buddhism traveled, its cosmological, paranormal concepts and psychic powers blended and adapted to local beliefs and practices. Even today from Thailand to Tibet, magic and the psychic play an important role. While canonical and scholastic accounts of the paranormal are useful systemizations of the most prominent understandings of these powers and abilities, most Buddhists throughout history were much more likely to be familiar with miraculous events and extraordinary powers through the vast collections of popular Buddhist stories, which have been orally transmitted, written down, told, and retold throughout the centuries.

Chapter 2 provides a brief overview of the modern study of the paranormal beginning in the nineteenth century. Here, I explore some seminal research in the study of psychic phenomena, mediumship, spiritualism, NDEs, OBEs, ghosts, spirits, and reincarnation, primarily from the scientific perspective. I delve into the contemporary research of the seminal figures and organizations in Europe and North America that have engaged in the scientific study of the paranormal, such as the Society of Psychic Research, Charles Fort, J. B. Rhine, Charles Tart, Dean Radin, Ian Stevenson and the Division of Perceptual Studies, the U.S. government's funded research into the paranormal, and research into UFOs and the paranormal by Jacque Vallée and others. Laboratory experiments based on meta-analysis demonstrate statistically significant results above chance, which suggest that certain psychic abilities such as telepathy, precognition, clairvoyance, and micropsychokinesis are real. While lab results have been significant but generally weak in favor of psi, certain rare individuals appear to possess exceptional psi abilities. Moreover, there exists some evidence to suggest that meditation may enhance these abilities. Studies into reincarnation, OBEs, NDEs, apparitions, and mediumship, while "anecdotal," also suggest that consciousness may possess nonlocal aspects that operate independently of the brain. This has led to several of the leading psi researchers to conclude that physicalism or metaphysical materialism (the mind is the brain) must be wrong.

Despite polls indicating that most Americans believe in some aspect of the paranormal, academic and governmental studies of the subject are nearly nonexistent in the United States. This is no doubt because of cultural prejudices that mark out the paranormal as "fringe" and studies into the subject as "pseudoscientific." While laboratory research appears to demonstrate some albeit weak psi phenomena, the most dramatic occurrences of the paranormal happen not in the laboratory but out in the world, often during extreme stress or trauma or during altered states of consciousness. The paranormal is deeply embedded in our collective imaginations, and our knowledge of it comes from our own experiences and stories of the experiences of others. Through our stories of these extraordinary experiences (most often privately communicated among family and close friends) the paranormal is kept alive down the generations and across cultures.

Chapter 3 explores contemporary (primarily convert) Buddhist stories about psychic abilities such as clairvoyance, precognition, telepathy, and retrocognition. To provide some social and cultural context for the stories, I begin this chapter with some demographic data on the participants of the current study. Throughout the remainder of this chapter and the next, I arrange the stories according to the particular phenomenon (clairvoyance, precognition, telepathy, etc.). I begin with some light statistical analysis of the questionnaire responses to provide additional information concerning the frequency and context for such experiences. Then I turn to accounts of each phenomenon as described by participants in the questionnaire and interviews. For this chapter (and the next four), my approach shifts to contemporary stories narrated to me in the first person. Unlike the study of official sources, this approach is more akin to studies in living folklore and oral history. In this way, I explore the paranormal as narrated by living and breathing people and uncover the roles such phenomena and the stories about them play in their lives.

Outside of popular media, entertainment, and fiction, people encounter the paranormal primarily and most forcibly through their direct encounters with it and the stories they hear about it often from family and close friends.

INTRODUCTION

It is through this folklore of the uncanny, anomalous, spooky, and weird erupting and intruding into ordinary life through death, trauma, and intense altered states that the paranormal functions as a dynamic force in people's lives. As we shall see, for contemporary Buddhists these events and the stories about them are interpreted through a Buddhist lens wherein karma and rebirth play prominent roles.

Chapter 4 continues the exploration of contemporary tales of the Buddhist paranormal, focusing on OBEs, NDEs, and encounters with other beings, such as animals, spirits, ghosts, gods, and holy beings. Based on my survey and interviews, these types of encounters appear to be less rare than one might expect. When asked, "Have you ever had an experience that you think might have been a communication from a deceased person?" 43 percent of respondents (26 out of 60) responded in the affirmative. When asked, "Have you ever seen, heard, or felt the presence of any person living or dead who was not physically present?" 54 percent of respondents (36 out of 65) said "Yes." When asked, "Have you ever felt the presence, seen, or heard a nonphysical spirit, entity, or holy being?" 75 percent of respondents (45 out of 60) said they had. Sometimes these encounters happen in dreams; other times they are during meditation or altered states of consciousness or spontaneously occur. Of those who answered "yes" to some contact with a spirit or holy being, 70 percent have had such experiences during meditation or some other spiritual exercise. For some respondents, such encounters are rare (happening no more than five times in their lives), but for others they are much more common (occurring more than twenty times). Phenomena range from merely sensing the presence of a spirit, ghost, or deceased relative to full-sensory visitation from a holy being, such as Amitābha, Avalokiteśvara, Padmasambhava, or Mahākāla. These encounters are not merely oddities or trivial anomalous occurrences but often transform people's entire lives.

Chapters 5 and 6 are more in-depth studies of two contemporary practitioners of Buddhist meditation and ritual whom I interviewed. Chapter 5, "The Yogin," is about the life experiences of Rick Repetti, a philosopher, scholar, meditation teacher, yoga instructor, therapist, and psychic virtuoso. Rick grew up in a low-income public housing development in Queens, New York City, in a large Italian American family.[15] His first awakening to the paranormal occurred as a teenager. This life-changing event propelled Rick on a spiritual journey and the passionate study of and engagement with meditation, yoga, psychedelics, and Buddhism, culminating in his contact with a spiritual community led by Ram Dass, Hilda Charlton, and Joya Santayana. Within this community, Rick immersed himself in spiritual disciplines such as meditation, fasting, and yoga, which led to numerous mystical and psychic experiences including clairvoyance, telepathy, precognition, and encounters with supernatural entities.

Chapter 6, "The Gift," is about Kat Smith (a pseudonym), who since her earliest memories has felt a close connection with the spirits of the deceased. Kat grew up in the Washington, DC, area and lived and studied in Montreal, Canada, for a number of years before immigrating to New Zealand. In her younger years, Kat had numerous and intense psychic experiences, which led to her misdiagnosis and years of being prescribed harmful medication that dampened her psi abilities. She was able to break free of this troubled past and while traveling in Southeast Asia discovered the occult practices of Thai Buddhism. Existing alongside the tradition of orthodox Theravāda Buddhism in Thailand, the Thai occult involves magic, curses, amulets, spirits, and ghosts, wherein the powers of the deceased can be ritually placed into objects to work for the good or ill of others. During our interviews, Kat related to me her early experiences and otherworldly encounters within the world of the Thai occult.

Chapter 7 is both a conclusion to the current study and a prolegomenon for future study of the paranormal based on a phenomenological approach. Specifically, I propose phenomenology as a bridge between the humanistic and scientific study of the paranormal that avoids dogmatic belief, whether religious or scientific. Moreover, since the paranormal is an integral part of human experience, such an approach has wider implications not only for the study of the paranormal in general but also for human inquiry into the unknown that breaks down artificial disciplinary boundaries and hierarchies.

The postscript provides autobiographical accounts of my paranormal experiences, including precognition, telepathy, clairvoyance, chaos magic, poltergeist activity, encounters with Mahāyāna holy beings, and experiments with psychokinesis.

ONE

The Paranormal in the Indian Buddhist Tradition

CURRENT SCHOLARLY CONSENSUS places the life of Siddhartha Gautama, the historical Buddha, at sometime around the fifth century BCE. According to legend, Siddhartha was a prince in the northeast of India who became disillusioned with worldly life, renounced his position in society, and became a wandering ascetic in search of permanent release from the endless cycle of death and rebirth. At first he studied meditation with some renowned teachers of the day, but after mastering the various methods he attempted, he realized that they did not lead to permanent release. Next, he practiced severe asceticism, and after nearly starving himself to death also realized this method would not allow him to succeed in attaining his goal. Finally, he sat under the "Bodhi Tree" by the banks of the Nirañjanā River and vowed not to move until he attained enlightenment. On the night of Siddhartha's awakening, he gained various clairvoyant powers, such as being able to witness his past lives and the universal workings of karma. In the final watch of the night, through the destruction of the defilements of hatred, greed, and delusion, he attained the ultimate bliss and supreme peace of nirvana.

Following his attainment of awakening, the Buddha began his forty-five-year-long mission to teach the Dharma, the truth he had realized to attain nirvana. During his career as a teacher, it is said that the Buddha performed many miracles and demonstrated several powers attributed to his mastery of meditation, such as the ability to read minds (telepathy), see things from a distance (clairvoyance), and even fly through the air. To understand the meaning and significance of these powers for Indian Buddhists, we need to locate them within the wider discourse on yogic powers in India and their function within Buddhist cosmology. After establishing this context, the remainder of this chapter looks at the role of psychic powers in Mainstream, Mahāyāna, and Tantric Buddhism in India.

The Indian Context

We find accounts of psychic abilities and encounters with nonhuman intelligent entities in the Vedic *Saṃhitā*s, the earliest strata of north Indian literature beginning from 1500 BCE.[1] The Vedic world was filled with numerous gods, demons, and spirits, and the ancient sages were believed to possess special powers, foremost among them the ability to hear (*śruti*) the eternal, sonic vibrations of the Sanskrit Vedic hymns. In the great Indian epic, the *Mahābhārata* (c. third century BCE–third century CE), we find accounts of sages, heroes, ascetics, yogins, and gods who have the power to fly, enter other beings' bodies, control the elements of nature, and multiply their forms.[2] These powers are variously called in Sanskrit *bala* (power, strength) *vibhūti* (power, manifestation of power), *vīrya* (might), *prabhāva* (force), and *yoga*.[3] By the time of the *Mahābhārata*, the renouncer traditions both within Hinduism and among heterodox schools such as Buddhism and Jainism had emerged. These traditions maintained that sentient beings were endlessly reborn into various states of existence according to the law of karma, the idea that beneficial actions bring forth positive results and harmful actions bring forth negative results. This cycle of rebirth (*saṃsara*) was viewed by renouncers as painful (*duḥkha*), and therefore they sought permanent means of liberation (*mokṣa*) from it. To gain this release, renouncers gave up attachments to material pleasures, engaged in various forms of ascetic denial, and practiced some form of mental discipline, concentration, or meditation. These disciplines were broadly understood as various types of *"yoga,"* meaning in this context the "yoking/restraining of the mind." It was a widely held belief that the practice of such yoga would result in the attainment of various "yogic powers."

An important orthodox account of yoga and yogic powers can be found in the *Yogasūtra* of Patañjali and its commentary by Vyāsa (c. second century

BCE–fifth century CE), the foundational texts for the classical Yoga system. In the *Yogasūtra*, Patañjali outlines an eight-limbed (*aṣṭāṅga*) spiritual path to liberation that begins with observances, discipline, postures, breath control, and withdrawal of the senses and culminates in the fixation of awareness, meditation, and ultimately meditative absorption (*samādhi*). Through the practice of the final three (collectively referred to as *saṃyama*, "concentration of the mind"), numerous yogic powers (*vibhūta/siddhi*) were believed to be attainable.[4] Interestingly, the *Yogasūtra* mentions that some people are born with such powers, while others can also attain them through drugs (*oṣadhi*), mantras, or ascetic practices (*tapas*).[5] Some of the yogic powers attained through *saṃyama* that Patañjali mentions are the ability to fly, telekinesis, invulnerability, telepathy, precognition, knowledge of past lives, invisibility, super hearing, X-ray vision, psychic entry into another's body, communication with animals, super strength, and ultimately omnipotence and omniscience.[6] Traditionally there are eight major powers a yogin is said to be able to obtain, which Vyāsa in his commentary describes as (1) miniaturization (the ability to become minute), (2) levitation, (3) magnification (the ability to become huge), (4) extension (the ability to touch the sun and the moon), (5) irresistible desire (the ability to do such things as pass through earth as if water, etc.), (6) mastery (control over the elements and the ability to resist the control of others), (7) command (the ability to control the appearance and disposition of material things), and (8) wish realization (the ability to make whatever one desires real).[7] The theoretical basis for these powers is found in the metaphysics of Sāṃkhya philosophy, which underlies classical Yoga and often forms the explanatory basis for such powers in the *Mahābhārata*.[8] According to this view, two fundamental principles exist: consciousness (*puruṣa*) and primordial matter or nature (*prakṛti*). Through restraint and concentration, one is believed to gain knowledge of nature and the workings of *prakṛti*, which in turn gives one mastery over nature and her powers. It was within this wider context of beliefs about karma, rebirth, and yogic powers that Buddhist views of supernormal powers developed.

The Buddhist Cosmos

From earliest accounts, we see that the Buddhist multiverse is inhabited by a vast array of nonhuman intelligences hierarchically arranged throughout countless realms and dimensions within an infinite ocean of spacetime. Many of these beings can and do interact with human beings in various ways and capacities. Moreover, spiritually advanced humans, such as Mahāmoggallāna (one of the Buddha's chief disciples), who possess superhuman psychic abilities attained through meditational mastery, can of their own choice interact with these beings and travel to their worlds.[9] In these countless realms of becoming, the law of karma and rebirth reigns supreme. In the remainder of this chapter, we first explore the Indian origins and nature of this Buddhist multiverse and the integral role "the paranormal" plays within it. Next, we address traditional Buddhist cosmology and the myriad creatures it contains. Following this, we investigate in some detail the "higher knowledges" (*abhiññā/abhijñā*) and "supernormal powers" (*iddhi/ṛddhi/siddhi*) that advanced meditators were believed to attain through their practice in the three main phases of Indian Buddhism.

In traditional Indian cosmology (both Hindu and Buddhist), time and space are limitless and filled with innumerable worlds, which go through vast cycles of evolution and devolution. The time it takes for a world realm to complete its cycle of evolution and devolution until its destruction by fire is called an eon (*kalpa*). The exact number of years in an eon was a matter of debate and various thinkers estimated between 1,344,000 and 1,280,000,000 years.[10] Once a world realm was destroyed, another began; many Indian thinkers speculated that this process had no origin or end but went on forever.[11]

Indian Buddhists recognized various classes of world realms (*lokadhātu*) distinguished according to their number of worlds. For instance, in the Pāli text called the *Mahāniddesa* (356) there are fifty categories, beginning with a world realm consisting of just a single world, up to a world realm of fifty worlds.[12] Beyond fifty, the text mentions a world realm of a thousand worlds, two thousand worlds, three thousand worlds, etc. The commonly occurring compound "thrice-thousandfold world realm" (*tisahassī lokadhātu*) was interpreted by the Indian Buddhist monk Buddhaghosa as multiplicative, stating that such a world realm would consist of 1,000,000,000,000 worlds.[13] Franklin Edgerton has observed that the Sanskrit term *trisāhasra-mahāsāhasra*, which he translates as "a (world system) consisting of a triple thousand great thousand (worlds)" occurs regularly in Mahāyāna sources.[14] Other contemporary scholars also attempt literal translations of the term and avoid assigning it an exact number.[15]

Indian Buddhists imagined that each of the countless worlds in this infinite multiverse possessed the same basic structure.[16] All world realms, including our own known as the "Sahā world realm" (sahā lokadhātu), are divided like a three-layered cake: the bottom layer is the realm of desire (kāmadhātu), next is the realm of form (rūpadhātu), and on top is the formless realm (arūpyadhātu). The realm of desire is the phenomenal world of the five senses, which possesses a symmetrical topography. At the center of our world resides a massive mountain called Mount Sumeru or Mount Meru. Surrounding this mountain are seven rings of mountains divided by seven seas. Beyond the mountains and seas are island-continents located at the primary compass points. Encircling the outer edge of the Sahā world stands a massive range of iron mountains called the Cakravāla.

The realm of desire is further subdivided into six states of rebirth (gati) inhabited by gods, demigods, humans, animals, ghosts, and hell beings. Six classes of gods dwelled on or above Mount Meru. The demigods, envious and warlike beings, reside below the gods on Mount Meru. Below Mount Meru are four island-continents inhabited by humans, animals, ghosts, and various intelligent humanoid creatures, such as demons (yakṣa), centaurs (kiṃnara), serpent deities (nāga), giant birds (garuḍa), celestial musicians (gandharva), and celestial maidens (apsaras). Indian Buddhists believed they inhabited the southern island-continent called Jambudvīpa (the Rose Apple Island). Also within the realm of desire wander the "hungry ghosts,"[17] an unfortunate class of spirits depicted in Buddhist art as piteous creatures with huge bellies and tiny mouths and throats. Because of their excessive greed in former human lives, they are doomed to constant hunger and thirst. Beneath Jambudvīpa are various extremely hot and cold hell realms, where the wicked are repeatedly dismembered, boiled, crushed, burned, drowned, and killed by other various and sundry methods (all horribly painful) until their evil karma has been expiated.[18] Indian Buddhists imagined that the basic structure of our world, both in terms of its various levels and topographical features, are the same for all worlds. According to Luis Gómez, "The universe of the classical Buddhist Indian imagination was a system of parallel worlds all of which shared a similar structure."[19]

Rebirth into these various realms is taken as a given and driven by the forces of karma (Pāli: kamma; Sanskrit: karman; literally meaning "action"). Karma, rebirth, and cosmology all assume what Rupert Gethin refers to as "the correspondence of psychology and cosmology."[20] This is the notion that a being's general psychological state, established through various karmic forces, determines in which cosmological realm that being resides. In this sense, there is no "objective" or "external" world "out there." Any particular world as phenomenologically experienced is generated by the collective karma and intersubjective psychologies of the beings that "inhabit" that world. Thus, in the bad states of existence (*durgati*), the greedy are reborn as hungry ghosts, the hateful are reborn in the hells, and the ignorant return to life as animals. Good actions lead to rebirth in the heavens, and the practice of calm meditation causes rebirth in the form and formless realms (discussed subsequently). Moreover, the physical characteristics of a world realm are dependent upon the virtues of the beings that inhabit it.

Above the realm of desire is located the realm of pure form, where divine beings abide in sublime bliss. This realm was further divided into four main levels corresponding to the four stages of concentration (*jhāña/dhyāna*) attained through the practice of "calm meditation" (*śamatha*). Early Buddhist meditation is of two main types: "calm" (*śamatha/samatha*) and "insight" (*vipaśyanā/vipassanā*).[21] The practice of calm meditation leads to four levels of trance (*dhyāna/jhāna*) characterized as follows:

1. One-pointedness, happiness, joy, examination, and applied thought at the first level
2. One-pointedness, happiness, and joy at the second level
3. One-pointedness, happiness, and equanimity at the third level
4. One-pointedness and equanimity at the fourth level

When one can achieve the fourth level of meditative trance, one is able to enter four different types of formless realm (each further realm represents a higher level of meditation):

1. The sphere of infinite space
2. The sphere of infinite consciousness
3. The sphere of nothingness
4. The sphere of neither-cognition-nor-non-cognition[22]

The second type of Buddhist meditation is "insight." The goal of insight meditation is to gain an understanding of the true nature of reality, namely, that all things are impermanent, unsatisfactory, and not self. When the fourth level of trance is achieved through calm meditation and is combined with insight, one gains access to the six higher knowledges (discussed subsequently).

Psychic Powers in Indian Buddhism

About a century after the Buddha's final nirvana, the Buddhist community began to split into various sects and schools based on disputes around monastic discipline and doctrine. By the beginning of the first millennium CE, numerous Buddhist schools coexisted on the Indian subcontinent. Although differing to some degree in their monastic codes and some finer doctrinal issues, these Mainstream Buddhist schools adhered to the same basic beliefs and practices. One of these schools, the Sthāviravāda, transplanted in the third century BCE to Sri Lanka and became the Theravāda school. From there, it subsequently spread to Southeast Asia, where it continues to this day in Thailand, Myanmar, Cambodia, and Laos. In the following discussion, I use the Theravāda school's texts, the Pāli Canon, as my primary source of information on the Mainstream Buddhist view concerning psychic powers.

As we have seen, the ability to acquire various psychic powers through the practice of meditation was a widely held belief in India since ancient times. About this belief in Buddhism, Bradley Clough writes: "The overall acceptance of the idea of attainment of certain extraordinary psychic powers by those adepts who have reached advanced stages of meditation is one of the most ancient and consistent features of South Asian Buddhism, from the early Pāli texts to treatise of the later phases of the Mahāyāna in this region."[23]

Although central to much of Indian Buddhist belief and practice, many modern scholars have not addressed these powers in any sustained way. Both Clough and Nathan Katz state that this is likely attributable to an academic prejudice that viewed early Buddhism as rationalistic and nonmystical.[24] Katz writes: "Following from a prejudice that Buddhism, or at least that part taught by the Buddha, was thoroughly rationalistic and non-mystical, many scholars ignored or even denied the existence of the considerable body of canonical references to these 'higher knowledges' (*abhiññā*), and especially to the 'psychic powers' (*iddhi*)." However, according to Katz, these knowledges and powers are an indispensable element of Indian Buddhist thought.[25] The remainder of this chapter investigates the *abhiññā* (Skt. *abhijñā*) and *iddhi* (Skt. *ṛddhi*) in Indian Buddhism in its Mainstream, Mahāyāna, and Tantric forms.

Mainstream Buddhism

In the Pāli Canon of the Theravāda school, we find a traditional list of five (or six—see later discussion in this chapter) higher knowledges:

1. Supernormal powers
2. Divine ear
3. Mind reading
4. Recollection of past lives
5. Divine eye
6. Destruction of the cankers[26]

Indian Buddhists maintained that any practitioner of concentration-based meditation (whether Buddhist or non-Buddhist) could attain knowledges 1–5, and therefore they considered them "mundane" or worldly forms of higher knowledges.[27] To this list of five a sixth "supramundane" higher knowledge was often added exclusive to Buddhist practice: the knowledge of the destruction of the "cankers" (*āsava*).[28] In Buddhism, the cankers or "influxes" are the mental defilements that are believed to keep one bound to the cycle of rebirth. They are often listed as three: sensual desires, desire for continued existence, and ignorance. Upon the destruction of the *āsavas*, one attains nirvana, the unending state of bliss and final permanent eradication of suffering and rebirth. This knowledge is supramundane because it leads to the ultimate soteriological goal of the Buddhist path.

According to Pāli sources, the *abhiññās* are acquired through the practice of *samatha* meditation at the fourth level of trance (*jhāna*), resulting in mental equanimity within the realm of pure form. *Samatha*, or calm meditation, is a form of concentration meditation whereby the adept trains the mind to attain one-pointed focus. The fourth stage is the pinnacle of this practice and is the access point to both the higher knowledges and the formless realms. The *Sāmaññaphala Sutta* describes attaining the *abhiññās* at this stage thus: "When the mind is thus concentrated, pure, cleansed, free of stains, free of corruptions, supple, pliant, steady, and unperturbed, one directs and thoroughly turns the mind to knowledge and vision."[29]

Once this is done, one creates a "mind-made body" (*manomaya-kāya*) and extracts this body from the physical body like pulling a sword from a scabbard, or a snake shedding its skin.[30] The description of this body strikes me as highly suggestive of what many moderns would refer to as the "astral body" (I'll return to this idea in chapter 4). Having created this body, one is then able to access the various supernormal powers with it. The *Sāmaññaphala* provides a stock description, which appears in many places throughout the Pāli Canon, in the meditation manuals of the Theravāda tradition, and in the Mahāyāna.[31] It reads:

> Being one he becomes many, or having become many he becomes one again; he becomes visible or invisible; he goes, feeling no obstruction, to the further side of a wall or rampart or hill, as if through air; he penetrates up and down through solid ground, as if through water; he walks on water without breaking through, as if on solid ground; he travels cross-legged in the sky, like the birds on wing; even the Moon and Sun, so potent, so mighty though they be, does he touch and feel with his hand; he reaches in the body even up to the heaven of Brahmā.[32]

There are numerous examples in the Pāli Canon of these powers being displayed by the Buddha and several of his chief disciples. For example, in the *Sutta Piṭaka*, we find the Buddha's faithful monk-servant Ānanda asking the Buddha if he could reach the Brahma world of gods in both his "mind-made body" and his physical body.[33] The Buddha replied that he could. This example is also telling in that the Buddha asserts the ability not just to "astral project" to this divine realm but to go there in his "ordinary" corporeal form. In the *Udāna*, a story is recounted that once when the Ganges River was flooding, the Buddha with his retinue of disciples flew across it.[34] Although these powers were not required to attain nirvana, many of the Buddha's disciples possessed them, and they were often employed to convert and teach people the Buddha's Dharma.[35]

The next higher knowledge is the "divine ear" (*dibbasota*), or clairaudience.[36] This psychic ability allows one to hear and understand the speech of others at great distances and even in divine realms. Although it could be used to experientially confirm the existence of other realms, Clough points out that it appears to be the least significant of the higher knowledges mentioned in the Pāli sources.[37]

The third higher knowledge is mind-reading (*cetopariyañāṇa* or *paracittavijānana*), or telepathy. This ability of the Buddha to discern the thoughts of others plays a prominent role in the early tradition as a means for the Buddha to directly witness the results of karma and to teach others effectively. This was also a vital skill used to discern if someone had truly attained the highest state of nirvana.[38]

The next three *abhiññā*s (recollection of past lives, divine eye, and destruction of the cankers) are collectively known as the "three knowledges" and play a significant role in early Buddhist thought.[39] In one prominent account of the Buddha's enlightenment found in the *Verañja*, *Bhayabherava*, and *Mahāsaccaka sutta*s, he is said to have realized these three knowledges in successive watches of the night. Thus, in the first watch of the night, the Buddha was able to discern many thousands of his past lives in explicit detail.[40] According to Katz, "The knowledge of former lives (*pubbenivāsānussatiñāṇa*) is essential in the formulation of Buddhist doctrine. Without it, there could be no teaching of *kamma* [karma] and rebirth."[41] Because the Buddha could directly experience in memory all these lives, he could experientially validate how his previous actions led to his future rebirths—ideas foundational to Buddhist teaching. Related to this knowledge, Clough cites references in Pāli sources referring to adepts who can even "remember" their future lives.[42] Although not labeled as a specific ability in the canonical sources, this is highly suggestive of the psychic power of precognition. It also raises some thorny philosophical issues related to precognition and free will, which I discuss in more detail in chapter 5.

In the second watch of the night, the Buddha is said to have attained knowledge of the divine eye (*dibbacakkhu* or *cutūpapārañāṇa*) or clairvoyance. The *Sāmaññaphala Sutta* describes this experience with the stereotypical formula: "He directs and turns his mind to the knowledge of the passing away and rebirth of beings. With the divine eye, which is purified and surpasses the human, he sees beings passing away and being reborn; inferior and superior, fair and ugly, happy and unhappy in their destinies as *kamma* directs them."[43]

In this way the Buddha was able to directly perceive the workings of karma and rebirth for countless beings throughout the cosmos, seeing those with negative karma reborn in the lower states of animals, hungry ghosts, and hells and those with good karma being reborn in pleasant divine abodes. Thus, the divine eye also confirms Buddhist cosmology and teachings on karma and rebirth. Anuruddha, the Buddha's most advanced disciple in this knowledge, was said to be able "to see" a thousand worlds.[44] Modern psi researchers refer to such abilities as "remote viewing," something that the United States Intelligence community has researched and successfully deployed for years (see chapter 2).

The sixth and final higher knowledge is the knowledge that destroys the cankers (*āsavakkhyayañāṇa*), those mental defilements (*āsava*) of sensual desire, the desire for continued existence, and ignorance that inhibit the attainment of nirvana. The *Sāmaññaphala Sutta* describes this knowledge with the following formula: "He knows as it really is, 'these are the *āsavas*.' He knows as it really is, 'this is the cause of the *āsavas*.' He knows as it really is, 'this is the destruction of the *āsavas*.' He knows as it really is, 'this is the path leading to the destruction of the *āsavas*.' And through this knowledge and vision, his mind is liberated from the *āsavas*."[45]

As mentioned earlier, Buddhists viewed the previous five higher knowledges as "mundane" and attainable by non-Buddhist yogins, while this sixth higher knowledge they declared "supramundane" (*lokuttara*) and achievable only by Buddhist adepts. In this sense, the destruction of the cankers is synonymous with the attainment of nirvana, the bliss that is the permanent end of rebirth and suffering and the *summum bonum* of early Buddhist praxis. However, Clough rightly points out that early Buddhist sources contain alternative means to attain nirvana.[46] Whereas some passages declare that the higher levels of trance (*jhāna*) wherein one attains the formless realms are required for liberation, others mention Buddhist saints who attain nirvana by "insight" (*paññā*) alone, without even achieving the fourth level of trance needed for the higher knowledges. In fact, at the time of the Buddha's final passing away, only sixty of the Buddha's five hundred enlightened disciples were said to have attained nirvana through the cultivation of both trance states and insight.[47] Thus, although the higher knowledges play an important role in early Buddhist theory and practice, their attainment appears to have been viewed as the rare achievement of those particularly skilled at forms of concentration-based (*samatha*) meditations.

Mahāyāna

In addition to the Mainstream Buddhist schools, sometime beginning in the first century BCE a new type of Buddhism emerged, the Mahāyāna, which radically departed from the Mainstream Buddhist schools in some essential ways. The origins and character of early Mahāyāna are still being debated within the academy,[48] but we do know that by the early centuries of the Common Era some of the basic features of this new Buddhism had developed. We may divide these into three broad categories: (1) a new cosmology, (2) a new philosophical outlook based on emptiness (*śūnyatā*), and (3) a new view of human perfection, the Bodhisattva Ideal.[49] In order to understand the role of psi in the Mahāyāna, we must first understand its new religious orientation.

The ultimate goal of the Mainstream Buddhist schools such as the Theravāda is to follow the Buddha's teachings and become an enlightened saint (Pāli: *arahant*; Sanskrit: *arhat*) who attains the final release of nirvana. The Buddha upon his final nirvana is believed to be gone forever beyond the cycle of birth and death (*saṃsāra*), with only his teaching and bodily relics remaining behind. Before the Buddha of the current age, there were thought to be countless buddhas of the past. In the far future it is believed that the next buddha will appear, named Maitreya (Pāli: Metteyya), who will once again teach the Buddhist Dharma. Since time is endless, this succession of buddhas is also thought to extend endlessly from the past into the future (with only one buddha occurring at any time). Buddhas before awakening in their final birth are believed to be extremely rare individuals who long ago vowed to postpone their final nirvana as saints in order to become fully enlightened buddhas in a time when the teachings had been lost. Thus, in the far future, these beings, who had accumulated countless powers and abilities through their vast store of merit, would reintroduce the Buddhist Dharma to the world. These extremely rare religious virtuosos, who have vowed to postpone their enlightenment, Buddhists call "bodhisattvas" (Pāli: *bodhisatta*), literally "beings (who exist) for enlightenment."

While in early Buddhism the spiritual status of the Buddha and the saint were considered more or less equal (both had attained the same state of nirvana), it seems that over the centuries the status of the Buddha increased with a corresponding decrease in the status of the saint. By the time of the Mahāyāna's appearance, the new Buddhists viewed the goal of sainthood to be an inferior goal to that of completely awakened buddhahood. Thus, a new religious goal was conceived: that one should become a bodhisattva and strive to become a completely enlightened, omniscient buddha for the sake of all beings. One who set out on this quest was thought to have taken "the bodhisattva's vow," to undergo innumerable lifetimes perfecting the various virtues and skills required to become a buddha. It is likely that this new ideal was inspired at least in part by the popular collection of past life stories of the Buddha known as the *Jātaka Tales*.

In the mature Mahāyāna, buddhas are thought to attain a "nonabiding nirvāṇa" that is neither outside of *saṃsāra* nor within it. This is because buddhas are thought to possess three bodies:[50]

1. Manifestation bodies, or bodies of magical creation (*nirmāṇa-kāya*), which appear in the worlds to help ordinary suffering beings.
2. Enjoyment bodies (*saṃbhoga-kāya*), which appear in pure lands, or "buddha-fields" (described in what follows), which can be accessed by highly developed spiritual beings, i.e., advanced bodhisattvas. We could say these are "cosmic buddhas."
3. The Dharma Body (*dharma-kāya*), which is the body of ultimate truth. It is the ultimate nature of reality.

Manifestation buddhas like the historical Buddha, Siddhartha Gautama, manifest in different worlds and appear to perform the deeds of buddhas such as renouncing the world, attaining enlightenment, teaching, and passing into final nirvana. Cosmic buddhas spend countless eons in pure lands sending out manifestation buddhas; whereas Dharma Body buddhas, being coextensive with reality itself, do not do anything at all. According to Mahāyāna cosmology, there are countless buddhas and advanced bodhisattvas throughout all time and space. Through meditative trance (*samādhi*), bodhisattvas can have visions of these beings and travel to their lands. Some of the more well-known celestial buddhas are Maitreya, Amitābha, and Akṣobhya.

An important characteristic of Indian Mahāyāna Buddhism is a belief in special worlds called "buddha-fields" (*buddhakṣetra*).[51] A buddha-field is a world that either contains a buddha or has the potential to contain one. Given the limitless merit and power of the buddhas, buddha-fields possess structures more conducive to religious practice than ordinary world realms and are often described in fantastical terms as being made of diamonds, jewels, and other precious substances.⁵² Mahāyāna Buddhists believe the most virtuous humans are reborn in buddha-fields like Amitābha's Happy Land, where the trees are made of jewels, lotus ponds are scattered across the perfectly level ground, and palaces float in the sky.⁵³ Surrounding the infinite numbers of buddhas in their buddha-fields are retinues of advanced bodhisattvas. Unlike ordinary human beings, these bodhisattvas possess the power to instantly transport themselves to other worlds, and this is a common motif occurring in Mahāyāna *sūtras*.⁵⁴ Some of the most popular advanced bodhisattvas are Avalokiteśvara (bodhisattva of compassion), Mañjuśrī (bodhisattva of wisdom), Tārā (the saviouress), and Kṣitigarbha. If prayed to, these beings are believed to be able to save one from calamity or aid one along the path to enlightenment.

The Mahāyāna philosophy elaborated by the Madhyamaka school reinforced the notion that the "external world" is mere appearance, since all phenomena lack inherent existence or independent essence (*svabhāva*) and therefore are characterized by their emptiness (*śūnyatā*). However, it was the Mahāyāna Yogācāra school that takes the equivalence between cosmology and psychology to its logical extreme: the belief that all the innumerable worlds with their different levels and, indeed all phenomena, are merely the product of thought (*cittamātra*).⁵⁵ The illusory nature of all things is at times expressed in Mahāyāna sources in terms of one or more of the following comparisons: all phenomena are like acts of magic, a mirage, the moon reflected in water, space, an echo, the city of the Gandarvas, a dream, a shadow, an image reflected in a mirror, and objects created by psychic powers.⁵⁶ The last of these comparisons highlights the Buddhist acceptance of the traditional Indian belief that through mental discipline one is able to attain psychic powers.

The bodhisattva's path was thought to begin when one awakens the "mind of enlightenment" (*bodhicitta*). This was conceived of as an altruistic act motivated by "great compassion" (*mahākaruṇā*) to attain complete buddhahood to save all beings. This vow begins the path of the accumulation of merit, whereby the bodhisattva acquires vast stores of good karma through countless lifetimes of self-sacrifice and practices various perfections. One of the earliest lists of these perfection we find in the *Perfection of Wisdom Scriptures* (*Prajñāpāramitā Sūtras*), where six perfections (*pāramitā*) are mentioned: (1) giving (*dāna*), (2) morality (*śīla*), (3) patience (*kṣānti*), (4) vigor (*vīrya*),

(5) meditation (*dhyāna*), and (6) wisdom (*prajñā*).⁵⁷ In the later tradition, such as in the *Scripture on the Ten Stages* (*Daśabhūmikā Sūtra*), this list gets expanded to ten by including (7) skillfulness (*upāya*), (8) vow (*praṇidhāna*), (9) power (*bala*), and (10) knowledge (*jñāna*).⁵⁸ The *Scripture on the Ten Stages* maps the ten perfections onto a list of ten stages a bodhisattva must advance through to attain omniscient Buddhahood:⁵⁹

Stage (bhūmi)	*Perfection* (pāramitā)
1. Joyous	1. Giving
2. Pure	2. Morality
3. Luminous	3. Patience
4. Radiant	4. Vigor
5. Difficult to Conquer	5. Meditation
6. Approaching	6. Wisdom
7. Gone Afar	7. Skillfulness
8. Immovable	8. Vow
9. Good Intelligence	9. Power
10. Dharma Cloud	10. Knowledge

Over countless lifetimes, a bodhisattva masters each perfection and advances through the stages. At each successive stage the bodhisattva attains various powers and abilities. In a description of *The Scripture on the Ten Stages*, Donald Lopez writes:

> Over the course of ten levels, a bodhisattva achieves extraordinary powers, powers that only multiply on the slow ascent toward Buddhahood. On the first level, for example, a bodhisattva can see one hundred buddhas in an instant, can live one hundred aeons, can see for one hundred aeons into the past and future, can go to one hundred buddha lands, illuminate one hundred worlds, and can bring one hundred beings to spiritual maturity in an instant.⁶⁰

At the third stage, Luminous, the bodhisattva achieves the fourth *jhāna* and the first five higher knowledges: the supernormal powers (*ṛddhi*), divine ear (*divyaśrota*), mind reading (*paracittajñāna*), recollection of past lives (*pūrvanivāsānusmṛti*), and the divine eye (*divyaṃ cakṣus*).⁶¹ Noticeably absent from this list is the sixth higher knowledge, the destruction of the cankers, which leads to nirvana. Since the Mahāyānists' new religious goal was the omniscient awakening of a fully enlightened buddha and not the nirvana of the Mainstream Buddhist, it appears that Mahāyānists avoided attributing the sixth knowledge to bodhisattvas.[62] In addition to these five higher knowledges, bodhisattvas at this stage can "see many hundreds of buddhas, many hundreds of thousands, millions, billions, trillions of buddhas, by great vision and willpower."[63] Seeing these buddhas, bodhisattvas honor them, make offerings to them, listen to their teachings, put these teachings into practice, and teach them to others. In this way, bodhisattvas accrue incalculable stores of merit and advance along the path to the next stage.

Har Dayal has discussed the evolution of the higher knowledges in the Mahāyāna in some detail.[64] Dayal's general thesis is that the Mahāyāna adopted the stereotyped descriptions of the higher knowledges from earlier tradition and expanded on them. Just as the "Great Vehicle" (mahā-yāna) expanded Buddhist cosmology to contain not just an infinite temporal series of buddhas but countless buddhas, buddha-fields, and bodhisattvas throughout all time and space, expanded the philosophical notion of "no-self of persons" (anātman) to the emptiness (śūnyatā) of all phenomena, and expanded the path to enlightenment to take countless lifetimes of practice, it in the same way vastly expanded the supernormal powers and wonder-working miracles of the bodhisattvas. In the Mahāyāna, bigger is definitely better.

We find evidence of this expansion of the bodhisattva's powers (ṛddhi) in the *Bodhisattvabhūmi*, a chapter of the massive *Yogācārabhūmi* attributed by tradition to the bodhisattva Maitreya transmitted through the Yogācāra philosopher Asaṅga but likely a composite work compiled between the third and fifth centuries CE.[65] About the mature Mahāyāna view found in the *Bodhisattvabhūmi* Dayal has some intriguing remarks:

> This was the high-water mark of wonder-mongering in Buddhism. This development is easily explained by the natural tendencies of the uneducated masses and the Indian thinkers' ingrained love of exaggeration.... It is possible that some genuine psychic phenomena were observed, and superstition erected the vast superstructure of marvels on this slender basis. The authentic testimony of reliable scientific investigators seems to show that thought-reading, levitation and other strange phenomena can be witnessed on rare occasions in India and other countries.[66] However that may be, the accounts of *ṛddhi*-wonders as given

in the Buddhist treatises adds a ton of sensationalism to an ounce of truth. The final outcome is the systematic catalogue of miracles in the *Bodhisattva-bhūmi*.[67]

This passage warrants some analysis before we investigate the expanded list of powers discussed in the *Bodhisattvabhūmi*. First, this passage is unusual for Dayal's *Bodhisattva Doctrine*, an erudite study of the bodhisattva doctrine in Sanskrit literature (for which SOAS, University of London, awarded Dayal a PhD in 1930). In this book, Dayal is foremost a textual scholar and rarely attempts to locate "real-world" sources for the Mahāyāna's exuberant religious imagination. However, after his disparaging classist ("uneducated masses") and racist ("Indian thinkers' ingrained love of exaggeration") remarks, he suggests that "some genuine psychic phenomena" could have been observed as the basis for the "vast superstructure of marvels" erected by superstition. The result is Buddhist Sanskrit treatises adding "a ton of sensationalism to an ounce of truth." Dayal's evidence is the "authentic testimony of reliable scientific investigators" into psychic phenomena. Thus this passage simultaneously demonstrates Dayal's commitment to a modernist Eurorationalism and his concurrent acceptance of the emerging Anglo-European scientific study of the paranormal (see chapter 2). Dayal's conclusion is that the *ṛddhi* powers found in Sanskrit Buddhist sources may have some basis in the actual lived experience of Indian Buddhists. If psi phenomena are indeed universal to human beings (as I suggest), then Dayal may be correct in this hypothesis.[68] We will revisit this theme in later chapters of this book.

The *Bodhisattvabhūmi* divides the *ṛddhi*s into two main categories: powers of transformation (*pāriṇāmikī ṛddhi*) and powers of creation (*nairmāṇikī ṛddhi*).[69] Powers of transformation take sixteen different forms:[70] (1) The ability to shake any dwelling or realm of existence (hungry ghosts, animals, humans, gods, etc.), up to an infinite number of worlds and universes. (2) The power to emit flames from the upper or lower body, while simultaneously shooting streams of water from one's limbs. This feat was famously demonstrated in Mainstream sources by the Buddha in what is known as the "Miracle of Pairs" (*yamaka-prātihārya*). Included in this power is the ability to cause one's body to glow and emit multicolored rays of light. (3) The ability to illuminate any structure or realm, up to infinite worlds and universes. (4) The power to make visible to others infinite worlds, buddha-fields, and universes. (5) The power to transform any of the four elements (earth, water, fire, and wind) into a different one, transform sounds into smells, tastes into touch, etc., including the ability to transform dung into food and ordinary stones into precious gems. (6) The power to pass through any wall or obstacle and ascend to the highest heavenly realms. (7) The ability to reduce or increase the size of anything, such as making a mountain the size of an atom or expanding a single atom to the size of a mountain. (8) The ability to make all things and forms enter into one's body, including the spectators who witness this. (9) The power to assume the appearance and ways of speech of whomever the bodhisattva is preaching to. (10) The ability to become invisible and visible to others, appearing and disappearing as many times as desired. (11) The power to control creatures as they choose, causing them to come, go, stop, and speak in any way they wish. (12) The ability to control and exceed the ṛddhis of others, except for more advanced bodhisattvas and buddhas. (13) The power to bestow intelligence and understanding on those who lack it. (14) The power to confer mindfulness on those who need it. (15) The ability to bestow material comforts and free beings from disease and other calamities. (16) And finally, the power to emit light rays that relieve and assuage the torments of all creatures in the lower realms of existence.

The powers of creation are said to manifest in two ways.[71] The first is the ability to create a phantom body (kaya-nirmāna), which can be similar or different from one's ordinary body. This illusory body can assume any characteristics the bodhisattva deems beneficial to other beings, appear to whomever the bodhisattva chooses, and perform all the regular functions of an ordinary being. The second power of creation is the power to generate a voice that preaches the Buddhist Dharma. This voice, melodious and clear, can sound like the bodhisattva or assume the tone and mannerisms of anyone the bodhisattva chooses to preach Dharma or rebuke those who are slack in their spiritual discipline. According to Dayal's analysis of the Mahāyāna Sanskrit sources, the two chief functions of all the supernormal powers are to render service to others and convert them to the Mahāyāna.[72]

The features of the Mahāyāna so far discussed—its expanded cosmology, its new religious ideal of the bodhisattva, assertion of the illusory nature of phenomena, and new vision of buddhahood—I refer to as the "Standard Model of the Mahāyāna." The maturation of this standard model, which I call the "Mature Standard Model of the Mahāyāna" (MSMM), in my view is best exemplified by the Mahāyāna sūtra known as *The Supreme Array Scripture* (Gaṇḍavyūha-sūtra), which was extant in India by the fifth century CE.[73]

THE PARANORMAL IN THE INDIAN BUDDHIST TRADITION

The Supreme Array is the story of a merchant's son named Sudhana, who quests for enlightenment in ancient India. During his travels, Sudhana visits fifty-three different spiritual guides and has numerous visionary experiences of the cosmos. Elsewhere, I summarize the worldview of *The Supreme Array* as follows:

> From the viewpoint of the *Gaṇḍavyūha*, because all things lack an essence (*svabhāva*), all worlds, realms and beings are illusory manifestations of the *dharmadhātu* [the Dharma realm]. As ultimate ground and locus, the Dharma realm is the totality of everything divided into hierarchically arranged levels. These levels represent a spiritualized view of the universe wherein the physical world is miraculously transformed into an infinitely reflecting, jewelled paradise. Although all levels interpenetrate each other, by representing the *dharmadhātu* as buildings or bodies, the *Gaṇḍavyūha* reveals a spiritual hierarchy wherein the more advanced beings inhabit spatially central or higher levels of architectural structures or human limbs. The most advanced beings, the bodhisattvas and buddhas, through their knowledge that all things are illusory, have the power (*adhiṣṭhāna*) to control, generate and manipulate reality. This power ultimately derives from their Dharma body that is one in essence with the Dharma realm. Both the *dharmakāya* and the *dharmadhātu*, from the point of view of their essence (*svabhāva*), are infinite, omnipresent, indivisible and inherently pure.[74]

The Supreme Array is a visionary narrative that demonstrates the Mahāyāna multiverse through baroque psychedelic descriptions rather than by philosophical arguments.[75] Although lacking philosophically rigorous arguments, the sūtra's worldview easily accommodates the main philosophical streams in Mahāyāna Buddhism such as Madhyamaka, Yogācāra, Tathāgatagarbha, and Chinese Huayan. Since its creation, *The Supreme Array* has been one of the most influential exemplars of the MSMM. The story was immensely popular throughout Asia and is prominently depicted in the Buddhist art and architecture of Tibet, central Asia, Japan, and Indonesia. Reliefs depicting scenes from *The Supreme Array* take pride of place on the gallery walls of Borobudur, the largest Buddhist monument in the world located in central Java.[76] *The Supreme Array* forms the final and most important section of the vast *Avataṃsaka Sūtra*, or *The Flower Ornament Scripture*, which is the foundational text for the Chinese Huayan School. *The Supreme Array*'s influence may also be found in the Chinese Chan (Zen) and Pure Land traditions.

Let us now look at the role of higher knowledges and supernormal powers in *The Supreme Array*, our paradigm of the Mature Mahāyāna.[77] The late Luis Gómez, one of the foremost contemporary scholars of the Mahāyāna, has written about "wonder-working" in the *Gaṇḍavyūha Sūtra* in two pieces written with thirty-three years between them.[78] In "The Bodhisattva as Wonder-Worker" (1977), Gómez demonstrates how *The Supreme Array* advances and synthesizes both the philosophical notion of the insubstantiality of phenomena and the powers of the bodhisattva found in early Mahāyāna sources. He writes, "Thus, the Gv [*Gaṇḍavyūha*] develops the view, expressed in other Mahayana sutras, that the very illusoriness of the world is . . . [the] foundation for the possibility of *ṛddhi*."[79] In discussing the link between *ṛddhi* and world illusion, Gómez translates a passage in the *Gaṇḍavyūha* in which the hero Sudhana praises the goddess Praśāntarutasāgaravatī: "Having understood that endless action arises from mind, that from action [arises] the whole multifarious world, that the world's true nature is mind, you display your own bodies conforming to the world. Having understood that this world is like a dream and that all Buddhas are like [mere] reflections, that all *dharmas* are like an echo, you move in the world without attachment. In an instant you show your own body even to [all] human beings in the three times."[80] Here we see expressed the Yogācāra dictum that world is "mind only," the Madhyamika notion that objects are illusory (given their lack of essence), combined with the *ṛddhi* power to multiply one's body. Thus, it is *because* the goddess realizes that all phenomena are mind only and insubstantial that she is able to create phantom bodies pervading the three times (past, present, and future).

As I discussed earlier in the section on Buddhist cosmology, *The Supreme Array* refers to the ultimate nature of reality as the Dharma Realm (*dharma-dhātu*). This Dharma Realm represents the simultaneous unity and totality of all illusory phenomena, which endlessly interpenetrate and inter-reflect one another. Advanced bodhisattvas and buddhas possess two types of bodies, the Dharma Body (*dharma-kāya/dharma-śarīra*), which is at one with the Dharma Realm, and limitless Form Bodies (*rūpa-kāya*), which can assume countless forms for the sake of liberating all beings. Although Gómez views the Dharma Realm / Dharma Body as a metaphysical foundation behind appearances,[81] I would argue that it represents a "groundless ground" and is therefore consistent with Madhyamika notions of radical insubstantiality (all phenomena lack independent essence, expressed as their "emptiness") and Lusthaus's interpretation of Yogācāra as a Buddhist form of phenomenology. Whereas other Indian systems based on nonduality, such as Advaita Vedānta and Nondual Śaivism, are happy to speak of pure consciousness as the metaphysical ground and foundation of all experience, *The Supreme Array* speaks of the Dharma Realm as either "divided into levels" (*dharmadhātu-talabheda*) or "undivided" (*asambinna-dharmadhātu*). In its divided aspect, it represents the totality of phenomena, and in its undivided aspect it represents the locus or "place" of all activity and experience. The Dharma Realm is the lifeworld, the totality of all phenomena as experienced by countless sentient beings. In this lifeworld, all phenomena are dreamlike, but nothing exists independently from consciousness (just as in a dream), yet consciousness itself depends on the appearance of phenomena, so it is not a metaphysical foundation of reality.

Although a single unity, the undivided Dharma Realm is like the empty set or zero in mathematics. As such it lacks any characteristics, but like a pregnant void it is full of limitless possibility. The Dharma Realm as groundless "pregnant void" connotes the sense of emptiness as implied by the Sanskrit Buddhist term "emptiness" (*śūnyatā*), which can mean empty, a void, a hollow, space, vacuity, a vacuum, deserted place, or barren woman.[82] In itself, this undivided Dharma Realm is nothing but the unified force and locus of the "realm of phenomena" (another possible translation of *dharmadhātu*) divided into its infinite and variegated levels. It is everything from every perspective in every dimension of spacetime throughout the boundless omniverse all at once. It's true nature is emptiness—its very lack of a true nature. In this sense, it is antimetaphysical or possibly a negative or apophatic metaphysics expressed as the groundless ground, the empty set, beyond thought and language but directly intuited by perfect wisdom. Since all phenomena are dreamlike and in constant flux, experience and its hermeneutical horizons are never fixed or static but constantly transforming. Likewise, human epistemology and ontology are never foreclosed—we are forever seeking greater understanding and knowledge.[83]

In summing up *The Supreme Array*'s view of reality, the bodhisattva's path, and its expanded notion of *ṛddhi*, Gómez writes:

Going beyond the common ground of the Mahāyāna, the *Gv* is trying to establish an equation between the true nature of *dharmas*, the *dharmadhātu*, the ultimate essence of Buddhahood, and the Bodhisattva's course (*cārya*) represented by the functions of the Form Body. To this purpose the sutra expands the notion or *ṛddhi*. The principal fruit of concentration and trance is presented then as the attainment of the faculty of reproducing reality. Thus the Bodhisattva's course is often described as consisting in the display of these fantastic manifestations, the *vikurvaṇa*, which show, on a cognitive level, the emptiness of all things (*dharmas*), while on another level ... bring about the release of numerous living beings.[84]

Thus, *The Supreme Array* fuses the notions of supernormal powers, the path to enlightenment, and the nature of reality into a unified vision. As Gómez writes elsewhere, "The master of meditation is also a master magician and a master of reality, and in this mastery lies the liberating power of meditation, as if *ṛddhipāda* were simultaneously the basis for liberation and basis for extraordinary, wonderous powers."[85] According to *The Supreme Array*, advanced bodhisattvas and buddhas are wonderworkers with nearly limitless power to generate and manipulate the very fabric of reality. We have seen that the use of the higher knowledges and supernormal powers in the Buddhist tradition have always played an important role in confirming the Buddhist worldview and in converting others to the Buddhist path. With the *Gaṇḍavyūha*, we witness the endpoint of many centuries of thought and practice culminating in a cosmic vision of a magical omniverse, which given its dreamlike nature, allows those who have intuitive insight into its true nature, the advanced bodhisattvas and buddhas, to become the ultimate thaumaturges.

The Standard Model of the Mahāyāna as depicted in its mature form in *The Supreme Array* has remained remarkably stable as "*the* Mahāyāna view of reality" for the last 1,500 years of Mahāyāna Buddhist history regardless of geographical location, culture, language register, sect, or school of Mahāyāna Buddhism being practiced. In its general form we find it in the *Avataṃsaka Sūtra*, *Lotus Sūtra*, *Perfection of Wisdom Sūtras*, *Laṅkāvatāra Sūtra*, and many others. Even later Vajrayāna (tantric) Buddhism in India, China, Tibet, and Japan all assume the worldview described in *The Supreme Array*. Moreover, since there are currently estimated to be over 300 million Mahāyāna Buddhists in the world, this worldview continues to exert a "real-world" influence on the beliefs and practices of a significant portion of humanity.

Indian Tantric Buddhism

Beginning around the fifth century CE, a new genre of Mahāyāna literature began to appear promoting innovative forms of practice, including rituals and meditation techniques for worldly gain and, later, for accelerated spiritual progress.[86] These new methods make extensive use of various kinds of sacred diagrams (*maṇḍala*), hand gestures (*mudrā*), sacred verbal formulas (*mantra*), and spells (*dhāraṇī*) as concrete expressions of the nature of reality. Much of this practice revolves around the visualization of various buddhas and other holy beings, and the use of creative imagination plays a key role in the process of realization. There is also a proliferation in the number and types of buddhas and other deities, including ferocious or "wrathful" buddhas and bodhisattvas in the later phases. Great stress is laid upon the importance of the guru or religious preceptor and on the necessity of receiving the instructions and appropriate initiations from them. In later texts, a spiritual physiology of energy centers (*cakra*) is taught as part of the process of transformation, which makes use of sexual yoga.

These changes were part of a larger pan-Indian religious movement generally termed "Tantra," which was to have a major impact on Hinduism, Buddhism, and, to a lesser extent, Jainism. By around the seventh century, the Buddhist form of Tantra came to call itself first the "Vehicle of Mantras" (*mantrayāna*) and then the "Diamond Vehicle" (*vajrayāna*).[87] Buddhist Tantra represents a special path that arose within Mahāyāna Buddhism, which while generally embracing the same aims claimed to provide a rapid means to achieve the goal of omniscient buddhahood through its distinctive techniques. In the early Buddhist tantric texts, we see elaborations of visualization techniques and methods that are presaged in *The Supreme Array*, which may have functioned as the inspiration for them.[88] Some of these "proto-tantric" features found in the *Gaṇḍavyūha* are elaborate descriptions of sacred circles (*maṇḍala*), an emphasis on the absolute obedience to the spiritual guides as gurus, a description of a secret spiritual society (organizational esotericism), and a hint of sexual yoga.[89]

We can summarize several key features that serve to distinguish Buddhist Tantra from other forms of Indian Buddhism:[90]

1. Use of sacred verbal formulas (*mantra*), visualization techniques, and initiation rituals
2. Use of sacred diagrams (*maṇḍala*) and hand gestures (*mudra*)
3. An emphasis on secrecy (esotericism)
4. Revaluation of the value of the body and skillful use of negative mental states
5. The importance of the guru as preceptor and initiator into secret practices
6. The use of impure substances and objects in its later phases
7. The use of ritualized sex and sexual yoga in its later phases

Various classificatory schemes have been used within India and Tibet to organize the vast array of Buddhist tantric texts, which can provide a rough chronological guide to the development of Buddhist Tantra in India.[91] One scheme divides the texts into five categories: Kriyā, Caryā, Yoga, Mahāyoga, and Yoginī tantras. In the large class of the Kriyā, or "action," tantras (second to eighth centuries CE), rituals and this-worldly goals are the focus. In the Caryā, or "practice," tantras, both outward rituals and inward visualizations are taught, and increasing emphasis is placed on the attainment of buddhahood (soteriology) as opposed to merely worldly goals. The most important text of this small class is the *Mahāvairocanābhisaṃbodhi Tantra* (approximately seventh century CE), also called simply the *Mahāvairocana Tantra*. The primary buddha and sacred circle (*maṇḍala*) focus on Vairocana, a cosmic manifestation of the historical Buddha who first appears in the *Flower Ornament* and *Supreme Array* sūtras. The Yoga tantras (approximately eighth century) are focused on liberation, develop the "five families" of directional buddhas, and continue to emphasize Vairocana as the central figure of the *maṇḍala*. In the Mahāyoga, or "Great Yoga," tantras (end of the eighth century CE), fierce and semifierce buddhas and sexual elements appear for the first time. The most important text of this class is the *Guhyasamāja Tantra*, which places Akṣobhya with his Vajra Family at the center of the *maṇḍala*. Also, in this class we find recommendations to employ forbidden substances such as alcohol, meat, and bodily fluids in rituals.

The Yoginī tantras appear in the ninth and tenth century CE and are thought to represent the final phase of Indian Buddhism.[92] Here we find the continued ritual use of sexual yoga and impure substances; the appearance of fully developed wrathful buddhas such as Hevajra, Heruka, and Vajrayoginī placed at the center of the *maṇḍala*; the use of cremation ground practices and ornamentation adopted most likely from tantric Śaivism, and an important role given to female buddhas, female deities, and spiritual beings often called yoginīs ("female practitioners of yoga") or ḍākinīs ("female sky-goers"). So, for example, visualization *maṇḍalas* may have male and female buddhas such as Hevajra and Nairātmyā in sexual union surrounded by eight yoginīs or a female buddha such as Vajrayoginī or Kurukulla standing alone at the center. An important text from this class is the *Hevajra Tantra*, which recommends sexual yoga and the manipulation of internal spiritual physiology and emphasizes the role of feminine spiritual powers. Other important tantras of this class are the *Kālacakra Tantra* and the *Cakrasamvara Tantra*.[93]

Around perhaps the tenth century, a new Buddhist tantric ideal of human perfection arose known as the mahāsiddha, or "great adept," who through the antinomian practices of the Yoginī tantras were believed to attain full buddhahood in this life.[94] Since the mahāsiddhas sought realization of the innate (*sahaja*) pristine nature of reality, sometimes their methods are referred to as the "Innate Vehicle," or *Sahaja-yāna*. A legendary account of the most famous mahāsiddhas was composed by the Indian master Abhayadatta in his *Lives of the Eighty-Four Siddhas*, which has survived in Tibetan translation.[95] The mahāsiddhas were first and foremost laypeople who rejected the status quo, scholasticism, and celibacy; engaged in sexual yoga; and ingested forbidden substances. Through these practices famous adepts like Saraha, Tilopa, Naropa, and others were believed to attain great magical powers (*siddhi*) and the ultimate goal of the "Great Seal" (*mahāmudrā*), a direct realization of ultimate reality, characterized as "great bliss" (*mahāsukha*). The lives and teachings of the mahāsiddhas gained tremendous popularity in Tibet, especially in the Kagyu school, having a major impact on the development of Tibetan Buddhism, which is tantric through and through.

Siddhas were great magicians, alchemists, and masters of enchantment who wielded superhuman powers to teach others and display the true nature of reality. With the development of the siddha ideal in late tantric Buddhism, we witness a movement away from the more traditional Buddhist language of *iddhi/ṛddhi* and the adoption of the term *siddhi* ("accomplishment"), the common expression used within tantric Śaivism for the psychic and magical powers of these Buddhist saints.⁹⁶ In addition to possessing the usually *ṛddhi* powers such as the ability to fly,⁹⁷ some mahāsiddhas possessed special powers such as the capacity to attain physical immortality, to generate "inner heat" in the body,⁹⁸ to control their dreams (dream yoga), and to project their consciousness out of their body into other people or other realms at the time of death.⁹⁹

Magic

Buddhist Tantra has always had a close association with the practice of magic. About this connection David Gray writes:

> For at least two centuries, around the 5th century CE, Buddhists produced a growing number of works focusing on magical formulas known as *dhāraṇī* and ritual practices that employ them. These gradually became more sophisticated, leading ultimately to the composition of the "esoteric sūtras" and tantras. Many of the early Buddhist tantric scriptures, which later were labeled "ritual tantras" (*kriyātantra*), are basically grimoires, compilations of magical rituals which were purported to achieve various worldly ends.¹⁰⁰

In later tantric practice, these "worldly ends" would be integrated with Buddhist soteriology, so that we witness a fusion of psychic powers, magical ability, and spiritual attainment. However, it would be a mistake to consider magic a uniquely "tantric" feature of Indian Buddhism. As Sam van Schaik has recently elaborated at length, magic has always played an important role in the Buddhist tradition.¹⁰¹ Moreover, the presence of magic and nonsectarian magicians, sorcerers, witches, and various other magic users in Indian literature is both widespread and ancient.¹⁰² In some Pāli and Sanskrit sources, we even find rival ascetics accusing the Buddha of being a magician.¹⁰³ As Fiordalis indicates, the accusation is obviously pejorative but may demonstrate a grudging respect for the Buddha's psychic abilities. Probably the most famous display of the Buddha was his "Twin Miracle" at Śrāvastī, where he is said to have risen in the air and emitted fire from the top half of his body and water from the lower half, alternated them, and then illuminated the cosmos.¹⁰⁴ On the same occasion, the Buddha also magically created countless other buddhas arrayed throughout space performing various miracles.[105] From these accounts and others like it, we see that the Buddhist tradition maintained that the Buddha on occasion would use his powers for spectacular effect. However, we should put these in context with a passage in the *Kevaṭṭa-sutta*, where we find the Buddha declaring that the greatest type of "miraculous display" is the teaching of the Dharma itself.[106] Thus, the use of miracles, magic, and various powers are considered secondary to and instrumentally related to converting and teaching people the message of the Buddha.

It appears that the Indian traditions distinguished between magic as acquired by casting spells and the attainment of psychic powers through yogic concentration. However, when we arrive at the tantras, such sharp distinctions begin to break down. Often magical rituals are described as requiring high levels of concentration and visualization to be effective. In van Shaik's study of a Tibetan book of Buddhist spells dating from the tenth century found at Dunhuang in central Asia, he specifies several different types of spells paradigmatic of various categories found within the tradition for centuries. For example, the book describes divination, clairvoyance, fortune telling, and spells to cure various illnesses, cure demonic possession, control the flow of rivers and springs, find treasure, control others' emotions (love and hate magic), become invisible, summon spirits, bring rain, conceive a child, protect an unborn fetus, aid in study, and protect travelers.[107] Other types of magic found in the tantras include rituals, charms, and formulas to protect one from snake bites and poisons and spells for harming or killing one's enemies.

Conclusion

In this chapter we have surveyed some of the primary canonical and scholarly literature addressing the paranormal in Indian Buddhist literature. We have seen that in traditional Buddhist cosmologies the multiverse is teeming with various nonhuman intelligent beings of all sorts, according to the inexorable law of karma. Also, from its earliest formation, through the Mahāyāna and up to the late tantric phase of Indian Buddhism, supernormal powers, psychic abilities, and magical powers have always been present. These features would continue to play an important role as Buddhism spread from India to Southeast, Central, and East Asia. Everywhere

THE PARANORMAL IN THE INDIAN BUDDHIST TRADITION

Buddhism traveled, its cosmology and notions of the paranormal and psychic blended and adapted to local beliefs and practices. Even today, from Thailand to Tibet magic and the psychic play an important role. While canonical and scholastic accounts of the paranormal are useful systemizations of the most prominent understandings of these powers and abilities, most Buddhists throughout history were much more likely to be familiar with miraculous events and extraordinary powers through the vast collections of popular Buddhist stories, which have been orally transmitted, written down, told, and retold throughout the centuries. In India collections like the *Jātaka* stories (previous birth stories of the Buddha), the various collections of *avadāna* stories (heroic tales and past lives of Buddhist figures), and the Pāli *Pettavathu* (karmic ghost stories) were important vehicles of this rich narrative tradition.[108] Likewise, to name just a few examples, from Tibet we find countless *rNam-thar* (biographies) of tantric Buddhist saints such as Rangjung Dorje (1284–1339), the Third Karmapa, and the famous Milarepa, who among his many feats killed numerous relatives through black magic to avenge his mother before meeting his guru Marpa.[109] From China we know of hundreds of Buddhist miracle stories from the early medieval period, stories of great thaumaturgy, miraculous stories about the *Lotus Sūtra*, and deathbed testimonials about Amitābha's Pure Land.[110] We have stories of Buddhist wizards from Burma and numerous modern biographies of forest meditation masters endowed with extraordinary powers from Thailand.[111] In the next chapter, we shift focus and investigate the contemporary Euro-American fascination with and scientific study of the paranormal, beginning in the eighteenth century.

TWO

The Enchanted West

The Contemporary Scientific Study of the Paranormal

IN HIS *The Myth of Disenchantment: Magic, Modernity, and the Birth of the Human Sciences,* Jason A. Josephson-Storm systematically dismantles the discourse of modernity's "disenchantment" by tracing the genealogy of this academic myth and demonstrating how some of the most "scientific" and "rational" thinkers of Europe and America since the seventeenth century have engaged with the occult and paranormal.[1] For example, eminent scientists, philosophers, and academics such as Francis Bacon, Isaac Newton, Marie Curie, Jean Baptiste Perrin, Charles Richet, Henri Bergson, William James, and Sigmund Freud were deeply interested in magic, spirits, and spiritualism. Moreover, during the last two centuries, as theorists were formulating the concepts of modernity and disenchantment, others (think Aleister Crowley) were leading revivals in the occult, magic, and spiritual mediumship. Even those responsible for creating the myths of disenchantment and modernity were often highly knowledgeable of and interested in magic, mysticism, and the occult.

This interest in the paranormal was not restricted to an elite few from bygone generations. Based on a YouGov survey from 2015 and Gallup poll data from 2005, Josephson-Storm concludes that *"only approximately a quarter of Americans are* not *believers in the paranormal."*[2] Thus, Josephson-Storm argues that the "disenchantment of the West" is a modern myth and that the West has always been "enchanted." In this chapter, I delve into an investigation of this Enchanted West by outlining some of the seminal figures and organizations in Europe and North America that have engaged in the scientific study of the paranormal.

Society for Psychical Research

One of the oldest and most prestigious organizations devoted to the scientific study of psychic phenomena is the Society for Psychical Research, founded in 1882 by academics and intellectuals in the United Kingdom.[3] Although largely a response to the explosion of popular interest in Spiritualism in the mid-nineteenth century, the society has dedicated itself to the study of numerous psychic phenomena, such as telepathy, hypnosis, clairvoyance, physical manifestations during séances, apparitions, and hauntings.[4] Some of its notable members have been J. J. Thompson (discoverer of the electron); William Crookes (discoverer of thallium); Andrew Lang (folklorist); Arthur Balfour (prime minister, 1902–1905); Camille Flammarion (French astronomer); the classicist Gilbert Murray; the physicist Sir Oliver Lodge; the Nobel laureates Henri Bergson, Lord Rayleigh, and Charles Richet; Charles Lutwidge Dodgson (Lewis Carroll); Sigmund Freud; and Marie Curie.[5]

Society members Edmund Gurney, Frank Podmore, and Frederic Myers published an early landmark study titled *Phantasms of the Living* (1886), which contains details of 702 apparitional encounters.[6] In *Phantasms*, the authors coin the term "crisis apparition" for the ghostly appearance of loved ones, close relatives, or friends who were later discovered to be dying or in mortal danger. According to Gurney, crisis apparitions are a type of hallucination telepathically generated by the dying or endangered person. Following this study, the society compiled the "Census on Hallucinations," the largest survey of its kind, which investigates the chance probability of apparitional manifestations coinciding with a crisis. The likelihood of these events happening merely by chance the society claimed could be ruled out through rigorous statistical analysis.[7] Another important early study was Fred Myers's posthumously published *Human Personality and Its Survival of Bodily Death* (1903).[8]

In 1885, the American Society for Psychic Research (ASPR) was founded in Boston. Notable members include the psychologist and philosopher

William James, Sigmund Freud, and Carl Jung (honorary members); Chester Carlson (the inventor of xerography); the quantum physicist David Bohm; the psychologist Gardner Murphy; and the dream researcher Montague Ullman. According to the society's website, it investigates "the prevalence and meaning of extraordinary human experience from creativity, hypnosis, dreams and states of consciousness to telepathy, clairvoyance, precognition, psychokinesis, healing, and the question of survival after death."[9] Now located in New York City, the ASPR maintains an extensive library and archive and has published the *Journal of the American Society for Psychic Research* since 1884.

Charles Fort

Charles Fort (1874–1932) holds a unique place in the Western history of the occult, or what has been called "Western Occulture."[10] Fort was a man whose search for the unexplained became an obsession. An avid reader of newspapers, journals, magazines, and any stories of strange phenomena, Fort spent untold hours at the New York Public Library and the British Library in London reading and taking thousands upon thousands of notes. Fort's primary interest was in collecting accounts of what he called "sunlight mysteries," strange events or anomalous occurrences that happen to everyday people during the ordinary course of life. Fort's goal was not to explain these phenomena as much as to point out how both traditional religious thinking and the scientific explanations of the day failed to account for them. For Fort, the supernatural was hiding in plain sight, but dogmatic belief prevented most people from seeing it. In the words of Jeffrey Kripal, Fort "was an intellectually promiscuous adventurer, a journalist of the metaphysical in search of what we might call, with only slight apologies to Freud, the parapsychology of everyday life."[11]

Fort wrote a number of books based on his compiled data, beginning with *The Book of the Damned* in 1919.[12] "Damned" in the title refers to anomalous data excluded by science and religion because they cannot be sufficiently explained by them. In this work, Fort recounts reports of frogs and other strange objects falling from the sky; tales of giants, fairies, poltergeists, and airships (UFOs); stories about the disappearance and reappearance of people; and people spontaneously combusting (all occurring since 1800, Fort's historical cutoff point). Following *The Book of the Damned*, Fort wrote *New Lands* (1923), *Lo!* (1931), and *Wild Talent* (1932).[13] In *New Lands*, he further elaborates his notion (introduced in *Damned*) of the "Super-Sargasso Sea," a place above the earth where objects materialize and then descend from the skies, and his theory of continents existing above the earth's skies. In *Lo!*, Fort explains his notion of "teleportation" (a term he coined) to the Super-Sargasso Sea as a way of accounting for humans and ships disappearing, the appearance of strange animals (cryptozoology), cattle mutilations, and poltergeists. He also develops a new cosmology wherein Earth is stationary and surrounded by a hard shell. In *Wild Talents*, Fort continues his strange tales of poltergeists, spontaneous human combustion, animal mutilations, vampires, ghosts, werewolves, witchcraft, and psychic murder. Here he largely abandons his notion of teleportation in favor of the idea of "wild talents," the thesis that primitive humans developed various psychic abilities, such as psychokinesis and telepathy, in our distant past as a survival mechanism.

Anyone familiar with Fort's tongue-in-cheek writing style, his wit, and his biting critiques of the science and religion of his day will recognize his antiauthoritarianism. It is likely that he developed his various theories merely as rhetorical foils to attack the authoritarian positions of science and religion. In his writing, fact and fiction, imagination, and reality blur into one another. More important than his bizarre theories are his endless tales (meticulously recounted and documented) of the truly strange and unexplainable events that are happening seemingly everywhere in the world all the time. It is not surprising that contemporary science fiction writers have mined Fort's books for material.[14]

In summing up Fort's collected works, Kripal writes, "Fort thus brings the fantastic into the real world, or better, he shows that the real world is already fantastic, and always has been. By doing so, he dissolves the boundaries between the imaginary and the real and scatters endless seeds of metaphysical confusion."[15] As the arch "Comedian of the Fantastic," Fort has inspired a cult following of "Forteans," and the term "Fortean phenomena" is now commonly used by parapsychologists and psychic researchers for anomalous events such as psychic powers, UFOs, cryptozoology, balls of light, apparitions, biological oddities, animal rain, and spontaneous human combustion.[16]

The Laboratory Study of Psi: J. B. Rhine, Charles Tart, and Dean Radin

J. B. Rhine

In the early twentieth century, paranormal research advanced into the laboratory. Joseph Banks (J. B.) Rhine (1895–1980), the father of modern parapsychology, stands out as the single most important individual for establishing the laboratory study of psychic phenomena in the United States. Initially a botanist, Rhine and his wife, Louisa, became fascinated by the paranormal in the 1920s, and Rhine switched careers to study mediumship and psychic phenomena. In 1927, Rhine accepted an offer to work at the newly instituted Department of Psychology at Duke University. There, disillusioned with the studying of mediums, Rhine established laboratory protocols for the study of what he called "extrasensory perception," or ESP. With the help of Karl Zener, a perceptual psychologist, Rhine developed a set of cards with various symbols on one side (Zener cards) to test students' ability to accurately guess these symbols.[17] Often the results were merely according to random chance; however, certain exceptional subjects were witnessed to score well above chance. Using such statistical methods over thousands of trials, Rhine was able to establish the high statistical probability of ESP (telepathy and clairvoyance). Rhine published his results in a landmark study, *Extra-Sensory Perception* (1934).[18]

Following the success of his *Extra-Sensory Perception* in 1934, Rhine secured funding to establish the Parapsychological Laboratory at Duke University and began studies on precognition and psychokinesis (PK).[19] In 1937, Rhine founded the *Journal of Parapsychology*, and his book *New Frontiers of the Mind* (1937), Rhine's popular account of his lab's research findings, was published.[20] This was followed shortly by the much more technical response to various criticisms, *Extra-Sensory Perception After Sixty Years: A Critical Appraisal of the Research in Extra-Sensory Perception* (1940) by Rhine and others.[21] In 1957, Rhine proposed the founding of the Parapsychological Association and in 1962 started the Foundation for Research on the Nature of Man (FRNM), which continued as an independent organization after Rhine retired from Duke in 1965. For thirty years, FRNM functioned as a parent organization to the Institute for Parapsychology and in 1995 was renamed the Rhine Research Center.[22]

Rhine's contributions to the scientific study of the paranormal were substantial. He founded the first research lab in an academic setting devoted to the study of psi; he developed standardized experimental procedures for psi that could be replicated by others; he was able to isolate and identify substantial evidence for telepathy, clairvoyance, precognition, and psychokinesis in a laboratory setting; and he developed a network of researchers through his founding of the *Journal of Parapsychology* and the international Parapsychological Association. From his many decades of research, Rhine asserted three fundamental points concerning the nature of psi (the "Rhinean Doctrine"): (1) psi is nonphysical, (2) psi is unconscious (it cannot be willed or controlled), and (3) psi is universal (although some people appear to be more gifted at it than others).[23]

Charles Tart

Following the work of Rhine, a new generation of paranormal researchers took up the laboratory study of psi. Charles Tart (b. 1937), professor emeritus at the Institute of Transpersonal Psychology in Palo Alto and Psychology at the University of California at Davis, is one of the leading researchers in the fields of altered states, transpersonal psychology, and parapsychology.[24] He has held several other academic positions, including Bigelow Chair of Consciousness Studies at the University of Nevada in Las Vegas, visiting professor in East-West psychology at the California Institute of Integral Studies, instructor in psychiatry at the School of Medicine of the University of Virginia, and a consultant on government-funded parapsychological research at the Stanford Research Institute (now known as SRI International).[25] He is one of the founding figures of the field of transpersonal psychology, and his scientific research has investigated a wide range of phenomena, including altered states of consciousness, hypnosis, dreams, telepathy, precognition, remote viewing, and out-of-body experiences (OBEs). Tart is the author of numerous books and over 250 journal articles. His edited volumes *Altered States of Consciousness* (1969) and *Transpersonal Psychologies* (1975) are considered classics in the field.

Through his writings and research, Tart has aimed "to build bridges between the scientific and spiritual communities and to help bring about a refinement and integration of Western and Eastern approaches for knowing the world and for personal and social growth."[26] This goal is clearly apparent in one of his most recent popular books, *The Secret Science of the Soul: How Evidence of the Paranormal Is Bringing Science and Spirit Together* (2017), first published in 2009 as *The End of Materialism: How Evidence of the Paranormal Is Bringing Science and Spirit Together* (2009). In *The Secret Science*, Tart draws on his five decades of research to argue for the reality of psi, the importance of "essential science" (as opposed to what he calls "scientism") for its study, how psi is evidence of the spiritual (nonmaterial) nature of mind, and how psi research could help bring science and spirituality together.

Tart begins *The Secret Science* by introducing what he calls "The Western Creed" as a psychological exercise in the affirmations of a strictly materialist universe, devoid of creator, supernatural beings, meaning, or purpose, wherein the mind is the brain, physical death is the end with no afterlife, and all moral judgments are subjective.[27] In his formulation, Tart assumes that the logical stance of belief in the Western Creed would be selfishness and hedonism without addressing possible alternatives such as secular humanism or existentialism. Tart also associates the creed with a dogmatic adherence to materialist science, which he calls "scientism." As an alternative to this Tart proposes "essential science" (which he also calls "essential common sense"), based on careful observation, experimentation, prediction, and peer review. Thus, Tart sees in essential science the tools and methodologies to study the psychic or nonmaterial (spiritual) aspects of the mind. Moreover, Tart maintains that although essential science is the ideal, numerous "pathologies of thinking" and "pseudoskepticism" (in the form of a dogmatic adherence to scientistic materialism) can and often do interfere with scientific research into the paranormal.

In subsequent chapters of *The Secret Science*, Tart discusses what he calls "The Big Five" psi phenomena (chapters 6–10), which in his view have been established with scientific experimentation beyond any reasonable doubt: telepathy, clairvoyance (remote viewing), precognition, psychokinesis (PK), and psychic healing (PK on biological systems). In discussing these forms of psi, Tart addresses important lab research he and others have carried out demonstrating the very high probabilities that these phenomena do exist. Although lab results often demonstrate weak results, with participants scoring perhaps an average hit rate for targets of 30 percent (when a 25 percent hit rate according to chance would be expected), even a 5 percent difference above chance over many trials results in odds way above chance in favor of some unknown psychic influence (telepathy, precognition, clairvoyance, etc.). Here Tart addresses a common critique by debunkers of these statistical methods: "If 'There's got to be something wrong with the statistics!' as dedicated pseudoskeptics often loudly proclaim, most fields of science are in bad trouble, because they use the same basic statistics."[28] In other words, the mathematics of probability used in psi research is the same math that science in general uses to study significant effects, such as the effectiveness of a new pharmaceutical drug.

In *The Secret Science*, Tart describes one of his early telepathy experiments, designed to test his hypothesis that the delayed results of testing were causing the "extinction" effect of psi ability. Tart postulated that in earlier experiments initial positive psi results dropping off and returning to results not significantly above chance could be caused by test subjects not receiving immediate feedback when their methods were successful. Tart wanted to see if "people could be trained to use telepathy more effectively by giving them immediate feedback on how they were doing," which would thereby overcome extinction of the psi.[29] By choosing participants who demonstrated some preexisting ability and giving them immediate feedback, Tart was able to produce results that were far above probability and did not diminish over time. Moreover, some of the participants "showed suggestive signs of getting better with the feedback training."[30] This result strongly suggests that talented individuals could be trained to improve their psychic abilities.

In the second part of *The Secret Science* (chapters 11–16), Tart addresses the "Many Maybes" with regard to psychic phenomena: "postcognition" (nonordinary means of recollecting past events), out-of-body experiences (OBEs), near-death experiences (NDEs), after-death communications (ADCs), mediumship, and reincarnation. In one of Tart's early experiments in OBEs, he was working with an exceptional subject he calls Miss Z, who claimed to frequently have OBEs during sleep. Under observation in a sleep lab, Miss Z woke from sleep and was able to correctly identify a five-digit number that had been written on a piece of paper and placed on a high shelf above her bed. As Tart notes, "The odds against guessing a five-digit number by chance alone on one try are a hundred thousand to one, so this is a remarkable event!"[31] Likewise, regarding the other phenomena, Tart discusses a number of remarkable case studies suggestive of the mind existing separately from the brain. In summing up his view, Tart writes, "I believe that psi phenomena like clairvoyance and PK are the means that link the transpersonal and the physical; that is, our mind has an intimate and ongoing relationship with our body, brain, and nervous system through what I've termed auto-clairvoyance, where 'mind' reads the physical state of the brain, and auto-PK, where 'mind' uses psychokinesis to affect the operation of the physical brain."[32] Thus, after many decades of research, Tart concludes that evidence for the existence of psi is beyond any reasonable doubt, and such evidence provides compelling reasons to believe in a transpersonal spiritual (nonmaterial) reality.

Dean Radin

Like Charles Tart before him, Dean Radin (b. 1952) is one of the premier scientists in the world studying psi phenomena. Radin received his BS in electrical engineering from the University of Massachusetts, his master's degree in electrical engineering from the University of Illinois, and a PhD in psychology from the University of Illinois. Since completing his PhD in 1979, he has held positions at AT&T Bell Laboratories (Bell Labs) and later at GTE Laboratories (now Verizon) researching advanced telecommunications. While at Bell Labs, Radin began publishing some of his psi experiments and presenting the findings at the meetings of the Parapsychological Association and Society for Scientific Exploration.[33] After holding positions at Princeton University, the University of Edinburgh, the University of Nevada, Interval Research Corporation, and SRI International (where he took part in classified government research on psychic phenomena), Radin joined the staff at the Institute of Noetic Sciences (IONS) in 2001, where he is currently chief scientist.[34] He also holds the position of distinguished professor of transpersonal and integral psychology at the California Institute of Integral Studies (CIIS).[35] He is the author or coauthor of hundreds of technical articles, over a hundred peer-reviewed journal articles, four dozen book chapters, and four popular books: *The Conscious Universe* (1997), *Entangled Minds* (2006), *Supernormal* (2013), and *Real Magic* (2018).[36]

Highly relevant to this study is Radin's *Supernormal: Science, Yoga, and the Evidence for Extraordinary Psychic Ability* (2013), wherein he compares his findings from psi research to the *siddhi*s as described in Patañjali's *Yogasūtra*, cites numerous examples of psi abilities from the Buddhist and Hindu meditation traditions, and investigates the psychic abilities of contemporary meditators.[37] Radin begins his study with a provocative question: "Was the Buddha just a nice guy?"[38] This sets the stage for a discussion of psychic powers found in the Indian traditions and the modern research on them. As a contrast between contemporary views, Radin points out that the Dalai Lama in his conversations with neuroscientists has made it clear that he assumes the reality of certain psychic abilities, which as materialists the neuroscientists reject.[39] As a scientist, Radin is convinced that the way to move the debate between traditional religious understandings and modern science forward is through empirical evidence. According to him, "Laboratory data amassed over many decades suggest that some of what the yogis, mystics, saints, and shamans have claimed is probably right. And that means some of today's scientific assumptions are probably wrong."[40] This is the central thesis of Radin's book, and the force of his arguments comes primarily through data compiled from carefully controlled laboratory experiments he and other scientists have performed over many decades and from the statistical analysis of those data. Radin employs powerful tools and methodologies from science, such as meta-analysis and the mathematics of probability, to demonstrate the likelihood of psi phenomena. The results strongly suggest the reality of psi and are potentially paradigm shifting for materialist-oriented sciences.

In part 1 of *Supernormal*, Radin summarizes the Western reception of yoga (chapter 1), the perennial philosophy; altered states in shamanism, psychedelics, and extreme sports (chapter 3); and mysticism and miracles (chapter 4). In chapter 5, "Unbelievable," Radin explores the Western scientific bias against the possible existence of psi. When discussing the stigma and taboo around the academic study of the paranormal, Radin writes: "In spite of the fact that opinion surveys consistently show that a majority of the world's population is fascinated with psychic phenomena, fewer than 1 percent of the world's accredited universities have even a single faculty member known for his or her scientific interest in these phenomena."[41]

In his discussion of the various reasons for this taboo, Radin addresses long-standing biases entrenched in the dogmatic adherence to a type of mechanistic materialism, which have led to the repeated disavowal of even the possibility of psi. He points out the often-blatant ignorance or disregard of the existing body of evidence for psi by some scientists and the "sunk cost bias" of professional skeptics (whose careers are based on debunking psi), who attempt to explain away any positive evidence for the phenomena. Radin, as a psychologist, also discusses the Myers-Briggs Type Inventory of personalities in relation to psi phenomena. In this regard, some research suggests that "intuitive-feeling" types are much more open to the mystical and the paranormal, while the category of "sensing-thinking-judging" (STJ) types are much less open to such phenomena. Evidence appears to indicate that most corporate-, private-, and public-sector executives are STJ types and therefore adverse to funding psi-research-related projects.[42] The remainder of part 1 is devoted to descriptions of the *Yogasūtra* and the *siddhis*. Here Radin speculates that certain individuals may have natural psi abilities. He writes: "I suspect that there are those among us who have high-functioning siddhis gained not through extensive meditation practice but through raw talent. Like Olympic athletes or Carnegie Hall musicians, these people are rare. Based on my experience in testing a wide range of participants in laboratory psi tests, I'd estimate that perhaps one in ten or a hundred thousand have exceptional skills comparable to the traditional siddhis."[43]

In part 2 of *Supernormal*, Radin surveys the scientific research on precognition, telepathy, psychokinesis, and clairvoyance in relation to the *siddhis* and meditation. In summarizing a meta-analysis of data collected from 309 "forced-choice" experiments to test for precognition conducted from 1935 to 1987, Radin writes: "Among the 309 forced-choice experiments, the combined result showed a small but repeatable effect, with odds against chance of 10^{25} to one. That's ten million billion billion to one. This means that the target was hit far too often for it to be considered a chance effect, suggesting that on average this group of people demonstrated a real skill—in this case, precognition."[44]

"Free-response" experiments for precognition conducted in various labs over several decades obtained similar positive results with odds against chance often several million to one.[45] Radin then goes into a detailed account of presentiment experiments he and others have conducted using measurements of unconscious physiological responses, such as skin conductivity, eye movement, and brain activity, to various visual and auditory stimuli. Meta-analytical data demonstrate statistically significant positive results in humans and animals of physiological responses to stimuli beginning *before* the stimuli were presented, thus demonstrating some type of unconscious presentiment of the future. Moreover, in a study Radin conducted with two groups—meditators and nonmeditators—the results indicated a dramatic difference in brainwave activity of meditators, who were able to gain a presentiment of random stimuli on average 1.5 seconds before it occurred. About this Radin writes: "This outcome supports the idea that these meditators were accessing future information in a way that is consistent with the first siddhi described by Patanjali."[46]

In his survey of experiments to test telepathy (chapter 10), Radin recounts that the British Society for Psychical Research began testing for telepathy in the 1880s. However, in the 1970s, such tests were greatly advanced with the development of the "ganzfeld." *Ganzfeld* is a German word meaning "whole field." Gestalt psychologists developed a ganzfeld as a mild form of unpatterned sensory stimulus to test visual and mental imagery. Using halved ping pong balls and headphones, experimenters could cover the eyes and ears of subjects and submit them to a soft pink light and "pink" noise (a kind of swooshing sound), while they relaxed in a seated position. In a short amount of time, this mild form of sensory deprivation caused subjects to enter a dreamlike, visionary state of awareness. Psi researchers postulated that subjects in such a state would be more receptive to receive telepathic messages sent to them from someone else nearby but sensorially removed from them. For decades these studies were largely unknown outside of a small group of parapsychologists, but in 1994, two psychologists, Daryl Bem and Charles Horton, did a meta-analysis of ganzfeld telepathy experiments that was published in the mainstream journal *Psychological Bulletin*, wherein they found positive evidence for telepathy with odds against chance calculated at 48 billion to 1.[47]

In chapters 11 and 12 of *Supernormal*, Radin discusses psychokinesis (PK) in living and inanimate systems. For example, numerous studies have been conducted on remote staring or intentionality, wherein someone at a randomly selected moment will stare at someone through a monitor screen for a set period of time while physiological responses such as skin conductivity and heart rate of the person being stared at is measured. About a meta-analysis of such studies, Radin writes: "In 2004, psychologist Stefan Schmidt and his colleagues from the University of Freiburg Hospital, Germany, published a meta-analysis of all known distant intentionality and distant staring experiments in the *British Journal of Psychology*. In a total of fifty-one studies conducted between 1977 and 2000 by multiple laboratories, involving some 1,394 pairs of participants tested in individual sessions, the combined odds against chance were 15,600 to 1." Similar studies on distant healing and prayer have been conducted with positive results. Here, Radin invokes the notions found in quantum physics of "nonlocality" and "spooky action at a distance," arguing that some type of comparable mechanism might allow for consciousness to function in similar ways.[48]

In his treatment of psychokinesis on the macroscales in inanimate systems, Radin states, "The bottom line about macro-PK is that the jury is out."[49] In other words, Radin does not consider the current evidence for people being able to move everyday objects like coins, pieces of paper, furniture, etc. with their minds sufficient to warrant macro-PK's existence. However, according to Radin, studies of micro-PK using computerized random number generators (RNGs) have yielded significant positive evidence for PK. For example, "field consciousness" studies pioneered in the 1990s by Roger Nelson at Princeton University postulate that when a number of subjective consciousnesses obtain a certain level of collective coherence (think group chanting, meditating, drumming, singing, watching a sporting event, taking part in a festival or religious ritual), this coherent "field of consciousness" will cause a similar coherence in physical reality. To detect this, RNGs are used because they are physical systems built to produce maximum randomness. Therefore, if significant deviations from randomness are detected in an RNG simultaneous to the generation of a coherent field of consciousness, it can be assumed that the consciousness field is affecting the physical system, resulting in nonrandomness or increased physical coherence. According to Radin, over one hundred field consciousness experiments have been conducted, with cumulative results demonstrating some mental effect on the physical (PK) with odds against chance "far beyond a million to one."[50]

Advancing the study of field consciousness to the next level, Roger Nelson began the Global Consciousness Project (GCP) in 1998. The aim of the GCP is to measure deviations from randomness of RNGs around the world during planetary coherence of consciousness events caused by world events such as major sporting competitions like the World Cup, natural disasters like the Asian tsunami of 2004, and terrorist attacks like 9/11 in the United States in 2001.[51] Based on the outputs of about sixty-five RNGs placed around the world in relation to 415 separate world events collected as of September 2012, the results demonstrate "an unambiguous deviation from chance, with odds against chance of 284 billion to 1." According to Radin, "This suggests that when a sizable proportion of the planet's population focuses their mental attention toward the same event, then the amount of physical coherence in the world also increases."[52]

As further evidence for micro-PK, Radin describes several experiments performed by him and others using two-slit experiments based on the quantum measurement problem (QMP). The classical two-slit experiment in physics shoots light particles (photons) toward two very small slits. When not observed, the photons act like waves and leave a probability distribution on the other side of the slits. However, when observed, the waves "collapse" and act like particles that "choose" one slit or the other. Radin and others postulated that mental attention alone without any direct observation would have the same effect. Experiments were conducted with experienced meditators and nonmeditators, and the results indicated much higher odds against chance that meditators could remotely affect the behavior of the light.[53]

In summing up his findings in *Supernormal*, Radin states that after a century of research the existence of clairvoyance, precognition, telepathy, and PK is "far beyond any reasonable scientific doubt." Concerning the relationship between psi and meditation, Radin, citing the research in India of Serena Roney-Dougal with fifty-two yogis and twenty-eight Tibetan monks, states that evidence suggests meditation's influence on psi ability with odds against chance at 8,500 to 1.[54] Thus, he maintains that both the Buddhist and Hindu traditions appear to be right when they claim that advanced meditation can lead to enhanced psychic ability.

In his conclusion to *Supernormal*, Radin discusses how psi phenomena challenges what he calls "the eightfold path of science," eight doctrinal assumptions that have supported a generally accepted scientific worldview based on our everyday common sense or "surface" view of reality.[55] These are: *realism* (that the external world is objectively real independent of observation), *localism* (objects are completely separate, and there is no "action at a distance"), *causality* (the arrow of time dictates that all causality moves from past to future), *mechanism* (everything can be understood in terms of causal networks like the gears of a clock), *physicalism* (everything can be described with real properties existing in space and time), *materialism* (everything, including mind, is made up of matter and energy), *determinism* (there is no free will, and all events are determined by preceding states), and *reductionism* (objects are made up of ever smaller objects, down to subatomic particles, with causality always moving upward from the microscopic to the macroscopic). However, Radin points out that all eight of these have been challenged by quantum physics. Moreover, now that quantum effects are being seen on macro and biological scales, Radin suggests that all of reality might behave according to the strangeness of the quantum world. As he argues in his earlier book *Entangled Minds*, the weirdness of the quantum world with its "spooky action at a distance" may be a means of understanding how psi works. In discussing various possible alternatives to monistic materialism, Radin points out that both panpsychism and monistic idealism as metaphysical systems would better accommodate the reality of psi. Drawing on the ideas of the physicist John Wheeler, Radin also suggests that at its base level, reality might be informational rather than material, an idea Wheeler coined with his catchy phrase "it from bit."[56] However, in his final analysis, Radin does not offer a new theory to explain the reality of psi but more modestly suggests that the ancient contemplative traditions and modern scientific inquiry both have a part to play in advancing human understanding of the psychic.

Ian Stevenson and the Division of Perceptual Studies

In 1967, the psychiatrist Ian Stevenson (1918–2007) founded the Division of Perceptual Studies (DOPS), a research unit of the Psychiatry and Neurobehavioral Sciences at the University of Virginia's School of Medicine. Through the DOPS, Stevenson carried out research on the mind-body connection, "focusing on phenomena suggesting that contemporary scientific hypotheses concerning the nature of mind, and mind's relation to matter, may be seriously incomplete."[57] Over the course of fifty years, Stevenson wrote a dozen books and more than two hundred scientific papers. He is most famous for his research on "cases of the reincarnation type" (CORT) and his groundbreaking study *Twenty Cases Suggestive of Reincarnation*.[58] Since the founding of the DOPS, a team of researchers has carried on Stevenson's empirical studies of paranormal phenomena investigating CORT, near-death experiences (NDEs), out-of-body experiences (OBEs), mediumship, crisis apparitions, deathbed visions, and various psychic phenomena such as telepathy and precognition.

In 2018, researchers at the DOPS published the book *Mind Beyond Brain: Buddhism, Science, and the Paranormal*, showcasing their research.[59] In chapter 2 of *Mind Beyond Brain*, the psychiatrist Bruce Greyson, who was the director of the DOPS from 2002 to 2014, summarizes his research on NDEs and concludes that conventional physicalist neurobiology fails to account for important features of NDEs.[60] More recently, Greyson reflects on the implications of the NDE in his book *After: A Doctor Explores What Near-Death Experiences Reveal About Life and Beyond* (2021).[61] In chapter 3 of *Mind Beyond Brain*, the psychiatrist Jim Tucker summarizes his and Ian Stevenson's research into CORT and DOPS's database of over two thousand cases from all over the world of children with past-life memories.[62] Tucker recounts the particularly intriguing case of the American boy James Leininger, who at the age of two began having nightmares about dying in a fiery plane crash as a World War II U.S. Navy pilot shot down by the Japanese. Tucker has written about James in his book *Return to Life: Extraordinary Cases of Children who Remember Past Lives* (2013) and more recently in his *Before: Children's Memories of Previous Lives* (2021), which combines two of his books on reincarnation, *Life Before Life* and *Return to Life* (2005).[63] The journalist Leslie Kean has also written about James and Tucker's research on him in her book *Surviving Death* (2017), which was the basis for the popular Netflix series of the same name.[64] Based on his studies into children with past-life memories, Tucker cautiously maintains that such cases "contribute to the body of empirical evidence that some aspects of the mind may transcend the physical body as currently understood, and perhaps even survive death."[65]

Mind Beyond Brain also contains chapters by Emily Williams Kelley on mediums, apparitions, deathbed experiences and by Edward Kelly discussing psi phenomena such as ESP, telekinesis, and precognition.[66] Here Edward Kelly narrates experiments with Bill Delmore, a gifted psychic who was able to score 180 hits out of 508 tries on a machine that randomly illuminates one of four buttons (the probability of this based on chance is about one in ten million).[67] Edward Kelly is also one of the authors of *Irreducible Mind: Toward a Psychology for the 21st Century*, an 832-page compendium of paranormal phenomena.[68] According to Kelly, the data in *Irreducible Mind* "demand a major overhaul of the physicalist worldview."[69] More recently, Kelly and colleagues authored *Beyond Physicalism: Toward the Reconciliation of Science and Spirituality* (2015).[70] In this book, the authors discuss several metaphysical positions (both modern and traditional), settling on what they call "evolutionary panentheism" as the best model to accommodate psi phenomena, many traditional "spiritual" worldviews, and contemporary science.

In the conclusion of *Mind Beyond Brain*, David Presti suggests that the significance of the data from the DOPS's paranormal research lies in the apparent deep interrelationships among mind, consciousness, and physical reality, which we simply do not understand within our present scientific framework.[71] Presti then asserts that because Buddhist cosmology takes phenomena like rebirth and telepathy seriously and Buddhist philosophy discusses at length the relations between consciousness and the world, these elements of the Buddhist tradition should be part of the dialogue between Buddhists and scientists. This interest in Buddhism highlights the wider context for *Mind Beyond Brain*, which evolved out of a daylong symposium in 2010 at Serenity Ridge Retreat Center of the Ligmincha Institute in Virginia, sponsored by Geshe Tenzin Wangyal Rinpoche, a Tibetan Bön master. Also, part of this zeitgeist are the dialogues that neuroscientists and the Dali Lama have engaged in over several years beginning in the 1980s. However, while *Mind Beyond Brain* is an excellent summary of DOPS's research, its discussion of Buddhism is minimal.[72] In fact, reading *Mind Beyond Brain* was a major motivation for my writing this book. Written from the Buddhist studies perspective, the current study explores in detail Buddhist approaches (both ancient and modern) to the paranormal so that they may be compared to the recent scientific investigations in a more nuanced and sophisticated manner.

U.S. Government Research Into the Paranormal

The private and public sectors are not the only arenas for the contemporary study of the paranormal. In her book *Phenomena: The Secret History of the U.S. Government's Investigation Into Extrasensory Perception and Psychokinesis* (2017), Annie Jacobsen chronicles programs and projects sponsored or funded by the CIA, Defense Department, and other U.S. agencies into the reality of ESP and psychokinesis. Following World War II, the U.S. Defense Department developed a keen interest in psi phenomena and in subsequent decades funded numerous classified ESP research programs with scientists such as Andrija Puharich and J. B. Rhine. In the 1970s, the CIA took the lead in investigating psi through the Stanford Research Institute (now SRI International), where both Charles Tart and Dean Radin have carried out classified research. At the time, SRI, located in the heart of California's Silicon

Valley, was the second largest Defense Department research institute in the country after the RAND Corporation. In 1972, SRI was contracted by the CIA to study ESP, which resulted in the now well-known research into and deployment of "remote viewing." Already by 1975, the CIA concluded from these investigations that "a large body of reliable experimental evidence points to the inescapable conclusion that extrasensory perception does exist as a real phenomenon."[73]

Two distinctive features of the SRI's research program into psi were the high caliber of the scientists and the exceptionally talented psychics they worked with. The lead psi scientist at SRI was Harold ("Hal") Puthoff, a thirty-five-year-old laser physicist who had previously worked for U.S. Navy Intelligence and the National Security Agency (NSA). Research at SRI began when Douglas ("Ingo") Swan, a New York artist and psychic, contacted Puthoff through a mutual associate. Puthoff, who was interested in quantum biology, was curious about the possible parapsychological effects between animate and inanimate systems, so he invited Swan to come to SRI to be tested. While at SRI, Swan was able to remotely view and sketch a magnetometer (a device that detects quarks), buried below him under five feet of concrete, and affect the readout of the machine simply by concentrating on it—a feat demonstrating both clairvoyance and psychokinesis—much to the amazement of the scientists present. Weeks later, after Puthoff wrote up the results of the experiment and circulated it among some colleagues, he was contacted by two CIA agents about starting a project into the study of ESP and psychokinesis. On October 1, 1972, the CIA awarded SRI a contract for $49,909 for an eight-month research project, and Puthoff's colleague, Russell Targ, joined the study.[74]

Puthoff and Targ's next exceptional subject was the infamous Israeli-born Uri Geller. In the 1970s, Geller was an international phenomenon famous for his psychic abilities of telepathy, remote viewing, and psychokinesis, particularly his ability to bend spoons seemingly with his mind. Handsome and charismatic, Geller's stage and television performances captivated audiences around the world. Although a preeminent showman, Geller always maintained that his psi abilities are real, and right from the beginning of his career people were polarized into true believers and skeptics. The skeptics maintained he was at best a good stage magician and at worst a blatant fraud. In the early 1970s, Geller's high profile caught the attention of the CIA, which wanted SRI to test his abilities.

Puthoff and Targ carried out nine days of tests with Geller between December 1, 1972, and January 15, 1973. According to declassified CIA reports, Geller was able to identify hidden objects well above chance (at times with a million- or trillion-to-one odds) and was also able to influence a weight-measuring balance with his mind.[75] When the Pentagon learned of these test results, there was deep skepticism about Geller's "powers," and after other scientists at the Pentagon tested Geller, they concluded he had no special abilities. This disagreement over Geller's psi highlights a prominent theme in Jacobsen's book concerning an ongoing battle within the U.S. intelligence community between the "goats" and the "sheep." This distinction was first coined in 1942 by the experimental psychologist Dr. Gertrude Schmeidler, who "created the term 'sheep' to refer to individuals who were confident about the possible reality of ESP and PK, and 'goats' to refer to those who doubted the existence of any so-called anomalous mental phenomena."[76] Early researchers into psi and PK discovered that one's belief system affected experimental results. For the sheep this was often understood to implicate the entangled and complex nature of consciousness, while the goats interpreted this as a sign of systematic bias of the "true believers" in studying psi phenomena. In the case of Geller, scientists at the Pentagon were accusing Puthoff and Targ of being naive sheep duped by Geller's trickery.

Geller was tested again in 1975 by a group of nuclear weapons scientists at Lawrence Livermore National Laboratory, located in Livermore, California. The scientists wanted to see if Geller was able to psychokinetically influence technology such as lasers and magnetic tapes. A declassified document describes one of these tests, in which magnetic computer cards were placed in sealed lead containers to see if Geller could influence them. The report states that "the magnetic pattern stored in the iron oxide layer of a magnetic program card was erased." However, much more worrisome was the fact that during the course of these experiments several of the scientists began experiencing paranormal events at home after hours, such as objects flying across the room, floating orbs of light, apparitional figures appearing, and other poltergeist-like events. These phenomena were never adequately explained. Moreover, two scientists at the lab viewed their paranormal events as signs that they should not design nuclear weapons and quit their jobs.[77] These bizarre events aptly demonstrated to the U.S. Defense Department the potential "real-world" effects of paranormal phenomena.

As impressive as Swann's and Geller's performances were to the SRI remote viewing team, the superstar of the program, Patrick Price, soon redefined the realm of the possible regarding remote viewing. The story as told by Jacobsen is that in 1972, shortly before Christmas, Swann and Puthoff were out buying a Christmas tree for the SRI office, when the tree salesman, who introduced himself as Pat Price, said he was following what they were doing at SRI and that if they ever needed any help, they should contact him because he could "handle anything."[78] Six months later, during a remote viewing test using map coordinates with Swann, Puthoff received a call out of the blue from Price in Lake Tahoe. Puthoff was so surprised by the timing that he decided to test Price by giving him map coordinates of a cabin in West Virginia supplied to Puthoff by a contact on the East Coast. Three days later, Puthoff received a letter with a detailed remote viewing from Price that did not describe the cabin but instead provided a description of a top-secret NSA base just down the road from the cabin. In a follow-up phone call, Price was even able to supply the name of the base as "Sugar Grove," the names of three personnel at the base from their desk tags, and some labels on folders stored in filing cabinets at the base![79]

Following this demonstration, Price came to work with Puthoff and Targ, performing some amazing feats of remote viewing,[80] including one occasion when he supplied detailed descriptions and drawings of a super-secret Soviet atomic bomb laboratory at Semipalatinsk, which were all later confirmed as accurate from satellite photographs.[81] After Price left SRI, he began working directly for the CIA on projects still classified and died under mysterious circumstances in 1975, when he was fifty-seven years old.[82] In an article written over twenty years later (once details were declassified), Russell Targ refers to Price as being "among the ranks of the psychic superstars." For Targ, Price's astonishing psychic abilities demonstrate how remote viewing "is an example of the near-omniscient ability of consciousness to transcend our ordinary awareness of space and time."[83]

In 1978, the Department of Defense (DoD) took over the remote viewing program, which ran until it was shut down in 1995. Codenamed Star Gate, the remote viewing program continued to produce some significant results employing individuals with exceptional psychic ability, such as Joe McMoneagle, Gary Langford, and Angela Dellafiora. However, after external review in 1995, researchers concluded that "the remote viewing phenomenon has no real value for intelligence operations."[84] As is often the case with other psi phenomena, the true "signal" of real information from remote viewing was often mixed with the "noise" of erroneous information. In this regard, the paranormal is often unpredictable and erratic, possessing an almost trickster quality to it.[85] While exceptional subjects at times produce truly amazing results under controlled conditions, most often the psychic and paranormal erupt during real-world events involving extreme situations such as trauma, profound altered states of consciousness, and intense emotion. Nevertheless, declassified U.S. Defense Department reports on psi research amply documents the occurrence of numerous paranormal phenomena.

Although the majority of the research doubtlessly remains classified, the U.S. intelligence community continues to be interested in the paranormal. At least two recent areas of research are known to the wider public. One is the U.S. Navy's research into intuition and premonition, the so-called spidey-sense. Based on observations in real-life combat situations where some individuals seem to "sense" the danger of hidden explosive devices or eminent attack, the Office of Naval Research in 2014 began a four-year, $3.85 million research program to explore intuition and premonition.[86] Another is the Department of Defense's research into Unidentified Aerial (or Anomalous) Phenomena (UAP), more commonly known as UFOs.

UFOs and the Paranormal

Many trace the start of the modern UFO era to the pilot Kenneth Arnold's sighting of nine silver, crescent-shaped disks flying in formation near Mount Rainier in Washington State on June 24, 1947.[87] However, researchers such as Jacques Vallée and Charles Fort have noted well-documented accounts of "flying ships" from the 1800s and earlier. Indeed, some ufologists suggest that encounters with UFOs date back as far as recorded history.[88] Despite thousands of credible cases collected for over seventy years worldwide by expert eyewitnesses backed up by radar data and other physical evidence,[89] many Americans still consider belief in the existence of UFOs to be part of the "lunatic fringe," and the subject within the academy has been treated with the same taboo status as the paranormal. This attitude is in part attributable to the U.S. government's successful debunking attempts, beginning in the late 1960s following the Condon Report and closure of the U.S. Air Force's Project Blue Book.[90]

For many, this dismissive attitude changed after the *New York Times* published the article "Glowing Auras and 'Black Money': The Pentagon's Mysterious U.F.O. Program," by Helene Cooper, Ralph Blumenthal, and Leslie Kean, in late 2017.[91] This shift in social perception was also facilitated by the release of footage of U.S. Navy fighter pilots' encounters with UAP, such as the "Tic-Tac," "Go Fast," and "Gimble" videos, which were later confirmed as authentic and then officially released by the Pentagon.[92] Following the *New York Times* article, numerous news outlets picked up the story, including the television program *60 Minutes*, which aired the show "Navy Pilots Describe Encounters with UFOs" in May 2021.[93] Some of the chief personalities behind the current shift in public opinion have been Christopher Mellon (former deputy assistant secretary of defense for intelligence); Senator Mark Rubio (Florida); the former U.S. army counterintelligence special agent Luis Elizondo; the investigative journalists George Knapp, Ross Coulthard, and Michael Shellenberger; and the documentary film maker Jeremy Corbell.

This sudden surge of interest caused by the disclosure of the U.S. government's secret study of the UFO/UAP phenomena and film releases of Navy footage caught the attention of the U.S. Senate, which added, "The provision in Senate Report 116-233, accompanying the Intelligence Authorization Act (IAA) for Fiscal Year 2021, that the DNI, in consultation with the Secretary of Defense (SECDEF), is to submit an intelligence assessment of the threat posed by unidentified aerial phenomena (UAP) and the progress the Department of Defense Unidentified Aerial Phenomena Task Force (UAPTF) has made in understanding this threat."[94]

In the subsequent report, "Preliminary Assessment: Unidentified Aerial Phenomena," released on June 25, 2021, by the Office of the Director of National Intelligence, the Unidentified Aerial Phenomena Task Force analyzed 144 cases acquired from military incidents occurring between 2004 and 2021. The Task Force was only able to identify one contact as a "large deflating balloon."[95] The other 143 UAP remained unidentified. Some of these phenomena demonstrate speeds, maneuverability, and signal management (the ability to jam tracking technology) inexplicable by current science. Concurrent to the release of this public document, the House Intelligence Committee received a much more detailed classified briefing. While many UFO enthusiasts were disappointed by the Pentagon's lack of disclosure, the public report clearly demonstrates that UAP are a real concern of the U.S. intelligence community, and their origins, intentions, and nature remain unknown to the most advanced military in the world. Since this time, the U.S. Defense Department has established the All-Domain Anomaly Resolution Office (AARO) to investigate both military and civilian sightings of UAP.

Then in June 2023, a former high-ranking intelligence officer named David Grusch turned whistleblower and came forward with amazing allegations that within the U.S. Department of Defense is a secret UAP crash recovery and reverse engineering program that has been in operation for over eighty years and functions outside of congressional oversight.[96] According to Grusch, this program has not only recovered at least a dozen craft of nonhuman origin but also possesses the bodies of their nonhuman pilots.[97] These claims led to a congressional hearing on July 26, 2023, where Grusch repeated these allegations. Also, in the same hearing, two former Navy pilots, Ryan Graves and David Fravor, testified on their encounters with UAP.[98] The Pentagon's AARO denies Grusch's claim that there is such a program or that there is any proof that UAP are technical craft of nonhuman origin.[99]

Serious investigators of the UFO phenomena have long known of an inexplicable connection between UFO encounters and paranormal events.[100] Already in 1975, Jacques Vallée, the French scientist, scholar, and world expert on UFOs, wrote: "What happens if we examine the files of UFO sightings with an open mind regarding such 'psychic components'? We find that phenomena of precognition, telepathy, and even healing are not unusual among the reports, especially when they involve close-range observation of an object or direct exposure to its light." Probably the most well-known example of this is Uri Geller, who claimed to have been inside a UFO and received his paranormal abilities from exposure to a mysterious light beam from the sky. Other examples Vallée mentions are an engineer who after an encounter with a UFO claimed to possess psychokinesis and the ability to astral project his consciousness out of his body and a medical doctor who reported experiencing telepathy, levitation, and electrical appliances malfunctioning after a close encounter.[101]

In the book *American Cosmic: UFOs, Religion, Technology* (2019), D. W. Pasulka recounts her experiences with "Tyler D.," a man who claimed "that his connection to off-planet intelligence helps him create biotechnologies." Tyler told Pasulka that he owns over forty scientific patents and has created new advanced technologies, including applications that have been used to cure bone cancer. At the start of *American Cosmic*, Pasulka narrates how Tyler took her and her friend James Master blindfolded to an undisclosed location in New Mexico, which is supposedly the crash site of a UFO in 1947. Master, an endowed chair of molecular biology, heads a laboratory at one of the world's top universities, is a successful inventor, and has a "global reputation for pushing the boundaries of science and biotechnology." Tyler brought them to the crash site to look for metal fragments of the craft. Pieces of exotic materials were recovered by James, who later analyzed them in a lab. About these metals, Pasulka writes: "James's preliminary analyses of the materials, months later, made it hard to believe they were made on Earth. In fact, he said he wasn't sure, given their structure, that they could be made anywhere—and certainly not on Earth in 1947. That's how weird they were, and how they defied conventional explanation. They were just ... anomalous."[102]

American Cosmic thus highlights the ambiguous nature of the UFO phenomena—they appear to be both subjective and objective, psychological and material. Jacques Vallée realized this over a half-century ago—that UFO encounters, like the folklore of meetings with fairies, demons, and angels, are profoundly paranormal and psychic, but they also leave behind physical evidence. About Vallée, Jeffrey Kripal writes: "What Jacques Vallee came to know, in other words, could not be explained as something strictly objective or subjective. It was both. And it was neither. When Vallee writes of the paranormal ... he is not thinking of purely internal states or subjective conditions, however interesting and profound. He is thinking of fundamentally anomalous events that routinely appear on radar screens."[103]

UFOs are not only associated with psi phenomena but also with paranormal events such as poltergeist phenomena, cryptids, and apparitions. George Hansen discusses this "unbounded" quality of the paranormal in his book *The Trickster and the Paranormal* (2001). Hansen writes: "Bigfoot sightings, cattle mutilations, and UFO flaps are some of the largest paranormal manifestations. With them, no clearly defined group of people is involved but rather participation is 'unbounded.' Any number of people can be witnesses; the phenomena occur over indefinite areas and for indeterminate periods of time. These are often exotic and confusing, and the conditions surrounding them are ill defined and unstructured."[104]

A well-known example of such conditions John Keel documents in his *The Mothman Prophecies: The True Story of the Alien Who Terrorized an American City*.[105]

In 1966 and 1967, citizens of Point Pleasant, West Virginia, reported numerous sightings of a strange, winged man dubbed "the Mothman" and countless UFOs and other paranormal events. These anomalous occurrences climaxed in the tragic collapse of the Silver Bridge on December 15, 1967, resulting in the deaths of forty-six people.[106]

Probably the most famous example of unbounded paranormal activity is Skinwalker Ranch, a remote 512-acre property located in Utah. Currently the basis of a popular History Channel series,[107] Skinwalker Ranch has been the site of countless paranormal events over many decades including poltergeist-type activity, UFOs, the appearance of cryptids, strange glowing orbs of light, cattle mutilations, animal disappearances, and more. Many of these events have been documented in the book *Hunt for the Skinwalker* (2005) by Colm Kelleher and George Knapp.[108] More recently, the U.S. government's secret research into Skinwalker Ranch is described in *Skinwalkers at the Pentagon: An Insider's Account of the Government's Secret UFO Program* (2021) by James Lacatski, Colm Kelleher, and George Knapp.

Skinwalkers at the Pentagon provides the inside story of the U.S. government's contracted study of UFOs discussed in the *New York Times* article of 2017. In the *Times* article, the organization erroneously credited with the $22 million contract is the Advanced Aerospace Threat Identification Program (AATIP), headed by Luis Elizondo.[109] The actual program to receive this money from the Defense Intelligence Agency was the Advanced Aerospace Weapon System Applications Program (AAWSAP), which was contracted out to Bigelow Aerospace Advanced Space Studies (BAASS) and ran from 2008 to 2010. During those two years, AAWSAP's research not only covered the physical aspects of UAP but also the paranormal and psychic phenomena associated with them. According to Lacatski, Kelleher, and Knapp, "an enormous body of data concerning the psychic and paranormal connections to UAP interactions currently exists at the Defense Intelligence Agency."[110] BAASS paid particularly close attention to Skinwalker Ranch, which was at the time owned by Robert Bigelow, the founder and head of BAASS.

One of the most fascinating aspects of *Skinwalkers at the Pentagon* is its documentation of what has come to be known as "the hitchhiker effect." Numerous individuals who have visited Skinwalker Ranch and experienced anomalous phenomena upon returning home continue to experience paranormal events as if something (a "hitchhiker") had attached itself to them, analogous to some type of psychic infectious agent. About this Lacatski and colleagues write, "All five actively serving intelligence agency personnel who visited the ranch during the AAWSAP BAASS program experienced profound anomalies while on the property. And even more importantly, all five brought something home with them."[111] One of these agents was Jonathan Axelrod (pseudonym), a senior aerospace engineer in naval intelligence. About Axelrod's experiences, the authors write: "For more than a dozen years following his July 2009 and subsequent trips to the ranch, Axelrod's wife and (then) teenage children were subjected to nightmarish 'dogmen' appearing in their backyard; to blue, red, yellow and white orbs routinely floating through the home and in the yard; to black shadow people standing over their beds when they awoke; and to a relentless barrage of loud, unexplained footsteps walking up and down the stairs in their house." Another agent was Juliett Witt, a Pentagon operational test and evaluation analyst and Department of Defense target sensor specialist, who on return from Skinwalker in 2009 began experiencing intense poltergeist activity in her home, such as wine bottles flying across the room, the television switching on and off, lights flickering, and books and clothes being found moved to different locations of her house. These phenomena, according to Lacatski, Kelleher, and Knapp, have continued to this day.[112]

Another frightening aspect of the hitchhiker effect was the negative impact it appears to have on people's physical health: "It can be unequivocally stated that a large number of people who brought something home from Skinwalker Ranch also began to experience autoimmune disease in one or more family or household members." Studying these physical effects and others from close encounters with UAP led the AAWSAP medical team to conclude that the human body could be used as an untapped reservoir of "objective" information related to UAP encounters. This breakthrough allowed AAWSAP scientists and medical consultants to pioneer "the strategy of treating the immune system as a trillion-cell information processing organ . . . capable of recording (and subsequently reporting) insults from UAP experiences."[113]

The study of Skinwalker Ranch and UAP is ongoing. We are currently witnessing a dramatic sea change in attitudes toward UAP in popular opinion and an unprecedented openness by the U.S. Department of Defense about their interest in UAP and paranormal phenomena. Whatever the future holds in this area, it promises to be interesting and to profoundly challenge numerous assumptions current science has about the nature of reality.

Conclusion

In this chapter, we have looked at some of the institutions and individuals in "the West" who have systematically studied the paranormal over the last 140 years: the Society for Psychical Research, Charles Fort, J. B. Rhine and the Parapsychological Association, Charles Tart, Dean Radin, Ian Stevenson and DOPS, the U.S. intelligence agencies, and the U.S. Department of Defense. We can define these inquiries as broadly scientific or at least empirical (and in the case of Rhine, Tart, and Radin, who have studied psi in laboratory settings, as scientific in the stricter sense of the word). Laboratory results based on meta-analysis demonstrate statistically significant results above chance, which suggest that certain psychic abilities, such as telepathy, precognition, clairvoyance, and micropsychokinesis, are real. While lab results have been significant but generally weak in favor of psi, certain rare individuals appear to possess exceptional psi abilities. Moreover, there exists some evidence to suggest that meditation may enhance these abilities. Studies into reincarnation, OBEs, NDEs, apparitions, and mediumship, while "anecdotal," also suggest that consciousness may possess nonlocal aspects that operate independently of the brain. This has led several of the leading psi researchers to conclude that physicalism or metaphysical materialism (the mind is the brain) must be wrong.

Despite polls indicating that the majority of Americans believe in some aspect of the paranormal, academic and governmental studies of the subject is nearly nonexistent (for example, given the Pentagon's annual budget, the $22 million for AAWSAP is minuscule).[114] This is no doubt attributable to cultural prejudices that mark out the paranormal as "fringe" and studies into the subject as "pseudoscientific." Hansen has argued that the stigma around paranormal research is an aspect of its "trickster" nature.[115] Likewise, Vallée has pointed out the absurd quality of UFO encounters, and Lacatski and colleagues refer to the "Oz Factor" (distortions in perception, time, and space) associated with anomalous phenomena.[116] Indeed, the most dramatic occurrences of the paranormal happen not in the laboratory but out in "the field," that unbounded arena of the lifeworld, and are often catalyzed during moments of extreme stress, trauma, or profound alterations of consciousness.

Throughout human history and across the globe, stories are told of premonitions and visitations happening in dreams; "crisis apparitions" appearing when a friend or relative is dying or endangered; near-death experiences leading to spiritual revelations and psi abilities; and intense meditation or psychotropic substances inducing telepathy, clairvoyance, or visitations from other beings. Thus, the paranormal is deeply embedded in our collective imaginations, and our knowledge of it comes from our own experiences and the stories of the experiences of others. It is through our stories of the paranormal, often privately communicated among family and close friends, more than anything else, that the paranormal is kept alive for our collective humanity throughout the generations and across cultures. This is no less true for contemporary convert Buddhists today as it was for their Buddhist ancestors from centuries ago. Now that we have established some of the modern context by investigating the Western scientific studies of the paranormal, we are ready to explore some contemporary tales of the paranormal as told by modern Buddhists.

THREE

Tales of Psychic Phenomena

WHEREAS THE FIRST TWO CHAPTERS deal with formal accounts of the paranormal from canonical Buddhist sources and modern scientific studies, for this chapter and the next three my approach shifts to contemporary stories narrated to me in the first person. Unlike the study of official sources, this approach is more akin to studies in living folklore and oral history. In this way, we can explore the paranormal as narrated by contemporary people and uncover the roles such phenomena and the stories about them play in their lives. Outside of popular media, entertainment, and fiction, people encounter the paranormal primarily and most forcibly through either their direct encounters with it or the stories they hear about it, usually from family and close friends. Through this folklore of the uncanny, anomalous, spooky, and weird, we learn how the paranormal erupts into ordinary life during moments of death, trauma, and intense alterations of consciousness to dramatically affect the course of people's lives. As we shall see from our stories, contemporary Buddhists often interpret these events through a Buddhist lens wherein karma and rebirth play prominent roles.

In this chapter, we explore contemporary Buddhist stories about five psychic phenomena: clairvoyance, precognition, telepathy, retrocognition, and psychokinesis (PK). In the next chapter (chapter 4), we look at Buddhist tales of out-of-body experiences (OBEs), near-death experiences (NDEs), and encounters with animals, ghosts, spirits, deities, and holy beings. The following two chapters (5 and 6) are each in-depth explorations of the paranormal through the life stories of two contemporary practitioners of Buddhist meditation and Buddhist ritual. For the remainder of this study, I use two primary sources of data: responses from an online, anonymous survey titled "Buddhism and the Paranormal" through the SurveyMonkey website, open from July 30, 2019, to February 14, 2021; and interviews conducted between March 3, 2021, and November 9, 2022, through the internet via the Zoom video conferencing application. To provide some social and cultural context for the following stories, I begin this chapter with some demographic data on the participants. Throughout the remainder of this chapter and the next, I have arranged the stories according to the particular phenomenon (clairvoyance, precognition, telepathy, etc.) and provide some light statistical analysis of the questionnaire responses to provide additional information concerning the frequency and context for such experiences. Then I turn to accounts of each phenomenon as described by participants in the questionnaire and interviews.

The Survey and Interviews

This research project began officially with the launch of the online survey "Buddhism and the Paranormal" on July 30, 2019, through the SurveyMonkey website. Simultaneous with the survey going live, I posted notices about it on the website H-Buddhism and on social media such as Facebook, Twitter, and Instagram, and I emailed several meditation centers and Buddhist monastic institutions, primarily in North America and New Zealand. On the front page of the web address for the survey I provided an information sheet that included a brief paragraph about myself, a project description and invitation, participant identification and recruitment, project procedures, data management, participant's rights, a human ethics statement, and my contact details. The project description, invitation, participant identification, and recruitment were worded as follows:

PROJECT DESCRIPTION AND INVITATION

This project aims to investigate accounts of paranormal phenomena reported by contemporary Buddhists throughout the world. Inspired in part by the recent publication of the book *Mind Beyond Brain* by David Presti, *et alia* (Columbia

University Press, 2018), I aim to write a monograph that will complement the research in this book.

I would like to invite you to participate in this research by filling out an anonymous online survey. At the end of this survey, you will be asked if you would like to participate in a confidential 60-minute interview, which may be recorded. Please note that if you do wish to be interviewed, your survey answers will no longer remain anonymous to the researcher. However, the researcher will keep your identity and the identity of your organization strictly confidential.

PARTICIPANT IDENTIFICATION AND RECRUITMENT

In order to take part in this study you must be at least 18 years old. Also, you should have some interest in and/or involvement with Buddhism, and have had at least one unusual, anomalous, or paranormal experience you would like to share.

The first question of the survey required a "yes/no" response to confirm that participants had read the information sheet and consented to the terms of the survey. All the remaining questions were optional and could be skipped. The next nine questions were general demographic questions to obtain information concerning participants' age, home country, and Buddhist identity and practice. The total number of responses to the survey was 115, although not all the questions were answered by all participants. Eighty-nine people answered the second question, "How old are you?" The youngest age reported was eighteen years,[1] and the oldest eighty, with an average age of participants of forty-five years. Of the ninety-three people who answered the question "What is your gender?," 68 percent were male, 31 percent female, and 1 percent agender. Of the ninety-four people who answered the question "What country do you live in?," most (45, or approximately 48 percent) said they live in the United States of America. The breakdown for other countries was as follows: 11 from India, 8 from the United Kingdom, 6 from New Zealand, 4 from Taiwan; there were two people each from Canada, Thailand, Japan, Australia, and Singapore and one person each from Myanmar, China, Czechia, France, Greece, Poland, Russia, and the Philippines.

The next several questions were about Buddhist identity and practice. In answer to question 5, "Do you consider yourself a Buddhist?," 70 percent

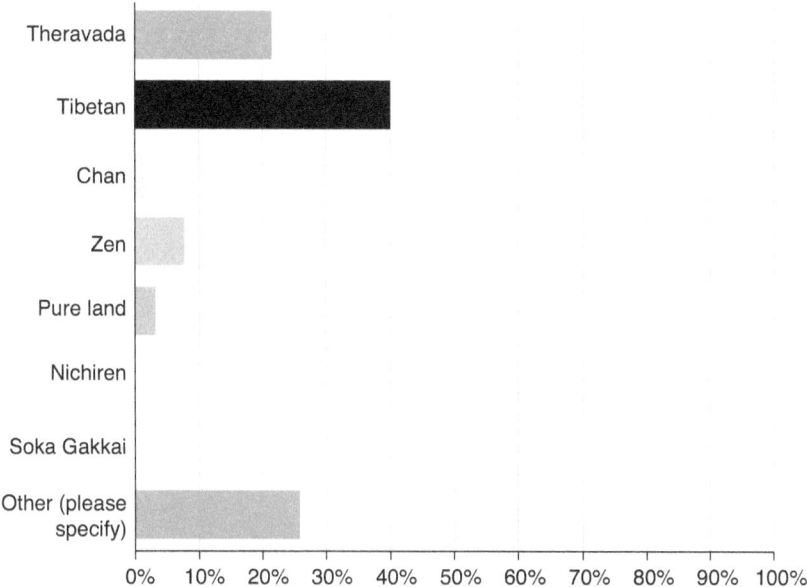

FIGURE 3.1 Types of Buddhism.
Question 7: What type of Buddhism do you practice. Answered = 65. Skipped = 51.

answered "yes" (67 out of 96). Of those who identify as Buddhist, 89 percent converted to Buddhism, while only 11 percent grew up in a Buddhist household. When asked, "What type of Buddhism do you practice?," of the 65 respondents, 40 percent chose "Tibetan," and just over 20 percent chose "Theravada" (see figure 3.1: Types of Buddhism). Other traditions selected were Zen (7.7 percent), Pure Land (3.1 percent), and Chan (1.5 percent). A significant portion of people chose the "Other" category (26 percent, or 17 out of 65). In specifying the "Other" selection, people mentioned a variety of eclectic practices such as "psychedelic," "Early Buddhism," "A combination of sectarian practices," "Shingon and Thai Forest," "Pragmatic Buddhism," "Tendai," "Thai Lanna Buddhism," "a generic Mahayana," and "nonsectarian." Of those who identify as Buddhist, when asked, "Are you a monastic or lay Buddhist?," 85 percent selected "layperson," only 6 percent selected "a monk or nun," and 9 percent chose "Other." In the Other category, respondents specified "ordained lay minister"; "a Yogi"; "Japanese ordained"; "electronic musician, artist and shaman"; "neither monk nor layman"; and "Lay lama."

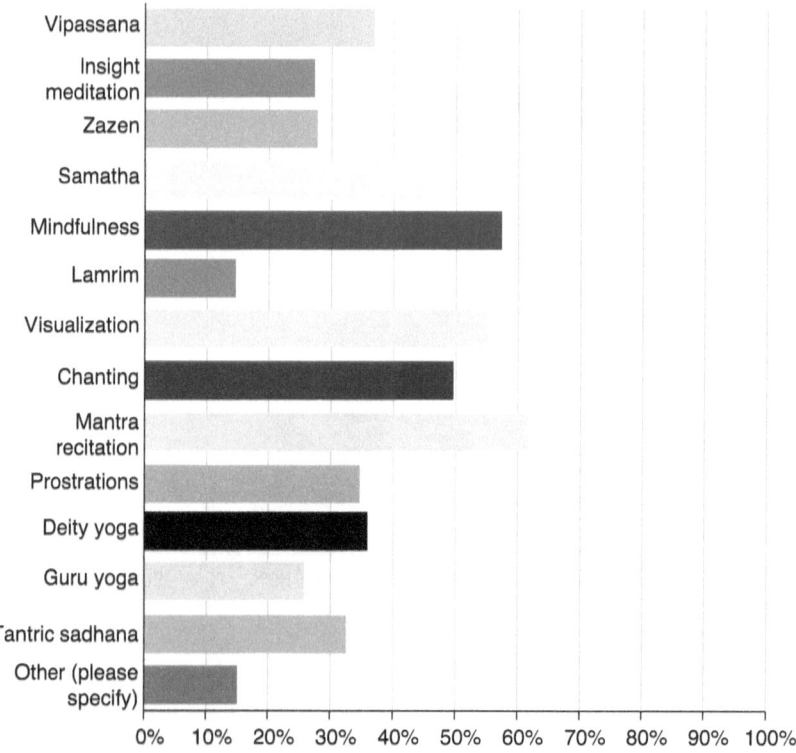

FIGURE 3.2 Buddhist Practices.
Question 9: Do you engage in Buddhist practice such as meditation, chanting, visualization? Answered = 89. Skipped = 27.

In answering question 9, "Do you engage in Buddhist practice such as meditation, chanting, visualization (tick all that apply)?," a wide variety of practices were chosen (see figure 3.2). The most popular practices were mantra recitation (62 percent), mindfulness (57 percent), visualization (55 percent), chanting (49 percent), samatha (44 percent), and vipassana (37 percent). Some of the other common practices selected were deity yoga (36 percent), prostrations (35 percent), guru yoga (26 percent), tantric sadhana (33 percent), and zazen (28 percent). In the "Other" (26 percent) category people mentioned the following: "psychedelic assisted meditation"; "Divine Abodes (Brahma Vihara Bhavana)"; "open monitoring / choiceless awareness"; "Trukhor Tsa Lung"; "copying scriptures"; "bodhi [sic] building in sports"; "Buddhist studies, pilgrimage, etc."; and "Study of scripture, generosity, ethics, generating positive social emotions (maitri, etc.), etc. etc."

A number of caveats and qualifications about the survey should be mentioned at this stage. The sample is obviously selective or purposive, rather than random. I was particularly looking for self-identified Buddhists or practitioners of some form of Buddhism who'd had some experience of the paranormal. Participants self-selected with a desire to disclose this information about themselves (albeit anonymously). Filling out the survey required a working internet connection and some basic proficiency in reading and writing English. As with an earlier survey I conducted for a previous book,[2] there were numerous responses shortly following my post advertising the survey that appeared on the academic list H-Buddhism. This suggests that a significant portion of the participants could represent what Charles Prebish calls "a silent sangha in America," that is, academic scholars of Buddhism who also either identify as Buddhist or practice some form of Buddhism.[3] Traditionally this has been a "silent sangha" because academics of religious studies have been reticent to disclose religious affiliation or faith commitment for fear that this would compromise their perceived objective and disinterested study of religion. Although it is more in vogue these days to admit a commitment to Buddhism or Buddhist practice than it once was, many Buddhist studies scholars doubtlessly continue to remain silent about their Buddhism in any formal academic context. This is probably even more the case regarding experiences of the paranormal, which we have seen is a highly taboo subject despite the widespread popular belief in the reality of paranormal phenomena.

The biases in the selection process for the survey are reflected in the results. The majority of the participants are from countries where English is the primary language. Also, of those who identify as Buddhist, 89 percent state that they are converts, and the vast majority are laypeople (85 percent). Thus, a significant portion of the respondents likely fit the category of American "convert Buddhists," which scholars of American Buddhism have previously discussed in some detail.[4] Although the current survey does not ask about ethnicity, racial identity, or income levels, we know from other sources that American convert Buddhists tend to be white, upper middle class, and highly educated.[5] Therefore, it is likely that a significant number of the survey respondents represent this cohort. However, this sample's characteristics are not necessarily detrimental to the current study. Since we are interested in contemporary Buddhist stories about the paranormal in relation to traditional canonical accounts and modern science, the "new Buddhism" of contemporary Anglo-American converts may be a particularly apt demographic to study. This group as a whole has been deeply steeped in the modern "Western" scientific outlook while simultaneously engaging in the serious practice of Buddhism and therefore has had to negotiate between these two worldviews. Moreover, as we will see in the following pages, for this group as for their Buddhist predecessors the paranormal is alive and well.

At the time of their interviews, the ten interviewees were between their early twenties to seventies in age and were evenly divided regarding gender, with five women and five men. Seven identified as Buddhist (five laypeople, one Buddhist nun, and one Buddhist monk), and the other three were practicing or had practiced some form of Buddhism or Buddhist meditation. None of the Buddhists were raised in a Buddhist household but came to Buddhism as adults. Six interviewees were living in the United States, three in New Zealand, and one in Canada. Ethnically, nine identify as primarily White/European and one as Chinese. All were fluent in English, with a socioeconomic range between low to middle class. In this and the following chapter, I draw on information obtained from seven of the interviewees; I reserve two interviews for the biographies in chapters 5 and 6.[6] The Buddhist monk I interviewed was Ajahn Chandako, an American-born Theravādin Buddhist and abbot of Vimutti Monastery in Auckland, New Zealand. Vimutti is part of the Thai Forest Tradition founded by Ajahn Chah in the lineage of Ajahn Mun.[7] Although he did not disclose any of his own experiences with ESP or the paranormal, Ajahn Chandako was an invaluable source of information concerning contemporary folklore from the Thai Forest Tradition, which is now an international community with monasteries in Thailand and around the world.

Clairvoyance

According to the *Oxford English Dictionary*, clairvoyance is

> 1. A supposed faculty attributed to certain persons, or to persons under certain mesmeric conditions, consisting in the mental perception of objects at a distance or concealed from sight.

2. Keenness of mental perception, clearness of insight; insight into things beyond the range of ordinary perception.[8]

Applying these definitions to our discussion of the Indian Buddhist sources (chapter 1), we can classify the "higher knowledges" of "divine ear" (more technically "clairaudience") and "divine eye" as forms of clairvoyance. During our interview, Ajahn Chandako mentioned a monk from the Thai Forest Tradition who is said to have developed the divine eye through concentration meditation (*samādhi*): "Particularly there was one monk, who I stayed with and who I knew, and his name was Luang Pu Dtun.... Luang Pu Dtun spent most of life living in solitude, and he had a lot of time for developing *samādhi* and developing psychic powers. He lived in the jungle of Northeast Thailand, and he is reputed to have the ability to see beings arising and passing away according to their *kamma*, which I think is credible."[9]

Likewise, the U.S. government's studies and deployment of "remote viewing" (see chapter 2) also would fit the *OED*'s definitions of clairvoyance. According to both ancient Indian sources and contemporary U.S. government declassified documents, certain people appear to be naturally gifted at this ability; however, through proper training, it seems that others can also acquire this talent.[10] Clairvoyance and precognition are closely related abilities in that the first concerns perception of objects or events distant in space, while the second is about perception that is distant in time (specifically the future). For the current study, I reserve clairvoyance for remote perception of contemporaneous objects and events and precognition (see next section) for perception of future objects and events.

A well-known example of clairvoyance in Buddhism is found in the Tibetan tradition of divination (Tibetan: *mo*). One of the participants in my study, Karma Lekshe Tsomo, related to me some of her experiences with Tibetan divination. Karma Lekshe (b. 1944) is an internationally known and highly regarded American Buddhist nun and professor of theology and religious studies at the University of San Diego, where she specializes in Buddhist Studies. She is also a social activist for Buddhist women, the cofounder of the Sakyadhita, an international association of Buddhist women, and the founding director of the Jamyang Foundation, an international organization to support the education of women in developing countries.[11] During our interview, Karma Lekshe spoke about her experiences with Tibetan oracles, which I quote here at length:

KARMA LEKSHE TSOMO: So you know in Tibetan culture... they have a tradition of divination where they go to a high lama and ask a question, and the lama will give them a reading. There are different ways to do it. Some of them use nothing. They can just tell straightaway. But the classical formula is the *Book of Mo*. And it has been translated into English and has been published. But they will have the Tibetan version—I don't know how many versions there are—but they'll roll the dice and get a page number and they'll turn to that page number and read the divination. Sometimes they can pull it out of their head. They also have a tradition of *lha bab*, I guess you would call them "diviners." Literally, it means "the deity descends." The oracles they call "*lha bab*," which means "deity descends." They channel some god or other. Like for example, I was living in Dharamsala, I was a student, very poor... and I had five hundred rupees in a cabinet, and it disappeared. And someone was staying with me. A Tibetan nun. And I didn't know what to do because I wanted to know if I could trust this person. And that was like all the money I had at the time, right?

D. E. OSTO: Right. You needed it for food, right?

K: Exactly. So I mentioned it to my Tibetan friend, and she said, "Why don't you just go to a *mo*?" And I said, "Well, okay." It turned out that her mother was best friends with a local oracle. She was a woman; most of them are women. I used to be the English secretary for one of them, the Nechung Oracle. That is a whole other story—talk about paranormal! Holy moly! We are going to need more than an hour here.

D: [laughs]

K: But in any case, I said, "Okay, what do I have to do?" And she said, "We'll go up at eight o'clock in the morning and you consult her, and it will be fine." So we went up, and it was really interesting. The woman was married but childless, and her husband acted as her ritual attendant preparing the offerings. There is a book about this, and there is even a film about the Nechung Oracle.... Well, that is the state oracle, and... that is another story.

So, we went up to Ugyen, that was her name, and she drank *chang*, which is barley beer, and milk together. Ewh! And she was wearing big furry boots. And she had a bronze chest plate. She had a big furry cap. And she was chanting all kinds of texts. And then at some point, she left, and the deity descended into her body, and you could tell that her whole character changed. And at that point we were invited, me and my friend, to ask our question. I think I was the first one to ask her. So I told this story that I had lost five hundred rupees, and I have someone staying with me and I want to know if that person took it or, how to get it back. And she talks in a twilight language. It is impossible for most people to understand. But I could understand just some words, but not the whole thing. But my friend who was Tibetan could understand everything, pretty much. And then that was it, and she called the next person. So then I just put the twenty rupees on the table and we left. And then my friend said that she said, "Don't put the black hat on the white person."

D: Okay?

K: Which means, "Don't accuse the innocent."

D: Oh, okay.

K: And she said, "The person who took the money, is a fourteen-year-old boy who lives next door, and his toes are deformed like this" [demonstrates with fingers curled in like toes].

D: Like curled in? Aha.

K: And, "It will be very difficult for you to get the money back." So I said, "Okay." So then I said, "Thank you very much," and went back down the mountain. And then I started looking at the neighbors. They had several boys in that family, Indian boys. And then I looked and sure enough there was one about fourteen years old and his feet were like that.

D: Wow.

K: And of course, I was very relieved that it wasn't my friend and nun. Of course, I don't know why I even considered it, but you never know. So anyway, there are many stories like that.

D: Did you ever get the five hundred rupees back?

K: No. They would have just denied it.

Here Karma Lekshe describes her encounter with a professional oracle in the tradition who enters a trance or possession state and is believed to receive information from a divine source. The procedure is formalized, and, for payment, the oracle imparts the needed information. In Karma Lekshe's story, Ugyen demonstrates an uncanny ability to provide specific details about the person who stole her money, which matched the description of a boy who was her next-door neighbor.

TALES OF PSYCHIC PHENOMENA

Karma Lekshe also told a story about a highly regarded lama providing specific information to a woman about where she could locate her missing passport. The following discussion took place:

K: Anyway... What happened was there were two famous lamas in town. They were both reputed to be bodhisattvas. One of them had wandered around India and into Tibet just like a wandering sadhu. But when his Holiness heard that he was in Varanasi, he immediately went to see him and bowed to him.

D: Wow.

K: And he is a remarkable figure. He has written many books. I had actually met him in Nepal just a few months before this.... He was famous for having no attachments at all. People would give him silver and gold and he would just throw it under the bed. He didn't care at all. And he was in this one room with just one cot, one bed, and that was it. So we went in and did three prostrations. And he said, "Get a grammar, get a dictionary, and learn Tibetan." And I think she was already a nun. And I was about to become a nun. And he said it three times, "Get a grammar, get a dictionary, and learn Tibetan." And we promised we would, and we did. We both did.

D: Wow. And this was the same person that came to...

K: Bodhgaya. One day, I saw him in the Mahabodhi Temple. I saw his brother in the Mahabodhi Stupa. And I sat down beside him, and we meditated together for I don't know how many hours. Like we went to another place. So then I heard this story that he had given a divination to a young American woman who had lost her passport. So she was really distraught because she was really far away from any emissary or anything. So some people advised her to go to him and ask for advice. "Get a *mo*," they said. So she went to him, made three prostrations, offered ten rupees or whatnot, and then posed her question, "I just lost my passport, how can I get it back?" He said, "Roll the dice." Then he looked at a text and said, "From the Mahabodhi Stupa walk in the southeast direction and you will come to a small village. In that village go to the second house on the right, and walk in the door and say, "I want my passport back." And you will get it."

D: Aha.

K: So, she was like, nothing to lose, right? She started from the Mahabodhi Stupa, walked in a southeast direction, came to a small village, walked in the second house on the right and said, "I want my passport back." And a guy pulled it out and gave it to her.

D: Wow! [laughs]. That's incredible.

These two stories highlight the popular belief in the efficacy of divination in Tibetan culture and the positive results that may be obtained through employing the clairvoyant abilities of either professional oracles or advanced lamas. However, Karma Lekshe also told me two other stories providing cautionary messages about the use of such abilities from a Buddhist perspective. The first one reads:

K: I had just lost my prayer beads, and these prayer beads had been with me for many years. I got them in Nepal. I traded my sweater for one, my brother's sweater, with one of those donkey guys, and I traded him for these bone prayer beads. And I was really attached to them. I had almost nothing in those days. My astrology books and almost nothing else.... And I was really broken hearted, because I really loved those prayer beads. So, somebody said, "Why don't you go to a *mo*?" I said, "Oh, that is a good idea!" Because they had told me the story about this girl, and she found her passport, so I went to this Tensen Gyaltsen I think was his name. And I posed my question and said, "I lost my prayer beads, how can I find them." And he rolled the dice, and he looked in his book and said, "They left you. Don't bother to look."

D: Aha. [laughs]

K: You know why? Because I was so attached to them.

D: Right. Right. It was time to say goodbye.

In this story, the Buddhist message is loud and clear: sometimes things are just gone, and one shouldn't be too attached to them. The next story cautions about monastics using clairvoyant powers for worldly gains.

K: Lots of people have these abilities since childhood. It is very onerous. They see it almost as a burden. I think I read this story, or maybe Mrs. Miller told us about it. That this young girl had this prescience. She knew what was going to happen. And one time she sat down next to someone in the dentist's office, and she could tell they were going to get hit by a car and killed the next day. But what could she do?

D: Yeah, you can't change it, so how could you say to someone, "Oh, you're going to get hit and killed by a car"? Yes, I have heard that. Sometimes people have near-death experiences or out-of-body experiences, or something happens to them like they're struck by lightning, and then all of a sudden they are prescient. But they can't change what is going to happen, and they can't tell a lot of people these things because they wouldn't believe them anyway....

K: That is also true of meditators. I have talked to people in Thailand who have meditated a great deal, and they get the lottery numbers.

D: Oh right! Yeah. Go on.

K: Some of them become very famous. But one nun came to me and, "You know, I get the numbers and they are always correct. What should I do? Should I use them? Should I help people to win?" I said, "You know, actually it is a great motivation to want to help others, but the precepts say that monks and nuns are not to engage in worldly arts." And that would be an example. That is why I stopped astrology.

D: Right. Because it is not Dharma. Yeah, I get that.

From Karma Lekshe Tsomo's stories we learn about popular Tibetan beliefs in clairvoyant abilities and divination. We see that it is not just advanced meditators who possess this power but that there are also professional oracles who are believed to channel divinities and receive information from them. While there is nothing prohibiting the use of these powers by laymen in Tibetan Buddhism, the overall framework of the Buddhist ethical universe determines the karmic results of such actions. Moreover, as is the case in the larger Buddhist tradition, monastics are forbidden to use such powers for worldly purposes.

To inquire into any clairvoyant experiences of the participants who took part in the online survey, question 10 asked, "Have you ever had an intuition, dream, or vision about something that you could not have known about at the time, but that you later learned had actually happened?" Of the 92 respondents, 71 percent replied "Yes" to this question. Of those responding in the affirmative, 43 percent said this has happened to them between 1–5 times; while 22 percent stated that this has happened to them over 20 times. When asked, "When the event(s) occurred was it during (tick all that apply):," 71 percent ticked "dreaming," 50 percent ticked "spontaneous," 47 percent ticked "meditation or spiritual practice," 21 percent ticked "altered state of

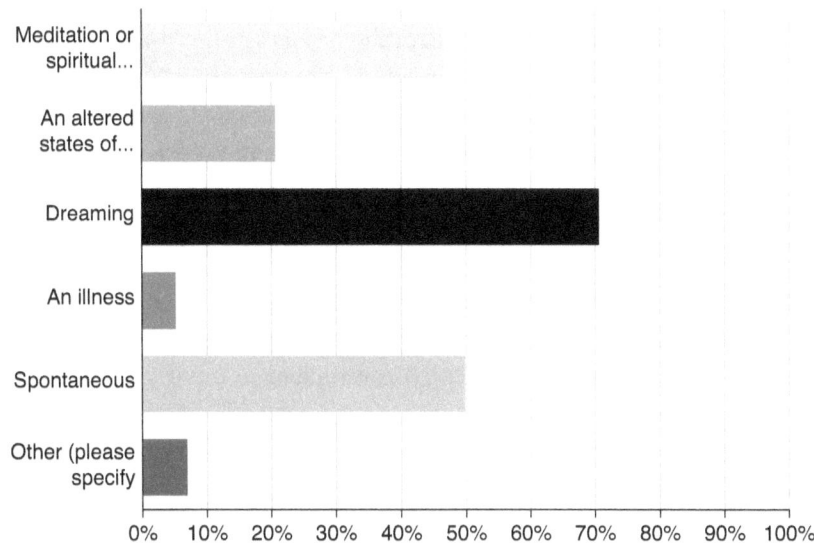

FIGURE 3.3 Occasion of Clairvoyant Experience.
Question 12: When the event(s) occurred, was it during ... Answered = 58. Skipped = 58.

consciousness," and 5 percent chose "an illness" (see figure 3.3). In the "other" category (7 percent) were included "intense stress and exhaustion" and "listening to a dharma talk while on retreat." This high incidence rate of clairvoyance reported during dreaming is suggestive. If some (as of yet unknown) "extrasensory" perception does exist, it makes sense that it would be more active when our ordinary five senses are "offline" during sleep.

To assess whether these experiences were strictly subjective or were also experienced by others (intersubjective), question 13 asked, "Did anyone else share the experience(s) with you?" Sixty-four percent ticked "no," 19 percent ticked "yes," and 17 percent ticked "sometimes." Given that most of the clairvoyant experiences reported occurred while dreaming, these responses would be expected.

Following these questions, participants were invited to describe their experiences in the space provided. Thirty-three wrote responses. Several of these I would classify as precognition, so I include them in the section below. Many replied with short answers such as "seeing the strings of karma"; "Shared dreams, dream visitation"; "Acts of revelation, answers to deep unresolved questions"; and "metanormal experience is normative to Buddhism."[12] However, some provided more detailed content, such as Mei's description of a recurrent dream she had as a child: "I was not a Buddhist at the time though. When I was a kid, younger than 10, I dreamt my friend's cat was lying on the side of the road and cars were passing by. I had the same dream for three continuous days. I went to my friend's house on the fourth day. I asked her about the cat. She told me the cat was run over by a car on the street three days ago. And the place was the same as in my dream."

Mei (a pseudonym) is a Chinese woman in her early thirties, currently living in Thailand, who converted to Buddhism as a young adult. Mei has also had precognitive experiences, which she related to me in our interview (quoted subsequently).

Similar to Mei's story about the cat, Elma (a pseudonym) wrote about two dreams she had concerning animals. The first is about her goldfish: "The very first time I experienced a [clairvoyant] dream was when our pet goldfish escaped the bowl early one morning, the dream image was of a bright orange fish floundering out of water.... On entering the kitchen, I found the poor fish beached on the kitchen bench." Because this dream startled her awake, Elma was able to find the fish in time and save its life. About this dream, Elma speculates, "I always wondered if the noise of the fish leaping from the bowl infiltrated my dream state," thus offering a possible mundane explanation. However, on another occasion Elma had this dream: "Another time I experienced a vivid dream of sheep scraping the ground for food, I awoke to find that an unexpected snowstorm had delivered a large volume of snow overnight. The storm caused havoc for weeks. There were no sheep around me at the time as I was not living in a rural environment. However, my children were at the time staying with their father on the family farm; the power cuts caused us communication problems for many days." The sheep at the family farm were in danger of both starvation and freezing to death because of the storm.

Elma is a European woman in her mid-fifties, living in New Zealand, who practiced Zen meditation for many years, beginning in her early thirties. For a while she considered herself a Zen Buddhist but currently does not claim any religious affiliation. In the survey she wrote that she'd had "multiple experiences of precognitive dreams that began shortly after I commenced the practice of Zen meditation around 1995." During our interview, Elma related some of these dreams and other paranormal events she has experienced (quoted subsequently).

Both Mei's and Elma's stories relate dreams concerning animals they knew dying a sudden violent death (Mei's neighbor's cat) or being in imminent danger of dying (the goldfish outside the bowl and the sheep on Elma's family farm). These clairvoyant dreams arose spontaneously in seeming response to emotionally charged life-or-death situations. Moreover, these dreams are not isolated incidents—both women also report other paranormal experiences involving precognition and encounters with other beings (quoted subsequently). While Mei and Elma each appear to possess some natural psi ability, Elma makes a definite association between the onset of her precognitive dreams and her initiation into Zen meditation.

Precognition

The *Oxford English Dictionary* defines "precognition" as "antecedent cognition or knowledge; (supposed) foreknowledge, esp. as a form of extrasensory perception."[13] Like clairvoyance, precognition overlaps with the Buddhist higher knowledge of divine eye, as well as the various forms of divination used within the Buddhist traditions. Probably the most substantial evidence for this ability based on scientific studies is the "presentiment" experiments carried out by Dean Radin and others (see chapter 2). Meta-analyses of these experiments demonstrate statistically significant physiological responses in humans and animals to stimuli beginning before the stimuli were presented, thus showing some type of unconscious presentiment of the future.

During our interview, Ajahn Chandako related a contemporary story from the Thai Forest Tradition of Ajahn Chah's possible precognition of a horrific plane crash in Thailand. The following discussion took place:

AJAHN CHANDAKO: Though predicting the future seems to be much more tricky, rather than seeing other realms that are happening in the present. It seems like predicting the future has more variables, so it is very difficult to do. But there was one occasion in Thailand when the queen was having her birthday, and she invited all the great meditation masters from the Forest Tradition at that time, especially a lot of the younger ones, middle-aged ones. So they were getting on a plane to attend her birthday in Bangkok. And Ajahn Chah was invited, and he refused. I mean no one refuses an invitation from the queen!

D. E. OSTO: Right! No one refuses a royal invitation!

AC: Why? He was healthy. There was no discernable reason why he didn't go. But then that plane crashed, wiping out a generation of all the up-and-coming meditation masters.

D: Wow!

AC: It was a national tragedy. And he was due to be on that plane. And so, some people speculated that he could see in the future. He never specifically said that. Well, at the time and before the plane crash happened, someone asked him, "Why didn't you go? It is a special occasion, why didn't you go?" "Ah," he said, "It is just leading people to die." And at the time it seemed like, what did he mean by that?

D: Yeah. What does that mean?

AC: Is that some Zen teaching? What does that mean?

D: [Laughs]

AC: Right? But then . . .

D: The plane crashes and everybody dies!

AC: The plane crashes, and then reflecting back, they said, "Oh, wow!" So people kind of speculated that he knew what was going to happen. It was also interesting if he knew it was going to happen, he didn't say anything to the others! [Laughs]

D: Yeah, right!

AC: Like how much can you affect the outcome of events? Sometimes the karmic momentum is so strong, you can't really stop that.

D: You can't interrupt that. Right. True. So, he wouldn't. I have heard that. This goes all the way back to Greek tragedy that sometimes when people can see things in the future, they have no ability to change them, so someone might see that there is a plane that is going to crash or a car crash, but it is almost like a curse because they know what is going to happen, but they can't change it.

This dialogue warrants some unpacking, since it raises two recurrent themes throughout this study. First, one might wonder why Ajahn Chah did not just tell people he had a precognition of the plane's crash. However, there are Buddhist monastic rules in their code of discipline (Vinaya) against declaring one's spiritual attainments. The issue of these monastic prohibitions came up a number of times during my interviews. For example, when talking to Ajahn Chandako about the Theravādin monastic rules (pāṭimokkha), the following discussion took place when I asked about the rules concerning claiming psychic attainments:

AC: If you knowingly lie about your attainments, the Buddha considered that to be one of the most serious offences that a monk or nun could do.

D: Yes, you could be immediately expelled for that.

AC: You are immediately expelled for that. Immediately you are no longer a monk or a nun. Immediately. So that was very serious. However, if it is true and you say it to others, it is a medium-level offense, called a *pacittiya* offense. Although the most egregious offenses are called *parajika*s; for example, killing a human being . . .

D: Wounding a Buddha or something . . .

AC: And so, the Buddha considered that to be one of the worst things that a monk or a nun can do, if you intentionally do it, because then you are doing it just to become famous or get donations, right? If your intention is lying. But if you actually do have psychic powers and you speak to laypeople about them, or even if you overestimate yourself, which is very common. People are sincere, but they actually overestimate themselves. But then you start talking about that with nonordained people, then the Buddha also considered that . . . it is an offense, a lesser offense.

Thus, while claiming false attainments is immediate grounds for expulsion from the order, even claiming true psychic abilities is a minor offense. Thus, in the stories related to me from the Thai Forest Tradition, Ajahn Chandako always refers to what others have said about a Forest meditation master's psychic ability. Many of these are from disciples of these masters or their fellow monastics who know them well. In this way these narratives constitute a contemporary folklore of the paranormal in the Theravāda tradition, which is nevertheless strongly rooted in the traditional canonical literature concerning psi abilities and encounters with other beings.

Another theme raised in the preceding dialogue with the Ajahn is the philosophical question concerning the relation between precognition and human free will. We can frame it this way: "If we are able to see the future, can we change the outcome, or is it predetermined?" Ajahn Chandako offers a Buddhist answer in the form of karma: "Sometimes the karmic momentum is so strong, you can't really stop that." This implies that when the karmic momentum is not too strong, future outcomes can be changed by present actions. Thus, karma dictates future events but not in a strictly deterministic way. This view supports the "Buddhist Soft Compatibilism" position on free will put forth by Rick Repetti.[14] I return to this issue in chapter 5, when I discuss a precognitive experience that changed the course of Repetti's life and eventually led him to become one of the leading contemporary academic thinkers on Buddhism and free will.

To inquire about precognition in my survey, I asked the following question: "Q15 Have you ever had an intuition, dream, or vision of something before it occurred, and that you could not have anticipated or expected to happen?" Statistical results were similar to the previous question on clairvoyance, but with a slightly lower number of people reporting precognition. However, as mentioned, many descriptions supplied under the clairvoyance question were precognitive, so if they were included in this question, the results would be roughly equal. Of the 81 respondents, 60 percent replied "Yes" that they had some precognitive experience. Of those responding in the affirmative, 32 percent said this has happened to them between 1–5 times; while 22 percent stated that this has happened to them over 20 times. When asked, "When the event(s) occurred was it during (tick all that apply):," 63 percent ticked "dreaming," 48 percent "meditation or spiritual practice," 45 percent "spontaneous," 15 percent an "altered state of consciousness," and 10 percent "an illness." Seventy-three percent reported that this was a strictly private experience.

Some of the descriptions of precognition were extremely brief, such as "Just dreamed that certain events would transpire" or "Auspicious signs predicting an event." Others provided a bit more detail: "Mostly talking deja vu. Seeing something that triggers a memory of seeing that exact same thing in a dream, sometimes years earlier. Feels weird and is distinct from 'hey, that looks familiar' "; "At the height of my practice I had precognitive dreams and waking experiences regularly, some far too complex, clairvoyant, and shared by others to be reasonably explained as coincidences"; and "I have had prescient dreams since my teens but they increased in frequency after my 'milam gyi naljor' (dream-yoga) retreat." One respondent mentions three different events: dreaming about a friend and being contacted by them, thinking of someone and then being called by that person, and even a "prophetic dream" predicting the COVID-19 pandemic's arrival in New York City: "1) Had a dream about a friend I hadn't seen in 15 years. He called me that afternoon. 2) numerous times I thought of a girl that used to work for me and she would instantly call me on the phone. This phenomenon still happens. 3) Had a prophetic dream where I was walking down W. 23rd St. in New York towards the Veterans' Hospital in the middle of the street and there were absolutely no people alive anywhere. A week later the corona virus arrived in New York."

Other replies to the survey were much more detailed. John is an ordained "lay lama" in the Tibetan Buddhist tradition; he is from the United Kingdom and is now in his seventies.[15] In the survey, he provides a detailed account of one of his prescient dreams:

> Many, many prescient dreams. Such as . . . Once, in retreat, I had this dream in several scenes: 1) I got out of a London Underground train somewhere north of London at a station called "Borough," just like the one in Southwark. My thought was that it was so far north of the Thames that it would escape confusion with the other Borough station. 2) A man in a "donkey jacket" was pointing out a multistorey car park next to the station and telling me about the Roman remains which were found on the site. We appear to be in Northampton. 3) I am in the office of a school. The office is filled with children. I ask to speak to the headmaster. A child responds, "Don't you mean The Mother?" 4) I am in the children's ward of a hospital. Amy, daughter of my friend Edgar, is there.

After outlining these four scenes, John then goes on to explain how each related to real-world people and events:

> As Edgar lives in Northampton, I write to him and ask if this makes any sense to him. Soon after the retreat, I visit him and he tells me that: 1) he grew up near Northampton station in an old part of the city called The Borough. It was demolished to make way for such buildings as the multistorey car park. 2) a friend of his who always wears a donkey jacket was a local historian who had just had a booklet published on The Borough. (Edgar showed it to me). 3) Edgar and his wife were considering home-schooling their daughter Amy. Her mother would be the teacher. 4) Amy broke her arm with a "green-stick fracture" and was briefly hospitalized.

It is unclear whether some of these scenes were clairvoyant of present or past events or prescient of future events; however, regardless of how we classify them, the dream imagery suggests access to some form of extrasensory perception. Note that although these images appear in a dream, the dream itself took place within the context of a Buddhist retreat, so its prescient imagery could have been induced from the prolonged and intense periods of John's meditations during the day.

Ayyā Mettikā is an American-born Theravādin Buddhist nun in her fifties who describes in her response a vivid precognitive dream of a stupa (Buddhist reliquary monument):

> [I had a] dream of being a sky-walker deva flying with two other such over a mountain forest area, us each cruising the peak and then swooping in to pay our homage to the ancient stupa of the Buddha Maitreya. I swooped in to pay my homage. Not long after word came of an ancient stolen stupa that had surfaced at an antique shop in Portland. Within two weeks, the stupa arrived at our temple hermitage, and was installed with relics of the Buddha which were then gifted [and] enshrined.[16]

Mettikā also related precognitive meditative visions connected to this dream:

> Persistent meditative visions of a forested entry road leading into a deeper forest. We had a dream of a forest monastery, or forest hermitage from years back, but this image was rising from the heart and felt like a real place, the beginnings, perhaps, of a concrete vision. Then we started getting third party invitations to visit a forest retreat land. Within a year, we finally bumped into the owner of that forest retreat land on a walking path down in the [name] Desert . . . and she invited us to come for our retreats. Three to four months later, on my birthday, we drove to visit that land for the first time. Driving in, I recognized the visualized image immediately and commented, "This is the place!" As it turned out, that very day, the owner wanted to speak about her heritage and that land. Today, more than ten years later, that road is the entry road to our [name] Forest Hermitage. And that ancient stupa [discussed earlier], has moved, from the temple hermitage where it first arrived . . . to our [name] Hermitage on the mountain's saddle. The forest and saddle are easily recognizable from the sky-walker deva dream. The stupa is from the Silla Dynasty, and [w]as originally dedicated to the

Buddha Maitreya. I pay my homage to the stupa daily, and it is as if I can feel the presence of the sky-walker devas around the land also doing so. I actively do not wish to be reborn as a sky-walker deva to perpetuate the attachment to this lovely forest, stupa and relics.

Here, the Ayyā's dream appears to be a precognition of both the ancient stupa dedicated to Maitreya that would be donated to her order and the location of their new hermitage. Her meditative visions of the place reinforce her dream experience. The "sky-walker devas" are a class of Buddhist deities that Mettikā both dreamed of and whom she can "feel the presence of" sharing her devotions to the stupa. This mention of nonhuman intelligent beings, which I discuss in detail in the next chapter, often occurs in relation to psi phenomena. This co-emergence at times makes it difficult to distinguish between what is psi and what is a "paranormal" encounter.

Ayyā Mettikā's statement that she actively does not wish "to be reborn as a sky-walker deva to perpetuate the attachment to this lovely forest, stupa and relics" contains a number of overlapping Buddhist themes. First, since she dreamed of being a sky-walker deva, the Ayyā is suggesting that this dream may be a premonition of her karmic propensity to be reborn as a goddess because of her attachment. However, since she is a Buddhist nun, her spiritual goal is to overcome all attachment and attain nirvana. Thus, her active intention not to be reborn as a goddess is meant to counteract the potential karmic fruition of her attachment. Here we see a further example of a "Buddhist Soft Compatibilism" concerning free will, implied by Ajahn Chandako and recently argued for by Repetti,[17] whereby the future is not strictly predetermined and where active intention can redirect one's karmic stream.

During our interview, Mei described three different precognitive experiences involving her husband. The first was a reoccurring hypnogogic experience that seemed to presage their future meeting. The following is a redacted version of our conversation:

MEI: Okay. So, I think paranormal phenomena in my experience is with my husband [laughs]. Before we got married . . . we both are Buddhists [her husband was raised in a Thai Buddhist household, and she came to Buddhism when she was twenty]. . . . So the experience was around 2017 . . . in August, so I guess the first . . . two times it was like in my dreams. And the third time was just during the day. I will tell you the details.

D. E. OSTO: Sure.

M: ... So, one time was like ... Before I fall asleep ... I don't remember when it started but it had been for a long time like that ... right before I fell asleep there would be an image suddenly appear in my mind far away, very slight coming. And then there is a shadow. So in the beginning when it happened, I feel kind of scared ... more like I feel shocked, but after a while I got used to it. So when that image shows up, I know, "Oh, I'm going to fall asleep." [Laughs]

D: So, there is light and then there is shadow? Is it like a clear bright light?

M: Yes. It is like a very bright light far away, and then there is like a person standing in front of the light, but you can't see the person. You can only see a shadow, and it is also far away, so you can't really see anything. Just like a shadow.

D: It is like an outline of a person behind a very bright light, but you can't see any of the details of the person?

M: Yeah, right. Exactly. So that had been for a while, and after I met my now husband, at that time I just got to know him [laughs]. So, one day suddenly, that image after it showed up becomes ... his face suddenly shows in front of me. So after that image it became his face showing in front of me very close. And so ever since then I don't have that image before I sleep anymore.

D: Right.

M: So that image disappeared ever since then.

D: So is it replaced by his image, or it was just that once that it happened, and then it stopped happening after that?

M: I am not quite sure. I think for a couple of times, it was replaced by his image, and then it totally disappeared. It didn't show up anymore.

D: Okay.

M: So that was one thing. I don't know if it means anything [laughs].

D: Interesting. It is interesting.

M: In the beginning I was kind of scared when it showed up because it is kind of like you don't know what that shadow is ...

D: Do you think it was him that was far away? Or do you think once you had met him, it stopped the other thing from happening? Do you have any ideas what the connection between the two might be?

M: I think maybe it was him [laughs].

D: Okay.

M: That is just my imagination. I don't really know.
D: I mean who knows? But it could be. Maybe it was like somehow precognition. You kind of knew on some level that you were going to meet him one day, but you hadn't met him yet, so he is always really far away, until you meet him, and then that goes away, because now he is actually in your life. You see him coming from far away. Who knows? But anyway . . . [laughs]
M: Because also that image suddenly . . . his face showed up for the first time, that was the last time the shade showed up. So first showed up the light and this figure, and suddenly became his face. It is kind of like I can only see this much in front of me, because I was dreaming, right? Not really dreaming . . .
D: Somewhere in between?
M: Right before I fell asleep. And then suddenly this figure suddenly appeared right in front of me, so I could see this person. So before that it was kind of like a sign for me to fall asleep.

This first experience one could interpret as a "hypnogogic hallucination" occurring in that suggestive state of consciousness between waking and sleeping. Mei sees a shadowy figure at a distance in front of a bright light, which is replaced with a close-up image of her future husband once they have met. She was frightened or shocked by the figure at first, then becomes somewhat indifferent. After meeting her husband-to-be and seeing his face replace the shadowy figure in this vision, the recurrence of the hypnogogic experience stops. Note that I offer the suggestion of a precognition of her husband, and she hesitantly agrees ("I think maybe it was him [laughs]"). This was a distinctive feature of my interviewees—their modesty in describing their experiences and their hesitancy in offering definitive interpretations. Often, they appeared truly puzzled by what happened to them but were willing to keep an open mind and offer provisional interpretations, fully aware of possible alternative explanations. In other words, my interviewees struck me as highly intelligent, rational people who were genuinely curious about the significance of their paranormal experiences. These events were often deeply meaningful to them, interpersonal, and life changing. They were happy to share their experiences with me but lacked the interpretive certitude regarding these events so characteristic of egotistical, narcissistic, and mentally unstable personalities. Whether one interprets Mei's experience as a phantasm of the hypnogogic brain, a precognition of her meeting her future husband, or a visitation of some being (the spirit of her husband? Another being in her life that was replaced by her husband?), Mei's experience was deeply meaningful to her as it seemed in her view to presage her meeting with her significant other.

Mei's second experience was a dream of her future husband's room before she had seen it.

M: It was dreaming.... I dreamed I went to visit him, but I don't quite remember, but he brought me to his room. We were not together yet. We were just friends at the time. So he brought me to his room. And then I said in my dream, "I feel so sleepy." Then he put me into bed, and he went out. So I could see the room layout, where the closet is, the bed is, the bookcases, I think. So I was curious about his real room—if it is like that. And also, the room entrance. So later, after we were together, I saw his room. It was kind of the same layout.

In the following discussion, Mei explained that his room in waking life had all the basic features of her dream-experienced room, but some of the details were different. Elma (quoted subsequently) described a similar dream to me, where some of the distinctive features were the same as a place in waking life, but not all. Appropriately enough, Mei was not particularly excited about this experience and did not offer any definitive interpretation. Was it a precognitive dream of her future visit to his room, a clairvoyant or out-of-body experience of his room in the dream state, or just a coincidence produced by her unconscious mind? As Dean Radin would say, "the jury is still out" on this event.

Mei's third experience was a waking vision that possessed some very distinctive and unusual features that seemed to presage a future event.

M: I think the last is the most mysterious one. So it was during the day, and we were talking. And then he was trying to kiss me. As soon as he kissed me, I suddenly had this image in my mind, and then I said, "Oh, I had an image in my mind!" Then I drew out a picture and showed him. So the picture was like ... let me see ... if I have the notebook. I'll draw it and show you. I can email you the real picture in real life. I remember a very dark red background, and flowers. But the flowers, they are lotus flowers, but it is different. I am Chinese. Chinese lotus flowers, I don't know if you know the kind of style. It's like a flower and big leaf . . . [draws a picture for me] . . . that's it.

D: Right.

M: This was more like veins in my dream. The leaves feel like flowers, but not really like flowers. . . . But it is kind of like a . . . Let me draw it . . . [draws another picture] . . . pardon for my really bad drawing . . . it's not so clear. I will show you the real picture so you can better understand what I am saying . . . you see, this is the lotus, and here are veins [shows me picture] . . .

D: Okay. Yeah right.

M: You see the dark red background lotus? So, that was like in my mind. . . . I don't know if it is clear for you?

D: Yeah. I can kind of see it.

M: So, these are leaves. And these are the flowers. But I have never seen leaves like these, especially for a lotus. So when it appeared in my mind, I was like, "What is that?" So I tried to explain to my at-that-time boyfriend. So I tried to draw it out and said, "So I had this weird image of this lotus flower, but the lotus flower's leaves don't really look like leaves of a lotus flower, but also look like flowers. They are gold and dark red background." That was a Friday, so I just told him. And on Monday, he brought me to a Thai temple, and then I saw what I showed you.

D: Right!

M: It is exactly like the lotus flower and the leaves and the same color.

D: So when you saw that in your mind, it was only just a part of what you saw at the temple. Because there is a creature underneath and flowers on top . . . It was like your mind's eye saw like one part of that. Is that it?

M: So, in my mind it was not totally the same . . . So if you see this picture like this [shows picture]. Here is the lotus flower. Right? In my mind it was this part [shows] and up here was the lotus [shows] flower.

D: I see. I see.

M: But the background and color are the same. And the leaves are like this [shows me], the same too.

D: Yep. Yep. So, it was like a snapshot of a part of that. And what is that? That piece of artwork in the temple? What is that of?

M: I can show you the whole picture [shows me] here.

D: Oh, it is at the entrance. And is that a dragon or some kind of guardian?

M: It looks like a dragon. Here are the leaves too [shown in picture]. And here is the flower.

D: So it was three days before, before you actually went to the temple.

M: Yes. It happened on Friday, and we went to the temple on Monday. Let me show you... [shows picture] This is what I had in mind of what a lotus looks like. That's how we [Chinese] picture lotus... especially in drawing it would be like this [draws and shows picture].

D: Yep.

M: So, it is totally different. And I never went to a Thai temple... nor any other Theravada temples before that. So I never saw lotus flowers like that. So that is why when it appeared in my mind, I feel the leaves are kind of strange, because they also kind of look like flowers [laughs].

D: Yeah. No. That is really interesting.

M: That was the last time. Yeah [laughs].

This account has a number of striking features. First, this vision or precognitive flash was spontaneously induced from a kiss from Mei's boyfriend (and future husband and father of her child), an event both emotionally and erotically charged. Second, the split-second vision is of a very distinctive piece of Thai Buddhist art, a lotus flower, which was completely unfamiliar to Mei.[18] Third, Mei is able to describe its shape and color in detail to her boyfriend and even draw a rough sketch of it to show him. And finally, Mei recognizes immediately the same artistic rendering of the lotus flower from her vision on the Thai temple they visited three days later, and she points this out to her boyfriend. Thus, we see that each of Mei's psychic experiences involves in some way her boyfriend (and now husband and father of her child). The highly personal and emotionally significant contexts for these phenomena are recurring themes in stories from people who seem to possess natural psi abilities. Often paranormal events in their lives involve close friends and family, major life changes, a birth, a death, or a life-threatening situation.

Like Mei, Elma's precognitive psi experiences involve someone very close to her—in this case her daughter and the events surrounding her conception and birth.

ELMA: I began Zen meditation in 1998, and it was a time in my life when I was just a young mum. I practiced meditation right through my last pregnancy.... It was a time when I started to realize that my concentration had improved, I was more at peace with myself, I was noticing things that I never really noticed before ... and I noticed that upon sitting I would get this little girl coming through to me, and ... I have never seen myself as psychic or anything like that.

D. E. OSTO: Right. You don't understand yourself in that way.

E: But anyway, this little girl comes to me in meditation, and she is asking me, "Are you ready for me yet?" And I kept pushing her away for two reasons: I wasn't sure what she was; I wasn't sure what she meant by am I ready for her yet. But I assumed it was a child that wanted to be part of our lives.

D: So, it was like a voice you were hearing when you were meditating?

E: I could see her ...

D: Oh, you could visually see her?

E: Not see her, but in my mind, I could see a picture of her. It wasn't a ghostly apparition or anything, it was just in my mind. I could see this little girl, and this little voice. And it would have been about six months she kept coming in; in the end I kind of gave in to her, I guess. And we decided we would have another child, so I guess maybe that was what that was about; this child wanted to come through. So that was fine.

Here we see that Elma's dream shares an important element with Mei's hypnogogic vision of a shadowy figure—both appear to presage the coming of someone very important into their lives. Elma also had a powerful precognitive dream during her pregnancy related to the birth of her daughter:

E: I became pregnant, and I hadn't had the easiest pregnancy as with my two other children, so I decided to hold off before getting a specialist in, because I needed to have a caesarean with this pregnancy. And I held off and I held off, and I must have been four months or five months pregnant, and friends said to me, "Have you decided on who you would have as an obstetrician yet?" And I said, "No, I haven't; I haven't really decided yet." But I had this very strange dream, a very, very vivid dream about a woman of Indian descent, and I dreamed I was on Bedford Avenue in Wellington.[19] It was really clear—the avenue, the trees, the road, the city traffic. I could see the houses, the old villas, and I could see down a side road to a garage. And I turned down this side road, and this woman came out to me, and she was greeting me arms opened wide, and she was saying to me, "My paintings, my paintings, you must come and see my paintings!" And I was lured towards her to enter this garage she was working from. And I had never seen the most exquisite colors; they were big canvases, and the colors—the reds, the blues, the yellows—they were all popping. And I woke up from that dream...

D: Okay. Interesting. Please go on.

E: And I am talking with my friend, and she is asking me, "Have you got an obstetrician yet?" And I am saying, "No, I haven't." And she is saying to me that "there is a consultant that my friend went to named Priya. She is in Wellington on Bedford Avenue somewhere and she does these really cool watercolor paintings. You would love her."

D: [Laughs] Wow! So how much before this conversation did you have this dream? Do you remember?

E: Usually my dreams are within three days. And there is nothing over two weeks. It is usually within that two-week frame, and more usually within three days. So I am thinking this would have been within the three days to a week mark, because it triggered that response right away, and that is what I find in reality—I get that trigger, and it is like, "Woah, that dream has just come back." And I had to take myself back into deep concentration to recall the dream. People probably think I am away with the fairies, but it all happens quite spontaneously...

D: Yeah. Wow. That is amazing. So, I am assuming that you went?

E: Yes, the story carries on. It is long. And Priya...I met her as well. This lady close to retirement, with eyes that appeared quite cloudy. And I thought, "Why am I trusting her to do my caesarian? You know this is crazy." But I trusted her because my dream connected me to her. She wasn't going to take me on as a patient because she was nearing her retirement. But she made an allowance for me because I had been so sick with hyperemesis, which is morning sickness where you just can't stop being sick. So I was always hospitalized to be rehydrated, so it was really rough. So Priya said to me, "I've been looking through your notes, and if you don't have a caesarian, and I am going to be quite straight with you, you will lose your life and your baby." So that was that. Pretty black and white, so I decided, "Yes, I trust this woman." And there in her waiting room is a little pile of [her] paintings, and we looked through while we were waiting.

Like Mei's dream about her boyfriend's room, Elma's dream about Priya's office shared important features with the actual place but was not exactly the same. Elma explained to me that Priya's actual office was on Bedford Avenue, in a villa (not down a side street in a garage as in the dream).[20] Also, Priya's paintings were not on large canvases on the walls but on smaller ones sitting on a table in the waiting room. However, the specific street, the artist, and the paintings were all very similar. Note also the timeframe of Elma's precognitive dreams average three days—the same amount of time that lapsed between Mei's vision of the lotus flower and her seeing it on the Thai temple.

Elma's story continues:

E: And eventually when it got to the time of giving birth, I started to go into labor early, and Priya had said to me, "If you go into labor early, you may not get me as your obstetrician, you might have to go through Wellington Hospital." But for some reason when we got to Wellington Hospital, Priya was there! And I just remember her standing in the hallway, arms crossed like this [demonstrates], and all the other staff—nurses and other people—were running around like crazy, and she was telling them what to do. So anyway, we went ahead with the emergency caesarian at this stage, and it turned out my daughter had the cord around her neck, and she was breech. So, I mean, it was just so lucky that she was delivered so beautifully by Priya. Then while I was in hospital afterwards, Priya came to me at about the third day, and she said, "Why did you choose me as your obstetrician?" And I told her about the dream just knowing that she would get it.
D: Aha. Right.
E: And the very next day she came in with a painting for me.[21]
D: Oh, wow. [Chuckles]
E: We've still got that painting, and my daughter knows about the story as well so . . .
D: Now, you said you didn't know if you were going to get her to perform the procedure, so was it just luck that she was there when you went there? Did you actually contact her, or had you no idea?
E: No, I didn't contact her. It was luck, sheer luck.
D: That she just was there when you got there?

E: And she said, "You are so lucky, Elma, it is my weekend off as well. I wouldn't normally come in, but I'm here." And there was no questioning it. And that is a really interesting question that you asked, because I never questioned it!

D: Yeah. Like there she was. Like she kind of had to be there, right? Because she was the one who was *supposed* to do it.

E: Yeah, it was planned beforehand. Why would she not be there? [Laughs]

These additional details add to the significance of Elma's dream. Elma's pregnancy was potentially life threatening to her and her baby, yet when she went into early labor, Priya was serendipitously at the hospital and successfully delivered the baby. Thus, Elma's dream seemed to be saying, "You *must* have this woman deliver your baby." Moreover, Priya's understanding of Elma's dream and gift of one of her paintings seemed to confirm the symbolic significance of the art in the dream. Finally, like Mei's experiences each being connected to her future husband, Elma's precognitive dream connects her meditative vision of the little girl:

D: Now do you think that that girl who was contacting you when you were meditating ... do you feel that was your daughter when she was born?

E: Yes.

D: Was there anything that made you when you saw her that was like, "Wow, you are the girl that was talking to me?"

E: Yes, the child that appeared in my dream was around three or four years old, she resembled my daughter perfectly around that same age.

D: So, she turned out just like you saw in the dream?

E: Yes.

D: Wow. How old is she now?

E: Twenty-one.

D: And she knows this story?

E: Yes, she does. My daughter has completed her bio-med degree with honors and is now studying at med school to become a doctor. On her most recent visit home she asked if she could take Priya's painting back to Auckland with her. I thought this was a great idea, both of us knowing the significance of the painting and the story.

These stories of precognition related to me by participants possess a number of important Buddhist themes. Karma is a central one, such as how karma relates to free will and future events. A connection between meditation and precognitive dreams and visions is another. The association of these phenomena with close personal relations is another Buddhist theme, perhaps not as obvious. This is because in Buddhism one's close friends and family are believed to be karmically linked to them not just in this lifetime but throughout many lifetimes. Thus, having spontaneous precognitive dreams and visions of future husbands or daughters would be understood as resulting from previous karmic connections.

If we put the responses to the clairvoyant and precognitive questions together, we see that for the people surveyed these experiences are fairly common, often occur spontaneously in dreams, but can be triggered by meditational or spiritual practice and more rarely by altered states of consciousness or illness. Most often these experiences were private (subjective) experiences, and therefore one might be tempted to dismiss them as wishful thinking, false memories, unconscious processing of subliminal information, or imagination. However, some of these experiences contain specific and veridical information that is difficult to dismiss as coming through some mundane (sensory) means.[22] Regardless of their ontological or metaphysical status, the precognitions reported were deeply meaningful for the people who experienced them and therefore possessed "real-world" effects in people's lives.

Telepathy

The *OED* defines telepathy as "the supposed communication of thoughts, mental images, etc., from one mind to another by psychic or other paranormal means; spec. the (supposed) ability to read others' minds" and cites F. W. H. Myers as the first attestation in 1883.[23] In the Buddhist tradition, telepathy corresponds to the third higher knowledge of "mind reading" (in Pāli: *cetopariyañāṇa* or *paracittavijānana*). We saw in chapter 1 that this was an important pedagogical skill of the Buddha and his advanced disciples and was also used to directly ascertain someone's level of spiritual attainment. In the West, telepathy has been studied by J. B. Rhine, Charles Tart, Dean

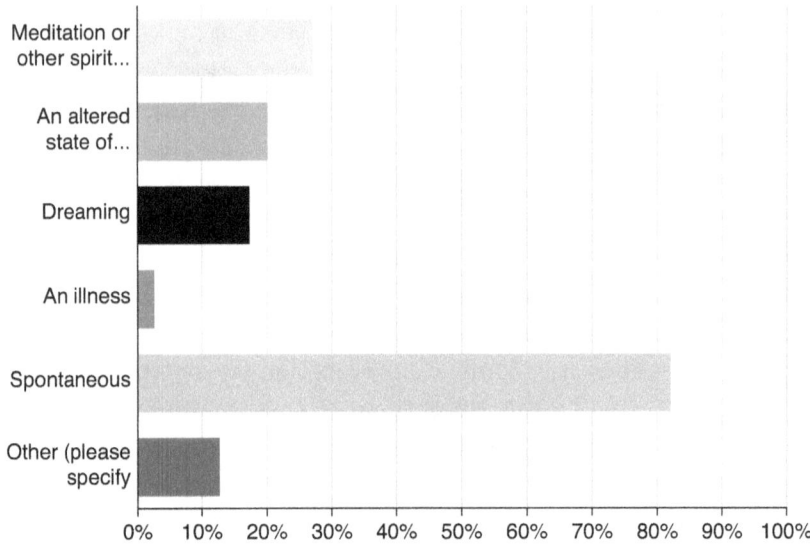

FIGURE 3.4 Occasion of Telepathic Experience.
Question 22: When the event(s) occurred, was it during . . . Answered = 40. Skipped = 76.

Radin, and others using various methods such as the ganzfeld experiments. Meta-analysis of these studies shows odds against chance many billions to one in favor of some extrasensory transfer of information. To assess if any of the survey participants have had experiences involving telepathy, question 20 asked, "Have you ever been able to sense, feel, or 'hear' the thoughts or emotions of others around you, or far away?" Of the seventy people who responded, 64 percent answered "Yes," and 43 percent of those who answered the next question on frequency of occurrence indicated that this has happened to them more than twenty times. The majority (83 percent) of these telepathic experiences occurred spontaneously, while only 18 percent said these events happened while dreaming (see figure 3.4).

When asked if anyone has shared these experiences with them, 55 percent of those that answered (22 out of 44) responded either "Yes" or "Sometimes." Thus, unsurprisingly, since telepathic experiences are relational (involving two or more minds), they seem to happen most often during waking life (unlike the clairvoyant or precognitive experiences reported) and involve some intersubjective element.

When asked to describe their experiences, some participants responded describing fairly mundane, spontaneous events, such as thinking of a root beer float (which they do not usually drink) and discovering that their wife was thinking of one at the same time, or someone wondering what time it was and then their friend spontaneously telling them the time, having experienced them as having asked out loud when they had only thought of it. Others reported "sensing" others' minds or empathically feeling others' feelings at a distance: "In conversing with or counseling individuals, I often sense a person's insights, obstacles, potential, or past experience" and "Under certain conditions my intuition becomes so dramatically heightened that I experience something I might describe as tele-empathy (feeling the emotional states of others at a distance)." One person specifically mentioned a heightened ability during "emotionally turbulent times," and another simply wrote, "When my husband was dying and unconscious." Here we see once again psi events' close connection to strong emotions and life-and-death situations. One respondent specifically mentions that their telepathic ability was heightened through "practice" and the use of "entheogens" (psychoactive substances used for spiritual purposes). There was only one specifically Buddhist response to this question: "Communication in dreams with loved ones, gurus and *dakini*s [Tibetan sky-walking goddesses]. Preternatural knowledge of death and beyond." However, under a different question, Ayyā Mettikā gives two detailed accounts of mind reading in the context of contemporary Theravāda Buddhism, which I discuss in what follows.

During our interview, Ajahn Chandako provided some fascinating insights into the development of telepathic ability according to the contemporary Theravāda tradition. The Ajahn additionally made some illuminating comments on the development of psi abilities through concentration (*samādhi*) and how he came to find accounts of such powers credible. Given the relevance of this subject for the current project, I cite from our conversation here at some length:

AC: When I first went to Thailand and toward the beginning of my exposure to Buddhist practice there was talk of deva, ghost realms, other realms, sometimes psychic powers, and I was like, "Yeah, maybe that is true, maybe not; I don't know." I put it in the basket of "I can't verify that," so I set it aside. I had plenty to work on in my own daily practice. I didn't really need any answers to that. As I spent a total of fifteen years in Thailand, and the longer I was there, the wider my range of acceptance of what is possible; it was expanded.

D: Right! Please elaborate.

AC: For a number of reasons. I will just try and systematically go through it. Of course, in the Buddhist *suttas*, the Theravāda Pāli *suttas* there are many, many mentions of psychic powers, and there are lots of stories from that era both in the *suttas* but also in the Vinaya, many, many stories. So there is a lot to work with there, probably easily researchable. But of course, that was thousands of years ago. So okay, how literally do you take that? Of course, also in the *suttas* you have *so many* mentions of other realms. There is no way it could have been added later. Clearly that is what the Buddha taught—multiple realms of existence overlapping each other generally based on the results of the *kamma* [karma] that we make. It is undeniable that is what the Buddha taught. It is another question of whether it is true or not. How do you verify something like that?

So, as I was staying in Thailand longer and longer, I had the opportunity to meet with and live with many of the great Forest masters. The reason I ended up in Thailand in the first place was first and foremost that was where Buddhism was thriving. There was the greatest collection of meditation masters I think anywhere in the world at that time. I think definitely anywhere in the world. So because of that, that is why I ended up focusing on the Thai Forest Tradition, rather than some of the other traditions. I started in Zen, I traveled in Tibet. But I settled down there (Thailand), particularly because of the meditation masters.

Having lived with a number of meditation masters and having come to completely trust them.... So, for example, the first year I was a monk, I stayed with a meditation master named Ajahn Piak. He was reputed to be one of the rare people with psychic abilities. He had very deep *samādhi*. And again, I stayed with him for about a year shortly after my full ordination. And in private I would ask him about some of these things—other realms or whatever and in private between monks he was allowed to talk about such things and even talk a bit about his own experience. And so it became more and more plausible that maybe these things really do exist.

In terms of psychic abilities ... one of the first psychic abilities that tends to arise with meditators is the ability to gradually become more sensitive to what other people are feeling and thinking. Even just normal meditators become sensitive, but in a very small percentage of people they can actually start to hear the thoughts of other people. And a more refined version of that is being able to tune in whenever you want to whichever person and very specifically know what they are thinking and feeling, but also it is almost like they can visually see the *citta*, or the mental energy, of another person so they can know for sure what stage of enlightenment that person is, how many defilements they have, how pure their mind is, etc. So it is not merely reading one's mind, hearing one's thoughts, although that can be part of it; it is more profound than that. They can tell, like Ajahn Piak can tell someone's level of *samādhi*.

To give you an example, when it first started arising for him, it was almost for him—as if we don't have enough thoughts in our own minds—right? He started to be able to hear all the thoughts of people in the audience. If there were a group of people in the meditation hall, he would start to hear all their thoughts. So initially it was like a cacophony. You have like twenty to fifty different radios going, which is not particularly, you know, conducive to being more peaceful [laughs]! But then with training, he was able to—a bit like a radio—tune in to certain frequencies. So it was like a skill that was developed to actually tune into this person or that person exclusively or just to shut it off. And again, it is not just a matter of hearing what someone is thinking but the idea that you can actually see someone's mental energy. Not so much like an aura, though maybe there is some overlapping with what some people think of as an aura.

D: Sure. Please go on.

AC: Like sometimes people talk about certain colors, and the colors will tend to indicate something. But generally, they are able to tell what level their mind is pure, impure, what their defilements are, what their *samādhi* is, and specifically what level of attainment they have reached. And that seems to be the only really reliable way to tell whether someone has attained certain levels of enlightenment . . . you look directly at their *citta* and see directly this is what level of purity they are at.

D: And the *suttas* talk about that right too? How the Buddha confirmed someone's level of attainment by directly apprehending what was going on in their mind?

AC: Exactly. Exactly. So, many of these phenomena you read about in the *suttas*, like there are some great stories, but they achieve a level of almost mythology.

TALES OF PSYCHIC PHENOMENA

Here we discover that although Ajahn Chandako has an extensive knowledge of the canonical sources of Theravāda Buddhism regarding psychic and paranormal phenomena, he did not dogmatically accept the veracity of these accounts but suspended his judgment. However, over the fifteen years he spent living with meditation masters in Thailand, he became more accepting of their credibility based on his own experience. Regarding psychic abilities in general, the Ajahn points out that although they are very rare, they do seem to arise in individuals who practice *samādhi*, the deep concentration techniques that traditionally have been associated with the development of these powers in Buddhism. Moreover, Ajahn Chandako gives a fascinating account of how the ability to read other people's minds arises. It begins at first as a type of general "tuning in" to the mental energy of others as unfiltered "noise." However, the Ajahn suggests that, as in the case of Ajahn Piak, this ability becomes refined over time so that one can tune into the minds of particular individuals at will. Ajahn Chandako also affirms the canonical accounts that this higher knowledge can be used to confirm the spiritual attainments of others.

During our interview, Karma Lekshe Tsomo recounted this story from her time studying Buddhism in India, which is suggestive of the "mind-reading" abilities attributed to some advanced Buddhist masters:

K: We would study these mostly Indian Buddhist texts—*Abhisamayamkara, Life of the Rinpoche . . . Madhyamakāvatara*—and all these amazing texts. And we were supposed to reflect on them. I would usually be doing retreat the rest of the day. But I would come up with this question in my head, and then I go to class the next morning, and we would always say some introductory prayers in the classical, traditional way, and then he [Geshe Ngawang Dhargyey?] would open the text and give the teaching for the day. So, a linear commentary, an exegesis line-by-line, word by word, really. But when I had a question in my head, he wouldn't open the text. We would say the prayers, and before he opened the text, he would answer my question to the whole class.

D: Right. Would he address it to you, or would he just be talking and it would be the answer to your question?

K: He would just answer it to everyone. This didn't happen just once; it happened many times. And I thought, "Okay" . . .

D: Right. But there was some kind of mind-to-mind telepathy? Like he knew . . .

K: I don't know whether I would call it telepathy or not. That is just a word, right?

D: Right.

K: But a kind of knowing, especially when you are very close to someone, especially in a teacher-disciple relationship, I think that there is something special that goes on, and they even talk about, "making your mind one with the mind of the guru." I am not a big wooshie guru worshipper. I am not that type. Actually, I am kind of allergic to it.

D: Yeah! Well, you've got good reason these days!

K: But you know this was the early days, when there were some really authentic teachers around.

D: Right, so you felt like there was a heart connection. Like there was real transmission happening there?

K: Yes. How he picked it up, I have no idea. Maybe a coincidence. I have no idea.

In the survey, Ayyā Mettikā provided two extraordinary anecdotes in relation to the telepathic powers of contemporary Theravādin meditation masters. The first is about Luang Po Jarun (1928–2016), a meditation master in the Thai tradition:

> Back in the beginning of this century, I had the experience of one-time meeting Luang Po Jarun in Thailand. I had heard that he was psychic. Going to meet him with my group, I experienced the turning of his mind-consciousness to mine and then [his] intaking through that beam of light vast amounts of knowledge about me, which I could also see, very, very quickly streaming out. I felt embarrassed about some of the things that were seen! But there was no sense of judgment, only intaking in the light of clear awareness. Still, my American sense of privacy and dignity got riled up!

Here Ayyā Mettikā experienced her mind being read by Luang Po Jarun as a "turning of his mind-consciousness" to her own and felt that personal information about her was transmitted to him through a "beam of light." Like using a fiber-optic cable to "hack" data, the master was able to tap into her mind-consciousness and gain access to her private thoughts and experiences.

On another occasion, the Ayyā experienced a type of mind-to-mind communication when she met Ajahn Maha Bua (1913–2011), also a Thai meditation master:

> Same time period in Thailand I went for winter retreat to the forest monastery of Luang Ta Maha Bua, who I had admired from afar, having read his book *Straight from the Heart* and appreciating his spirit. Upon meeting him in person, in the public Dhamma talk context, immediately as he looked at me, I felt a [mental] softball throw of the hard-hitting question: "What are you this disgusting, rotting, gross female body of filth?!"—which came together with a packaged illuminated image of a disgusting, rotting, corrupted, gross female body visible beneath the robes.
>
> I caught that and tossed the softball right back immediately with: "Hair of the head, hair of the body, nails, teeth, skin," and the developed meditation that came with it. That was well met, everything settled down, he asked me to sit up front with the monks and then offered a Dhamma talk on *adhisīla* [higher virtue] on my behalf. The topic was so well matching where I was at, and the monks and people told me afterwards this was his teaching style: read your mind, give a talk to help you indirectly in front of everyone (meanwhile others often know who is being talked about).

There is a number of overlapping Buddhist elements in this account of mind reading. First, we see a meditation master using his psychic ability to send a direct message to the Ayyā's mind. Note that actively sending a message is somewhat different than the higher knowledge of reading others' minds. However, in keeping with the metaphor of data transfer, we can imagine that an advanced psychic could send as well as receive data. This information Ayyā Mettikā receives both as verbal and visual. Verbally this is in the form of both a question and a challenge: "What are you this disgusting, rotting, gross female body of filth?!" This negative assessment of the female body is an ancient one in the Buddhist tradition. In her study of what she calls "post-Aśokan" Indian Buddhist hagiography, Liz Wilson (1996) argues that these ancient Buddhist stories establish a "gendered system of point of view" whereby the male "I" views the corrupt female body as object of contemplation in order to attain freedom from lust and attachment to the body.[24] These narratives reveal a moral dimension to the foulness of the female body, since in them the female characters are described as distracting males from the spiritual life with their physical beauty. However, this distraction can be nothing but "false advertising," for the true nature of the female body is corruption.[25] Thus, we see that Ajahn Maha Bua's challenge contains a traditional Buddhist attitude concerning the corrupt nature of Ayyā Mettikā's female body.

Luang Ta Maha Bua's "softball" thrown at Ayyā Mettikā's mind comes with a visual image of a rotting female corpse wearing monastic robes, emphasizing the corrupt nature of her body. However, the Ayyā "catches" this and throws back: " 'Hair of the head, hair of the body, nails, teeth, skin,' and the developed meditation that came with it." Here we see Mettikā sending her own psychic message, which seems to imply she also possesses this ability, unless the implication is that as a response to the Luang Ta's "softball," she is merely using the mental connection he has already established. Her answer is a direct reference to the meditation on the foulness of the human body (*asuba bhāvanā*) described by Buddhaghosa in his *Visuddhimagga*,[26] the fifth-century CE Pāli classic manual on the Buddhist path, which has been maintained as the standard of Theravāda orthodoxy since its conception. Thus, what we see here is a psychic version of what the Zen tradition calls "Dharma Combat," which occurs when two Buddhist practitioners (usually a Zen master and student) challenge each other on the teachings to test their level of enlightenment. Since Ayyā Mettikā's response was "well met" by Luang Ta Maha Bua and she was invited to sit with the monks, we can surmise that the Laung Ta's challenge was not malicious but meant to test the Ayyā's insight into the teachings.

From the survey and interview data we see that the majority of participants have had or do have telepathy-like experiences with some frequency. However, the bulk of these appear to be spontaneous and involve fairly mundane events among friends and family ("I was thinking of a friend, and they called me," or "I thought of a root beer float at the same time as my wife"). Less frequent and more dramatic are telepathic events involving strong emotions or life-and-death situations. From the monastic responses, we learn of a living tradition of folklore about Theravādin meditation masters with mind-reading powers. The personal charisma of these "forest saints" has been written about at some length by Stanley Tambiah.[27] In his study, Tambiah points out the close connection between Forest monks thought to possess psychic powers and the cult of amulets in Thailand. People seek out these masters to bless protective charms, which are then sold at high prices in Bangkok (see chapter 6 for more about amulets in the Thai tradition). A skeptic might claim that these masters' "psychic powers" are the result of the overactive imaginations of their disciples involved in the "cult of personality" surrounding these charismatic figures. However, contemporary accounts are consistent with the ancient canonical sources concerning these powers' connection to intense concentration techniques. Personally, I found my sources to be intelligent, sincere, and credible.

Retrocognition and Rebirth

The *OED* defines retrocognition as "knowing the past by supernatural or paranormal abilities" and once again cites F. W. H. Meyers with the first attestation in 1892.[28] Here I use it to refer specifically to people's memories of past-life experiences. In the Buddhist canonical sources, retrocognition corresponds to the fourth higher knowledge, "recollection of past lives" (Pāli: (*pubbenivāsānussatiñāṇa*), and as we have seen in chapter 1, it plays a central role in both the Buddha's enlightenment and Buddhist thought as the experiential basis for the doctrine of karma. In our interview, Ajahn Chandako gave me an example of a modern-day monk possessing this higher knowledge: "Ajahn Piak did have clear memories of his past lives including previous births within the Thai royal family." As discussed in chapter 2, the most extensive empirical investigations of past-life memories in children have been carried out in contemporary times by Ian Stevenson and Jim Tucker at the University of Virginia's Division of Perceptual Studies (DOPS). Related to this research is a recently published book, *Rebirth in Early Buddhism and Current Research*, by Bhikkhu Anālayo, a German-born Theravadin monk and highly regarded scholar of early Buddhism.[29] Part 4 of Anālayo's book is a fascinating case study of Dhammaruwan, who as a young child exhibited xenoglossia (speaking a language without any known prior knowledge of it), which is particularly relevant for our current discussion on retrocognition in contemporary Buddhism.

Dhammaruwan was born in Matale, Sri Lanka, in 1968. At about two years old, he spontaneously began to sit in meditation and recite Pāli texts, which he had not learned or heard recited by anyone. People realized when

Dhammaruwan was about three that he was reciting Pāli, and a number of recordings were made. His recitations were also witnessed by numerous people, including eminent Buddhist monks, two Sri Lankan presidents, and Ian Stevenson.[30] As an adult, Dhammaruwan lost this ability. According to his past-life recollections, he had learned to chant these texts as an Indian Buddhist monk 1,500 years ago during the lifetime of Buddhaghosa, the famed Theravādin commentator and author of the *Visuddhimagga*. About this Anālayo writes:

> According to Dhammaruwan's memories, he learned the Pāli chants in a former lifetime in India, where he had been born as the son of a Brahmin and trained in memorization of the Vedas. He had gone forth as a Buddhist monk and become a student of the eminent monk Buddhaghosa at Nālandā. After being trained as a *bhāṇaka*, a reciter, together with other monks who had similarly been trained, he was chosen to accompany Buddhaghosa from India to Sri Lanka. Having come to Sri Lanka, he stayed with Buddhaghosa at the Mahāvihāra in Anurādhapura, of which he remembers various details.[31]

I first learned of Dhammaruwan about five years ago from websites mentioning his story and providing links to audio recordings made of him chanting.[32] What struck me as most unusual was that his style of reciting Pāli was very different from the contemporary method employed by Sri Lankan monks. Anālayo, who personally knows Dhammaruwan from his time in Sri Lanka in the 1990s, describes his chanting in this way: "What was of considerable interest to me was his rather unusual way of chanting Pāli texts. Traditional Sri Lankan Pāli chanting tends to be quite swift; in fact often several monks chant together so that, when one of them has to take a breath, the others can continue. Dhammaruwan's chanting is in contrast very measured and slow. It is also much more melodious than standard Sri Lankan recitations."[33]

In his study, Anālayo first consulted a professional audio-recording and mastering engineer about the authenticity of the audio files. The engineer's conclusion was that the digital audio files were authentic copies of tape recordings made between 1970 and 1985 and that it would be extremely difficult and expensive to make convincing forgeries.[34] Following this discussion of the recordings' authenticity, Anālayo enters into an exhaustive comparison of the language and content of the recordings based on his expert knowledge of the canonical texts and manuscripts surviving in Pāli, Sanskrit, Chinese, and Tibetan. By investigating Dhammaruwan's errors, omissions, and additions, Anālayo concludes that the recordings are not based on any currently known editions of the Pāli texts. Moreover, the differences found in Dhammaruwan's recordings are consistent with what we know of the oral transmission of these texts in South Asia. Anālayo concludes: "In sum, the evidence surveyed above suggests that Dhammaruwan's chanting of these texts as a child is a genuine case of xenoglossy, in the sense of involving a recitation of material in Pāli that he did not learn and was not made to recite in this way in his present life in Sri Lanka." Based on this case and others he has reviewed involving children with past-life memories, Anālayo concludes that the collected evidence has "significantly contributed to changing the notion of rebirth from a religious creed to a reasonable belief."[35]

In my survey were two questions related to rebirth and retrocognition. In answer to question 57, "Have you had any other kind of experience that you think suggests life after death?," a number of respondents mentioned people they had met or heard about who seemed to recall one or more previous lives. For example, one person wrote, "I've had a handful of interactions with Tibetan tülkus that clearly suggest they remember something from their previous lives." Another wrote, "I have a friend who is a young Tulku at Tashi Lhunpo in India. I feel strongly that I met his former incarnation at Likir monastery several years earlier." This respondent recounts a specific incident with a child: "A three-year-old child spontaneously described to me her previous life when I was showing her pictures of travel to a Buddhist monastery. She later gifted me with a picture she had drawn of 'the world' resembling the Buddhist cosmology of Mt. Meru surrounded by islands, etc."

This respondent makes several observations concerning behaviors of children they knew of that appear to suggest knowledge of a previous life:

> It is uncanny how some children I knew are able to memorize texts as if they are simply recalling knowledge from a previous life. Their mannerisms also suggest connections, for example, the subdued monastic behavior of young monks and nuns, the way they instinctively know how to wear the robes, sit, use ritual instruments, etc. I know of substantiated cases of children born in Buddhist families (especially in countries where Buddhists are typically vegetarian) who have an aversion to eating meat from the time they are babies. If they are given

meat, they spit it up. I know of several cases where young children are taken for a visit to a temple or monastery at a very young age and refuse to leave, until their parents finally let them become monks or nuns.

These accounts, though not particularly compelling in and of themselves, suggest that popular stories of reincarnated lamas and children with preternatural abilities or habits continue to keep the belief in rebirth alive and well for contemporary Buddhists.

To inquire about the possible past-life memories of participants in my survey, question 48 asked, "Have you ever had a memory that you thought might be from a previous life?" Of those that responded (61), 64 percent replied "Yes." When asked about the number of times this has happened, of the 38 people who responded 42 percent said one to five times, 21 percent said five to ten times, and 21 percent said more than twenty times. When asked about the context, 71 percent of these respondents said that the memories had arisen spontaneously, 43 percent said while dreaming, 32 percent indicated during meditation or spiritual practice, and 26 percent indicated that they occurred during an altered state of consciousness. Thus, like the other psi phenomena discussed so far, we see a strong connection between retrocognition and dreaming.

When asked to describe their experiences, as usual, participants' responses were mixed, ranging from the brief to the elaborate. Some of the shorter responses were: "Places, faces, and objects were familiar and known"; "I dreamt I was me but not anywhere I had ever been"; "Powerful experiences of times, people and settings that I know of but yet have never lived in this life"; "I did a past life regression once and for the time those memories felt very real to me"; "Vivid dreams of times and places not my own. Or being in meditative states with similar qualities of reliving and déjà vu"; "Very vivid memory of two past lifetimes—one as a boy on a fishing boat in East Asia, one as a Buddhist monk"; "Recognizing landscape in Thailand that I dreamt while a child"; "Dreams of being a tailor in Italy, in the 19th century"; and "I have had multiple experiences of previous lives in Australia and Canada." Though intriguing, these accounts lack details and therefore are not particularly compelling.

When reading or listening to stories about psi, accounts of acquiring detailed knowledge of people, events, or places that could not have been known about through ordinary means (such as Dhammaruwan's xenoglossia) have always been the gold standard of researchers. So, are these brief descriptions examples of retrocognition? For those who experienced these phenomena, they were certainly compelling enough to leave an impression and suggest to them that they might have been. But the mind is a trickster, so who really is to say? Retrocognition is a difficult phenomenon to verify because even vivid and detailed memories often lack any specifics that could be checked.

Some respondents provided more details. Jane, a twenty-nine-year-old woman living in the United Kingdom, wrote: "I dreamed [of] my grandmother's house how it was in the 18th century, comparing it to images, [and] it looked exactly like that. [There was] no way for me to have known before the dream." Likewise, Rick, a sixty-three-year-old American man, had dreams suggestive of retrocognition: "As a child I recalled feeling very strongly that I'd lived in ancient times. As a teen, many dreams of another life with its own memories, continuous with themselves but separate from this life." In addition to these dreams, Rick wrote that "in meditation I once saw a series of my former lives."[36]

For Jason, a forty-nine-year-old Australian man, retrocognitive-like phenomena came in the form of an uncanny familiarity with certain places, people, and experiences:

> I'm not really sure I'd describe them as vivid memories, rather some places I have travelled and certainly people and lamas I have met seem very familiar. I also feel strongly connected to certain places, cultures and religious/spiritual teachers that don't seem easily explainable from the context of my current life. When I was a small child, around 7 years old, another child taught me to meditate and I spontaneously immediately experienced a blissful state, that I can still recall now. It was a powerful and familiar experience. I also had the typical experience of feeling like I had come home when I entered my first dharma centre. Many such experiences...

A much more dramatic experience of recognition is described by Kimberly, a fifty-two-year-old American woman: "Once I recognized someone from a past lifetime in a vastly different cultural context on a busy city street. In fact, we recognized each other simultaneously. As we spontaneously ran to embrace one another, we suddenly recognized the absurdity of the situation (our reunion under such totally different circumstances) and began laughing hilariously." This account is particularly noteworthy because it involves the simultaneous and intersubjective recognition of two people who by conventional standards should not have known each other.

In her survey responses, Ayyā Mettikā wrote about several retrocognitive experiences involving specifically Buddhist themes. The first three occurred as childhood dreams: "As a child, I dreamed repeatedly of being in a dark meditative transitional realm (... now I recognize it as a meditation state); living as a large water snake nearby some old underwater ruins, which I had some unknown attachment to be in that location from the past; ... [and] living on a baking red sun-dried old world at an outpost, watching out for and waiting for the next rare ship/portal ... (past or future?)."

The first appears to be the dream recollection of having attained a previous *jhānic* state of meditation. Note that the second dream is of being an animal—a snake attached to underwater ruins. Both rebirth as an animal and rebirth based on a previous attachment are commonly occurring themes in Buddhist narrative literature. Note that for the third dream Mettikā is unsure if it is a memory of the past or the future. Dreaming of a future life may seem odd, but recall Clough's mention of a reference in a Pāli text to a monk with this higher knowledge, who was able to remember future lives (chapter 1).

The next experience of retrocognition mentioned by Ayyā Mettikā occurred as a spontaneous vision while visiting a sacred Buddhist site: "At the ancient great stupa in Korea ... [I saw] the opening of a past life vision on site and the re-arising of my old great vows at that place, appearing in kaleidoscopic parallel vision with the real time present image of the site, and present intentions and dedications—like a colliding of the worlds, their jarring and opening, and then their reintegrating." Stūpas are Buddhist reliquaries containing the remains of buddhas, saints, or holy beings and are common pilgrimage sites for Buddhists to pay homage and acquire merit. In this psychedelic vision, the Ayyā experiences her "old great vows," which is suggestive of the bodhisattva's vows for supreme enlightenment found in Mahāyāna Buddhism. Since Mahāyāna has always been the dominant form of Buddhism in Korea, this suggestion gains further credence. However, as mentioned, Mettikā is a Theravādin nun now. Since she does not mention any tension between her old vows and new intentions and dedication, it seems as if this vision caused an integration of her Mahāyāna Buddhist path from the previous lifetime with the present Theravādin one.

TALES OF PSYCHIC PHENOMENA

In Ayyā Mettikā's final account of retrocognition, she describes recollecting past lives from her traditional practice of the *jhānas*:

> During a three-year retreat: one day, determined to try to practice the *jhāna* meditation methods I read about in the early Buddhist *suttas*; doing so, and then seeing a number of past lives. Seeing each one there was a lesson that tied to now (back then); some habit tendency or small fault in my moral conduct. Seeing the linking of karma from life to life related to these various small moral faults, habits or attachments. Feeling so much *saṃvega* seeing this and making an emotional and strong determination not to keep repeating the same!

Here we see three significant Buddhist themes. First, the Ayyā mentions attaining a recollection of past lives in the manner outlined in the canonical Pāli sources. Next, through this, she is able to witness the karmic links resulting from her moral faults, habits, and attachments. Third, from seeing these karmic consequences, she experiences *saṃvega*. This is an important Pāli term from early Buddhism, which we can translate as "aesthetic shock."[37] In early Buddhist sources there are accounts of *saṃvega* occurring in people as the result of an unexpected, shocking, or horrifying experience, often of death, decay, or impermanence. This feeling of *saṃvega* then motivates them to practice the Buddhist path and escape from *saṃsāra*, the cycle of death and rebirth. Thus, Mettikā's strong determination not to repeat her unskillful past actions is also a traditional response to the feeling of *saṃvega*.

Another participant, "Patricia," a seventy-six-year-old American white female, also mentioned recollecting being an animal in a past life during a meditation retreat in Kathmandu in the seventies. I quote here at length from our dialogue:

PATRICIA: One experience was a meditation course I did in 1974 in Nepal. Maybe you have learned of Lama Zopa and Lama Yeshe?
D. E. OSTO: Yes, I have heard of them. Please go on.
P: In any case, they started teaching every year a one-month course in November. And the living conditions were very poor, very primitive. We were basically sleeping on the dirt. It was pretty basic, right? But I remember they did some meditations on—the one month was very intensive, mind you. It was like from four in the morning until ten at night.
D: Wow. That is pretty full-on.

p: We did a lot of meditation. It still goes on. I wonder if it is anywhere near as intense as it was then.... And one of the meditations one day was, "Now you understand the nature of consciousness, now we want to trace our consciousness back..."

d: Yes. I see. Please continue.

p: You trace your mind-moments, you could say, mind-stream, back moment by moment from today, to yesterday, to last week, to last month, to teenage times, to childhood times, to baby time, to the moment of birth. And then keep going to the moment of conception. And from the moment of conception there is just one moment to the previous life, right?

d: Yes.

p: And then just keep going. Keep going back.

d: To remember past births, yes, I have heard of this.

p: A lot of people... it was quite an extraordinary course.... In any case, lots of monks and nuns came out of that course, and many of them are still ordained today, which is quite unusual, as you know, because the drop rate is very high. A lot of people, you know we weren't supposed to talk about it...

d: But a lot of people did! [Laughs]. That's great! I want you to talk about it!

p: Seven lifetimes back.

d: Seven lifetimes?

p: Seven is not difficult. To recall seven lifetimes is not difficult.

d: Wow!

p: If you can get your concentration going, it is a pretty mechanical process. And of course, it is very instructive, because we haven't always been human, right?

d: Were you able to recollect some of your past lives? Remember you are anonymous here, so no one will know!

p: I really... You shouldn't talk about it...

d: Alright. Okay, let me put it more abstractly then: So, when you mentioned the animal thing, that was because the other people that you talked to said there was a recollection of nonhuman births, like "I was a dog" or "I was a monkey"?

p: I mean, I remember being a rabbit and getting eaten by an owl. I mean, I didn't even know that owls eat rabbits.

d: Yeah, wow!

p: I was absolutely a rabbit, and I absolutely got eaten by an owl.

D: Yeah, that is intense!
P: You don't have to debate rebirth after that. You know it. You just know.
D: There was a real clarity to the experience of it?
P: Absolutely. A knowing. As if you were recollecting what you had for breakfast this morning, which I usually can't even remember these days!
D: [Laughs] Yeah, I know! I don't remember what I did yesterday now either!

In these contemporary Buddhist tales of retrocognition we learn of a wide range of experiences from uncanny feelings or dreams of familiarity with people, places, and events to full-blown recollections of past lives spontaneously arising or induced through meditation. While feelings of familiarity and dreams of other times, places, and lives do not seem that uncommon, much rarer are stories of people having detailed memories of previous lives arising spontaneously or through meditation. Rarer still are stories like Dhammaruwan's xenoglossia, wherein people exhibit verifiable knowledge or skills they could not have acquired through ordinary means. Although investigating children's spontaneous recollections of these memories remains the main focus of contemporary research, Anālayo points out that such stories are quite rare in the early Buddhist sources.[38] This may be simply because such accounts were not seen as particularly remarkable, given the widely held belief in rebirth. In the accounts given in the preceding pages from monastics and devoted Buddhist laypeople, we see the importance of such recollections for them as direct experiential evidence that confirms their beliefs in the doctrines of karma and rebirth.

Psychokinesis and Other Powers

As discussed in chapter 1, Buddhist sources mention a number of supernormal powers that one can attain through the practice of concentration meditation such as multiplying one's body, becoming invisible, flying through the air, walking on water, and passing through solid objects. Accounts of such things occurring in modern times are extremely rare, so I did not ask any questions about these powers in my survey. However, during my interview with Ajahn Chandako some of these were mentioned in reference to the development of psychic powers in general and in stories involving contemporary Thai Forest monks. Since these topics are particularly germane to the current study, in the following pages I cite at length from our conversation.

AC: According to Ajahn Piak, Ajahn Chah himself had quite a number of psychic powers. Although Ajahn Chah was very discreet, tight lipped, would never talk about them, right? Because people tend to get overly fascinated with them, because they are pretty fascinating! [Laughs]
D: [Laughs] Yeah! They are!
AC: But Ajahn Chah and so many of his generation, because it wasn't something that people doubted the existence of, it's just that you tried to keep them on track practicing the Dhamma, right? Don't get distracted by this stuff. So, Ajahn Chah would rarely if ever talk about his own psychic powers, but because Ajahn Piak had the ability to read Ajahn Chah's mind and see what was going on, he could see what Ajahn Chah was doing. So apparently Ajahn Chah was quite adept in that area as well.

Here Chandako makes an important point as to why Forest masters do not openly discuss psychic powers: the Buddha's teachings are for one's ultimate release from suffering, not to attain special powers. And because these powers are so interesting, talking about them openly could distract people from practicing Dhamma. However, since Ajahn Piak could read Ajahn Chah's mind, he could tell that he was adept at these powers. Here we find an account of someone using telepathy to discern someone else's psychic abilities.

Next, Ajahn Chandako discusses the development of these powers and offers a possible explanation as to how they might work:

> These powers usually if they are going to arise, they arise as a byproduct of meditation. In current times, like let's say the previous hundred years, 150 years, at least in the Forest Tradition, people don't intentionally develop them. Sometimes, but very rarely. The great energy of their time and their focus is on purifying their heart from the defilements, but sometimes in that process psychic powers start to develop, and they can give some attention to that and refining that. And I guess one way that I have understood it that makes sense to me is when on a very elemental level of physics it becomes more difficult to tell the difference between what is physical and what is energy. So, it makes sense to me that on the elemental level the distinction between what is physical and what is mental is not so clear. And so, if you develop a mastery of your mental capabilities then

okay, it kind of makes sense that you could translate that into having an effect in the physical realm. So that makes sense to me.

So many of the stories in the *suttas* that talk about being able to manipulate elements so that things that were liquid can be made solid, for example, walking on water. So when you hear stories of Jesus walking on water or Moses splitting the Red Sea to walk through them, I don't question that—it is quite believable to me, because we have examples of that in Buddhist history. At least walking on water, but also turning solid things into liquid, for example, being able to move through solid objects.

Here we see a view of psychic powers that is contemporary, traditionally Buddhist and pluralistic. The Ajahn draws on the notion in contemporary physics that at an elemental level there is no clear distinction between matter and energy. Then from this he supposes that there may not be a clear distinction at this level between what is physical and what is mental. As many have pointed out, certain aspects of quantum physics imply as much (at least the Copenhagen interpretation seems to suggest this). Following this, Chandako proposes that it makes sense that someone who develops their mental powers might be able to influence the physical realm. In contemporary terms, such abilities would be considered very advanced macro-scale psychokinesis (PK), also called telekinesis. Note that there is nothing unreasonable or irrational in this line of reasoning (only if one presupposes a metaphysics such as monistic materialism would such a mind-matter connection be impossible—in Buddhism and the lifeworld of phenomenology, there are no such sharp dichotomies between physical and mental phenomena). Next, Ajahn Chandako mentions the plethora of narratives in the Pāli scriptures involving people exhibiting forms of macro-PK such as making solids into liquids or walking on water. Finally, the Ajahn cites examples from the Torah and Christian Bible of Moses parting the Red Sea and Jesus walking on water. He finds these stories believable, making a comparison to Buddhist accounts and the possible nondistinction between mind and matter suggested in some contemporary physics. With this comparison, Chandako suggests that psi abilities are a human universal found not just in Buddhism but in other traditions such as Judaism and Christianity.

Following these statements, the Ajahn recounts some intriguing stories of contemporary Thai meditation masters exhibiting macro-PK abilities such as softening solid stone, levitation, and flight:

AC: There was one meditation master in Thailand, who wasn't part of the Forest Tradition, but he was well respected for his meditation. And he had a walking meditation path, and I guess at one end there was a big rock, and as he was developing these psychic powers, he was able to make the rock a bit more, not liquid exactly, but manipulate it enough so that he could put his foot right in it, pull his foot out, and leave a footprint [laughs] in the rock! As if it was like mud [laughs].

D: Yeah right. Wow.

AC: So, again, these things won't help you get enlightened, but they are kind of interesting just to see what the mind is capable of. One of the very rare things is actually being able to rise up into the air . . .

D: Levitate! Right.

AC: . . . [A] very believable example is Ajahn Mun's contemporary, actually his teacher, Dhamma friend, Ajahn Sao. And if I can remember the story correctly, Ajahn Sao . . . while in deep meditation it seemed that he was actually rising up. But he wasn't quite sure if this was just a perception in his own mind, or if physically . . .

D: Right, if he is physically lifting off the ground.

AC: Right, so what he did before his meditation was put a piece of paper in the rafters of his ceiling [laughs], and then during a meditation he would actually find out if he pulled the piece of paper down. And it turns out he was able to rise up and pull the piece of paper down, and then he realized that he actually was physically rising up off the ground.

Another example is [from] another very famous Ajahn Mun disciple, Ajahn Khao. So there was quite a well-known incident where a Thai fighter pilot from the Thai air force was flying a plane in the northeast area of Thailand, and he swears that he saw a monk floating in the clouds in seated meditation. Stationary, I think, but just kind of sitting there in midair! [laughs] And he went and reported it, and they looked at the coordinates, and the coordinates corresponded with the monastery directly below, which was the monastery of Ajahn Khao. And then the physical descriptions looked like Ajahn Khao as well. So that was a very famous story in Thailand.

After relating these stories, Ajahn Chandako further explains why monastics do not openly talk to laypeople about psychic powers and the necessary conditions for these abilities to arise:

AC: Fully ordained monks or nuns are not allowed to talk about our own attainments, whether it is psychic powers or states of enlightenment, or even *jhānas* with laypeople. You are not allowed to talk about that. We can talk about it with monks ourselves, but not with laypeople. The reason why was because even back in the time of the Buddha, the Buddha didn't want people to be sidetracked. Whether it is modern day or 2,600 years ago, people love this stuff. And so he didn't want people to be sidetracked, otherwise people would just be supporting the monks with psychic powers. There were *arhants* who had no psychic powers...

D: Yeah, right. It is really the *jhānas*, isn't it? It is the *samādhi* or *samatha* that is thought to lead to these powers. Like really high levels of concentration, isn't it?

AC: It seems to be more than that because in order to attain, say, any level of enlightenment, even the lower levels, to say nothing of fully enlightened *arhat*ship, then very good *samādhi*, *jhānas* are necessary. That seems to be a given. But in addition to that to develop psychic powers seems to be just an accumulation of a tremendous amount of good *kamma*. If you have a great repository of good *kamma* [from deeds] you have done in the past... it will just start to come up and manifest as psychic powers. So it seems to be the determining factor, even. Of course, you have to have deep *samādhi*, but in addition to that for psychic powers to develop usually what is required we generally call *pāramī*, just like an accumulation of the results of wholesome *kamma* we have done in the past.

D: Yes.

AC: And that of course for some people, even before they reach the first stage of enlightenment, they are already developing psychic powers, so it is not exclusively tied to how wise or how deep someone's insight has gone.

D: Yes, that meshes quite well with the Indian tradition too, the yogic tradition—this idea that it is a byproduct of very intense meditation and concentration but... it is not necessarily indicative of how enlightened you are.

Here the Ajahn reiterates the central importance of practicing Buddhism and the distracting potential of being overly concerned with psychic powers. He points out that another possible negative consequence of monastics disclosing their abilities is that laypeople would only donate to monks with special psychic powers (and ignore others who may be more worthy). He also mentions how in the Pāli texts we find enlightened Buddhist saints (*arhants*) without any powers. Finally, Chandako highlights an important aspect of the traditional Buddhist view of psychic abilities—although concentration-based meditation seems to be a central factor, it really depends on a person's previous good karma. If one has developed *pāramī*, the various perfections (see chapter 1) in past lives, one will have accumulated a vast store of merit, which can result in psychic ability. Nevertheless, powers per se are not necessarily a sign of spiritual attainment. One may have developed mental discipline and vast amounts of good karma through countless lifetimes but still lack the wisdom, insight, and compassion necessary for true awakening.

Conclusion

From the accounts in this chapter, we see that psychic phenomena are alive and well for modern convert Buddhist practitioners. Do these contemporary tales "prove" the existence of psi powers? As I mentioned in the introduction, "proof" is a term best left for deductive logic and mathematics. In the empirical world, the lifeworld of phenomena, veracity of events is established inductively and probabilistically. How likely are these stories "true" accounts of the paranormal? Well, all these stories could be considered true in the sense that they are based on actual events that happened to real people. Whether someone finds these stories compelling accounts of actual ESP and psychokinesis depends on several factors, including someone's metaphysical presuppositions and philosophical commitments, whether they find the narrator a credible source, the amount of detailed evidence presented, and the subjective and intersubjective nature of the phenomena. Note that these stories generally are very private and only revealed to close friends and family, who are often involved or related to the experiences in some way. And people tend to trust the people they love and are emotionally bonded to. This "human element," the interpersonal and intersubjective aspect of psi, cannot be overlooked. Nor can the often close association of these phenomena to strong emotions, dreams, altered states of consciousness (induced through meditation or other means), and life-and-death situations. Moreover, in the more dramatic stories we regularly see the massive impact these experiences have had on the course of people's lives. These "real-world" effects of psi make it extremely relevant when trying to comprehend the significance of this folklore of the psychic for contemporary Buddhists. They also suggest why in wider modern societies the "knowledge of the people" (a literal translation of "folklore") often trumps whatever the "scientific" viewpoint might be and why the popular belief in psi continues to this day.

FOUR

Tales of OBEs, NDEs, and Close Encounters

THIS CHAPTER INVESTIGATES contemporary Buddhist stories of out-of-body experiences (OBEs), near-death experiences (NDEs), and encounters with animals, ghosts, spirits, deities, and holy beings. As in the previous chapter, I address responses from the survey and also look more in depth at my conversations with interviewees. Once again for each of these categories there were a range of responses, and, often, different phenomena would overlap. Thus, the divisions between the different types of phenomena presented here is only for heuristic purposes. I suspect that the events that we today call "paranormal" are signposts to entire realms or dimensions of experience beyond our current understanding (see chapter 7). Some accounts in what follows appear more to be examples of the random weirdness that is simply part of human life, while others are clearly interpreted through a Buddhist lens and highlight themes specific to Buddhist thought and practice.

Out-of-Body Experiences

To inquire about OBEs in my survey, question 30 asks, "Have you ever had an experience of being outside of your physical body, so that you could see your body or your physical surroundings from a point of view outside of it?" Of the 67 respondents, 37 percent answered "Yes." When asked how often

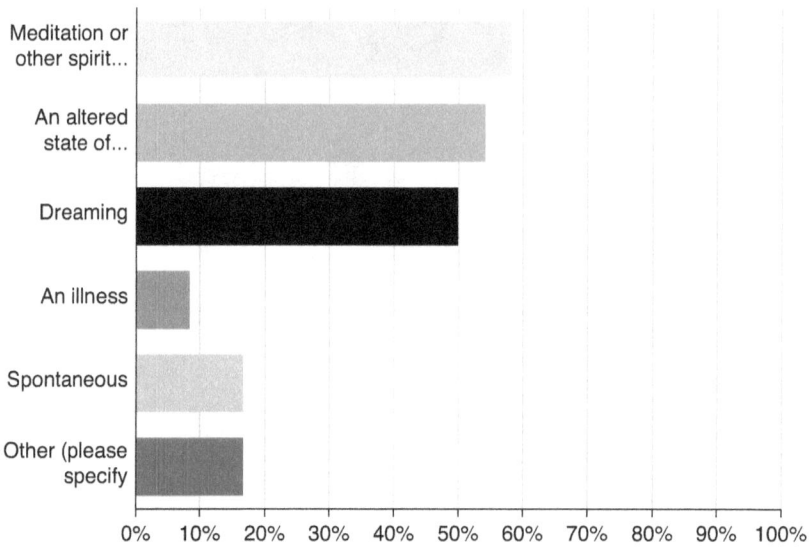

FIGURE 4.1 Occasion of OBE
Question 32: When the event(s) occurred, was it during . . . Answered = 24. Skipped = 92.

this had happened to them, of the 24 who responded, 8 said 1–5 times, and 7 stated that it had happened over 20 times. In answer to question 32, "When the event(s) occurred was it during (tick all that apply):," we see for the first time that "meditation or other spiritual practice" takes the lead, with 58 percent. Closely behind this are "an altered state of consciousness" (54 percent) and dreaming (50 percent). In the "Other" (17 percent) category, people mentioned "trying to go to sleep," "weed," "heart attack," and "in a subliminal state between waking and sleep" (see figure 4.1). Here we see once again that the hypnogogic state at the onset of sleep has the potential to trigger unusual experiences. Note that one might consider the OBE from the heart attack as a near-death experience (NDE), thus demonstrating the fuzzy boundaries between some of these anomalous phenomena.

The intentional induction of an OBE in contemporary times has often been called "astral projection" and the noncorporeal "body" associated with it the "astral body." These terms were first widely employed by the Theosophical Society in the nineteenth century.[1] Note the similarity (mentioned in chapter 1) to the Buddhist concept of the "mind-made body" (Pāli:

manomaya-kāya), attained at the fourth level of *jhānic* trance, wherein the adept can extract their mind-made body from their physical body "like pulling a sword from a scabbard" or like "a snake shedding its skin" (see chapter 1).

During our interview, Ajahn Chandako had some interesting comments about the contemporary practice of astral projection in the Thai Forest Tradition.

D. E. OSTO: So, I was wondering about the other things that are categorized as paranormal, or what is categorized as paranormal in the Western literature such as out-of-body experiences or near-death experiences. I know it doesn't map perfectly onto Buddhist understandings, but I know there is this idea of a mind-made body that one can generate, what we would consider an "astral body," which is then able to go other places. Do you have any recollections of stories or experiences like that?

AJAHN CHANDAKO: Yeah, sure. I have heard stories. Sometimes these things can occur almost like an innate ability. There as one monk, it seemed to be quite a believable story, where he was seemly able to rise out of his body and send his mind into the village or wherever it wanted to go and know exactly what people were talking about as if he was there; they couldn't see him. But then he could come back into his body. Also, one of the contemporary meditation masters, who is still alive, I think he had that experience as well when he was young. So it seems to be quite possible; also it seems to have the drawback of that it is very pleasant. So, you kind of leave this heavy physical body and basically can float and go wherever you want, right? How cool is that? But because it is so pleasant, if people do that over and over again, they start to lose a bit of touch with their physical body and their physical reality. They become a bit spacy, almost like they don't want to come back into their physical body. So it is not something that is recommended. It is actually discouraged just for that reason. It is definitely something that seems to happen, but it has those drawbacks, so in our meditation tradition it is discouraged.

Here the Ajahn gives two examples of people having this ability from the modern Forest Tradition but also is quick to mention that his tradition discourages its practice because its pleasant sensation can lead to a type of disassociation from the physical body.

Some of the brief descriptions of OBEs in the survey were: "Was looking at myself in *zazen* while I could see myself floating in front of my physical self from the third person"; "During *goma* or meditation this has occurred, physical senses go inward, and perceptions feel outside the body"; "We were floating on the ceiling looking down at our bodies lying on the floor"; and "Total integration with universal being. Arising transcendent free of physicality." Slightly more detail was given in this account: "My first meditation was *yoga-nidra* [yoga of sleep] with visualization and *pranayama* [breath control], triggering an OOBE. Afterwards, I've had many, often during meditation or entheogens."

Michael, a sixty-one-year-old American man, also recounts an OBE in relation to the ingestion of psychoactives: "The most prominent episode of this was on a high dose psilocybin experience where I very vividly and distinctly experienced being outside of my body while still in the same room, so it seemed as if I had the perspective of a camera mounted on the ceiling of the room I was in, pointed directly at my own head."

Linda, a seventy-one-year-old American woman, mentioned OBEs happening often for her, but then she became reluctant to give up control of her physical body: "This used to happen to me quite a bit, but I became hesitant to separate my consciousness from my body in this way (and risk relinquishing control over my body) and no longer do so." This statement also implies that she had some conscious control over her OBEs and was able to astral project in a manner similar to the Buddhist "mind-made body."

In her responses, Ayyā Mettikā relates three occasions where her consciousness was separated from her body (one of these I discuss in the next section on NDEs). The first reads: "During residential yoga training retreat in Europe as a very young adult entering my 20s, I used to love to walk the neighboring forest and nearby lake in the afternoons and evenings. In the night, in a waking dream state, my consciousness would rise and move around the land and lakes in the air."

In this account, the Ayyā describes "a waking dream" wherein her consciousness could move through the air. In this context, her terminology seems to suggest that this "waking dream" was much more vivid and realistic than her ordinary dreams, and the realism of the dream landscape reinforces this. These experiences also foreshadow Mettikā's precognitive dream of being a sky goddess and flying over a landscape she later recognized as the locale of her monastic order's future hermitage (see chapter 3, under "Precognition"). It also suggests that her dream of being a sky goddess may have been an OBE of flying over the location that would be the site of their hermitage.

Ayyā Mettikā's second experience occurred during Buddhist chanting as a nun in Sri Lanka and contains a number of paranormal elements:

> I had an incident at the time of the tsunami that affected Sri Lanka. At that time, while chanting, seeing the rising up of an old and powerful female "keeper of the history of the ages" kind of spirit/deva/goddess/divine being. Feeling the breath energy thicken and quicken, falling over backwards, and then appearing to others to be unresponsive for around an hour; meanwhile I was still able to see and hear, and even feel a little, but was not able to move, open my eyes, or speak. Others present were at first concerned I might have died or be dying, but then the monks apprehended that I was present and conscious but just not yet responsive. Although my eyes were closed, I could to a degree see them and felt there was communication by mind and heart, even if I couldn't speak or gesture.

In this story, we hear about a deep trance state induced through chanting, in which the Ayyā encounters a divine being and enters a catatonic state wherein she is nevertheless able to "see" the monks around her and communicate by "mind and heart." Thus there are aspects of visitation, clairvoyance, telepathy, and an OBE (although not quite). The state seems to sit somewhere between clairvoyance and a proper out-of-body experience. This is reminiscent of some of Patrick Price's remote viewing for the CIA (see chapter 2), where it is unclear whether he is remote "seeing" a locale or astral projecting to that place and then "looking around" with his astral body. In Mettikā's story, it seems that her consciousness was still very closely associated with her body but that she was able to "see" without using her physical eyes.

The two most detailed OBEs in the survey were provided by Angela Sumegi, whom I subsequently interviewed. At the time of the interview, Angela was a seventy-two-year-old Canadian woman and adjunct research professor of humanities and religion at Carlton University (and retired associate professor of religion). Born and raised in Jamaica, Angela's family immigrated to Canada in 1962. She completed a BA in art history (1976) and an MA in religion (1984) from Carleton University and a PhD from the University of Ottawa (2003). She also lived and studied in southern India for five years (1981–1986).

Upon returning to Canada, she raised three children, worked as a film producer, and taught at Carleton, the University of Ottawa, and St. Paul's University.[2] Her area of expertise is Indo-Tibetan Buddhism and the interface between Buddhism and Shamanism. She is the author of two books, *Dream Worlds of Shamanism and Tibetan Buddhism: The Third Place* and *Understanding Death: Identity and the Afterlife in World Religions*.[3]

Since Angela is an accomplished author and a good storyteller, I quote here at length from her original accounts. Angela describes her first OBE in the following words:

> The first time this happened, I was a grown woman. I had many times previously had the experience that on lying down and trying to go to sleep I would fall into a state of intense vertigo with a loud roaring sound in my ears—it was not a pleasant feeling, and I would shake myself awake to stop it, but as soon as I let myself try to drift off, it would happen again. Often, I would just give up and sit up in bed reading for a long while until I could fall asleep without that feeling. One night I was very tired, so tired that when the feeling came over me, even though it was quite scary, I thought, what the hell, just go with it—so I let the vertigo completely overtake me and felt like I was being sucked down into a dark hole.
>
> Then I woke up and tried to get out of the bed, but it was like my back was stuck to the bed, and in getting up, I felt like I was peeling myself slowly off the bed, almost like there were two halves of me. Anyway, when I finally got up and out of the bed and looked around, there I was sleeping on the bed. I got very excited at this because I was totally aware that I was completely conscious and aware, just exactly as I would be if I were awake. There was nothing dream-like about the experience; I was simply standing in my bedroom looking at myself on the bed.
>
> As an experiment, I walked over to my dresser and stared into the mirror, which of course reflected nothing but the furniture in the room. Now I was sure that I was functioning in what the Tibetans call a "thought body" and decided to try out some thought-body experiments—after all, if this was so, I should be able to fly or walk through walls. I tried jumping in the air to see if I could fly but just fell flat on my face on the floor. Then I tried to walk through the wall, and I put my hands up and pressed against the wall—nothing. Then I suddenly realized that due to the habitual tendency of identifying with my body, I had been trying to do these things with my body, not my mind. Then I simply thought myself on the other side of the wall, and of course, there I was. I walked to the

front door and looked out and thought about how far I could go, but the fear of leaving my physical body far behind stopped me, and I returned to my room, whereupon I experienced lots of rainbow lights and woke up in my physical body.[4]

In this account, Angela vividly describes what her first OBE was like. We see here that Angela's first impulse is to interpret this experience in the context of Tibetan Buddhism, which she was fully immersed in by this time of her life. Note her mention of the Tibetan "thought body" (Tibetan: *yid lus*), which is the analogous term to the Pāli "mind-made body" (Pāli: *manomaya-kāya*). In Tibetan Buddhism, this thought body is also the body that is believed to manifest during the *bardo* state between the death of the physical body and rebirth into a new body. Also, note how her description of her thought body peeling from her physical body sounds strikingly similar to the analogy in the Pāli sources of the mind-made body being drawn out of the physical body like a snake shedding its skin or a sword being drawn from a scabbard. The wider context for this experience is the tantric practice of "dream yoga," mentioned briefly in chapter 1. A detailed account of dream yoga is beyond the scope of this study;[5] however, it is worth pointing out that a major presupposition of this practice from Mahāyāna Buddhism is that there is no essential difference between phenomena arising in the dream state, and the phenomena of our waking life—both are ultimately lacking any essence or objective reality (they are empty) and are illusory and insubstantial fabrications of the mind.

Angela highlights how similar this experience was to her waking life by stating how lucid she was of her environment and that there was "nothing dream-like about the experience." Seeing her physical body asleep in bed made her realize she was having an OBE and prompted her to try out some "experiments" that transcended her habitual tendency to identify with her physical body. However, the fear of leaving her physical body too far behind (a recurring theme in accounts of OBEs) motivated her to return to it and led to her "waking up."

Angela describes her second account as follows:

The next time this happened, I was living in India with my family. On that occasion, having gone to sleep normally, I woke up and walked out into the large upstairs hall where my children had been playing. I picked up some socks from the floor and put away toys when my attention was drawn to a small window on one side of the room. I walked over and looked out—I could see a mountain far in the distance with a light right at the top, and I had an overwhelming feeling of wanting to go to that light—but then I woke up in my bed and was *extremely* surprised to realize that I had not been awake.

Of course, I wanted to immediately return to that state and go to the mountain, so I shut my eyes, trying to return to what I understood to be an out-of-body state—but when I shut my eyes, there was nothing but darkness, just like when you close your eyes normally. Anyway, I stayed like that for a little while, and all of a sudden, like someone just opened the curtains that were drawn over my eyes, there was light, and I could see my room, and I knew I was back in whatever state it was.

I leapt out of bed and ran through the door and around the corner, so fast that my body seemed to me to be like a streak of light, and then I was standing at the window wondering how to get to the mountain. Then I remembered that in a thought body, I just needed to think myself there. So I thought myself out the window and found myself flying through the night, kind of spread-eagled in the sky. I could feel the night breeze moving across my arms, and I can truly say that it was the most ecstatic feeling I have ever had in my life. I could see the tops of the coconut trees and the houses and streets around our house—and although it was my intent to be heading for the mountain, I think the distraction of looking around and loving the feeling interrupted the focus that would have taken me there because I suddenly woke up in my bed, and I could not get back again.

Like her first experience, Angela's second OBE is characterized by its vividness and resemblance to ordinary waking life. The appearance of the mysterious mountain generates in her a strong desire to go there, and she is both surprised and disappointed when she wakes. However, she is able to return to that dreamlike state, and by applying the principle based on the Tibetan thought body, she is able to "think" herself toward the mountain and experience "the most ecstatic feeling" of her life[6] as she flies toward it (flying is also a common theme in lucid dreaming and OBEs).

Unable to understand the significance of the mountain, Angela asked many people about it until one day about a year later, she asked a Tibetan lama in Canada:

Subsequent to this experience, I asked many monks and other people what to make of it, but no one had any answers for me. About a year or so later, I was back in Canada and met up with a great hidden yogi (Lama Karma Thinley), who simply asked me in what direction the window faced. I told him it faced directly southwest.

He then said, "Oh! That is Guru Rinpoche's Copper-Colored Mountain. When you go again, please ask him if there is any message for Lama Karma Thinley." He also advised me to return to India and to request of HH Penor Rinpoche a Guru Rinpoche empowerment, which I did.

Here Guru Rinpoche refers to Padmasambhava, the legendary eighth-century Indian tantric adept and founder of the Nyingma School of Tibetan Buddhism. His Copper-Colored Mountain of Glory (Tibetan: *zangs mdog dpal ri*) is his pure land located in the southwest, where devotees aspire to be reborn. When Lama Karma Thinley hears Angela's story, his response is indicative of the significance of such dreams in Tibetan Buddhism. Certain special dreams are considered different from ordinary dreams and are distinguished by their clarity and vividness.[7] In these special dreams of clarity, the thought body is able to separate from the physical body,[8] thus making these dreams portals to other dimensions whereby devotees may travel to pure lands and encounter holy beings.

The beings encountered and places visited are also indications of their karmic connections to the dreamer. This is why the lama suggests that Angela receive a Guru Rinpoche empowerment—to further strengthen her karmic bond with Padmasambhava. Note also that Lama Thinley does not draw any sharp distinctions between visiting the Copper-Colored Mountain in a dream versus going there with a thought body "in real life." When all phenomena are dreamlike and illusory manifestations of the mind, such distinctions become meaningless. Thus, dreams can be the means by which one can travel beyond the physical body (OBEs), not merely hallucinations of the sleeping brain. From Angela's accounts of her OBEs, we can discern that these experiences made a lasting impression and were deeply meaningful to her. And no doubt they played some role in inspiring her to write her first book, *Dream Worlds of Shamanism and Tibetan Buddhism*.

The reality of out-of-body experiences has been a part of the Buddhist tradition from its earliest days. From the accounts described here, we see that the phenomenon continues to this day for contemporary Buddhists. Since Buddhists past and present distinguish between the physical body and a mind-made or thought body, which can under special circumstances separate from the physical body, OBEs are more than merely the result of the hallucinating brain. The Tibetan tradition distinguishes between ordinary dreams and dreams of clarity, so when OBEs happen in the dream state, they allow the possibility to travel to other worlds and encounter other beings. Moreover, from the Mahāyāna philosophical perspective such experiences highlight the illusory and dreamlike nature of all phenomena and therefore can be both instructive and instrumental in advancing one on the spiritual path. Thus, OBEs continue to have deep religious significance for contemporary Buddhists.

Dying and Near-Death Experiences

Death and dying are important events in most religious traditions, Buddhism being no exception. In the Buddhist traditions, one's final state of mind at the time of death is crucially important because this "death-proximate karma" (Sanskrit: *āsanna-karma*) will be a strong determining factor for a person's next rebirth.[9] Stories in the Buddhist traditions speak about one's mental state in the final moments of life having the power to completely redirect one's future birth, either for good or ill.[10] Thus, a calm, clear, and aware mind that recalls good deeds or vows to perform future good deeds is the ideal mental state for a dying person; however, a hateful, greedy, afraid, or attached mind at the time of death could be disastrous for the next rebirth.

Narratives of paranormal happenings surrounding death and dying abound in the Buddhist traditions. In the Mahāyāna Pure Land schools, the moments before death are a crucial time to recall Amitābha Buddha and recite his name, so as to be reborn in Sukhāvatī, his pure land. The Chinese and Japanese Pure Land traditions are replete with stories of miraculous events taking place on the deathbed of the sincere Pure Land Buddhist.[11] In the Zen tradition, there are many stories of Zen masters sensing when they are going to die, and the Tibetan tradition speaks of enlightened lamas' physical bodies dissolving into the "rainbow body" at the moment of death.[12] In the Thai Theravāda tradition, miracles surrounding the death and dying of saints, such as the incorruptible nature of their remains, are often reported.[13] Likewise, there are countless stories of paranormal occurrences around death and dying in the modern Western literature.

TALES OF OBES, NDES, AND CLOSE ENCOUNTERS

My survey contained two questions related to death and dying. The first, question 40, asked, "Have you ever had an unusual experience at a time when you were seriously ill or near death, or thought that you were near death, or appeared to other persons to be unconscious?" Of the 64 people who responded to this question, only 14 of them (22 percent) said "Yes." When invited to describe their experience, only one account was close enough to the traditional notion of an NDE to mention here. A forty-nine-year-old Buddhist practitioner from Singapore wrote, "I was in a car crash (came out unharmed), but in the midst disappeared into another realm, with beatific beings radiating light and telling me all was at peace. My (earthly) life was distant as if in a dream." However, under the question about OBEs, Ayyā Mettikā described an experience that I consider to be a classic example. She wrote:

> [As] a young teen, I fell ill with late-diagnosis rocky mountain spotted fever (RMSF). This causes extreme illness, and at one point a near-death experience: rising from the body into welcoming and beautiful painless clarity and light, and then hovering above, looking back and seeing the body from above. I could also see through the nearby house walls and see my moving relatives (my first younger sister) through the walls. I could see my sister coming, opening the door, seeing what looked like a dead body, her shocked calling of my name, and then the fast snap of umbilical cord-like attachment snapping back with the belly-flop whiplash-like snap back into the body of sickness and pain, and seeing out of those eyes again.

Both of these NDE accounts describe the appearance of light, which is a commonly occurring theme in modern tales of NDEs. Here we see an obvious connection to the appearance of the "clear light" at the moment of death described in the *Tibetan Book of the Dead* (*bardo thol dol*).[14] Other recurring themes in modern stories of near-death experiences present in these two narratives are an encounter with other beings, rising outside of and above the physical body, entering another realm, the remoteness of earthly life, and the sensation of "snapping" back into the physical body. Note also that Ayyā Mettikā's story takes place when she was a young teenager. This is the earliest paranormal event she describes in the survey, and it indicates (along with her OBE as a young woman at a yoga retreat, recounted earlier), that her paranormal experiences occurred throughout her life from a fairly early age. However, once she became seriously involved in Buddhism, these events began to contain specific Buddhist elements and are interpreted by her through the lens of her Buddhist worldview.

Question 43 inquired, "Have you ever been with a dying person who seemed to see or hear people or other beings who were not physically present, or see places or events that were not part of the immediate physical surroundings?" Of the 62 people who responded, only 13 (21 percent) replied in the affirmative. Thus, for the survey sample, NDEs and deathbed paranormal events appear quite rare. Concerning deathbed phenomena, of the 13 who said that they had experienced something, none chose to describe the events. However, as mentioned in the previous chapter under telepathy, one respondent simply stated, "When my husband was dying and unconscious," without supplying any additional details. Does this mean she had some type of telepathic communication with her dying husband? Her statement would seem to imply this, but without further information, this is only conjecture.

Close Encounters

As we saw in chapter 1, the Buddhist omniverse is teeming with a vast menagerie of nonhuman intelligent life forms. The standard model divides the cosmos hierarchically, with the realm of sense desire containing the six domains of humans, animals, hungry ghosts, hell beings, gods, and demigods. In addition to these are various classes of demons, spirits, and celestial beings. Above the realm of sense desire, the realm of pure form and the formless realm contain their own classes of deities. With the advent of Mahāyāna and Tantric Buddhism, entire pantheons of holy beings, wrathful protectors, bodhisattvas, and buddhas evolved. Since the acceptance of these other intelligent nonhuman beings has always been a given in Buddhism, one could argue that encountering them would be more of a "normal," rather than "paranormal," event. However, a direct encounter with other nonhuman intelligent entities was likely not a common occurrence for Buddhists throughout history, and certainly such encounters in modern times would be considered by many to be anomalous, unusual, or at least of some particular significance. Thus, while somewhat sidestepping the problematic nature of our current nomenclature, I here proceed with a discussion of narratives concerning "paranormal" close encounters that contemporary Buddhists have had with animals, ghosts, spirits, deities, and holy beings.

Animals

Of course, there is nothing particularly paranormal about humans' interacting with other animals. However, on rare occasions people report experiences with domestic or wild animals possessing paranormal features or psi phenomena. In contemporary times, numerous studies have been conducted into the psi abilities of animals.[15] Moreover, cultures across the world and throughout history are rich with stories about human encounters with cryptids, that is, creatures known to folklore or legend but not substantiated by scientific observation. Bigfoot and the Loch Ness Monster are two widely known examples from Anglo-European cultures, but local legends and stories from traditional and modern communities are numerous and continue up to this day. The AAWSAP agent Jonathan Axelrod's family's seeing strange "dogmen" is a case in point (see chapter 2).

Traditional Buddhist narrative literature is filled with stories about nonhuman animals and their interactions with human beings. The *Jātaka Tales*, previous birth stories of Buddha, is one noteworthy example. In these stories, as in many Western fables, animals often possess human speech and act in decidedly anthropomorphic ways. In addition to these Buddhist fables, we also read about the Buddha and Buddhist saints interacting with animals in ways that demonstrate the supramundane nature of these holy beings. Two well-known examples are the *nāga* King Mucalinda (often depicted in Buddhist art as a king cobra), who shielded the Buddha with his hood while the Buddha was meditating during a rainstorm,[16] and the intoxicated elephant Nāḷāgiri, sent by the Buddha's evil cousin Devadatta to trample him.[17] In this famous story, the monk Devadatta has the king Ajātasattu's elephant Nāḷāgiri intoxicated and sent on a rampage to kill the Buddha, but just as the elephant is about to trample a little girl caught in his path, the Buddha calls to him and radiates loving-kindness (*metta*) at him.[18] Immediately, Nāḷāgiri is pacified and reverently approaches the Buddha, who teaches him Dharma and converts him to the Buddhist path.

During my interview with Ajahn Chandako, the following discussion took place related to this psychic connection between humans and animals and the role of intuition in the development of psi abilities.

D: Do you know stories of meditation masters and actual snakes? Like that when they are in the jungle, they develop a rapport with or friendship with the snake, so the snake kind of hangs out and looks after the practitioner or master?

AC: Well, certainly in terms of nonviolence. Animals in the jungle are extremely sensitive. They have to be for their own survival, so they have a high degree of awareness and tuning into other beings, so they can tell very quickly if someone is aggressive or not aggressive. Or if they have fear, that will tend to make the animals more afraid. So, one example of an animal that has a high degree of mental power is the king cobra. Tigers and king cobras are the ones that have the most. And king cobras can be huge, and when they rise up, they are about the same level as humans' heads. They are that big, so that king cobras seem to have rather advanced minds in order to be able to send mental energy out. And so it is almost like a basic psychic power, a rudimentary psychic power. There is a story of Ajahn Ganha. Ajahn Ganha was a disciple of Ajahn Chah, and Ajahn Ganha was staying in a cave; Ajahn Ganha is still alive, the most-famous-at-the-time master today. Ajahn Ganha was staying in a cave and a king cobra showed up. Sometimes these stories get exaggerated...

D: Sure.

AC: So, I think it was a king cobra that came up while he was meditating in a cave and was right in front of him. He just reached out and petted it. Even for a meditation monk that is a pretty gutsy thing to do.

D: [Laughs]

AC: [Laughs] Not your normal reaction! But there was just such a shared confidence in the *metta* and nonviolence that "we would never harm each other" so he could reach out, even though it was a wild animal, which usually don't like to be touched, but he could reach out and pet it.

This story about Ajahn Ganha is reminiscent of both the story about the *nāga* king Mucalinda and the elephant Nāḷāgīri. In all three narratives, a Buddhist holy person (the Buddha or Ganha) has a special relationship with an animal based on reverence and loving-kindness that transcends ordinary human interaction with nonhuman animals.

This conversation about humans and animals possessing an intuitive connection to each other led on to a discussion about the relationship between intuition and psi and about certain exceptional individuals having an innate talent for psychic abilities:

AC: It is like we all have the ability to develop intuition. Mostly we are taught not to trust our intuition, but if you have that ability, that is like the kernel or the seed of psychic powers that can be developed.

D: Yes, it is interesting how in wisdom traditions such as Buddhism they have been able to cultivate those kinds of intuitions to virtuoso levels. But it is very much like you said, of all the people that practice *samādhi* and all the people that meditate . . . only a very small percentage get psychic powers. That is interesting to me too—this idea that some people have that rare or anomalous thing, which because it cannot be scientifically tested must not be real. Just like there are extraordinary athletes and phenomenal virtuoso musicians, it makes sense to me that there are certain people who are extraordinarily gifted in certain ways like this. And if they practice intense meditation, it seems to amplify that ability in the same way that anybody can learn chess, but no matter how much they study and play chess, less than 1 percent are going to become grandmasters.

AC: Yes, to be like Mozart, you know? You could study music your whole life, but he was just born with it. He could visualize entire symphonies and just write them down. You know they would just come to him. How do you explain that? It is just innate, in the same way some people just have these innate abilities, and it's a matter of systematically developing it.

The idea that certain intuitions form the kernel of psychic ability connects human psi more closely to other nonhuman animals, who also seem to possess these sorts of intuitions, and supports Charles Fort's notion of "wild talents," that psi abilities are primordial ones that humans developed for survival purposes (see chapter 2). Ajahn Chandako's view also runs counter to certain New Age and theosophical notions that humans are spiritually evolving to possess psychic powers. Thus, according to the Ajahn and

Fort, psi may have evolved from latent intuitions in certain humans as natural abilities to sense and respond to their environments.

Ghosts and Spirits

Stories of ghosts and departed spirits are universal across cultures and throughout human history, and the Buddhist traditions are no exception. As mentioned in chapter 1, we find many stories in Buddhism concerning "hungry ghosts," those pitiful beings who, because of their excessive greed, have been reborn into a nightmare realm of perpetual hunger and thirst.[19] Unsurprisingly, these tales are generally about the demeritorious effects of bad karmic action. In the Western paranormal literature, there are countless reports of poltergeists, apparitions, ghosts, and spirits. Mediumship, the practice of contacting the spirits of the deceased, which gained widespread popularity in Europe and North America in the nineteenth century, possesses a vast literature by insiders and skeptics that is far beyond the range of the current investigation even to begin to explore.[20] Thus, we see that the belief in ghosts and spirits of the deceased is alive and well in the enchanted West. This popularity is reflected in my survey results.

When asked in the survey, "Have you ever seen, heard, or felt the presence of any person living or dead, who was not physically present?," 36 of the 65 respondents (55 percent) ticked "Yes." Of these, 50 percent have had this happen to them 1–5 times, while 32 percent have had this happen to them more than twenty times. When asked the context of these experiences, 68 percent of the responses were "spontaneously," 50 percent were "dreaming," 44 percent were while meditating or during some other spiritual practice, and 21 percent were "during an altered state of consciousness." When invited to describe their experiences, some of the shorter responses were: "I think I've seen what might be described as ghosts at least twice"; "It happens often in my dreams"; "Sensing a spirit in the house"; "Either with divination work, prayer work, pilgrimage etc. sometimes visible sometimes felt"; "Received initiation in a dream with departed master." One participant mentioned being possessed by a spirit, as has often been described in the literature on mediumship: "People come to visit me after they die. Some I didn't know they had died. One possessed my body to give her sister a hug."

TALES OF OBES, NDES, AND CLOSE ENCOUNTERS

A number of people mentioned contact with deceased family or teachers: "Grandmother offers advice in dreams"; "Days after both my father and my husband died, I felt them and heard them"; "My father came to speak with me shortly after his death. Others who have died have also done so"; "After my mother died, I occasionally felt her presence." Three of the survey participants provided longer responses. Jason, a forty-nine-year-old Australian man (mentioned in chapter 3), wrote, "After the death of my sister, I had several experiences of objects moving, glasses and plates on tables a few times, and one profound experience of autumn leaves in the shape of footprints of someone walking behind me." Rick Repetti, a sixty-three-year-old American man (mentioned in the previous chapter and the focus of chapter 5), describes two encounters with deceased meditation teachers: "When one of my first meditation teachers died, unbeknownst to me, he visited me in a light body, telepathically communicating to me that he died, and was saying goodbye. Another time, I sensed another of my deceased early meditation teachers' presence, then smelled her rare perfume. I've had many such experiences."

Steven, a thirty-five-year-old American psychedelic Buddhist,[21] describes two encounters he had while on ayahuasca journeys:

> I can think of a few cases of this. Most recently, and most prominently, during an ayahuasca journey I came into contact with two "ghosts": the first was the ghost of an ex-lover of mine that I was especially close with during our relationship. We had a bad breakup and had become estranged. She died (most likely by suicide, but I don't know for certain) about 18 months ago and I learned about it through a third party. I specifically requested to meet with her so I could say goodbye. My request was granted.
>
> During another ayahuasca journey I had the distinct experience of coming into contact with the "ghost" of my never-born baby brother. I'm an only child. I have for many years suspected my mother chose to have an abortion and not carry to term the fetus who would have been my little brother. I met him on accident. I hadn't requested it but in the context of the journey it made a lot of sense to encounter him.

A recurring theme in many of these stories is someone encountering a recently deceased person with whom one has a strong emotional connection, such as a lover, family member, or spiritual guide. From a Buddhist point of view, these are people one would have a strong karmic connection with. Sometimes these meetings only consist of sensing or feeling someone's presence. Other times, a departed person visits someone in a dream or during a psychedelic journey. Rarer still are spontaneous visitations or encounters while someone is meditating or engaged in some other spiritual practice. Are these experiences merely the results of the overactive imaginations of people in the throes of grief from having lost a loved one? Skeptics would like to say so. However, not all of these encounters are so easily dismissed.

Sometimes ghosts are just annoying. In my interview with Patricia (mentioned in chapter 3), she talked about living in Berkeley in the 1970s, in a big house with ghosts in the basement. Our discussion went as follows:

PATRICIA: And then I went back to Berkeley, and that was a time when there was a lot of buzz around paranormal experience, and I remember one time I was—not relevant to Buddhism exactly—but I was living in a house. You know how we used to live ten or twelve people in a house, right?

D. E. OSTO: I have read about that.

P: And I was living in a house like that, and we had ghosts in the basement. And they were really noisy! And so, we thought, "We gotta do something about this," you know? And someone said, "Just call Elizabeth Miller. Mrs. Miller will take care of it." And we all thought that was a good idea, and then somehow, I got designated as the person to call her.

D: [Laughs] Okay. Please go on.

P: So here I am calling Mrs. Miller and saying, "We've got ghosts in the basement, and someone said you would be willing to deal with them. So, I wonder if you can help us?" And she said, "Oh in the basement? Is that 27–28 Derby Street? Yeah? I've been there before. I'll be right over."

D: Wow! [Laughs]

P: And she came over and took care of it, and we never had a problem again. So, then we were so impressed that we decided that we would like to learn from her. So we would drive over to Sausalito every couple of weeks, and in her tiny front room we would converse with her, and she would teach us. She called herself a "white witch." And said that she was "working for the good." And she was relying on things like psychic self-defense, like Annie Besant [the second president of the Theosophical Society], and you know, some of that genre.

Here we see an example of the popular Western belief in ghosts (particularly in Californian counterculture of the 1960s and 1970s), combined with the revival of twentieth-century witchcraft, in what has been called Western "occulture."[22]

More germane to Buddhism were Ajahn Chandako's comments during our interview. Here, he spoke of the Thai meditation masters Lumpa Chorp and Ajahn Piak being able to perceive ghosts:

AC: Lumpa Chorp has many examples. There are also examples in his biography of, in a matter-of-fact way, oh he saw this whole group of beings from the ghost realm, and they were described as more like sad humans [laughs], not like haunting, fearful, or fear-inspiring beings but more just like ... they had their own society, lived in groups, seemed to look relatively human as if there were a whole other layer of reality superimposed onto what we can perceive.

D: Yes. I see what you mean, very traditional Buddhist cosmology.

AC: So, there is that and, of course ... many, many stories of devas, ghosts ... Ajahn Piak also talked about ghosts ... seeing ghosts for example at Wat Pah Nanachat, he noticed an unseen being who was like the—I mean ghosts are basically the leftover consciousness of a living being that—either call them ghosts—or say that they haven't taken rebirth yet. Either way, he described what that person looked like. He said it was a Westerner who had these particular features, and when it was checked with some of the older Western monks who had been in Wat Pah Nanachat, they said that it was a perfect description of a Western guest who had come to Wat Pah Nanachat when he was old and sick, and he had died there. And Ajahn Piak had described him basically as a little bit sad or depressed, which would fit for being in the ghost realm, right? Generally, if you are happy and bright you tend to have ...

D: A better rebirth! Rather than come back as a ghost! Right!

These modern accounts of Thai meditation masters' "seeing ghosts" conform to the traditional Buddhist understanding of hungry ghosts, who inhabit another realm (or as Chandako puts it, "a whole other layer of reality superimposed onto what we can perceive"), which nevertheless is not far removed from our own. Because this realm is one of the lower rebirths that results from excessive greed, the beings here are more pitiful and sad than scary. In Ajahn Piak's story, we find a particularly contemporary version of the classical Buddhist ghost, a Westerner who had died while visiting the monastery. However, this does not mean from a Buddhist point of view that every ghost encountered is a hungry ghost. Several Buddhist traditions accept an intermediate state between rebirths, which the Tibetans call *bardo*.[23] Thus, someone who encounters a recently deceased relative may be having a visitation from them, while their consciousness is in this in-between state before their next rebirth.

Spirits, Deities, and Holy Beings

As discussed in chapter 1, the presence of spirits and divinities is a ubiquitous feature of Buddhist worldviews since the earliest days. Similar to the Greek gods and goddesses, deities in early Buddhism are like superhuman beings with great power and longevity but ultimately subject to karma and rebirth, as are all sentient beings in *saṃsāra*. Although they come in many varied types from an array of different heavenly realms, a common term for such beings in Sanskrit is *deva* (feminine, *devī*). In the early Buddhist sources, these beings are regularly depicted as interacting with the Buddha and other human beings. Many were said to have converted to Buddhism and acted as protectors of the Buddha or Buddha's Dharma. We have already heard *devas* mentioned by Ayyā Mettikā and others in stories about other psychic phenomena (see chapter 3). With the advent of Mahāyāna and tantric Buddhism, entire pantheons of holy beings—buddhas, bodhisattvas, spiritual guides, protectors, and wrathful deities—emerged. From the earliest strata of the Mahāyāna in India, directly encountering buddhas and bodhisattvas was an important element of the spiritual path,[24] which has continued to this day in the Mahāyāna and tantric traditions. In Tibet, for example, the hagiographies of enlightened masters are filled with direct encounters with spirits, divinities, enlightened masters, bodhisattvas, and buddhas.[25]

Two participants during interviews mentioned the *nāga*s, a group of semidivine serpent beings having a special connection to Buddhism. The Indian mythology of the *nāga*s is ancient and widespread.[26] They are often depicted as part human and part snake and are believed to be able to take the form of either.[27] Powerful and beautiful beings, the *nāga*s reside underground or at the bottoms of lakes, rivers, and oceans. Although potentially dangerous, they are generally benevolent and often guard treasure or entrances into sacred places. *Nāga*s appear numerous times in the biographies of the Buddha and the *Jātaka* stories.[28] One of the most famous accounts depicted throughout the Buddhist world in art is the story (mentioned earlier) of the *nāga* king Mucalinda sheltering the Buddha from the rain with his hood. In Mahāyāna legend, the story is told of the Buddha entrusting the *Perfection of Wisdom* sutras to the *nāga*s at the bottom of the ocean, who centuries later gifted them to the great Mahāyāna philosopher Nagārjuna.[29] Stories of *nāga*s and their interactions with humans are a pan-Buddhist phenomenon that continues up to the present day.

During my interview with Paul, a forty-two-year-old American Buddhist and scholar of Tibetan Buddhism, the topic of *nāga*s came up a number of times. The first mention was particularly instructive:

PAUL: So honestly one of the things that really attracted me to Tibetan Buddhism was the fact that it combines in some ways, this really high-level philosophy, right? All these discussions of emptiness, and these really advanced meditation techniques, all of this sort of stuff, combined with this really crunchy granola feeling of the world. "Yeah, there is a *sadak* over there. There is a stream, that is where the *lu* live." Sorry, I am using the Tibetan terms; the *lu* are the *nāga*s; *sadak* is the place-lord. I really like that. Not so much on an intellectual but on an affective level of that part of the tradition.

D. E. OSTO: Right. The world is imbued with this kind of sentience and non-human beings that you can interact with . . . and there is that kind of ritual component too . . . When you were . . .

P: Can I just jump in for a sec . . . I am really glad you didn't say, "The world is imbued with this mystical thing."

D: Okay. Care to elaborate?

P: Because it doesn't feel mystical at all. It just seems to be the way the world is. I mean it is not mystical when I see my neighbor. It is also not mystical when maybe I think there is a *nāga* in the spring. For me this is an important part of it. It is not some highfalutin mumbo-jumbo like trying to create a mystical world. It is just like . . .

D: Right. Let me see if I can rephrase. You are not trying to reenchant the world. Maybe other people are just not paying attention to how the world is.

P: It's just how it is. So, if you hang out with Tibetans enough (or Indians and Nepalis), it is not so much about other people not paying attention; it's just everyone is paying attention and everyone sees this, so it is just normal.

D: Right.

P: Like *of course* there is a spirit in this tree. It just is. Like this isn't a topic of debate, it's just . . .

D: Right. It is just taken as a given.

P: It means you shouldn't pee on it, but not like, "*Ooo*, this tree is mystical!" Or special—it is just a tree with a spirit.

Here Paul makes an important point, which he reiterated throughout our interview—in the Tibetan worldview, the existence of spirits like *nāga*s is not considered something mystical or "paranormal" but just "normal," a given, everyday part of the world. By implication, then, it is only if you assume that a particular type of modern Western materialism is normal that such things as spirits need to be thought of as "paranormal." Later in the interview, Paul rephrases the same idea this way:

P: If there was a bull in my neighbor's yard that kept coming over and trampling my garden, I would build a stronger fence. Right? That's just what I would do to deal with that situation. So, to deal with the *nāga*s, I should build a little shrine, and then that would deal with the *nāga*s. It honestly doesn't feel paranormal. It feels just normal. It is just part of the world, right? As I conceive of it. And when I say that, it is more on an affective level, not a conceptual level. And when I try to think that that is not real, it seems awkward. Does that kind of help?

D: Yeah. It does.

Both *nāga*s and *deva*s came up during my interview with Ajahn Chandako.

AC: *Nāga*s seem to have a close relationship with Buddhist monasteries. They seem to be very supportive, and some meditation masters have real solid relationships with *nāga*s. . . . You go stay with him [Lupetan, the forest monk mentioned in chapter 3] . . . You know as monks we just pee in the forest. And he would say, "Don't pee over there because there is a *nāga* who lives over there, whom you might offend."

D: I've heard that too! There may be a tree deity there, so if you pee on the tree, you will insult them.

AC: Right. So, we have kind of monastic etiquette around all facets of our lifestyle. And there are few monastic etiquette rules around *devas*. For example, if we are doing walking meditation ... apparently *devas* like watching monks doing walking meditation. It is kind of peaceful ... I don't know [laughs].

D: [Laughs]

AC: It is kind of sweet, human beings trying to be their best. So, we are not allowed to pee right in the immediate area around our walking meditation path, because there might be a *deva* watching! [laughs] Little things like that.... There are examples such as Lumpa Chorp, who was particularly known for having very deep *samādhi*.... He loved solitude, so he spent a lot of time in caves to the point where he was fasting in caves, and there was a local female *deva* who was very concerned about his welfare and was regularly in contact with him and trying to encourage him to eat.

From both Paul's and Ajahn Chandako's interviews we see a very pragmatic and matter-of-fact approach to *nāga*s and *deva*s—you don't urinate on their homes or in front of them, you propitiate them if they seem to be offended or causing trouble, you follow necessary etiquette around them, and under the right conditions you can enter positive relationships with them. Thus, we see that belief in such beings is alive and well in the Tibetan and Theravāda traditions. Neither Paul nor the Ajahn mention specific personal encounters with *nāga*s or *deva*s, but from within their respective worldviews, people's directly encountering a spirit or goddess would be completely within the realm of possibility and, although probably thought unusual, wouldn't be considered "paranormal" in the commonly used sense of the word.

In my survey, when asked, "Have you ever felt the presence, seen or heard a nonphysical spirit, entity or holy being?," an astounding 45 out of 60 people (75 percent) responded "Yes." Of these, only 3 indicated that this had happened to them once, 15 said it has happened 1–5 times, while 12 stated this has happened to them more than 20 times in their lives. When asked about the context of these experiences, 70 percent (30 out of 43) of the respondents indicated that one or more had occurred during meditation or some other spiritual practice, 65 percent (28) said they happened spontaneously, 40 percent (17) said while dreaming, and 30 percent (13) indicated they occurred during an altered state of consciousness. When invited to describe their experiences, replies once again varied from the extremely brief to the more verbose. Some of the shorter responses were: "receiving advice from a 'deceased' guru"; "I've felt a 'sensed presence' many times during very deep meditations"; "Clear presence of being in the energy fields of such beings"; "a vision of my Guru who told me I had a gift as a teacher, at a time in my life before I had thought about teaching"; "during a period in my life I saw countless deities, gurus, and holy beings in meditation and chanting"; and "I feel them all the time, God, Gods, saints, sages, elders, angels, Buddhas, Bodhisattvas, Buddha nature/Natural state, nature spirits." Linda (the seventy-one-year-old American woman mentioned earlier) wrote: "the presence of the teacher, buddha, or bodhisattva is intentionally invoked in the process of ritual practice. It could be imagination, but it feels very real."

Two respondents gave more details about the context of their experiences with multiple entities such as spirits, saints, gods, gurus, and bodhisattvas. Rick Repetti writes: "Some of my deceased meditation teachers, as well as yogis, gurus, saints, deities, and sometimes unidentifiable nonphysical beings have appeared in my meditations, or when I was in altered states (when my practice was so serious that I was frequently in a meditative state throughout the active day), or just spontaneously."

Here Rick mentions various types of beings appearing spontaneously, in meditation, and while in altered states. I provide further details and contexts to some of these in chapter 5. Steven (the psychedelic Buddhist mentioned earlier) described his ability to invoke beings during psychedelic experiences. His account is reminiscent of early Mahāyāna Buddhists' attempts to contact buddhas and bodhisattvas by altering their consciousness through intense concentration, fasting, sleep, and sensory deprivation.[30] He writes: "During several of my more powerful psychedelic journeys I have directly contacted and interacted with several spirits/entities that matched the description of and self-identified as various gods and bodhisattvas. This happens pretty reliably, including upon request, meaning I seem to be able to induce the experience with focused intention and will as well as appropriate contextual setup and mental priming."

Several participants mention encountering specific Mahāyāna holy beings. One writes, "I have experienced visions of Amitābha." As mentioned in chapter 1, Amitābha is the Buddha of the Western Paradise, Sukhavātī, and the central figure in the Pure Land Buddhist schools of East Asia. In these schools, a vision of Amitābha is an extremely auspicious sign of one's karmic connection to the Buddha and likely rebirth in his pure land. Another respondent writes, "When I first started meditating on Guru Rinpoche Padmasambhava, he appeared to me." Recall that Padmasambhava is the legendary Indian tantric master responsible for subduing Tibetan demons, transmitting the Nyingma teachings, and hiding numerous "treasure texts" (*terma*); he is considered by many Tibetans to be a "second Buddha." This person was likely engaged in tantric visualization practices, and the appearance of Guru Rinpoche would also be an extremely auspicious sign of one's spiritual progress. Unfortunately, they did not provide more details about this appearance and their level of interaction with Padmasambhava.

Two respondents specifically mention Mahāyāna holy beings from Japanese Buddhism. One participant, a practitioner of Tendai Buddhism, states, "[I] have seen teachers change into Fudō Myōō, saw someone who may have been Benzaiten, have had daytime visions of hosts of bodhisattvas." Fudō Myōō (Sanskrit: Acala) began his career as a wrathful protector deity (*dharmapala*) of Indian tantric Buddhism closely linked to the Hindu god Śiva.[31] However, Fudō rose in prominence in East Asian Esoteric Buddhism, and in Japan he is especially revered in the Tendai and Shingon schools and is viewed in Shingon as a wrathful form of the cosmic Buddha Mahāvairocana.[32] Here the respondent mentions teachers changing into Fudō, which suggests the esoteric Buddhist goal of transformation into an enlightened being through tantric practices. Also, seeing one's teacher as Fudō Myōō would indicate a purified vision that is able to view one's guru as a manifestation of Buddha. Benzaiten is the Buddhist and Shintō patron goddess of literature, wealth, music, and femininity, associated with the sea; she seems to be a transplanted form of the Hindu goddess Sarasvatī.[33] Needless to say, an encounter with Benzaiten would be an auspicious sign.

Jane, a twenty-nine-year-old woman from the United Kingdom (mentioned in the previous chapter), also writes about Fudō Myōō: "My apartment building used to be attached to a temple, on the side of a room where there is a powerful image of the Buddhist deity Fudō Myōō. I am particularly attached to him, but I rented the room by chance, not knowing about the temple. Fudō consistently helped me throughout the months I lived there."

TALES OF OBES, NDES, AND CLOSE ENCOUNTERS

In this passage, Jane describes a fortuitous move close to a temple with an image of Fudō, whom she is "particularly attached to." She also mentions being helped by him but unfortunately does not supply any details. Jane also describes mysterious encounters with an old man dressed in white: "When visiting a shrine of gods, I am particularly attached to, I stumbled on a decrepit house full of rubble. A white-clad old man with a long beard (I initially thought it was a statue) told me, 'Welcome back.' I saw the man again, walking with a cane and dressed in white, on the last day I went there, more than six months after I'd saw him first. The main god of the shrine is an old man with a cane."

Here Jane's account implies that the old man may have been a manifestation of the god. Based on her account of Fudō, Jane likely lived for a time in Japan. If this were the case, the description of the old man suggests that the shrine god may have been Jurōjin, one of the Shichi-fuku-jin (Seven Gods of Luck), who is particularly associated with longevity.[34] But without further details, we can only speculate.

Two of my interviewees provided detailed accounts of interactions with Avalokiteśvara, the Bodhisattva of Compassion. During our interview, Wystan, a twenty-four-year-old Canadian-American Buddhist, described to me how his close relationship with Avalokiteśvara evolved over time. The following conversation took place:

WYSTAN: I was at my parents doing *metta* [loving-kindness] practice, the feeling of *metta* radiating it outward in all directions. [And then] I perceived this white light above me, and it felt like a separate presence that was beaming the *metta* back to me. I can't remember if in the moment I interpreted this loving presence as Avalokiteśvara, or that happened afterwards.

D. E. OSTO: Yeah. Okay. I was wondering if it was that being or Amitābha or something like that. Right.

W: Regardless of the ontological status of that presence, I considered it Avalokiteśvara beaming compassion and *metta* back at me.

D: So, it was an encounter? It felt relational?

W: Yes.

D: Yeah, that is intense.

W: Since then, there have been several more encounters along the same lines. Not so much with the diffuse luminous presence but more fully formed and vivid. I have had a couple of experiences where it seemed that that same presence was behind me, like interacting with me, or like putting hands on my shoulders.

D: Was that while you were meditating or spontaneous?

W: No, it was not intended, it just happened.

D: Weird. And they felt connected somehow, so that the presence from the light was the same?

W: Right. It was the same.

D: So, do you feel that that first experience opened a door or some kind of channel to that presence and then it carried on from there? Was that a definitive moment, or are they free-standing, separate events?

W: Well, it was sporadic, but within the past six months . . . they have actually become more frequent as time has gone on.

D: Interesting.

W: And like now occasionally a strong emotion will come up. When an afflictive emotion comes up, sometimes I will close my eyes, meditate, check in with the body, and then invoke the presence of Avalokiteśvara. And I will instantly feel this incredibly soothing energy just course through and like embrace the whole space of the body with this feeling of love and compassion.

D: Wow. That is intense. It is kind of amazing too how you went from this very "self-power" effortful meditation to shifting into this much more relational, in some ways kind of devotional, interactive relation. That is an interesting shift there.

W: I mean, yeah. I have to say there is still both, and predominately there is still self-power, I think. But there is this other element. And on that point initially I had a kind of allergic reaction to devotional practices like bowing or chanting. By the time of the end of my living with monasteries some of my favorite stuff was the bowing and the chanting and invoking of bodhisattvas' names. I loved it. . . . There was one other experience . . . I was reading a poem by Patrul Rinpoche, a Tibetan lama, a Dzogchen teacher, from I don't remember maybe nineteenth century, or eighteenth century. At the time, I was able to recall the verse from memory but . . . it was something about your mind itself is . . . or "Mind itself, nondual, pure and empty, luminous . . ."

D: Right! Very Dzogchen! [laughs]

W: Right. But after that it had something like: "Is the embodiment of Avalokiteśvara . . . something something something . . . chant the six-beat mantra . . ."[35] You know *Oṃ maṇi padme Hūṃ*. And then after reading that verse there was a sense of the boundaries dropping, and over the last year, I think, that sort of sense of the boundaries between inside and outside dropping away has been a daily part of my life.[36]

Wystan's story fascinated me because he is able to recount in vivid detail the relationship he developed with Avalokiteśvara over time and its connections to his rather intense meditation practice, devotional activities, and Buddhist philosophy.[37] These types of relationships, such as the great Tibetan scholar Tsongkapa's bond with Mañjuśrī, are typical of the Tibetan hagiographic literature. Although some modern interpreters of Tibetan Buddhism may dismiss such accounts as pious embellishment,[38] Wystan's story provides us with a living example.

One of the most intriguing descriptions of an encounter in the survey was provided by Angela Sumegi. She supplied more details of this experience during our Zoom conversation, so the following account is from our interview, which I quote at length:

A: So, the other story I will tell you has to do with actually how I came to study and eventually practice Tibetan Buddhism. I was born and raised in Jamaica in the West Indies. And maybe I was about eight years old, something like that. We lived in a big old Jamaican house, and my bedroom was separated from my parents' bedroom by a big dark dining room. I am sure it probably looked bigger and darker to me as a kid! [laughs] I am sure if I saw it again, I would be like, "Oh, tiny little dining room." But in my child's mind, my parents' bedroom was so far away, and a big dark dining room, and then my bedroom. And I was in bed one night sleeping, and I woke up to a sound at the door, and when I looked in my doorway there was this horrific, horrific looking creature. Kind of a giant with long claws, a person, but with long claws on both hands and feet, and holding a *daṇḍa*, a stick, and stamping his foot, and grimacing, and fangs and wild hair . . . I mean I took one look at him and thought, "Monster!"
D: Yeah!
A: And the only thing I knew about monsters is that they eat little children! [Laughs]
D: Yeah right! [Laughs]

A: I mean I was awake enough to throw the bedcovers over my head. I mean I just waited there shaking in my nightie for the monster to come and eat me. And after a while once the monster had not eaten me, I got enough courage to pull the covers down and take another look, and the doorway was empty, but you know when you hit a tuning fork, and you hear the *hhhmmm* [imitating humming sound]?

D: Yes.

A: The reverberation. So, I could hear the sound—we had wooden floors—and I could hear the stamping still reverberating in my ears, the sound of the stamping. Well of course I leapt out of bed and ran across the dining room and jumped into bed with my parents. And because I had absolutely nowhere to put that; that was not the result of anything I had seen; we had no television; I had no books with monsters like that.

D: No giant trolls or anything that would resemble that?

A: I mean, no. There was nowhere for me to put it. It was just lost in my subconscious. And many, many years later, while I was an undergraduate, I was in the office of my mentor and looking through a big picture book of Tibetan thangkas, and all of a sudden, I saw the monster! And the memory of the vision just immediately came back to me completely, strongly, because I thought, "That is the monster I saw! That is what I saw!" And the image was an image of Mahākāla.

D: Ah!

A: And I remember at the time feeling very confused. Because, of course, I grew up in Jamaica—no TV, no Buddhism anywhere, especially no Tibetan Buddhism. And I remember thinking quite ridiculously, "Gosh, is this what Jung means by the collective unconscious? What is going on here?" And even to this day, I honestly could not give any word of explanation, except that I thought, "This is interesting." And it inspired me to begin to study Tibetan forms of Buddhism, to go in that direction for my study as well as my practice.

D: Wow, that is intense.

A: Yes! [laughs]

What intrigues me the most about Angela's story is how there was no Buddhist context for this visitation, yet many years later as a young adult, Angela recognized the "monster" in a book of thangkas (traditional Tibetan paintings on scrolls used for teaching and meditation purposes) as Mahākāla, a wrathful protector deity believed to be a fierce form of Avalokiteśvara, the Bodhisattva of Compassion. Moreover, this recognition inspired her to pursue a lifetime career in Buddhist and religious studies.

Of course, one could say Angela's experience was "just a dream." However, in Angela's survey response she writes about it: "This could have been a dream, but it appeared to me that I was ordinarily awake in my room, with the presence of mind to physically throw the covers over my head, so I have thought of it as a type of waking vision." The lucidity of the experience and the sudden waking also suggest a hypnogogic hallucination, and we have already seen that this in-between state (*bardo!*) at the intersection of waking and dreaming is an opportune time for visionary experiences. But if this was a "mere hallucination," why did it look just like Mahākāla to a little girl living in Jamaica?

When I asked for more details about the monster, the following conversation took place:

D: But [Mahākāla] is Avalokiteśvara, right? That is a fierce form of compassion.
A: Yes.
D: But [he] has a diadem with the skulls and eyes and fangs . . .
A: Oh yeah. The monster that I saw, of course, had the third eye and the flaming hair, and the fangs, and all the rest of it.
D: So, the iconography was like the photograph of what you saw in the book when you were an undergraduate?
A: Yes.
D: But it is funny how as a child you were like, "This thing is going to eat me." But it's Avalokiteśvara . . . [laughs]
A: But it seems scary.
D: Right.
A: It is a wrathful figure. And of course, as a child I am just looking at the form. But also, something else that occurred to me later as I came to understand Buddhism, because Mahākāla is also a Dharmapāla . . .
D: Yes. A Dharma Protector.
A: A Protector. And the protector deities in the monasteries are placed in the doorways.
D: Yes, to stop evil influences from entering.
A: Exactly! So, there was Mahākāla in my doorway.

TALES OF OBES, NDES, AND CLOSE ENCOUNTERS

When I asked Angela for more details concerning her interpretation of this vision, the following illuminating discussion took place in relation to stories, interpretation, and karma within a Buddhist context.

D: Do you think that [Mahākāla] was an emanation to protect you, or was it a trigger that was planting a seed in you, so that you would go in that direction when the time was right, like a kind of precognitive experience, or a protective experience, or a visitation, or your own unconscious in a Jungian style? Not that you need a definitive interpretation, but do you have a gut sense of what was going on there? Or are you just like, "I don't know."

A: Well, the problem for me is that . . . I mean, despite the fact that I feel I have had very strange experiences, I don't feel like I have a psychic bone in my body. I don't hear people; I don't sense things . . . but I . . . When you ask for an interpretation, my intellect tells me whatever interpretation I might put on that, it is sort of *makyō*, what the Japanese call *makyō*, illusion.

D: Illusion, right.

A: For many of my dreams, I have consulted my guru . . . and I say, "Here is what I dreamed; and I know that what I want to do is share it with you, and then I can forget it." Because the stories that we make about things, about experiences, about whatever throughout our life . . . It is those stories that trap us; it is those stories that bind us. Whereas I would like to say, "Here was the experience; you asked me about it." But if I have more thoughts about it, then it is kind of like, "Am I someone special because Mahākāla is looking after me?" [Laughs]

D: Right. I see what you mean.

A: There is a lot of danger there. And not that I think there is any harm in the stories except it is possible it can instead of diminishing our sense of "I," it enhances it.

D: Self-cherishing? Yes. Yes.

A: And it makes of me something that I am really not . . . It is just imagined. Of course, everything I think about me is just imagined! [Laughs]

D: [at the same time] Is just imagined! [Laughs]

A: You know?

D: Yeah, I totally hear what you are saying. It is like in a way we can't live without the stories . . .

A: That's right.

D: But maybe if we hold the stories lightly, delicately, rather than gripping tightly.

A: Yes.

D: Maybe that is why too much interpretation is not good ... Just say, "Okay, this is what happened to me when I was eight; this is what happened to me as a young adult; this is where I am now." And that is all that needs to be said! [Laughs]

A: Right! It is kind of like, "That's all there is!" [Laughs]. . . .

D: So already in the few interviews that I have done ... one of the themes I've noticed that makes many of these stories in some ways Buddhistic is that there is an explicit or implicit belief or sense of karma. That things emerge due to karma and that karmic connections have significance. Also, the way we respond to things ... is very important. It is almost like it [the paranormal] amplifies the potential karmic impact that things can have. Is that your feeling? Is this in the background of your worldview?

A: Yes. I would say that karma is ... I mean, I remember once asking my root guru, "Why do I feel so happy when I see you?" And he just said, "Ah, some karmic connection."

D: Yeah, right. No big deal.

A: So I feel, for example, the experience that I had as a child may well be the residue, leftover karma, some experience that would ripen in the future if the causes and conditions are there. Because many things don't ripen, you know. Things plant seeds, but they don't have to germinate. So if the causes and conditions are there, and that is also kind of related to karma ... You know, that being said, I find the karmic framework an interesting and a good framework to work with. It is a good map, but map is not territory.

Angela's approach here is clearly Buddhist. Attachment to views is harmful, and especially the view that "I am special," because it leads to self-cherishing, which reinforces the false sense of self. All interpretations are merely provisional and relative truths. This is true even of karma, which may be a useful framework for understanding but from the ultimate truth of emptiness is also only relative. Note also that Angela (like Ajahn Chandako and Rick

Repetti) avoids a deterministic view of karma. Karma plants seeds that *may* come to fruition, but only if/when the conditions are right.

Conclusion

In this chapter, we read stories of out-of-body experiences, near-death experiences, and close encounters with animals, ghosts, spirits, deities, and holy beings. Whereas OBEs and NDEs seem quite rare based on the survey results, some type of encounter with other beings was much more commonly reported. These experiences ranged from simply sensing the presence of some being to full-blown waking visions of other entities. Since most of my participants are Westerners, is this high frequency of encounters representative of a phenomenon in the wider Anglo-American population? It is impossible to say. However, given the stigma attached to people who are too vocal about such encounters, numbers may be much higher than supposed. As I briefly mentioned, accounts of the paranormal are usually kept among close friends and family.

Several themes have emerged in our investigation of these contemporary Buddhist tales of the paranormal. These events seem to erupt into daily life often spontaneously in waking life and in dreams. Sometimes they appear to be triggered by life-and-death situations and altered states induced through meditation, illness, or psychoactive substances. They often are deeply personal and emotional, involving close family, friends, and teachers. They are deeply meaningful, sometimes changing the course of a person's life. And they are commonly interpreted through a Buddhist worldview within which karma, rebirth, and nonhuman intelligent entities play important roles.

One could argue that since most of my survey respondents identify as Buddhist, their worldviews would predispose them to interpret events through a Buddhist lens, which accepts the existence of nonhuman intelligent entities such as *nāgas*, ghosts, goddesses, and bodhisattvas. This is a "common-sense" version of what in philosophy of science has been called the "theory theory of knowledge."[39] Briefly stated, this is the view that one's theory determines what one can perceive and how it is interpreted. Thus, perception is always "theory laden." Buddhist philosophy is quite sophisticated and can easily respond to such a critique, but for now I merely point out that a predisposition to interpret phenomena in a certain way does not mean a priori that that interpretation is wrong. In other words, if your worldview accommodates the existence of OBEs, NDEs, psychic abilities, and nonhuman intelligent entities and you interpret a phenomenon through this lens, it is only necessarily incorrect (a hallucination, delusion, or misperception, for instance) if someone else assumes a different worldview where such things are impossible. However, if we suspend our metaphysical commitments and look at the empirical evidence, interpreting a phenomenon as, for example, an encounter with a nonhuman intelligent entity might be the best possible explanation, *all things considered*. Moreover, this critique also falls down because for several respondents, such as Angela, their experiences happened before any commitment to or even knowledge of Buddhism. This highlights another possibility that certain exceptionally sensitive individuals, who have had numerous psychic and paranormal experiences, might be predisposed to a Buddhist outlook because it can give a meaningful account of such events that does not necessarily imply that they are deluded, hallucinating, or mentally ill.

FIVE

The Yogin

THIS CHAPTER IS about the life experiences of Rick Repetti, a philosopher, scholar, meditation teacher, yoga instructor, therapist, and psychic virtuoso. Rick received his PhD in philosophy from the Graduate Center of the City University of New York (CUNY) in 2005. He then went on to teach at CUNY's Kingsborough campus, becoming a full professor in 2016. In addition to his numerous articles and book chapters primarily on Buddhism and free will, Rick is the author of *Buddhism, Meditation, and Free Will: A Buddhist Theory of Mental Freedom* (2019) and *The Counterfactual Theory of Free Will: A Genuinely Deterministic Form of Soft Determinism* (2010). He is also the editor of *Buddhist Perspectives on Free Will: Agentless Agency?* (2017) and the *Routledge Handbook on the Philosophy of Meditation* (2022).

I first learned of Rick Repetti in 2020, when I was preparing to teach a course on metaphysics at Massey University. While searching for books on Buddhism and free will, I discovered his *Buddhism, Meditation, and Free Will*. On the first page of the preface, I came across this passage:

> Certain experiences conditioned my interest in both free will and Buddhist philosophy: As a teenager, I had an out-of-body experience during my first meditation, followed by several precognitive and other otherwise mystical experiences connected with my subsequent, intensely disciplined meditation practice, which shattered my paradigm. *What kind of world is this?* If I could see a distant future

formed by many yet unmade choices of unrelated individuals, how could free will be possible?[1]

Intrigued, I emailed Rick and invited him to take my survey and be interviewed. Rick agreed, and we conducted several Zoom interview sessions over a three-week period in March 2020, wherein Rick described some truly amazing experiences, which I detail in this chapter.

Rick was born in 1958 and grew up in a low-income public housing development in Queens, New York City, in a large Italian-American family.[2] His first awakening to the paranormal occurred one day in 1973, when he was fifteen years old. This is how Rick described the event to me:

> How I got into this stuff at all—apart from being a teenager in the '70s and knowing about this stuff culturally a little bit—I was watching television one day and I saw a yoga class going on. I didn't even realize it. It was two beautiful women in leotards—that's what caught my fifteen-year-old eye. And they were doing yoga poses that were very sensual, and then I realized, "This is a class." I was just flipping through the channels, as we did back then. And there was this Asian-looking man, but his name was Richard Hittleman, like a western name, and he was the teacher. He was talking them through poses, and they would do them. And I thought, "Let me try it." I used to watch Jack LaLanne so I thought, "Let me try this." So, I did it.[3]
>
> And at the end of the class, I was lying in deep relaxation, and he guided us through. He did this thing with visualizing light on our fingertips and putting it into our *cakra*s while we were breathing, and bringing it from here to here [demonstrates the light moving through the body]. I literally had this phenomenal experience—it felt like the energy was *really* there ... like I wasn't imagining it—I really felt it. I felt these strong vibrations and whatnot. When he finalized this meditation, saying, "Breathe in and visualize this golden light in your fingertips. Bring it up here and exhale to this area," I felt my head almost explode where it kept expanding then contracting, expanding, contracting; then my body was expanding. Like the energy went into my body, which felt huge, and my head felt small, and it kept flipping back and forth, and then I popped right out of my body! [snaps fingers].

A number of elements in this account stand out as significant. Note Rick's age. A recurring theme with sensitives or "exceptional subjects" (as they are called by psychic researchers) is that their experiences and/or abilities seem to emerge at a young age. Moreover, these are often spontaneous events induced by some extraordinary circumstances. In Rick's case, from following a televised yoga class and relaxation meditation at the end of the show, he was thrown into a profound altered state eventuating in a full out-of-body experience. I was duly impressed and became even more so as further details came to light:

D. E. OSTO: Wow!! [in response to the above story]
RICK: And I was literally floating up in the air like a cloud of awareness looking down at my body while I am on the floor.
D: Oh my God! You had a full out-of-body experience.
R: Full out-of-body experience. I was just ripe. And I remember thinking, "There is a paranormal. There really is another world. This is what happens when you die."
D: Right! Right!
R: It seemed like a memory. It just seemed so *real*.
D: Right.
R: Like this was a moment of minienlightenment for me. Like, "There is not just this. There is *this*." [Laughs]
D: Yeah, right! And you were so lucid, rationally lucid too, it sounds like. You were reflecting on the process as it is happening.
R: I had very clear insight-type thoughts. And I remember thinking, "Death is not the end." Kind of like when people have near-death experiences, which I haven't felt yet, but this was . . .
D: You just kind of intuited it.
R: I immediately came to that recognition, "This is real. It is not just the body." And I thought, "I wonder how to get back in?"
D: [Laughs] Yeah, right!
R: I got a little afraid, and was like, "If this is like death, maybe I am dead!"
D: And then you went . . .
R: Swoosh [demonstrates with his hand as if going into something], right back in.
D: Yep.
R: And I lay there on the floor feeling like two bodies—the etheric or astral, or energy body, or whatever, superimposed over and inside my physical body. And I just laid there for a while just feeling both. Oh, I remember

also—I forgot to mention this—when I was in that place, I noticed certain things in the room that I hadn't seen. Like everything was transparent. So, there were things behind my dresser that had fallen and whatnot. And I remember looking around and feeling like I could see through things like there were two worlds—this one and that one. One that was light-like, made out of light, and the other one was physical. And when I came back after I had recuperated and I felt like, "Okay, I can get up now," I went and checked and the things that I mentally "saw." They were there.

D: They were there?

R: That piece of paper and whatnot, yeah. So, I don't know. I thought, "This was real."

D: That is amazing. And you were what, how old were you?

R: Fifteen.

D: Fifteen? Wow! That is intense.

R: Yeah.

D: Yeah, that by itself would change someone . . .

R: I hadn't read about any of this stuff.

D: Yeah, because some of the characteristics are just *classic*. There is a large body of data that people have collected about out-of-body experiences, and this fits the general pattern. And the kind of energy body versus the physical body that is often described maps perfectly onto your experience.

R: Yes.

D: So, that is intense. So what happened after that? I mean, that is the kind of thing that changes somebody's whole life.

R: I am who I am now because of that.

D: [Laughs] So that one event . . .

R: Yep.

Following this experience, Rick began a quest to learn more about yoga, meditation, and Asian religions. His first stop was his local library, where he found several books that had inspired an entire generation of young Americans, such as Ram Dass's *Be Here Now*, Iyengar's *Light on Yoga*, Paramahansa Yogananda's *Autobiography of a Yogi*, Robert Pirsig's *Zen and the Art of Motorcycle Maintenance*, and Shunryu Suzuki's *Zen Mind/Beginner's Mind*. He read D. T. Suzuki and Alan Watts's books on Zen and anything else he could

THE YOGIN

find about Eastern thought or meditation. Alongside this intense reading, he taught himself yoga and began practicing meditation.

Rick told me how he fell in love with *Be Here Now*[4] and how Ram Dass's account of his LSD experiences inspired him to experiment with psychedelics. Commenting on this, he laughingly told me the book made him think, "I can try LSD and that it was safe." Adding psychedelics to his yoga and meditation, Repetti claims created a "synergy," which I interpret to mean that these mind-altering practices alchemically combined to ripen Rick for the psychic and paranormal events that would soon follow.

Rick quickly became the "meditation/yoga/LSD guy" among his campus and high school friends, sharing his newfound passions with fellow spiritual seekers. Then one day a few months after his initial OBE, one such friend invited Rick to come along to a meditation group he had heard of in Greenwich Village led by a teacher who had lived in India for many years studying with spiritual masters. Rick was keen, so the next Thursday evening he and his friend made their way to the basement of St. Luke's Church in the Village for a meeting. There was some singing and chanting, and then a woman named Hilda came out, gave a talk, and led a meditation.

Hilda Charlton (1906–1988) was a well-known spiritual guide who taught classes in meditation and prayer in New York City for twenty-three years.[5] Charlton was born in London and moved to the United States with her parents when she was four years old. At eighteen, she began her professional dancing career in the San Francisco area. In 1947 she traveled to India and toured as a dancer for three years. Following this, she remained in India for fifteen years studying with various gurus such as Sri Nityananda, Sri Mahadevananda, and Sri Sathya Sai Baba. Upon her return to the United States in 1966, Hilda began teaching meditation and prayer in New York City, first at St. Luke's Church and then from 1976 to 1987 at the Cathedral of St. John the Divine.

This first encounter with the group had a profound impact on the young Repetti:

R: I went in and there was a lot of déjà vu when I went into the meditation meeting . . .
D: Sure, like you recognized them . . .

R: It felt like I recognized them from another lifetime! And it was just an overwhelming feeling—a kind of connectivity—that I just like [snaps his fingers], "Drank the Kool-Aid," and the teachings ...
D: [Laughs]

This first meeting also resulted in Rick drastically changing his lifestyle: "When I went to the first meeting ... I got sold on purification. So, I became a vegetarian, a celibate, I quit smoking, I quit drinking, I quit doing drugs, I quit everything. Because in that very first day ... Hilda ... quoted him [Sai Baba] as saying something like, 'Psychedelics are like plastic grapes, compared to wine,' or something like that. And something clicked in me [snaps fingers]."

Following this intense first encounter, Rick became a regular at the meetings. Unbeknownst to him at the time, Hilda was one of a trio of teachers in the New York City area who often taught together and shared many of the same students. Repetti quickly became tightly bonded with a core group of serious practitioners. His regular engagement with these people marked the beginning for Rick of a period of intense psychic and paranormal phenomena. From our discussions, Repetti attributes these events to three interrelated factors. First, he postulates that he may be psychologically predisposed to these phenomena through previous karma. Second, he sees an association between his intense meditational and purification practices and these phenomena (some of these were directly induced through meditation, whereas others occurred spontaneously). Particularly, he mentioned to me the practices described in Patañjali's *Yogasūtra* (see chapter 1 for details). And third, he sees his association with these other like-minded practitioners as creating a "gestalt" imbued with extraordinary potential to induce psychic and paranormal phenomena. In his words:

> A lot of these things happened to me not when I was meditating (many things did happen to me when I was meditating), but so many of these other experiences happened in the period of my life where I was living an almost monastic lifestyle. . . . I attribute them to the practice with people who were also pretty sensitive, psychic, you know spiritually evolved kind of thing, and I think there is some kind of—I don't know what it is—but there is some kind of gestalt activity thing. You know when you meditate with people, when you do psychedelics with them, you know something happens.

I should say here, for the sake of full disclosure, I find Rick's explanation entirely convincing based both on the research I have done on psi and paranormal phenomena and on my personal experiences. As I have outlined in the previous chapters, there is a strong connection between intense meditation practice and these phenomena. Moreover, as modern researchers have pointed out, some individuals ("exceptional subjects") are much more prone to psi. Whereas the default Buddhist explanation for this is karma, modern psychic researchers would likely attribute this predisposition to genetic inheritance. From my several hours of conversation with Rick, I found him to be extremely rational and very modest in cautiously offering explanations for the phenomena he experienced. Often, he seemed genuinely perplexed as to the ultimate cause or significance of much of what happened to him. Nevertheless, despite his general skepticism, he stands by the veracity of his experiences. In other words, while he admits he may not truly understand what happened to him, the fact that significant paranormal events did take place he accepts as the simplest explanation in many cases. This kind of "double vision" about these past events as both skeptic and experiencer Rick nicely summarizes by calling himself an "agnostic gnostic."

After about six months of going to Hilda's group, Rick met the other two teachers of the spiritual triumvirate. About the first, the following conversation took place:

R: I went there for a few months, and I was talking to one of my best friends, Barry, "You got to go, you got to go, you got to," and finally I talked him in to coming. And when we got there, Hilda wasn't there. Ram Dass was there in her place.
D: Wow.
R: And he introduced himself, and a lot of them already knew him. And he said, "Hilda has a cold or something and she asked me to cover for her today."
D: [Laughs]
R: I'm in the right place!
D: And you had no idea that they were connected?
R: No! I had no idea that he had anything to do with her.
D: Wow.
R: And that was the first time Barry went, and Barry had read *Be Here Now*, so he was like, "I'm sold on this."

Ram Dass (1931–2019), aka Richard Alpert, a Harvard psychologist, psychedelic researcher, and famed "homegrown" American guru and author of the hippy classic *Be Here Now* (1971), hardly needs introduction.[6] Alpert rose to infamy as the colleague and co-researcher of psychedelics with Timothy Leary under the auspices of the Harvard Psilocybin Project in the early 1960s.[7] After their dismissal from Harvard, the psychologists spearheaded the psychedelic revolution among members of the American counterculture. Then in 1967, Alpert traveled to India, met his guru Neem Karoli Baba, and returned to the United States as Ram Dass, becoming an American teacher of Hindu and Buddhist spirituality. His book *Be Here Now* (one of many) became a counterculture classic and influenced the lives of millions of young spiritual seekers. Dass continued to teach and serve others until his death in 2019.[8]

Around this time, Rick met the third teacher, Joya, when Hilda brought her to the group one evening. Rick remembers feeling an immediate and powerful connection to Joya: "When I saw her, I felt like I knew her. I felt this tremendous energy connection with her. It was like lightning had walked into the room or something." Colette Dowling writes at length about the relationship between Joya Santayana (given name, Joyce Green) and Ram Dass in a 1977 article for the *New York Times*, "Confessions of an American Guru."[9] About Joya, Dowling writes that she was "a Jewish housewife from Brooklyn in her mid-thirties who'd been married to an Italian Roman Catholic since she was 15" and that she "had a faculty that made her, at least to Ram Dass, fascinating in the extreme. She went into trances." According to Dowling, Hilda Charlton introduced Ram Dass to Joya in her Brooklyn apartment. When they arrived, Joya was deep in *samādhi*. When she arose from her trance and saw them, the first thing she did was shout, "What the hell do you want?"[10] From this moment, Ram Dass was hooked.

During their interview for Dowling's article, Dass confessed that he was for a time completely taken in by Joya's charismatic personality. During this period in New York together, the two were inseparable and often seen holding hands and being affectionate to each other. When Dowling asked both if they had a sexual relationship, Joya emphatically denied it, while Dass demurred to give a direct answer. Regardless, it was obvious to their followers that their relationship was intimate and intense. However, by 1975 their spiritual romance was over, with Ram Dass claiming in *Yoga Journal* that he had been seduced by her "combination of powerful charisma and chutzpah."[11]

At the time of Rick's first meeting with Joya (1973/1974), all three teachers—Hilda, Ram Dass, and Joya—were on good terms and teaching (sometimes together) a loose-knit group of students and spiritual seekers, who would move freely among them. It was during this time in Rick's life of intense practice with these people that his psychic and paranormal experiences reached a fever pitch.

Rick described this period of his life (1974–1978) as a time when he had "many meditative trances, out-of-body experiences, and related psychic phenomena (telepathy, shared dreams, etc.)." He told me that it was as if he was living in some type of "psychic zone" within which he had numerous "samadhi experiences, continuous consciousness through the waking/dreaming/dreamless cycles, flow states, déjà vu-like recollections throughout the day about phenomena just before they arose, endless synchronicities, visions, seeing auras, etc." Repetti emphasized to me that he had had so many of these experiences that he has forgotten most of them. However, the events he does remember and related to me stand out for their vividness and detail. During our conversations, Rick was not prone to boasting, and his demeanor was often matter of fact. He provided recollections of events as accurately as he could remember them, adding little commentary as to their deeper meanings or significance. However, in emphasizing the intensity of daily life in this "psychic zone" he did have this to say: "These things were happening to me all the time, and if I took the experiences that I had in one day and distributed them to a hundred different people, I would convert one hundred different people into believers in the paranormal. That is how rich that was for me at the time. All the things that had happened to me in those years, it was the norm."

Some of Rick's most profound experiences came in the form of precognitive dreams. The first one he related to me involves Joya. What I found particularly intriguing about several of Repetti's accounts is the fine-grained level of detail and the mention of others sharing in these experiences. Whereas many of my survey respondents claimed to have precognitive experiences, often these are entirely subjective recollections, with the details being vague or entirely missing. However, a distinctive feature of exceptional or sensitive subjects like Repetti is their ability to recall specific information, such as we will see in the following story. Since Rick is a particularly good narrator, for much of what follows, I quote at length from our dialogues so that the reader can get a sense of the storytelling.

R: I remember being very touched, very connected with her [Joya] and meditation and everything. And then I forgot about her. And a few months later—this was in the first year of my being in this group—I had this dream where I got into a car, like a little Volkswagen, with my friend Barry and two or three other people who I recognized from Hilda's *satsang*, as we called it. I never knew them personally, but in the dream, I got in the car with them, and we drove to a certain place in Brooklyn that I had never been before, because I had only been living in Brooklyn for a year or so. And it is big—like a city. But I recognized the area that we went past that I knew. We were in a place I had never seen, and there was an IHOP [a chain restaurant]; I remember seeing that. And then we went down certain streets, and we stopped at a street corner. And in the dream, I didn't know I was dreaming. It was lucid; it was really very brilliant. One of those kinds of dreams that feels more real than the waking state.

D: Yeah, right. More real than real.

R: Even though you don't know that you are dreaming. There are two uses for me of the word "lucid" . . .

D: So, it was vivid, but you didn't know it was a dream.

R: No, I didn't realize that I was dreaming. So, in the dream when we got to the street corner, I remember getting out of the car and looking at the intersection sign—Avenue L and East Seventy-Second Street (I had never been in that neighborhood)—and having a déjà vu while I was looking at it like, "I know this." It was déjà vu, and I knew what house we were going into—there were brick stairs; there was a carved wooden door. We went inside, we went down a black wrought-iron staircase into the basement; it was dark; there were twenty-odd some people sitting in lotus poses and whatnot on the floor; there was a little elevated platform, and Joya was sitting on it in lotus pose; there were pictures of yogis and whatnot behind her; candles, incense, and everything. We came in; we sat down, and we just went into a state of meditation, which was an incredible state of meditation. When it was over with, one of the women who was there, who I recognized from Hilda's meetings, but I had never spoken to her—she had blonde hair and green eyes—she came over to me and she said, "How did you like the meeting?" And I said it was awesome, right?

D: Mm hmm.

R: When I woke up, I told my friend Barry about it. I said, "Remember that woman, you know, who came with the black hair, Joya? Well, I had this weird dream," and I started telling him about it, and his eyes were popping out of his head, and I kept saying, "Oh, what?!" He was like my best friend at the time. "What?!"

"Just keep telling me, I can't say anything" [he said].

D: [Laughs]

R: So, I told him the whole story and he said, "Look, I can't say anything. You will understand more later. You have to go tell Patty." Patty was the girl who brought us to Hilda's. The one who said, "My friend knows this woman, she goes there in the Village." So she was somehow connected to her. So, I told her, and her eyes were popping out of her head. She kept stopping me and saying, "Did someone put you up to this? Is this a gag?"

D: Mm hmm. Go on.

R: "What the hell are you and Barry . . . What is this about?"

D: Yeah, what is this about? Yeah.

R: So, I told the story and she said, "You just completely described Joya's house, the street corner, the outside, the inside, the basement, how the meetings happen." She said that they are by invitation only. That is why they couldn't tell me about it.

D: Oh, my God!

R: "I think I have been invited!"

D: Yeah! You were! [Laughs]

R: "Still, I have to run it by Joya before we can let you actually come," [Patty said.] I said, "Okay, I am happy with that." So, then I got approval, and I went there, and Barry had been going all along, not all along—I don't know how long, but he had been going already. And I went in the car with Barry and a couple of his friends. They were the same people in my dream . . .

D: This was a premonition. This was prescience. You were basically living the experience in the dream before . . .

R: Precognition. The ride there we passed the IHOP, we stopped at Seventy-Second and Avenue L, I recognized the house, the spiral staircase, everything. The meditation was exactly the same. And when it was over, that same lady . . .

D: The same woman . . .

R: The only difference, which is really—you know when a precognition doesn't happen because you adverted it, because you had a precognition ...

D: Yeah, right! So, you get a paradoxical situation ...

R: This was one of those. Yeah, the paradox. This falsified my dream on one level, but it verified it in a *much stronger* way.

D: Okay.

R: Instead of, "How did you like it?" she said, "I had a dream you were here."

D: Oooohhh! [Laughs]

The level of detail in this story is impressive. Rick mentions the specific car he entered and the people with him, passing particular places, and the exact street address of the house he entered. Also, the description of the house in the dream matched exactly the actual location of Joya's meetings. Furthermore, he told his dream to two different people who were both astonished by the accuracy of this dream as it related to real people, places, and events. And then when Rick did go to the meeting, all the specific details of the dream matched the actual event down to practically every detail, including the woman coming up to him after the meditation, but only this time in "real life" saying, "I had a dream you were here," instead of "How did you like it?"

From his telling of this story, it seems like the experience of going to this meeting must have felt like one long déjà vu for Rick. Of course, there are many possible ways a skeptic may attempt to debunk that this dream was a true precognition, and Repetti himself confessed as much for a number of his stories over the course of our conversations. However, as an "agnostic gnostic" Rick feels like many of these experiences provided enough evidence to convince him personally of their veracity, although he freely admitted that they may not convince others.

A number of Repetti's stories involved telepathic experiences, in the sense of both passively being able to discern others' thoughts and actively sending thoughts into others' minds. For example, Rick described to me having a telepathic conversation with his girlfriend once at her parents' house:

R: And they all hang out in the basement [laughs]. And we were hanging out in the basement, just me and her, and I started "think talking" to her.

D: Okay. Please go on.

R: And she didn't realize it, and she was "think talking" back to me. We had a good conversation, a good four or five rounds, when she finally thought that was going on, and I said something like, "It took you a while to realize," but I didn't say it, I just thought it. And she got really frightened, and she said verbally, "Stop! Don't do that!"
D: Ah, so you were talking to each other in your heads?
R: We had this whole thing . . . telepathically, yeah.
D: Wow.

On another occasion, Rick was with some of his meditation friends in the subway when a drunk and menacing guy started hitting on one of their female friends. Rick described it to me this way:

> There were three or four of us, I mean, we were all hippy, yogi-looking people from Woodstock only with the beads, you know. And, um, there was really this rough ghetto, gangstery kind of guy, who was drunk and stood over the hippy girl and was trying to flirt with her, and he was being very harassing and whatnot. And my friends were all like peaceniks and whatnot. I remember thinking . . . well I felt pretty strong, and I know some of my friends do, I kind of whisper to my friend on one side and on the other side, "Let's project the thoughts into his head, 'I have to pee, I have to pee.' And I am going to visualize squeezing his bladder." [Laughs] And um, we shouldn't have done it, it was really stupid, but we all did it, and then the train pulled into the station, and the guy blurted out, "Sorry, I love talking to you, but I have to pee! And I got to go," and he ran out the door, right? [Laughs] I figure he is drunk; he might have liquid in him anyway, but I mean silly little things like that.

One of the most interesting discussions we had on telepathy relates to a group experience Rick had where he attempted to project an image into the minds of the people he was meditating with:

R: Okay, I remember once when I was a teenager at *satsang*, a number of us had these little satellite meetings—weekly meditations at someone's house. I ran this little yoga club kind of thing. So, we do sun salutations and whatnot and meditation. And it was just yoga and meditation, no lecturing or anything like that. We would just get together. I would lead the postures, I would briefly initiate meditation, but most of us were meditators already, so it was just quiet after a minute or so. So, I remember once, intentionally thinking of a Buddhist deity, Tārā, and visualizing her very strongly. And I was trying to make it so that in my mind that I was telepathically sharing that image with about a half a dozen yogis there. When it was over, I just said, "I was just curious, how was the meditation?" And like everybody there said, "I saw a green like Buddhist deity kind of thing."

D: [Laughs] Oh my! Wow!

R: [Laughs] Yeah. So that stuck with me. That was something I tried to do, and it happened.

D: Right. Right. Wow. That's phenomenal. So . . .

R: [Laughs]

D: So, did they give much detail of what they saw? Because obviously once the first one says that they did, it is going to predispose others to that account.

R: I don't remember the details. All I remember is that a number of them (maybe not all of them) but at least three or four of them, said, "Yeah, I saw that too!" One of them said, "I just saw green." And other said, "I saw some Buddhist mandala kind of thing with a green buddha in the middle." They were all on target, but at least three of them said, "I thought it was Tārā."

D: Ah, okay. So they knew what it was.

R: Yeah [chuckles].

D: Wow. That's amazing. Yeah. It is funny that they talk about the—the Merry Pranksters—in [Tom Wolfe's] *Electric Kool-Aid Acid Test*—have you read that? Where they talk about "the group mind?" Yeah, they did all that tripping together and after a while they were all telepathically linked to each other.

R: No, me and a few of my friends who did psychedelics together a lot were linked and had a lot of experiences like that. But the people in that particular group, a lot of them might have been acid freaks or something, but I never tripped with any of them.

D: Right, but the meditation had the equivalent kind of thing. The heavy *sādhanā* practice . . .

R: And we were in the same community, so there was a lot of synergy there.

During this period of intense psychic and paranormal activities, Rick had an encounter with what appeared to be a homeless man, but in retrospect he suspects he may have been some advanced spiritual being:

R: So now I am on the train. It is empty except for this one homeless person. He seemed like a kind of hobo or whatever. You know, the people that carry all these bags.

D: Mm-hmm.

R: They've got all this patterned clothing, they look grubby and unshaven, and matted-looking hair, sloppy, dirty, not a matted yogi. And a real urchin who kind of lives in . . . a lot of them live in the subway, and they only come out late at night. Late at night they will take the train because nobody is on it. They will sleep on the train because they feel safer and whatnot. So there was this one guy at the opposite end of the train. I was on one end, and he was on the other. And I would just sit there, put my legs up on the seat, and you know, kind of go into deep meditation. But I felt something about this guy, and he was older. I mean I was, I don't know, about eighteen, seventeen, or whatever. And ah he looked like maybe in he was in his fifties or something, sixties, I don't know, you know, gray beard and everything. So in my meditation, I sort of projected myself out of my body over to where he was. I felt like I was above him and kept showering him with light and blessing him, right?

D: Mm-hmm. Please continue.

R: And when we got to my subway stop out in Brooklyn almost an hour away, I got up and walked off the train, and he jumped up and got off the train and came over to me as I was walking toward him, because that is where the exit was.

D: I see.

R: And he said, "I know what you did. I know who you are. Thank you so much. To complete what you did, you have to eat a piece of bread." He had rye bread, right? And he was so smelly, greasy, grungy looking, that I did not want to touch anything.

D: [Laughs] I can relate to that. What happened next?

R: And I was like, "No thank you. That's quite alright." And he said it like two or three times, he tried to insist. And I kept saying no, and then he like changed into a different voice, and he said something. I don't even remember the way he worded it. But he said something like, "*This is a deeply karmic important thing, you will understand it at some point,*" or something, "*but you must eat at least one bite of this bread.*" And I felt like he had turned into some kind of master soul or something, a bodhisattva or something. So I said, "Okay." And I took the bread and took a bite out of it. As I was doing that, he walked past me. I turned around . . .

D: And he wasn't there. He was gone!

R: And he was gone. And you know the subway platform—it was an elevated train.

D: Right.

R: So, I leaned, I crouched down over the edge, and I looked underneath. He wasn't anywhere. There was nowhere to hide.

D: Right. Nowhere to go. You have to go out the exit to get down. It is the only way down.

R: Nowhere to go.

D: Yeah.

R: Yeah. He exited this realm. [Laughs]

D: [Big sigh]

R: So now when I told my friend, Barry . . . he said to me, "Think about it. You saw him. You smelled him. You heard him. You touched him. And you tasted a piece of bread from him. You used all five senses." He said, "That is what the bread was for . . . so that later, when you doubted your experience, you would know that it wasn't that you had a . . . a false awakening, or something like that."

D: Yeah. Dreamt it.

R: "You had all five of your senses operating." That is a pretty good theory, because I still haven't figured out what that was about. [Laughs]

D: [Laughs] Wow. That was a lot. And that was in that time too, that real intense time?

R: Yeah, I was in that place.

In this story, we have what at first glance appears to be merely an odd encounter with a homeless person but that shifts into high strangeness when this person seems to vanish into thin air. These raised platforms on the NYC train system are quite high off the ground, and the only way down is through designated exit stairs. It is inconceivable that someone could climb down any other way, and jumping would likely be fatal or, at the very least, cause critical injury. Of course, according to his own testimony, Rick was the only witness to this encounter, but the multisensory nature of this event seems to mitigate against his having had an elaborate hallucination or a vivid dream experience.

As mentioned, Rick's life at this time was filled daily with spiritual experiences, expanded consciousness, precognitions, telepathic events, strange synchronicities, and deep trances. He told me once when meditating one-on-one with Ram Dass that he entered a profoundly altered state of expanded consciousness and that when he arose from his trance it was eight hours later. On another occasion, he went to the Twin Towers to have lunch with a friend, and while in a bookstore on one of the sublevels suddenly felt that the building was about to collapse on top of him. With visions of falling concrete and people screaming, Rick ran from the Towers in mortal fear, thinking it was really happening. This visionary experience, he told me, he had entirely forgotten until the events of September 11, 2001. However, young Repetti's life changed dramatically in 1976, when Ram Dass, Hilda, and Joya "broke up" as a teaching trio.

Rick related to me the profound faith he had in his teachers and his shock and dismay at their falling out. He was still a teenager at the time, and he compared his feelings and conflicting emotions around this dissolution to a kid whose parents were getting divorced: "Yeah, and they were like a trinity of teachers. I thought of my relationship to them almost like Jesus's disciples and Jesus or something. I mean I had this tremendous faith in them. When they split up it was like parents getting a divorce. I was a teenager, nineteen when they split up, and I didn't know what to do. So I kept seeing all three of them."

However, after a while Ram Dass stopped having meetings, and when Hilda found out Rick was still seeing Joya, she gave him a hard time and eventually banned him from coming to her group. Rick described to me his disillusionment and sense of being lost without his community of spiritual seekers and the negative psychic repercussions of this sense of alienation:

> Once I no longer had a *satsang* for support, I started having ... I was so psychically opened at the time; I was having all these experiences. But without that kind of safety net ... I was kind of "lost psychic guy in the world." With my psychic sensitivities, I was safe as long as I was with that group all the time. Away

from them, I was just in the world with all kinds of weird things happening to me. So I started having negative experiences, almost like negative supernatural experiences, negative precognitive dreams. I felt like I was battling demons all night in lucid dreams, vivid I should say.

Around the time of the three teachers' split, the community also lost an important member named Raja. Raja was a Sri Lankan meditation teacher who ran a pizza place in the city, the proceeds of which were donated to an orphanage. Rick used to volunteer at Raja's restaurant regularly and knew him well. During this tumultuous time of the community breaking apart and people choosing sides and teachers, Raja became unwell and had to be admitted to the hospital. Rick went to visit him and recounted to me the following:

R: Raja was a meditation teacher, and when he was sick in the hospital, I remember seeing light come out of him. He had an aura about him and light coming out of his eyes, and I thought maybe he is near the end or something. That is just an intuition that I had. And within a matter of months, you know he was home from the hospital, but within a matter of months, I didn't hear anything about him being ill anymore, I thought he was okay, because he was out of the hospital. And I had a . . . it was like a dream, but it was one of those nights where I was pretty lucid the whole night.

D: Right. I get it. Please go on.

R: And in the "dream" [makes quotes with fingers] Raja descended in a column of rainbow-colored light like sparkles, formed almost like one of those Star Trek teleporters . . .

D: Oh yeah. Teleporters. Yeah, right. "Beam me up, Scotty!" [Smiles]

R: He like beamed down glistening; he turned into kind of a rainbow body of light and telepathically said to me, "I left my body, and I came to say goodbye." But it wasn't in words, it was in thoughts.

D: I understand. Go on.

R: And he just showered me with love, and I felt this tremendous love for him, and then he went back up. And then the next day, I went to one of those forbidden Joya meetings, and when I walked in, Joya was sitting there and she said to me, "Your friend Raja died last night."

This account possesses several paranormal elements. First, Rick sees an aura around Raja and light coming out of his eyes. This vision gives him a premonition that Raja may be dying. The connection between this intuition and the aura is not explained. Perhaps Rick felt like he was perceiving Raja's astral body separating from his physical body. Then "within a number of months," Rick has a "dream" in which he is visited by Raja appearing in a beam of rainbow-colored light. Rick places the quotation marks around the word "dream" to indicate that this experience had a different phenomenology from his regular dreams. It was during a period when he often felt awake all night long, with his dream experiences having a vividness making them seem much more real than ordinary dreams. Rick's reference to a "rainbow body" is suggestive of the Tibetan belief that certain very advanced lamas can dissolve their physical bodies at the moment of death into a rainbow body of light and enter the Clear Light.[12] Moreover, within this dream-vision Raja telepathically communicates to Rick, showering him with love and letting him know he has died. This is then confirmed the following day by Joya the moment Rick entered her meeting.

Before going into details about this next phase in Repetti's life story (*Lebensgeschichte*), I want to mention a profound experience of retrocognition Rick told me about that he shared with a close friend. This event provided experiential support to Rick's belief that his psi abilities are related to his karma acquired from past lives involving yogic practices:

R: So, we were sitting in her room, and we were sitting across from each other and doing this thing. Ram Dass had taught us this little exercise where you just sit across from a person, and you just make eye contact, and you don't say anything. It is a Gestalt psychotherapy thing. I think that is where he learned it. You try to become totally comfortable with the other person, where you don't feel a need to speak or react or smile or anything like that and you just notice what that is like in yourself and in them. And if you are sensitive, or you do it when you are on LSD [chuckles], it is going to be very different. So we would do that every now and then. And this one time we were in that kind of space, but I kind of went into an altered state where I felt like I passed through some kind of barrier. It is hard to describe. But it looked like to me that I was seeing superimposed over my physical body, and I was kind of this big spherical globule of awareness around myself. And looking at my body from the inside but also the outside—it was kind of weird—but seeing superimposed on me one figure after another, which I recognized. Now at the time, I recognized them. Now I don't even remember. I have vague episodic memories of some faces. This was a long time ago.

D: I understand. How long ago was it?

R: I was a teenager. I am sixty-three now. And I thought that they were previous lives of mine.

D: Uh-huh. I was going to ask you that.

R: Yeah. And a number of them looked like bearded yogi type, you know, matted hair, like one after another, and they all seemed like me [chuckles]. And there were *dozens* of them in a row, and there were some interspersed beings who didn't look like yogis, but I don't remember how many dozens of faces. They would come and last for a brief period and then morph into another one. And she saw the *exact* same thing. Because we compared notes afterwards.

D: Yes. I see what you are saying.

R: Yeah. And she said, "I saw several of these . . ." And she described several of them, and she said, "I just knew that they were you."

D: Wow, that is so weird. That is so weird. [Laughs]

R: This is the woman that I had this synergy with.

D: I get it. That connection.

In this story, Rick again recounts events not merely experienced subjectively by him alone but shared with someone else. Tellingly, this person Rick is exceptionally close to. As with other accounts of psi and paranormal phenomena discussed in this book, when experiences are intersubjective, they often involve people who are close friends and family. It seems as if our emotional bonds with others connect our minds and perceptions to one another in ways that we do not yet fully understand. Again and again, this theme occurs in experiences of telepathy, precognition, clairvoyance, and nonordinary encounters, especially when traumatic, life-threatening, or sometimes life-ending events occur. In fact, it is this shared quality of Rick's experiences I find so compelling about his accounts.

As mentioned earlier, Rick's experiences took a dark and frightening turn at the dissolution of his community. He began having terrifying nightmares of battling demons. During the day, at times he would see people's auras being attacked by demonic forces. He felt alone, isolated, and trapped in a frightening world, like a character in a scary movie like *Devil's Advocate*.[13] One nightmare kept occurring every Thursday night (the night Hilda held the meetings that he was no longer allowed to attend). He would wake from these dreams feeling like he was clawing his way out of Hell, unable to breathe or remember the content of these horrifying night terrors. Then one night on his way to watch a late-night movie with a friend, Rick noticed a church from his cab window and immediately recognized it:

R: So, one night me and a good friend of mine were hanging out in Greenwich Village at Washington Square Park, it's a kind of hippy hangout and it was like almost midnight, and we had a newspaper and we saw there was a movie we wanted to see uptown, so we said, "Yeah, let's go!"

So we hopped in a taxicab, and the cab was moving just a few blocks from that neighborhood when I saw this church, and I remember the nightmares I couldn't recall on waking when I was rushing out of Hell, and landing in my bed, the reverse of falling. And I said, "Stop the cab." And my friend is like, "What?" I said, "Stop the cab. Sorry we have to get out."

We paid the guy, we got out, by then we were like a block or two away from the church, and I told him about my dreams. I said, "That church. Just seeing that church reminded me of my nightmares."

And the whole memories of the nightmares came back to me. The nightmares were that we would be coming out of Hilda's meeting, which was in a big church, and walk down the block and walk into another church, which was smaller, and it was this church that I had just seen. And we would go inside, and it was a church with altars and crucifixes, but there was a bar in there, and all these people were dressed up like Hollywood actors or something in fancy clothes. It was like a cocktail lounge, and everyone had goblets of red wine in their hands, and there was this guy, who was kind of like some kind of satanic leader of them, like a priest kind of guy. And I would see him, and he would look at me and make eye contact with me, and it felt like he was trying to suck my soul right out of my brain, and he would smile with an evil grin. And I felt this force coming from him trying to take over me, and I would jump out of that dream; that is what I would wake up from.

D: Yes. Go on.

R: It was the Devil trying to grab my soul!

D: Yeah! Yeah! It sounds like something right out of a scary movie!

R: Yeah. That was the dream.

D: That was the one that you couldn't remember and kept waking up from?

R: Right. And that was the way I remember it; it was a recurring dream. So when we got there around midnight, I am standing in front of the place outside, and looking. And there was a big red painted door, and there was a kind of rectory entrance, and I could see through the window. And I could just tell that this was the place. I absolutely knew it. I felt it in my bones. And we were just kind of whispering out there because it was late, and a window opened on the second floor, and a guy in sunglasses, dressed completely in a suit; he had cufflinks on his shirt, in a dark room at midnight, opens the window and says, "Can I help you?"

D: Woah! [Laughs]

R: He had a really deep scary voice.

D: Yeah right. "*Can I help you?*" [imitates a deep, scary voice]. Right yah, aha. Go on.

R: "*Can I help you?*" [imitates the voice]. And I said, "You know, I have been having these weird dreams. Is there something going on in this church on Thursday nights? Because I had some dreams about this. Some kind of meetings here having something to do with something spiritual or paranormal, or whatever." And he said, "Actually, there is a minister here from down South, who has been holding classes here on the Bible and the paranormal on Thursday nights."

D: Oh my God.

R: And I said, "Oh, interesting." And my friend, I had told him the story, grabbed my arm in fear, you know? And he looked at me as if he was afraid to look back up. And I said, "Don't be afraid. Don't show him any fear." No wait, that happened a moment later. So, the guy, after I told him that, said, "It sounds like you are connected with this place. Would you be happy to come here tomorrow, and I will give you a tarot card reading?" And I said, "I am not sure about that, but I'll think about it." But I was like *I am not going in there!*

D: [Laughs] Hell no!

R: Right? That's when my friend grabbed my arm. And I said, "Don't show any fear." And when we looked back up, the guy was gone. And that wasn't even the freaky part. So now, we leave to go to the movie, and we had walked a block or two downtown to go to the church, and Washington Square Park was further downtown, so we crossed—it was right on the street corner, it takes up half the city block. We stepped out into the street to walk back to the park and talk about this, and we got right in front of it, and a manhole cover right there exploded, a good twelve to fifteen feet of fire as wide as the manhole cover shot up into the air right in front of us, and the manhole cover fell right back down into the place it came from.

D: Like right back on the hole?

R: Yep. Right where it came from. Right in the spot; it was no longer sticking out or anything. And my friend was like, "Holy shit!" And he took a knife out of his pocket and wedged the manhole cover open and lifted it up to look in there. And there was nothing in there. It was maybe three or four feet down, and there were some wet papers or leaves or something, I don't know. Nothing. And we were like, "Let's get the hell out of here!" And we left. [Laughs]

The events of this story are triggered when Rick spots a church from his cab, which sparks an immediate recognition and recall of his recurring nightmare. In the dream, he leaves the church grounds where Hilda was holding her Thursday night meetings (at this time at the Cathedral of St. John the Divine, located at 1047 Amsterdam Avenue, in Uptown Manhattan), and goes to another smaller church. But inside this other church there is a bar, and everyone is dressed up like movie stars. Here he is confronted by a satanic figure who appears to be the leader of some cult, and Rick senses he is trying to steal his soul.

The building that Rick recognized as the church in his dream was the Episcopal Church of the Holy Communion, designed in 1844–1845 and built in the Gothic Revival style. It is a New York City historic landmark building located at Sixth Avenue and West Twentieth Street. Upon approaching this church, Rick and his friend are confronted by a mysterious and foreboding figure from an upstairs window. Following this interaction, a manhole cover is mysteriously blown fifteen feet into the air by a column of flame only to fall back exactly in place—an apparent supernatural event witnessed by both of them. Needless to say, this was a terrifying experience. However, this would not be Rick's last experience involving this church—it turns out that his nightmare was yet another precognitive dream of something still years away from happening.

After Repetti's experience outside of the Episcopal Church of the Holy Communion and "other really freaky experiences like that" (one can only imagine!), he began practicing what he calls "reverse *sādhanā*." *Sādhanā* is a Sanskrit word meaning "accomplishment" or "performance." In the religious context it refers to spiritual practice aimed at a particular goal, and it appears regularly in both Hindu and Buddhist tantric sources. Since Rick was constantly being overwhelmed by these negative psychic and paranormal experiences, he felt like he needed to dampen down his psychic sensitivities somehow. Reasoning that his strict vegetarian, straight-edged lifestyle and his concentration-based meditation practice amplified his psychic sensitivities, Rick began eating meat, drinking alcohol, and using drugs again in order to reverse this process. He described it to me in these words:

> I started eating meat, and drinking beer, and smoking pot, and doing LSD again. And I did that for a while figuring that if all the other stuff I did turned me on, this will turn me off. I wanted to turn off all my psychic antennae. I just figured I need to become invisible to these people, or beings, or whatever they are that are targeting me. *I am just going to shut this down.* And that is what I did.
>
> And I remember reading a bunch of things that were clues that that would be a way to do it. I remember this Indian saint Rama Krishna used to eat meat and smoke cigars or some pipe to stay in his body. So I remember getting that idea from that. That, "That was what I need to do to shut down. I'll do this reverse *sādhanā* thing." And it worked. It took a while.
>
> I remember I used to be so feeling psychic that when I was breathing, I felt like I was drawing life-force, *prāṇa*, into my fourth *cakra*. You know, into my chest, with almost every breath. It took months for me to feel like that thing . . . I remember once when that finally felt like it had ended, it felt like I had another set of lungs that just shut down [laughs]. . . . So, after going back into drugs and this and that—I tried to become a worldly person—it was like being born again in the flesh, not in the spirit.

When I asked Rick if he continued any spiritual practices once he began his reverse *sādhanā*, he told me that he kept up his postural yoga for health and fitness, reciting mantras, and meditation. However, his meditation practice shifted from a mainly Hindu concentration-based meditation to Buddhist mindfulness/insight practice. Rick explained to me that this shift was brought on by his disillusionment with gurus precipitated by the breakup of his teaching trinity and by an insight he had gained about how he had been clinging onto his psychic experiences as signs of his spiritual attainment. The following discussion took place about this:

R: And as soon as I left that trio of teachers when they split up and I was on my own, because I started having all these weird negative experiences, it made me suspicious about that whole approach, that Indian yogic approach. Hindu yogic approach, which is oriented toward out-of-body experiences, astral projection, psychic powers, and I remember reading in one of those vipassana-type books, I forget who the author was, some guy at a retreat during the Q&A time with the teacher, said to the guy who was complaining that when he started his practice he used to have all these rich psychic experiences, and *prāṇa* and whatnot, and they are not happening anymore. And the teacher said to him something like, "Yes, and where are all those experiences now?" Right? I forget how it said it, but the point was, "What is the point of all that?"
D: Yeah, right. I hear that.
R: Having them, not having them . . .
D: Totally. There is a cherishing of them, a clinging to them.
R: Right. Clinging to those things. And I remember having an insight, like my out-of-body insight—this is the thing about vipassana—you get these insights, and there is this kind of gestalt shift in you. And I remember just reading that and thinking that I had all these experiences—positive ones and now negative ones, and when I read that I thought, "That whole thing was a mistake." I had plunged myself toward all that stuff as if they were marks of my spiritual advancement or something. And then I realized, I felt lost with all that stuff. And that one little thing that I read, I was like, I don't have a *saṅgha*, but I am just going to practice this. This is safe. I will stick with mindfulness, vipassana. I will keep my simple yoga *āsana* practice for my body.
D: For sure. Keep your body fit.
R: I am just going to keep a simple yoga practice and mindfulness and stay away from gurus and teachers. And I stayed away from teachers and gurus for at least twenty years.

Rick also mentioned to me that even during his reverse *sādhanā* he kept up his recitation of mantras. The two that he has used regularly since his teen years are the Tibetan *maṇi* mantra (*oṃ maṇi padme hūṃ*) and the Christian mantra from his Catholic upbringing, *kyrie eleison*. Another practice important to Rick during his years as a PhD student was a Buddhist loving-kindness (*metta*) meditation. Rick explained to me that over the years his meditation practice has varied, sometimes involving concentration-based practice and at other times employing a more "open monitoring," as in Dzogchen, or mindfulness practice. Although Rick said that he does not consider himself a Buddhist, he has practiced various Buddhist meditation techniques since early adulthood, and most of his scholarship revolves around Buddhist thought and free will. Thus, Buddhist practice and worldview have had a significant impact on his life.

In the early 1980s, even though Rick had successfully dampened down his psychic sensitivity with his reverse *sādhanā*, his paranormal experiences did not entirely end. In fact, one of the most profound events—witnessed in a precognitive dream—was yet to come. Tellingly, Repetti continued to have these types of dreams throughout his life despite his conscious efforts to "shut off" his abilities. In sleep, the conscious will is taken offline, and the ordinary world of sense perception recedes from view, giving the unconscious free rein. As we have seen in this study, our nightly suspension of the waking world allows on rare occasions for a select few to access extrasensory information through their dream worlds.

In 1981, Repetti began working as a truck driver delivering oil to large residential addresses in Manhattan. Strangely, one of his first deliveries was right next door to the Episcopal church of his nightmares. Around the church Rick still felt extremely apprehensive and sensed that this delivery was not merely a random coincidence but foreboded something ominous. However, this event was soon forgotten, and life went on for Rick, who when he was not working threw himself into his new party lifestyle with the same gusto as his previous asceticism during his renunciate yogi teen years. And then one night in 1982, he had a strange dream:

R: A cousin of mine who was into meditation and psychedelics—we used to play a telepathy game where one of us would imagine a color and the other one would have to guess it. And we always got it right. [Laughs]

D: [Laughs] You were just like 100 percent accurate?

R: Yeah, 100 percent. Well, we had done mescaline together many times. And we were cousins, and you know, we hung out almost like best friends around that time and . . . I had a dream one night with my cousin in it. I had a dream that he was on my oil truck, I mentioned that oil truck to you.

D: Uh-huh. I remember. What happened in the dream?

R: We got into an accident where the truck crashed into a fence, and he went through the windshield and landed on the hood of the truck. And when I woke up the next morning, I called his mom to say hello and I just mentioned casually, "You know I had this weird dream last night with your son," and I told her the dream. And she said, "No way! Hold on a second. Vincent! [a pseudonym] Tell your cousin Ricky the dream you just told me you had." And he told me the dream; it was the exact same dream.

D: He had the same dream?

R: The exact same dream.

D: Wow.

R: And then like maybe a year later, him and a couple of his friends started, like the boss that owned the oil company, he had some younger brothers who were my cousin Vin's age; they were his friends. They were all a few years younger than us. And they started coming down to the yard in the morning and asking the drivers to take them out with them as a helper for the day, and you know, make twenty-five bucks. You know, if you help the driver, he will throw you some cash, whatever. And Vin asked me a lot. Now I wouldn't take helpers, because they slowed me down. Usually, we would get paid by the delivery, not by the hour.

D: Right. You didn't want anyone to slow you down.

R: And I kept saying, "No, no, no." One day I went out, I made my first delivery, and I had a problem with the truck, the front end. And I had to go back to the shop. So I went back to the shop, and Vin was there and goes, "Oh man! I am so glad you had to come back! I got here late; I missed all the drivers. You're my cousin, you have to hook me up, you have to hook me up. Come on, Ricky, please, please!" I said, "Alright." I finally took him with me, and we went out, we made a bunch of deliveries. I was going to bring him to Hilda's for the first time. I was still visiting Hilda's occasionally. I would go maybe once a year, just to see my friends who were still there.

D: I see. Go on.

R: He had heard about it and he wanted to go, because we had had those psychic experiences together. And right after the last delivery, we were driving back to the shop, we got on the highway. And that front end problem, I don't know what happened, but the front end, they thought they fixed it, but they didn't. Like the fender was rubbing against the tire or something like that. Something went wrong, and something scraped against the tire, and the tire shredded apart, and those tractor trailer tires are huge, so once there is no air in the tire, that axle will go down maybe four feet. So that is what had happened. Like a boom! The tire went flat, and the truck started veering to the left, and I am holding the steering wheel with all my might. I must have been doing nearly sixty miles an hour on the highway. You can't jam on the brakes with a tractor trailer or else it will jackknife.

D: Gotcha.

R: So, I am holding the steering wheel with all my might, and I am hitting the brake, but not too hard, and all of a sudden, the steering wheel snapped. That is how much pressure there was.

D: It just broke?

R: It just disconnected. I had no steering. And the truck started going all the way to the left, and I looked at my cousin, and he looked at me, and we both remembered the dream.

D: [Laughs] Holy shit!

R: And I said to him, "This is it." And then we crashed. We crashed into the guardrail and then hit a bridge abutment. And he went right through the windshield and landed on the hood. Just like we had dreamt.

This precognitive dream story stands out as the most exceptional I have ever heard in my research. In it we hear about two people, psychically linked family members, who first share the same dream of a truck crash and a year later both experience the exact same crash in real life. Fortunately, Vincent survived the crash without any permanent disability. When Rick and I were discussing the philosophical implications of this experience, he mentioned that from their shared dream, he knew when it was really happening that if he didn't hold the wheel for as long as he possibly could, the crash would be fatal.

THE YOGIN

Then some months after the truck crash in late 1983, Rick returned to the address next door to the church for another oil delivery. This time he saw a security guard outside the building and several people busily unloading equipment and bringing it inside. Curious, Rick walked up to the guard once he was finished to ask what all the fuss was about. Rick details what happened next:

R: So, after the delivery I walked over to the security guard and I said, "What is going on in here?" And he said, "You haven't heard? It's all over the news. This is that brand-new disco like Studio 54, it's called the Limelight. It's opening up this Friday night. Frank Sinatra is going to be there . . ." And I was like, "Oh my God!"

D: Wow.

R: In my dreams there was a bar in that church.

D: Oh yeah! Of course! Because they are making it into a club. Gotcha.

R: Night club, bar church in my dream! Oh, that is the other thing I forgot to say. In the dream I would walk in, and it seemed like there was Gregorian chanting going on, but when I would go in, the lights would go on and it was this nightclub environment. And I remember thinking—this was such a chilling thing—like I was lured in by something. I was tricked. It was like a bait-and-switch kind of thing.

D: Like, "Oh, it's a church. No, it's actually a satanic nightclub!" [Laughs]

R: Which is really precognitive or prescient of my life at the time, because by that time, I was someone who hung out in nightclubs. But I didn't want to go to that place, but then I thought, "I have to go and see. I just have to go and see."

D: Right. I totally understand that. You had to find out.

R: So, I told my girlfriend at the time all about it. She thought I was crazy, but we went [several months later in 1984]. And she was a party girl, and we were in that party circuit like Studio 54 and that whole kind of thing, but I was like, "I don't want to go to that place, but I have to go and see." And we went, and it was decadent—you know they had all the trimmings of the church—the statues, the alcoves, and everything. But there were people in there snorting cocaine, all kinds of sexual things were going on in corners.

I felt like that character in that Al Pacino movie that I told you about *Devil's Advocate*. Women were all around me who were seductive looking, beautiful women. And there is all this decadent activity going on. It just felt sinfully wrong like. I don't know. I was frightened. Nothing was happening, but I kept thinking there were people there who were on staff. They had the thing in their ear, and they were talking to each other. I kept feeling they were looking at me. It might have been just paranoia, because of my dreams.

Finally, I was like, "Alright, I have seen enough. I don't like this place." And I told my girlfriend, "Let's go." So, just at that point this one guy, who I thought looked like the guy in my dreams. I thought was either one of the bosses there or one of the managers or something. He walked across the dance floor, stood right in front of me, like two to three feet away from me. The guy in my dreams had on a tuxedo and a red bowtie, and his hair slicked back like Bella Lugosi, I swear to God. *This guy* was the guy in my dream. He came up to me and looked me in the eyes, and he gave me that same exact grin. And I remember feeling the same way I felt in my dream, and I remember trying to feel an inner strength like, "I can resist you!" And he just burst out laughing and walked away.

D: He just burst out laughing and walked away?
R: He just burst out laughing as if he had defeated me and walked away. And I told my girlfriend, "That is the guy!" And she said, "Nah, nah. That was just some gay guy checking you out." And I said, "No, no. I recognized him. That was the guy." She just didn't believe in that stuff.
D: Yeah. It sounds like it. Quite a skeptic. But . . . Yeah go ahead.
R: He left, and I realized that he had defeated me, because those dreams petrified me, made me shut myself down, and I ended up being one of those decadent people hanging out in places like that.
D: Right! Right! So, you felt like you let that fear drive you, and then he got you where he wanted you to be.
R: Yeah. I had lost my faith. I should not have lost my faith. That is what I thought, you know?

With this event, Rick's recurring dream about the church had come full circle, revealing the nature of its precognitive content.[14] He began having this nightmare in 1977, and then in 1984, he finally walked into the church, now transformed into the Limelight nightclub (which would soon become infamous for the rampant drug use at its events). Thus there was at least a six-year gap between the onset of the dream and its dramatic real-life climax when Rick finally met the man wearing the red bowtie. Significantly, Rick interprets the man's laugh as a defeat. The dark forces at work in his life had succeeded in scaring him away from his spiritual practice, causing him to lose his faith and willingly commit himself to hedonism. Rick had turned to the Dark Side of the Force.

This experience was another major turning point in Repetti's life. He realized he had gone too far with his reverse *sādhanā* and was playing into the hands of otherworldly demonic forces. What he needed now was to try to understand what had happened to him and to make sense of these psychic and paranormal phenomena. So that same year (1984), Rick enrolled in university and began studying philosophy. He threw himself into his studies with the same passion that drove first his teen asceticism and then the hedonism of his twenties. He became intensely analytical and told me that this "left-brain type focus further diminished the frequency and magnitude" of his psychic experiences. He went on to complete his PhD in analytical philosophy in 2005.

It was no accident that Rick ended up specializing in Buddhism and free will. Buddhism became a major influence in his life when he turned away from his more Hindu, yogic concentration practices and the desire for psychic abilities. Also, some of his most intense and confusing psychic experiences involved precognitive dreams (Joya's meetings, the truck crash, and Limelight), which caused him to question the possibility of free will. As he stated to me, "That is why I started studying free will, because I was like, how could you have free will if I saw things five years in advance?! Or even two weeks in advance?!"

Since undertaking his academic career, Rick told me that his psychic experiences have significantly reduced but have not entirely gone away. He said that usually about once a year or every six months or so, "something weird" happens. For example, he told me that around the time when he was finishing his PhD (2003–2005), he dreamed that a friend was imprisoned, and when he woke up and went to get his mail, there was a letter from this friend from jail. And then in about 2005, he had a dream that a colleague in his philosophy department who specializes in psychic phenomena was having an oil delivery when the truck (another oil truck dream!) slid on the snow and crashed into his house. In the morning he told his girlfriend about the dream, who mentioned it to his colleague. Astonished, the professor told her that exact event had just happened to him.

During the end of our three hours of interviews, we had an opportunity to reflect on the larger arc of Rick's life story:

D: It seems to me that a lot of analytic philosophy that you have done, you threw yourself into developing this other part of your mind as a bulwark against . . . like the agnostic bulwark against the gnostic experience, like the "ag" to counteract the "nostic" [laughs].

R: I love that idea, Dee. Thank you. Yeah, I have always been trying to figure out what is this thing going on in my life, this kind of schizophrenia, you know? It is almost bipolar or something. But that makes sense. But also in recent years, since the more reading I have been doing, and studying and learning about things like Vedānta and various Buddhist ideas, I realize that I would have been better off if I had done more of this reading *years ago*.

D: Yeah, right.

R: Because from a certain nondualistic perspective, the waking world, the dream world, astral world, all of it is equivalent to dreamworlds. They have a degree of reality all based on your karma, so the analogy I would tell people frequently freaking out on acid, I should have applied it when I was worried about the Dark Side coming to get me. I did my reverse *sādhanā* because I thought, "Those things are real! They are not hallucinations."

D: Right. I see what you mean.

R: At the time, I thought that these things are more real than the physical world. They are scary as shit, and I am not ready for it, so I am just going to turn the dial on that. But ya know, [big sigh] I am learning. Still learning [laughs].

D: In a sense, that is the whole Buddhist emptiness thing—it is like it doesn't matter. And it is what I found with the psychedelics too—how for people who are psychedelic Buddhists, emptiness levels all playing fields. So, no matter what you experience, it is just as unreal as anything else. So in one sense you can learn something from it, but don't cling on to it, because ultimately it's all emptiness. It's all conditioned phenomena, and under analysis it just dissolves. So it is an equalizer that way. It seems like we are going to end [our interview] pretty soon; I just want to check in to see where you are at now. Because it seems like in a way that you're at a stage where there is a lot of reflection going on as a way to try to integrate these different phases in your life. Would that be true?

R: No, that is exactly what is going on. I don't have a recipe for how I am doing that. It is just kind of happening in my life at this time. . . . I threw myself into academia, I told you, even when I went back to school, that was my new anchor, analytic philosophy. So, like you said, it kind of helped me with the agnostic part, but now that I don't have anything to prove, I am working on still . . . Did I tell you I have a contract with Routledge for a handbook on the philosophy of meditation?

D: Yes, you mentioned that.

R: I always thought that when I start working on the philosophy of meditation stuff, my meditations are going to be about that, it is going to be a more reflective period of my life. It is almost like when you know that you are in the later part of your career, you can do the things you always really just want to do, and you didn't do that. And just being in that zone is a very integrative place for me. And then you appear at the same time. This is synchronicity, you know?

D: Yeah, right. I know exactly what you mean.

R: You getting me to talk about all this is very helpful to me right at this time that I am working on that book [his next monograph on the philosophy of meditation].

Rick Repetti is by far the most psychic person I met during my research for this project (or ever), and I am not afraid to say that I was truly impressed by the richness and detail of his paranormal experiences, especially his clairvoyant and precognitive dreams, which appear to provide highly specific details. Particularly compelling accounts include other people sharing the dream, such as his cousin Vincent (is this a case of astral travel?), or Rick providing the details of a dream that are confirmed by third parties. Personally, I found Rick's life story compelling and highly entertaining (I often thought while writing this chapter how it would make a great feature film). His initial OBE and teen foray into yogic asceticism and American guru devotion in the 1970s, followed by his hedonistic lifestyle in the 1980s, map nicely onto the zeitgeists of those decades. His stories include precognition, telepathy, clairvoyance, otherworldly and demonic beings, gothic churches and decadent nightclubs, all against the backdrop of New York City. At times

I couldn't help being reminded of the movie *Constantine*, starring Keanu Reeves.[15]

I found Rick as a person to be highly intelligent, thoughtful, lucid, and quite modest about his experiences. Tellingly, to this day he does not claim to understand how the things that happened to him are possible or what their deeper religious or philosophical significance might be. From his over forty years of Buddhist practice, Rick appears to have developed a certain level of nonattachment and sense of humor about these extraordinary events. While walking that razor's edge between agnostic and gnostic, Rick remains both deeply critical and profoundly curious about the deeper spiritual and philosophical significance of the paranormal.

SIX

The Gift

THIS CHAPTER IS based on three interviews I conducted with Kat Smith (a pseudonym) in 2021 and 2022. Growing up in the 1980s in the Washington, DC, area, Kat admits she was a "weird kid," whose strangeness was in part positively reinforced by her family, who told her from a young age that she had "The Gift." However, her parents seemed somewhat ambivalent about Kat's gift, and as she grew into young adulthood her psychic sensitivities became pathologized, leading to hospitalizations and medication, which dampened down her psi. Struggling through her twenties, Kat was eventually able to break free of the pathologization and medicalization of her gift and move away. After living and studying for a time in France and Montreal, where she completed a degree in French, Kat immigrated to New Zealand.

Kat's early connection to the spirits of the deceased drew her from a young age to Catholicism and as a young adult inspired her to get a degree in mortuary science and work for several years as a funeral director. In her thirties, Kat traveled to Thailand and discovered the Thai occult. Existing alongside the tradition of orthodox Theravāda Buddhism in Thailand, the Thai occult involves magic, curses, amulets, spirits, and ghosts, wherein the powers of the deceased can be ritually placed into objects and work for the good or ill of others. Although the Thai occult is primarily about power through the manipulation of unseen forces, the laws of karma still pertain: those who abuse this power and harm others suffer the consequences of their negative actions. However, those who are able to establish mutually beneficial relationships with spirits are able to promote and foster the acquisition of good karma for both the spirits and themselves.

Unlike Rick's stories in the previous chapter, Kat's experiences are less dramatic and focused on a particular period of her life and more about her ongoing relationship with unseen forces. This relationship manifests both in Kat's interactions with the deceased and through her psi abilities of precognition and claircognizance. During our first interview, Kat spoke at length about her relationship with deceased spirits enshrined within Thai amulets and statues she has acquired over the years. At the time, she was working in a metropolitan area of New Zealand as a librarian. However, by our third interview, Kat had left that job and was working full time doing divinations as a Lenormand card reader.

Throughout our three hours of discussions, Kat and I covered many topics, including the Thai occult, similarities in occult and spirit work across religions and cultures, gender and socioeconomic differences in attitudes toward psi and the occult, the medicalization and pathologization of psychic abilities, and the relationship between psi and encounters with nonhuman entities. I found Kat to be highly intelligent, thoughtful, and lucid. We quickly developed a strong rapport, leading to some lively and intellectually stimulating conversations. Kat was often modest and reticent to discuss her own experiences, but I was nonetheless able to extract some interesting details of anomalous happenings. Her approach to unseen forces and psychic abilities was more matter of fact and integrated into her daily life, rather than involving stories of the paranormal dramatically intruding upon the mundane world. For Kat, the paranormal was normal—an ever-present reality that she lives on a daily basis. She seemed decidedly unconcerned about trying to prove the reality of the paranormal or substantiate her experiences as "real." She took it as given that different people have different views based on their backgrounds and experiences. For her own part, she is open-minded and accepting of pluralism, and although she does not identify as a Buddhist, Kat's own worldview is ethically grounded in karma but nondogmatic, remaining open to the endless mysteries of the universe.

Since our conversations covered several topics touching on the social, economic, and gendered aspects of the paranormal, this chapter adds important nuance to the current project that transcends the specificities of Kat's own biography. For this chapter, I've decided to stick closely to my interview transcripts and follow the natural flow of our conversations, interposing my own commentary where it seems appropriate. In this way, the style of this chapter is somewhat akin to one of Joe Rogan's marathon podcasts—sometimes rambling but hopefully both engaging and informative.[1]

First Interview

D. E. OSTO: So yeah, as I was saying, thanks for agreeing to do this interview. I don't have any set questions or anything like that. It's more about just us having a chat in a safe space where we can talk about any kind of experiences that you might have had. I'll just ask you questions as we go, and we'll see how it goes. My interviews usually are about an hour long. If we get really into it and it goes past time, then we can always reschedule another one to keep the conversation going. My plan is once I collect all the interviews to go through and transcribe them.

KAT: Great. I guess in terms of paranormal experiences or just experiences in general with Buddhism definitely for me started when I started meditation. I mean I have always done some form of meditation. I've done a variety of meditation techniques, and I guess that kind of opens you up in general. At least I think it opens you up to the potential for different types of experiences. But I am quite an enthusiast and collector of Thai Buddhist amulets. I have a lot [laughs]. And I know that they are not strictly Buddhist, but they are kind of within that realm.

D: Yes. Although not widely known by many Westerners interested in Buddhism, amulets are a part of the tradition. I remember when I was at Harvard Divinity School reading about amulets in the Thai tradition in Stanley Tambiah's *Buddhist Saints of the Forest and the Cult of Amulets*.[2]

K: And that is where my interest lies in Buddhism—it has always been from a Thai perspective generally. And after . . . I guess the first ones I bought were probably about ten years ago. And I was, and still do, primarily collect ones that are considered *prais*,[3] so they have human remains in them. Or the hair of monks, you know, all that kind of ephemeral stuff like things that belong to monks or to the temples themselves, or were used in any sort of specific ritual, but mostly ones that have to do with having human remains. The idea is that ghosts can assist you in this life, so that they can improve their karma. This was always really interesting to me, so I started buying these about ten years ago. And that is when it sort of started.

D: Was that the first time you went to Thailand? I am assuming you went to Thailand to buy them.

K: That would have been the first time, and I made quite a lot of connections, and thanks to Facebook and stuff like that. You know, you can be friends with everybody on Facebook.

D: [Laughs] Yes! So true. Please go on.

K: Well, I became friends with a guy and his partner who, his husband's Thai, and my friend is English. But I guess I was sort of in that whole scene. I am not sure if you are aware of Peter Christopherson? He was living in Thailand at the time. He is an English musician who was into the more paranormal side of Buddhism. I kind of made friends in that scene, and I started to get a few of these objects, and they probably are considered repulsive to your average Westerner, because they have human remains in them.

D: Right. I can see that.

K: Sometimes quite discernable human remains, or they are treading that line of very, very taboo. Although I suppose in the Thai context—I don't know, I guess you can extract Buddhism from the Thai people, but it is deeply, deeply interwoven in their lives, at least with the people I know. And the context I have been in, it is so deeply interwoven that it is almost anything goes—or at least it seems it.

D: You mean with the magical or supernatural realm? What we would call that?

K: Yes.

D: A lot of Westerners when they study Theravada Buddhism get a very sanitized, Protestant version of what Buddhism is. But on the ground, it isn't really like that. Did you have any problems importing some of these things, since they were human remains?

K: No, I've managed to get around them. [Laughs]

D: Okay [laughs]. Good on you.

K: And I suppose ... No, I don't find it dodgy. I don't find it taboo personally.

D: Right.

K: But I am respectful that other people *definitely* would. I mean, I have had a long history of dabbling in different kinds of magic. Ever since I was a teenager. In the nineties, there were those Llewellyn books [a publisher of books on various occult topics]. And I grew up in the States, so I had access to lots of metaphysical bookstores. Where I grew up, we had lots of botanicas, and lots of Latino influence, so there was always a mixture of magic with whatever, Catholicism generally. So that never struck me as odd—that there are some occult or magical elements in Buddhism. For me it was, "Of course there is." I never stopped to question it, but the things that I have imported or brought in are human or animal remains.

I mean human remains, when you start getting into things like the *luk krok*,[4] which are remains of babies, fetuses, or people who have died in accidents, or body parts that are really easily able to be discerned like, "Oh those are someone's fingers" or "that's their hair," I was almost immediately like, "This is great, because now I have heaps of ghost friends." I mean in my house, I treat them as if they are like anybody else. I mean not like everybody else, but we all live together. You know so I feed them and take care of them, and light incense for them, do good works for their behalf, pray *kata*[5] towards them, and things like that. I meditate with them in mind occasionally. And of course, they do things for me.

So, I suppose that is where it all started. I do still buy some; not as many as I did. It can be quite costly depending on what is going on; especially, the Thai government is cracking down on a lot of the more human remains, the more necromantic type of stuff. I suppose Thailand with its monarchy and everything has got this image they want to give to the rest of the world. And probably every time in the news when somebody has tried to bring babies' fetuses into another country, they are like, "Oh shit, this isn't really what we are about."

Although Kat briefly mentions at the start her practice of meditation, suggesting that it "opens you up to the potential for different types of experiences," she quickly shifts to her real passion—her collection of Thai amulets. The kind she is particularly interested in are called *prai*, those that contain human remains. These amulets and other artifacts such as figurines and statues also containing remains or other objects associated with the dead are part of Thai occult practice and constitute a form of what in Anglo-European discourse has been called necromancy. Broadly, necromancy is the communication with the dead especially to gain information about the future. The word carries associations with "black magic," magical practices carried out for nefarious purposes. The Thai occult also has this popular association with black magic and may be practiced to harm others. However, the strong and pervasive belief in karma has led to forms of magical practice working with the dead that aim to be karmically beneficial (or at least neutral) for both the living and dead ("white magic").

Through forging a relationship with certain deceased individuals by means of amulets or other *prai*, a living person can gain insight into events at a distance in time and space, protection, or other types of aid from the deceased. In exchange for their efforts to help another, the deceased attain beneficial karma, which hastens their rebirth into a better state. However, because these magical practices involve human remains, regardless of whether they are "black" or "white," there are strong social taboos associated with them. This transgressive aspect of magical practices involving human remains seems to hold true across numerous cultures and historical periods. This is a topic that Kat and I discussed in some detail.

K: So that is kind of where it started, and I did have, do have, a lot of experiences with it. And it is just part of my life now. So I kind of accept it as normal. And everyone else I talk to in the amulet community in the Thai Buddhist realm also just kind of live with these experiences.

D: Are these apparitional experiences? Are those the kind of thing we are talking about, or sensing other presences or something else?

K: Yeah. Sensing other presences, the presence of maybe your ghost that you are personally taking care of. And I think for me, I've got at least a dozen or more human ghosts that I care for and take care of, as well as various animals; I've got cats, rats, and dogs, and all kinds of stuff. And you know they are meant to take care of your house, take care of the property, warn you if there is danger, or keep things out. . . .

I have thought a lot about land spirits, which you find in Thailand . . . where that overlaps with . . . in the Māori context; [such as] where and how do I introduce these spirits to Māori land spirits? You know because we're living with other types of land spirits [here in New Zealand]. So, also making arrangements to introduce these foreign ghosts, who are coming from a totally different environment, to the land spirits that we've got here. So, it is kind of a time-consuming process, not strictly Buddhist. But I think it is interwoven into Buddhism such that it can't be divorced from the two. The prayers to the ghosts or the prayers to even a particular monk or temple that I have a lot of items from, or objects from—it's all Buddhist. It is all Buddhist prayer; I sit in Buddhist meditation. So I don't think that even though these things predate Buddhism in a lot of ways, I don't think they can be divorced.

D: I see what you mean. I totally agree.

K: I suppose I would have to ask people who grew up in Thailand what their thoughts on that were, but at least from my perspective, I don't think they can. So that is kind of where I am at with it.

D: Okay. I am curious because I only know a little bit about this topic. So is the idea then, say you acquire some type of amulet that has some remains in it? Obviously, there is some kind of karmic connection the spirit has with the remains. Are they bound to those remains, or is that the link that connects you so that you can have a karmic relationship? Do they have an option to opt out even though you have a bit of them? Or . . . How does that work?

K: I think from what I know from the monks who are doing these rituals . . . Apparently what they do is let's say there's an accident or a suicide—these are your preferred remains. This is only because of the nature of suicide or accident. In terms of Theravada Buddhism, these types of deaths are cases when you are likely to have an angry spirit. Where you can have a person who's angry that they've been, you know, taken; they have been taken out of life basically.

So let's say that there's a suicide. A monk will come and get permission from the family, generally. And then he will take those remains, pray over them . . . I suppose it varies from monk to monk, or tradition to tradition . . . exactly what they're trying to accomplish. Basically, they placate that person's spirit and make them not angry. They make them not an angry ghost or an angry spirit that hangs around suffering and causing trouble, and they negotiate with them. Like, "If we make your body available to other people, they're going to pray for you. They want to do good deeds for you. They're going to raise your karma. You're going to do good things for them. You're going to grant them their wishes or you're going to make sure their house doesn't get robbed or bring them money, or attraction," or whatever it is in exchange for this kind of reciprocal relationship. And I suppose they do have the option to opt out and be like, "Nah, I'm just going to, you know, not do this." So, in that case, I suppose they return the remains to the family . . . or in the case of babies,

I suppose they would in the event of the mother's living, and the mother didn't die, return it to them. So it is quite reciprocal, but it is dependent on the monk or lay practitioner having that knowledge, having a lineage, having been trained by particular masters to even be able to do these kinds of things.

D: Mm-hmm. So, once you acquire an amulet or an object—that sounds like it's a big commitment.

K: It's a responsibility.

D: Yeah, right. Because you're part of the deal, you're part of the contract, or the agreement the spirit made.

K: Yeah, I suppose there is. I mean, you can dress them up so they can be quite fancy looking, you know, wrapped in gold, or they can look painted or molded into clay, like, little molds where they have a shape and stuff. But the ones that I'm mostly interested in are quite raw, quite feral looking, like things that are made in secret in the forests. It's not strictly human remains. I mean, there's oils, or there's ones made of clay, there are some made from the grounds of a certain temple or have been made by a certain monk. Also trees and other plants have spirits. So, you've got *devas* and other kinds of almost fairy-type things that live inside plants.

You're in a reciprocal relationship, so to take on one of these things is quite a responsibility. And it's like, "Whoa, can I actually take this on? Can I do this? Can I take care of this person?" Because you're agreeing to raise their karma for them. Because now they can't do it for themselves.

[Being in a relationship with these ghosts] at times I will have a feeling of something. Or, you know, something will happen or not happen. And I'll say, "Well, that's as a result of my reciprocal relationship with these spirits." And there's all kinds of examples in Thai culture of people being shot at, but because they were wearing a particular amulet, the gun doesn't work; or they don't get in a car accident; or they're just saved by the skin of their teeth. Those are the kinds of things that people usually report. These stories make a particular temple more famous than another temple or a particular prayer more effective than another prayer....

I guess to be in a relationship with some of these amulets you're, you know, praying the Triple Gem, and you're doing really traditional Buddhist prayers to even begin. So, yeah. It's been like that for me for a little over ten years, but I'm somebody who's probably always had experiences.

THE GIFT

Here Kat describes how the *prai* are formed by ritual specialists (both monastic and lay), who through the appropriate rituals broker a contractual relationship with the recently deceased person and then bind that person's spirit through their remains to an object such as an amulet. The person who then purchases this amulet has a responsibility to look after the spirit and help the ghost acquire the merit needed to move on to a better rebirth. In exchange, the ghost can offer protection and useful information to the amulet's owner. In this way, these necromantic practices become enfolded into an overarching Theravādin Buddhist worldview based on karma and rebirth.

In the following discussion, I ask Kat about her upbringing and how her childhood experiences led to her current interest in the Thai occult.

D: So what gravitated you towards the Thai occult? Was it a childhood thing? Were you aware of the presence of others, spirits, or ghosts around you from a young age? Or was there an event in particular that drew you into a relationship with the deceased?

K: So, I guess I was kind of always a weird kid. I was raised by a mother who was a Baptist and a lapsed Catholic, or a non-Catholic father because his family was Catholic. And I became really, really interested in Catholicism pretty young, because I was drawn to the ritual. I mean, I think we must have done something like gone to a mass or must have been invited to like a church or something. And I was like, "Wow! Incense. What big statues! Magical people! Yeah, I'm really into this!" And much to my mother's horror, I was like, "I'm going to RCIA class or CCD class."

And I did that when I was really young, probably thirteen or fourteen, and I was really into the ritual of it. All the ritual appealed to me. Saints, relics appealed; the whole magic of Catholicism and growing up in DC, with its really high levels of, really high populations of Latino, mostly people from Ecuador, Mexico, Honduras, things like that. Where you have botanicas[6] . . . I had one that I could walk to. And I was like, "Yeah, this is it, this is what I'm about." And I knew that really early on.

Really early on I remember having experiences of hearing other things, and my parents never thought that I was ill.[7] They never said, "Let's take you to a doctor," thinking I was mentally ill. It was accepted to some extent. Because I had, you know, aunts that would read tea leaves or read cards. So, my mother despite being a Baptist, which has kind of got a bad rap in the U.S. as being quite extreme, wasn't really like that. She encouraged it, and they were like, "Oh you've got a gift. So, we're going to let you do these things," which was great.

And I can't imagine how bad it could have been if they would have reacted badly when I was a kid and didn't have heaps of agency. So, I did the Catholicism thing. And I hate to use the term "folk Catholicism," because it sounds like I'm looking down on other people. But I'll say "Catholicism on the ground" has quite a lot of magic in it. And that was and to some extent still is something that I *definitely* believe in. I mean, I definitely had a relationship to saints, Catholic saints or folk saints, in the same way that I do with Buddhist saints or monks that have reached enlightenment. Both traditions have statues with their hair or their body parts in them. There are lines of similarity where you've got, let's say, Catholic saints with uncorrupted bodies or they have magical properties. You touch it, and something happens to you. Same thing with the Buddhist saints or masters or people who have reached enlightenment. You know, you've got a little bit of their hair, a little bit of their robe or some rice that that was in their rice bowl, something of them in the very same way. I have relics of them, and I have a couple of Catholic first-degree relics.[8] Managed to get a few. Yeah. First-degree relics of Catholic saints, when you compare them to Buddhist relics, they're very similar. Yeah, you know, people who have reached a certain state by what they've done here on earth, their remains are, for lack of a better word, magical. They contain something of their essence, enough that it can affect our lives.

So, I've kind of just always been like this. I've always been reading cards or communing with something or investigating something. I went to esoteric meetings; I spent a lot of time in metaphysical bookstores. These things never really struck me as odd. I have a high tolerance for the taboo, so I was never put off by the potentially taboo nature of Thai occult Buddhism, which can sometimes get . . . you know, people are horrified, even Thai friends of mine here in New Zealand. Sometimes when I have invited them over and I have a living room where the stuff is set up on an altar space. They're like, "Oh my God, my mom said I'm not supposed to talk about this stuff. This stuff is bad, you know." And I forget. And I'm like, "I'm sorry." So, even amongst other Buddhists, they're kind of like, "Oh, I don't know about that. That's, that's necromancy."

THE GIFT

Here Kat touches on several aspects from her childhood and early adulthood that shed important light on her current fascination with the Thai occult. The first is her "weirdness," which seemed to draw her naturally to the magic and ritual of Catholicism. She also mentioned how she "heard other things" when she was young, but her parents, particularly her mother, accepted these experiences as a "gift" and not a sign of mental illness, which was fortuitous for Kat. She also points out the strong similarities between the Catholic and Buddhist veneration of saints and relics. And indeed, this is the case, as shown by important studies on the subject by Peter Brown on medieval Christianity and Stanley Tambiah on modern Thai Buddhism.[9] Kat mentions how she also has acquired some Catholic relics and is still drawn to this aspect of the tradition. She also touches on the taboo nature of the Thai occult even for some of the Thai Buddhists she knows.

In the next section, I make the comparison of her interest in magic and the occult to notions found in Indian tantra and ask about her experiences with Buddhism. She also discusses her work as a funeral director and her lifelong interest in and connection with the deceased.

D: So can I ask... It strikes me as almost kind of tantric. That for you, there's always been a draw toward tantric practices such as magic and the ritual use of human remains. Is that true?

K: Yeah. It seems that way; I totally agree.

D: And you are right, there is this really strong overlap between saints and relics and things like that. But was there something about the Buddhist worldview and maybe karma and rebirth that you found more attractive than, say, Catholicism? Or do you have your own views on these things, and they dovetail with some of these Buddhist ideas? How do these interests fit into your Buddhist practice? Like you've mentioned that you do meditation and stuff, too. So how do these things relate? I know, that's a very open-ended question...

K: But no, I get that. I did end up probably, when I was in my late teens, abandoning the more Catholic aspect of everything, because it's quite punitive with things like original sin. Also, certain teleological issues which (although I didn't realize it at the time) I was beginning to move away from. And I did a retreat probably when I was maybe sixteen or seventeen. It was a Buddhist retreat, and I think it was Pure Land

Buddhism. Maybe it was like a week or so and I was like, "Okay, well I have a strong feeling that I'm moving towards this kind of world," knowing that Buddhism like Christianity is really broad and really individual in some ways. But that's when I started going into different types of Buddhism. I tried Zen Buddhism. I did a retreat with that. And like Pure Land, I didn't really stick with that for too much. It didn't really hit me the right way. I did go into more tantric practices. . . .

I was a funeral director in the U.S. for a long time, so I've always kind of worked with the dead. Well, I did that for about ten years, and I suppose that I was led into that as a result of feeling like working with the dead was my role here. Here in this life, I mean. I guess maybe like a psychopomp [a guide of souls] or something like that, but I really just was in service to the dead and taking care of their bodies. You know? I felt like that was good work to do. It felt like true work for me. Like it was the right thing for me to do. And I had a background as a bookseller. I would do that weekends, which is how I got interested in library work . . .

D: When you were . . . Can I ask, when you were a funeral director, did you feel a connection to the recently deceased and have experiences around their bodies and things like that?

K: Yes. I worked in a family-owned funeral home at the time, and there was an unusual number of women who worked there. Typically, funeral homes are very much a cismale workplace. So, I did work with an unusual amount of people who identified as women, and we all were always talking, not talking, but we were always communicating with the people we were with. They were not just the deceased to us or just inert objects in the room. They were *people* still, and quite often, you know, we would be receiving those people very, very soon after their death.

D: Yeah, right. They'd be very, I mean, karmically, they're still very much linked to their physical remains.

K: And sometimes when you work . . . because we would do embalming and things like that, you know, sometimes you had to tell them, "Do you know that you're dead? I just want to let you know that you're dead before we start this because . . ."

D: Right. It was like you were saying, "I'm not doing this *to you*. I'm doing this to your remains."

K: Yes. Exactly. And I wondered if some of them just were not sure. It was like, I would tell them, "I just want you to know, you're dead now. Now we have to go through this process." Or, "We need to do this, because you are dead. And you know it's good for you to know that you're dead."

D: Yeah, right. I understand what you mean.

K: And yeah. And then I do think, especially in the case of children, because again, we did have quite a lot of kids or babies, young people, suicides, and accidents, unfortunately. For I was always like, "We just want you to know that you're dead, because you've had a big shock, you know." Or, "You got hit by a car; you're dead now."

D: Of course. Because they didn't have a chance to mentally prepare for dying.

K: Yes. And I mean I'm a firm believer that . . . I think because of my tantric practice and a lot of ways which are informal, but I'm quite deeply into it. . . . People think all tantra is just about sex; it's like, "No, actually a lot of it is just dealing with human remains."

D: Yes. The charnel-ground practices, for example.

K: Yes. The charnel ground. Yeah. And I always felt very close to that. I always felt a bit like that was my role. And a lot of ways that people who end up working in charnel grounds or, even further back in time, working with human remains were kind of a bit . . . they were a bit *tapu*. So, I suppose I've always kind of felt a little bit *tapu*, like maybe this is just what I do. I don't do it now, but it's still a very big part of my life. But definitely within the funeral home or at a cemetery, I always feel something. And I spent a lot of time walking through cemeteries and definitely feel something. So I think I'm somebody who just has a proclivity towards it anyway.

I was never afraid of death and the dead, you know, the process of people dying. At funerals or whatever, I would never cry. I was never really upset by it; I was pretty pragmatic about the whole thing, like, well, "This is for the living, so that their loved ones also know that they're dead now." And I don't mean that disrespectfully, but it's like, a way for the living to adjust to the change.

Here Kat explains her gradual drift away from Catholicism toward Buddhism and her long-held connection to death and dying. This connection she describes as if it were her calling, the thing she is meant to do, regardless of the taboos surrounding death. When talking about this, Kat uses the Māori term *tapu*. *Tapu* is a word common to Polynesian languages and is actually the source of the English word "taboo," introduced to the lexicon by Captain James Cook from his encounter with the Polynesian term *tapu* in the late eighteenth century. In Māori culture, *tapu* has a wide semantic range capturing the sense of both sacred and forbidden. Human remains are always considered *tapu* for Māori. Even though both Kat and I are American immigrants to New Zealand, I knew immediately what she was referring to, since *tapu* is one of many Māori words commonly used by English-speaking New Zealanders.

In the following final excerpt from our first interview, I press Kat a bit for details of the type of connection she has with the deceased through the occult artifacts in her possession.

D: Do you feel that being more psychically sensitive, it's almost a requirement that you actually put effort into developing these kinds of positive relationships with spirits to protect yourself against possible negative influence?

K: Yeah, I suppose. Probably. I can only speak for myself. But yeah, I think if you have a positive relationship with some of these phenomena, it's probably more protective. I definitely try to do things to protect myself. I think people who have these experiences anyway probably should protect themselves in whatever way they need to, whether that's wearing something or carrying particular stones, or whatever it is, such as saying prayers to protect yourself. It's probably beneficial for them to do that, to protect yourself.

I think as far as precognition goes . . . I definitely feel like, because I have an active relationship with, I guess an unseen world, it's kept me from, you know, getting into trouble. Like sometimes, I might have a thought like, "I'm not going to go down this street today." And instead of the street I usually go down, I take a different one, and good job because, you know, there was something bad that would have happened.

I find money, and that's kind of my feedback—money, finding it. And I keep a record of all the money that I find. Sometimes it's just coins, other times it's big notes or other things. You know because money extends beyond just cash; sometimes it is other things of value. But that is my feedback that we're in right relationship with each other and that we're working together. This is the way they give me feedback like, "Yeah, carry on, go down this road, or keep doing that thing." So, there is this feedback that I've tried to develop, like if we're all working together and I'm engaged with this unseen world. You know, I will look for money, and if I find it, then I will carry on the way that I am. If I don't find these kinds of feedback, I have to think, "Well, is everything working the way that it should? Am I doing right by these people that I'm trying to take care of? Am I doing right by my own practice, by my own ritual?" So, I try to find those kinds of ways to communicate without necessarily having some sort of, you know, telepathic experience. Sometimes I get clues in dream worlds, that happens too. Yeah. But I think that probably differs from person to person, I guess.

D: Now, when you feel connected or in contact with this unseen world is it . . . Can you describe more phenomenologically what that's like? Is it more like a felt sense? Do you visually perceive other beings? Are there other kinds of apparitional activity, like things moving around? Can you think of any examples you could share?

K: Sure. Quite often I hear knocking on the windows or on the door, and that used to freak me out a lot. One of the first amulets when it came in the mail . . . I had ordered it. It is from someone's skull . . . There's a piece of their skull cut from the third eye in a circular shape; I still have it. I brought it in the house, I did some prayers, I invited it into the home and said, "You live here now. You're staying with me now. So come on in." That whole day there was this knocking on the windows that was like this [demonstrates by knocking on a table]. Not like a leaf or something mundane hitting the window . . .

D: There was a "bump, bump." I know what you mean.

K: It was like rapping, and I'm like, "You can come in." You know, we have this whole dialogue where it's like, "Do you need help coming in? Like what's going on? You can come in," and eventually it stopped. That is the kind of stuff that happens to me.

I mean, I don't know what the spirit's experience was like. You know, we're speaking in another language. I mean, I don't know if that person spoke English, I don't speak particularly good Thai. So aside from prayers, which are really formulaic and set in stone, you say those things, and it's meant to say, "Come on, you can come in the house." Aside from that, it's kind of mental, because that's where we're meeting on that level and in that kind of place. So sometimes it seems like they're a bit unsure of what to do with themselves. So there's a lot of knocking, knocking on the door, knocking on windows. And it's like, "You need in, or do you need out?" kind of like having a cat [laughs]. It's constant . . .

D: Yeah, right! [Laughs] First you're in, then you're out, then you're in . . .

K: And then they get used to it, and then it's like, "Well, you can come and go as you like, you don't need me to tell you what to do. You know, I'm going to feed you. I will pray for you in exchange for you watching out for the house while I'm at work," and all that other kind of stuff. I also let them know, "You can move about; you have permission to move about, you can eat; you know, this is your food. This is your space." And things like that.

So, there are also dream states. Like, occasionally, I'll have dreams and I can differentiate between dreams that are about myself, like in a Jungian sense where everybody is an aspect of me, versus a premonitory dream or dream work, where someone's coming into my dream and giving me a message or telling me something. I can usually tell the difference between . . .

D: What is the difference that you notice?

K: The difference is, when I wake up there's a different felt sensation where it's like "Oh, that was somebody telling me something" versus "Ah, that was a dream sequence, which is about me, and my inner processes."

D: Yes, I've heard this before. Also, often when people have precognitive dreams, they're more vivid. And when they wake up, there's a sense that, "Yeah, this wasn't just my unconscious. I was receiving information from somewhere else."

K: Yes. Also, for me, it comes to be kinesthetic. Sometimes, if I touch somebody, I know something, or I'll be like, "That doesn't feel right. What's going on with you?" Like kind of an . . .

D: Okay, kind of like their energy?

K: Yes. It is energetic. It's yeah, it's almost like an electric shock, but you're getting haptic feedback where you're like, "Oh, that's a feeling; there's something that's going on for you." And I definitely experienced it a lot with my partner. Sometimes even touching it's just too much and I just try to avoid it, because it's way too much. I get too much coming in. So again, protection, I think in general, for people who live like this is probably good. Even speaking to people or being in their space when they are home sometimes is like, "Wow, I'm getting too much. There's *a lot* of

you coming in here. There's a lot of you in here and I'm picking up heaps of it."
D: Like too much information? Like you're overstimulated?
K: Yeah. Sometimes it feels like that. So I try to protect myself using talismans or sometimes stones and stuff like that to just keep an aspect of myself from getting too overwhelmed by other people both living and unseen. It makes life easier; I guess people call it being an empath. I guess that's the way that we describe that now.

Here we learn more about Kat's life with the spirit world and other psi experiences. For her the unseen world is very real, and she is actively and daily involved with the spirits in her care. She describes how knockings and other signs indicate a spirit's presence. Sometimes she receives premonitions or visitations in her dreams. She recounts how over time her relationships with her ghosts develop through mutual feedback, understanding, and care. While she feeds and prays for them, they look after her, giving her feelings when to avoid certain places, showing her where to find money, and protecting her house. Kat also speaks about protecting herself by using amulets and other objects. Being an empath and someone with psychic sensitivity, she can feel things in certain places such as cemeteries or people's homes or by physically touching someone. Sometimes these feelings are overwhelming, so forms of protection are beneficial for her.

In this final excerpt from our first interview, I press Kat on the karmic implications of working with the deceased, who are connected to her *prai* objects.

D: Do you feel that this view of karma gives you a good ethical framework to understand how these relationships work and how you feel you should be? Such as how a person should relate to others both, say, on this side and the other side?
K: Yes. I mean I definitely think that you don't have to be ethical for sure. I mean you can do whatever you want, but if you have these gifts, or you're using tools, or you're developing these relationships, you can choose to be a bit dodgy or commit crime. You can use these kinds of gifts, or use talismans, or these cultivated relationships to do bad. Sure, you can do bad with them. Yeah, I mean if you have, let's say, an amulet that you

know is all about, let's say, invisibility, and I don't mean invisibility like "now I'm invisible" but invisibility in the sense of nobody notices that I'm here. And I love those, and I use them a lot because I walk around a lot. The city I live in is pretty safe, but . . .

D: You're safer when no one notices you are there.

K: Exactly. And there are times where I can walk anywhere and I'm not bothered because I'm invisible. I am not seen for whatever reason. I am literally visible in the physical sense, but to others around me I am invisible.

D: It's like psychic invisibility, or you're in their psychic blind spot?

K: Yes, something like that. And I could use this ability for bad. I could go steal stuff, or I could, you know, do whatever. But if I use those gifts or I use that object to steal, it's not going to whitewash the crime. I'm still collecting karmic debt on that, perhaps more. I don't know if the crime is worse because it was easy.

D: Yeah. Right. I see what you mean.

K: Like sure if you have these gifts, or you've developed these kinds of relationships, sure you can go rob somebody; you can go do all kinds of stuff, and nobody's going to bother you. Nobody is going to stop you. It's kind of a bit worse. I mean, so I think there is probably, at least for me, a desire to try and do better with it because it's much harder to do better with these kinds of things. I think if you live this way, then it is easy to do bad. I mean, I could get all kinds of help to do bad, and perhaps it would be easier to rob, lie, or cheat or use things like *metta* to try and persuade people to do what I want. Could be a lot easier. It's hard being good, you know?

D: Yeah. But in a karmic scheme, that's a bit of a false economy, isn't it?

K: Yeah, it is.

D: Because for whatever gains you get, you're always gonna pay for it more.

K: Yeah, that's it. Yeah, at the end of it.

D: Yeah. You know, do you want to pay now or later? The smart choice is actually to generate merit and . . .

K: Right.

D: Karmically, and I guess because you're entering into these relationships that are supposed to be mutually beneficial. You know, you're not enslaving spirits and saying, "I am your master, you must do this." It's like, "Hey listen, I will take care of you. I will help expiate your negative karma

THE GIFT

that is holding you back; in return, you do this thing for me. You do this thing for me, and it's a win-win." Yeah, it's not black magic; I guess in the sense of black magic as trying to acquire power for power's sake. Well, if it is a power, you can always choose how you're going to use it.

K: Yeah, I suppose. And I do think that people probably do bad with it. I mean especially for ones that provide protection or invisibility or sleight of hand or whatever. Sure, I'm certain that people do all kinds of shit and get away with it, but it's like, "Do I pay for this now or do I pay for it later?" You know, sure these spirits will help you and that they will help you do bad. But you're bringing both of you down, and also you're probably going to be held extra responsible because you are using these kinds of gifts (and they are a gift) to do bad things. When you rob somebody, you're hurting that person you've robbed; plus, if you're involving a kind of a spirit alongside of it, now you've implicated at least three people in your crime.

D: Yes. You, the victim, and then your co-conspirator spirit.

K: Yes. And I suppose they don't have as much agency as we do here. I imagine you lose certain types of agencies when you aren't in a body anymore. So, I mean, at what point do you say, "Well, I've now roped this other person into my misdeeds," and then you would be holding them back for longer. I suppose, yeah, you have to take those kinds of things into consideration. So I would like to think and certainly amongst other people I know, they try to do good, or they try to be better. They try to gain those merits to live, you know, a better life, or a kinder life, or a more sustainable life or whatever. Yeah, but certainly not everybody, certainly not everybody does that.

During our first interview, Kat taught me a lot about the Thai occult through sharing her passion and interest in it. By explaining her upbringing as a "weird kid" in the DC area, I learned about her lifelong connection to the unseen world and her attraction to the deceased, human remains, and the relics of saints. From an early age this manifested through her involvement with Catholicism and ripened with her experience as a funeral director. With time she came to discover Buddhism and after exploring different traditions found her natural home in the liminal practices of the Thai occult. However, despite its magic and ritual involving human remains, the Thai occult falls solidly within the moral universe of Theravāda Buddhism and the dictates of karma and rebirth. Thus, those who are wise enough to consider the karmic implications of their actions develop reciprocal relationships with the spirits. Through these relations, the living gain protection and aid in exchange for their prayers and offer the deceased an opportunity to acquire the necessary merit to lead them to a better rebirth.

Second Interview

During our second interview, we talked at some length about the gendered aspect of the Thai occult.

K: And interestingly, in terms of Kālī, I do have one Thai amulet that was made by a woman, actually. So generally women don't make these amulets because of where they sit, I suppose in relation to what is practice, women can't become monks, for example, they can be nuns.
D: But they can't be fully ordained.
K: Yes. And in a place like Thailand, where most male people are going to become a monk for a period of time . . . I forget what the percentage is but it's a very high percentage, almost all will go.
D: Yeah, yeah, like 80 or 90 percent.
K: And, they kind of sit in that place. If you're someone who identifies as a woman, you never reach that place, and you can never do certain things such as make amulets. Most of these are made by men by tradition, I guess I would call them cismen, as they're the ones who are making, creating, blessing, and then dispersing these amulets into the public. I have only a couple that were made by women who are in the Thai Forest Tradition. So, these are women who would identify as or call themselves nuns, but a lot of people don't consider these to be blessed or to have any sort of significance. Now, I bought these. Here's two examples made by two different women [shows them to me]. This one, which is like a little *bucha* statue of a mother, and she would have died pregnant, right? So, the dirt, well, this is kind of shaped and baked clay, so maybe it is cemetery dirt. Cemetery dirt, probably necromantic dirt, probably some powdered plants all baked like this clay, and it'll be baked into this statue. And there is [a] little shawl made from the clothes she was wearing when she died.

THE GIFT

D: Okay.

K: And inside, we can't see it, but inside there's going to be a mass of probably bone. And probably some scrolls with prayers, things like that baked into this statue. This was made by a woman. And I paid, let's say, like five dollars, five New Zealand dollars.

D: I see.

K: Because it's made by a woman.

D: Yes, I see what you mean.

K: So, it isn't as good. You know, why get that one? You can have that one. And that's really interesting to me because when I talk to other friends and actually, 99 percent of them are people who identify as males, cismales. Who are into the amulet, let's call it a lifestyle where, I mean, lots of big money is trading hands. I'm pretty small potatoes when it comes to this. The most I've ever paid for one would have been about three thousand U.S. dollars. That's the highest I've paid.

D: Wow.

K: Which is objectively a lot, yes. And the hand, for example, that was probably about six hundred U.S. dollars. It is probably one of my favorite things. I'll find it while I'm talking . . . So, it's really not a lot of money when we talk about some people are paying ten thousand U.S. dollars, a hundred thousand U.S. dollars. This is a major industry in Thailand, especially recently, as the Chinese market has gotten involved, and they have this taste for amulets, especially the nine-tailed fox and stuff like that.

This is another set of *mala*s [beaded necklace] made by a significant monk. That is from one of my favorite monks. Probably made from elephant bone. It's got to be probably sixty to seventy years old at least, with a little glob of *prai* oil. So, it came from a human body and it was rolled into a little ball.

D: I see. Please go on.

K: A sticky looking little ball. But anyway, these are all made by male people. And interestingly, the Kālī example I have, also made by a woman, and it's black. It's got her painted on it [shows me].

D: Yes. I think I can see it . . .

K: Not super clear. I'll try to take a photo, but [it's] made by a devotee to Kālī and it's got some script written with a paint marker. It has some scrolls, some gemstones, some little bone chips, and things like that. Again, this, which is quite big. I mean, it's like two inches approximately. Really beautifully made. You can see that it's been pressed into a really nice shape. It cost me five bucks again, maybe even three U.S. dollars, because it was made by a woman. And speaking to friends who are into this, they easily can say "Women can't make them, because they menstruate" or that "Women aren't as able to memorize the scripture as well. Women can't become monks. Women are, they shouldn't be touched by monks, or monks shouldn't touch them." And there's all these litanies of reasons why women just can't make amulets.

D: I see what you mean. It is very patriarchal.

K: Yeah, yet these work, these work, or they have a presence, like any of those that a male has made. So I find that really curious, and I've gotten into quite a few online debates about that. Some people think women can't own them, they can't even use them, and things like that, so I find that really fascinating.

D: Yeah, let's see. It seems that the Theravāda tradition is very patriarchal that way. Whereas in the Indian religions, the more left-handed tantric and the śāktā worship, seems less so. It's hard to know, because people will say that things were more egalitarian and even, you know, women would be worshipped as goddesses. But a lot of these groups, because they were esoteric organizations, we don't really know what they were doing. Because they're secret for a reason. But my guess is that it's not always that way. And that comes from the Indian tradition with the ideas of purity and pollution, and menstrual blood is polluting. And yeah, it's really interesting too because a lot of the left-handed practices invert all of those things. Because these substances are powerful, they use that power. And so there's this nondualist approach to that. If you're afraid of this and if you're still discriminating between what is pure and what is impure, then obviously you're at a much lower level, because it's all God, it's all Shiva, it's all Shakti, it's all Buddha. So, that's funny how there's that trickle-down effect that the monks, because they're closer to the Dhamma, right? They're closer to the truth, they're closer to Nirvana, they're closer to Buddha. So therefore, they have more spiritual mojo or something.

K: Yet at the same time, the most powerful ghosts, at least in the Theravāda tradition of Thailand, but probably also in Cambodia and Lao . . . but the most powerful, fearsome ghosts to deal with are women, pregnant women, especially . . . they are desirable to use for *puja*, for worship, because of their immense anger, their immense strength. They are the angriest ghosts. They are the ghosts that need to be placated, most seriously, but they're also the ghost that will grant your wishes to speak, answer your prayers or whatever with the highest efficacy.

So it's really interesting how a lot of the, the male believers, or the male people who are involved in buying this stuff have a really, really narrow outlook on like, I'll just say on women and in Thailand, the whole trans ladyboy community as well. They've got this narrow kind of like, "You all can do this, and this is what you do. And this is why you can't do this. But, man, if we want a ghost, you all are who we welcome with open arms!" Like their ghosts are very desirable. I just find it quite interesting. Once you hear people go into kind of their thoughts around women in the community, and of which there are not many. I have to admit, I probably only know one or two others. Women or people who identify as female, who are even into this as a practice, and neither are Westerners. But I just find it really interesting to think about.

D: Well and also there's the whole psychoanalytic take on things where there is the male suppression of the female/mother. You have the archetype of the beneficent mother, and then you have the wrathful mother, and so then you have the wrathful goddesses and the beneficent goddesses. Wendy Doniger, a scholar of Hinduism, she said Hindu goddesses fall into two main types. There's the "goddesses of the breast," who are very beneficent and auspicious. And then there's the "goddesses of the claw." They are the wrathful, terrifying ones. You know, Kālī with the lolling tongue that is dripping blood. And so, from the psychoanalytic perspective your mother is a very big deal. Some traditions try hard to suppress that power. But it seems to find a way out, one way or another.

K: Yeah, really.

In this passage, Kat and I discuss the gender disparities within the Thai cult of amulets. I interpret her several comments about how she "finds it interesting" as a polite way of pointing out the sexist and patriarchal notions concerning the making of amulets, their efficacy and use. The vast majority of people who make and use amulets are cismen (monks and laymen), while the rare amulets made by ciswomen are thought to be much less efficacious and therefore only sell for a few dollars. This notion that men are spiritually superior to women is a central feature of Theravāda Buddhism, where only monks are allowed to receive full ordination (the nuns' ordination died out centuries ago) and only men are believed to possess the spiritual "mojo" (power, ability) to produce powerful amulets. However, paradoxically it is the ghosts of women, especially pregnant women, and transfemale sex workers (Thailand's infamous "ladyboys") who are considered especially powerful once installed into an amulet. Like the left-handed tantric practices in India, the taboo and polluting nature of certain people (low class, untouchables, sex workers, people associated with the dead and human remains) is harnessed for magical purposes.

In the next segment of our conversation, Kat and I talk about the relationship between encounters with other nonhuman entities and psychic abilities, which Kat refers to with the Sanskrit term *siddhi*.

D: I thought it was really interesting how often people's experiences inform what they can accept and what they won't accept. And I was wondering, what were your thoughts on this? Because you're very much into this kind of practice with amulets, but you don't have as much experience with intense concentration and yogic disciplines that are believed to lead to telepathy, precognition, clairvoyance, or other psi types of phenomena. So, I was just wondering what your thoughts on that are.

K: With the *siddhi*s? I mean I guess I would call them *siddhi*s.

D: Yes, the *siddhi*s. That is a good Sanskrit term for them.

K: Yeah, I'm borrowing that word from Hinduism . . . but that's what I always think of them as . . . I find that quite interesting . . . I know people who are quite happy to placate a land spirit in New Zealand. For example, the *taniwha*, you know, like for example, when during lockdown last year, my partner and I went to the very far north to stay with his brother who lives in a very rural area, and there is a lake that goes through that area, and there's some eels there. Now those eels can't be touched, they can't be eaten, you can't throw things out to them, because if you do that, you're going to anger the *taniwha*, and that is just what we were told by more than one person. "You don't fuck with the eels." They belong to the lake, and that lake belongs to the *taniwha*. So you have people who are very happy to placate a *taniwha*, but then when you talk about precognition with them, they're like, "Oh no, that can't be true." I find that quite interesting.

D: [Laughs]

K: But the *taniwha* has got some sentience, right? It can get mad at you. You're going to follow some rules around it, but telepathy, "definitely, no way." Well, how do you think people communicate with the *taniwha*? I don't know. I mean, perhaps some of it is telepathy, perhaps some of it is in dream states. I really don't know. But I assume . . .

D: Because they are talking to them, like, we're talking to each other . . .

K: Yeah. I find that so interesting. And I have met so many people who are like that. Where I'm like . . . so I guess for me there's no line in the sand where I go, "This is as far as I can go, for everything else, there must be a rational reason for it." I'm not like that. So, say for example, I'm building a house, and I keep getting water damage. I would think instead of like just limiting it to, "Well, then there's a water spirit, or a *taniwha* or something that maybe I didn't get permission from, or that I have, I've crossed a boundary, or I've kind of pissed it off in some kind of way, or it's just not an auspicious direction to be building it." If I am getting a sense that something is not right with the unseen world, I would consider that within the realm of telepathy or a similar type of *siddhi* where this thing is communicating with me. It's giving me information. It's more than just about placating it; I would want to have a dialogue with it. Now you've done something, it's responded, you must respond again. I mean to me that's communicating with it. That's not just, you know, changing the direction of where I decide to dig that hole.

Here Kat talks about her experience with other people who are happy to accept the existence of sacred eels and land spirits but are skeptical about the existence of psi such as precognition or telepathy. Kat, however, doesn't draw any such "lines in the sand" to divide what she accepts as possible or impossible. This, no doubt, stems from her own lifelong psychic sensitivity and interactions with the deceased. Unlike some who may believe that certain lakes or eels are *tapu* (sacred) or that there are land spirits (*taniwha*) for cultural reasons, Kat has firsthand experiences, and her interactions with the unseen world and psi abilities seamlessly blend into each other. Moreover, Kat suggests that having a meaningful relationship with spirits, for example, implies some type of psi such as telepathy in order to be able to communicate with them.

Next, Kat further elaborates the relationship between *siddhi*s and interactions with the deceased in the context of Thai Buddhism.

K: Whereas in terms of *siddhi*s, I suppose, the use of amulets kind of belies to some level, I mean, it's considered pretty low level. I've said before I hate to say "folk traditions" because that becomes kind of a weird Victorian term for "poor folks." Yeah, well, you know uneducated country people. But within these kinds of traditions, local traditions, using amulets or ghosts is considered pretty low level. That is not higher-level prayer. That's not higher level moving toward reaching Nirvana, reaching some type of enlightenment. It's very low level. It has to do with love and luck and all that kind of very mundane earthly stuff.

But I suppose the thought is, if you use these amulets and you were praying and you're saying and reciting your *gāthā*, your mantras, your things like that, you'll eventually get rid of using the amulets altogether, because you've reached a higher state where now, you were more in line with dealing with more heavenly-type beings, rather than kind of earthly low-level spirits, ghosts, things like that. It is considered pretty low on the scale, I guess of things.

And that would kind of imply that if you have any *siddhi*, any sort of power like, like say precognition, if you're relying on an amulet, it's the ghost that's giving you the little whisper in your ear. Like there's amulets, they're called *phi krasue*, which literally means "whispering ghost." I have this one. So if I carry it with me, if I get a feeling or a voice literally in my head that says, "Don't go down that road." Or I've gone to the races, and it tells me the name of a horse that is going to win in a race. Then that's the horse to bet on. The whispering ghost will whisper things to you to tell you, to warn you, or to tell you when to do something. So, it's definitely not a *siddhi*; you're relying on that communication that you created. The care of this ghost belies his communicating with me and telling me all auspicious stuff because he has precognition, which is interesting.

But the ghost has been placated by a monk, right? So the monk has placated the body. The body is brought in by the family, and the funeral is performed and all that stuff in the end after that, the monk at the temple or in the forest, he goes through his own ritual because he's somebody with a *siddhi*; we have to assume the monk making them has the *siddhi*, the ability to communicate directly with ghosts as if we're talking now, and he bargains with that ghost and he says, "If you do this, if you agree to this, you allow me to do this. You know you're going to be able to get out of this loop that you're going to be stuck in otherwise." So, by the ghost's agreeing and communicating with that monk, who then through I would imagine prayer and other methods has [the] ability to communicate with the dead as a *siddhi*, by my carrying it around, it's the ghost who's telling me this, it's not through my own efforts. It's not through my own prayer, my own devotion, or my own ability to focus. I'm merely relying on these ghosts who I've agreed to take care of and bargain to keep me safe, to help me win the lottery.

At this point the conversation shifts, and we discuss the socioeconomic factors related to belief in "high strangeness" and Kat's devotion to Santa Muerte ("Holy Death"), a female deity and saint of folk Catholicism and Mexican neopaganism.

K: But to me, there is "no line in the sand," whatever you want to call say a *tulpa*, or a ghost, or whatever you want to call the *siddhi*s, you know, it's all possible, to me. I mean, I have an extremely high tolerance before I go, "Na, that's not real."
D: Right, I get that.
K: Yeah. I find that [range of popular and higher practices] really interesting within Buddhism. But I suppose it's like that within say Catholicism; you've got the tolerance for high strangeness, you know, saints for example, levitating and stigmata . . .
D: Exorcisms.
K: Exorcisms. Like, I mean, when you think about that stuff, *that* is weird shit. You know?
D: Yeah, definitely! And it's not like that doesn't exist anymore. That's still all a part of Catholicism, but you get a very kind of sanitized, almost like an upper-class WASPy [White, Anglo-Saxon, Protestant] Catholicism where it just ignores all those supernatural elements to it, and people just go to church on Sunday kind of thing.
K: Yeah. I find that quite interesting. And but I mean, I suppose where I grew up was [a] very Latino area with botanicas everywhere. And I have a very strong and long-term working relationship with Santa Muerte, which is my primary form of worship. I do tie her into Kālī worship. It is very tantric, and it's my practice. But I think, from day one, I was probably in a psychic space in an environment where that was going to be

part of my experience. But then I think it's a little bit more than just environment too. But, you know, I saw that post that you made on Facebook about growing up in a WASP neighborhood in Connecticut . . .

D: Oh, yeah.

K: Which is interesting because over time, I have had a lot of conversations with people. When I was at university, most of those people I knew who are like that, they don't have a tolerance for high strangeness.

D: Mmm.

K: And in that sense, it's very class oriented as well. And even within the Thai Buddhist tradition there is this layer of class in it as well, that it's like, "Well, if you believe in those ghosts, well you're probably either dumb, you're from a poor area where you're a working-class person, you're a prostitute, you're a gambler, or you're a professional thief," and same with devotion to Santa Muerte and things like that. It's like, well that is relegated to the level of the outcasts of society. So, I don't know. I'd actually have to really do some research into that. But even in New Zealand, I have noticed it. Once you get into that upper-middle-class WASPy kind of way of thinking, that's when the high strangeness stops.

D: And then, yeah, there's like an inverse relationship . . . the closer you get to "Suburgatory" the lower the tolerance for strangeness. Well, it's like since they're getting their power from their socioeconomic status, they have no need for the supernatural, right? So, it's like, "We don't recognize that this is even real," because they get their power elsewhere. They get their power from their social prestige or their income levels, or their Western-style education, where it is taboo to admit belief in the paranormal.

K: Something that I guess I have noticed that when you look at the cost of amulets and some of them are wrapped in gold or whatever. I mean you're talking about people spending ten, twenty, thirty thousand dollars, purportedly. And these are upper-class businessmen. They're like yeah, "I'll pay thirty thousand dollars to make myself invincible." Does it make them that way, or does it make them more money? I don't know. It falls under a really weird place, and I think about it quite a lot. Who am I interacting with? What is the background of people that I'm interacting with? And it's never a hard-and-fast rule, but typically it comes out of rural or kind of urban poor traditions, and those are the people primarily using it. Those are the people gaining windfall or I don't know. I'm not sure, but then I don't know what it's like outside Thai Buddhism. Tibetan tradition reminds me of "university Buddhism," the kind of stuff that you learn when you decide to take a meditation class. And it's not really about strangeness, it's about cultivating enlightenment, I don't know.

D: Yeah, I think there is that tradition in Tibetan Buddhism too, but I think there is also the white convert approach focused on meditation and enlightenment. There are aspects of Tibetan Buddhism that are more magical or shamanic. Meditation and Enlightenment Buddhism seems to be the kind pitched to and embraced by the middle class, the WASPy people. Perhaps they have the same ideas about the supernatural or magical elements, but they are just more hypocritical about it, because it's not okay to openly talk about it in their social circles. But it seems like these different practices from "high" and "low" traditions are all thrown into the mix, aren't they? Because you can't really separate them out one from the other—gender, class, race, culture, wealth, and power are all intertwined with beliefs about the paranormal. But I think our time is about up again . . .

Third Interview

My third interview with Kat took place in November 2022, over a year after the second one. I was not planning on a third interview, but when I asked Kat if she would supply me with some general information concerning her life chronology, she wrote rather laconically, "Involuntary hospitalization for psychosis at age 17." This statement intrigued me for a number of reasons. First, Kat had not mentioned this to me before, and it seemed that such a significant event must have had a huge impact on her. Second, I was curious to see how this hospitalization related to her psychic sensitivity. Third, having suffered a psychotic episode myself thirty years ago following an overdose on a Sri Lankan Ayurvedic medicine containing cannabis called *madana modaka*,[10] I was curious to know about her experiences with the mental health system and the stigmatization that often accompanies diagnosis with a mental health issue. And finally, I was interested in what effect any medications may have had on her sensitivity to the unseen. When I emailed Kat asking if she would be interested in discussing such topics in a third interview, she readily agreed.

THE GIFT

K: Any particular place you want to start?

D: You can just start where you feel like starting. You know, go back as far as you want. You grew up in the DC area, didn't you?

K: Yeah, I was born in DC. And grew up in the Northeast. I grew up there and lived there until my twenties, and then I moved to Baltimore, which isn't far. But between them, when I was a teenager, I lived for a while just out of Baltimore in Ellicott City, Maryland, one of the most haunted places in America.

D: Oh, Wow.

K: Yeah, well that's how they always billed it. And if you've gone to Salem or other haunted places, you'll have tours, and anybody you talk to who lives there will have some kind of story. Initially it was a logging area; there is a river that runs through it. There's a train line and late-1700s-type of buildings. It was quite an early settlement at some point, maybe in the early 1800s. Yeah. And I would as a kid quite often want to go there.

So, I would take the bus down there, because it's, I'd say probably if you were driving, it would take you forty-five minutes with no traffic to get there from DC. It's just outside of Baltimore. And I really loved it. I loved the idea that it had a great deal of paranormal activity and that it was haunted, so to speak.

It had cobblestone streets and very old brick buildings. The coffee shop that I would go to was an old funeral home. There's an Odd Fellows Hall, and strange things were said to happen near there. I was living in Ellicot and hanging out there when I had my first hospitalization. I was very taken with the place, I think. If I were to quote my mother, because she said it multiple times, that there was something about the place that really drew me to it, and there was nothing that anyone could do to take me away from that area.

It is like a small town, but there's a main street, and it was the main street that I would spend all my time hanging out and wandering around. And, like, when we talked about it many years later, my mother did think that there was something almost like the city itself was an entity. It had its own kind of existence. And it really sucked me in, and I thought that was interesting because I did feel that way, I don't know what it was. I mean I guess I've thought about like, "Well did I have a past life there?

What is it about this place?" I don't know, but I was very, very connected to that area, to that place.

Because it has a train line, it had a transient community, like a train-hopping community, and the majority of my friends were from this group. There was a metaphysical bookstore that I'd go to quite a lot. It's where I bought my first card decks and things like that. So it had a vibe of alternative people and just a ragtag group of people, you know, and I would spend quite a lot of time there.

There were definitely moments of paranormal phenomena that happened to me and other people. There was also, I have to fact-check, I can't remember now all the details, but there was the street itself, there was an abandoned or burnt-out girls' school or something like that. That was just ruins that people would go to in the woods. There's a lot of burnt-out or old buildings that had kind of fallen into disrepair. There was an Odd Fellows Hall. And . . .

D: What is that? The Odd Fellows?

K: They're like a secret society. They're a bit like the Masons or . . .

D: Okay. I get it.

K: . . . like those people who put the cloaks on their heads and the blinder glasses and stuff. Yeah. They're some kind of men's secret society. I don't know exactly what they do, but they do have quite a lot of old paraphernalia in their rituals. So, the Odd Fellows Hall was up a very steep flight of stairs. It was kind of like a lot of hills in Wellington, it was that kind of a thing.

D: A very steep hill, got ya.

K: And there were accounts from people who live there of often seeing a man falling down the stairs from the Odd Fellows Hall. It was really steep, you know. Like if you fell, you'd break your neck.

D: Yep.

K: And I saw him once. I mean obviously it was a ghost or some sort of repeat of an accident that had happened, probably a long, long time before. And that was something that most of us had seen, you know, you'd see this person falling from the stairs and you'd think, "Oh shit, someone's fallen." And then you go and there's nothing there.

D: Wow. How much detail could you see of the person? Did it seem really realistic, or were they kind of shadowy?

THE GIFT

K: It was realistic enough that it would stop you, and you'd think, "Oh my God, someone's just fallen." And you go to the place and there would be nothing there.

D: Right. I understand. Please continue.

K: So, it wasn't like transparent, or it wasn't just something out of the corner of your eye. It was enough that if you were with somebody else, they'd go, "Did you just see someone fall?" "Yeah, I think that we should probably go over there." And a lot of people had . . .

D: Did that happen to you? Were you with somebody else?

K: Yeah, it happened to me. Yeah. And it happened to almost everybody else I knew—they had all seen this guy. Who would continually fall, you know, quite often. And we just kind of put it down as a traumatic accident or a traumatic death maybe, and it was hanging around like it would just be on a loop maybe.

D: Yeah, on a loop. I have heard of that. I've read some different accounts of how sometimes it's not necessarily an entity but something like a karmic residue attached to a place. So it just plays repeatedly. But how do you distinguish exactly between a ghost and a karmic loop? It gets a bit tricky. But it's interesting to me that you mention multiple people seeing it, because I don't really believe in an objective reality. But whenever there's intersubjective experiences, that always piques my interest. That is not to say that purely subjective experiences aren't real or valid, but you know what the skeptics are like. If you report something that just happened to you, the first thing they're going to jump to is that you imagined it, or you were hallucinating, or blah blah blah. But as soon as somebody else experienced it too, it then gets . . .

K: Then it's complicated.

D: It's complicated and so much harder to explain away. Yes, well that's interesting, huh?

K: Yeah, they did used to . . . I don't know if they do anymore, but they used to have a haunted tour or a tour where everybody would see ghosts or have paranormal experiences. They'd just walk tourists around the city. They were definitely doing that in the late '90s early 2000s. I don't know if they're still doing it now.

D: Is that when you were there? In the '90s?

K: Yeah, late '90s, early 2000s. The city itself—it kind of sounds like one of those horror films or, you know, some sort of fantastical thing where you feel like the entire city's got its own individual personality. But a lot of people felt that way about that area. For me, I would often sense smells. That's something that happened to me quite a lot. It was one of the contributing factors. To me, being hospitalized was, you know, they called them "olfactory hallucinations." But I would smell something quite out of the ordinary; it wouldn't be attached to or explained by the environment itself. So, they were very, very specific smells. And I was like, "Does anybody smell that?" And people would say, "No." Or I would ask, "Is anybody wearing some sort of weird perfume?"

D: Were they bad smells or were they perfumy? Were they like cigar smells or something like that? Could you identify what it was, but you just couldn't find it in the environment?

K: Yes, I couldn't find it in the environment. Yeah, I would have cigars, or you know, maybe cigarette smells. I would have that for years where nobody in the area and nobody in the room would be smoking, nobody smoked. So it wouldn't be residual, you know. I would try to explain it away while I was there. Like wondering if somebody else in the building was smoking. Or perfumes, like really specific perfumes.

Here Kat describes how in her late teens she was strongly drawn to Ellicott City and the mystique of the place. Its haunted history drew the young sensitive there like a moth to a flame. Enchanted by its old architecture, she would wander the streets of the old city. Eventually she fell in with a group of bohemian travelers, and together they reveled in their alternative lifestyles and shared strange experiences, such as seeing the apparition of the man falling to his death down the steps leading to the Odd Fellows Hall.

Over time, Kat felt that the city itself possessed some type of sentience, which captivated her. She would often smell things—people's cigars, cigarettes, or perfume—but no one would be there. Note the similarity here to Rick's connection to the neo-gothic church in New York City (see chapter 5). It seems that psychically sensitive people are not just opened to psi phenomena and other entities but that certain places, such as buildings, towns, or geographical locations, can exert some influence over them. Such places like Ellicott City, Skinwalker Ranch, or the Bridgewater Triangle seem to function as psychic "hot spots" and are often associated with various paranormal phenomena.

In the next section of the interview, Kat returns to her childhood and upbringing. Here I learn that the accepting attitude of her family was mixed with a certain ambivalence toward her gift.

K: When I was a lot younger, when I was a child, I was described as, I mean, my family kind of described me as a spooky child.

D: [Laughs].

K: I was one of those strange kids, you know. And they encouraged it. I should say that they encouraged it in that they didn't . . . my interests in like occult stuff or ghost stories or mysterious disappearances, things like that, as a child they didn't discourage it. They didn't say "Oh, that's all fantasy" or "Don't be silly" or "That's evil or bad." They would actively buy me books or let me watch the documentary or whatever, but. . . .

As a younger kid, I guess like elementary school age, maybe, you know eight, nine, or ten. I would often tell my mom, "I didn't know you had people, over last night."

And my mom would say, "No, there was nobody over, just me and your dad."

And I would say, "Okay, well I heard a party going on last night."

"What do you mean?"

I said, "I heard a party. There was a party here, people laughing, like a lot of them and glasses clinking," and, you know, I could hear it outside my bedroom door when I went to bed.

There was no television that would have been heard, it wouldn't have been noise from neighbors or anything like that. It almost sounded like a dinner party. You know, women laughing; it was right outside my door. I could hear it. That carried on for quite a while as a young child to the point where my mother did take me to see an analyst. It was a Freudian analyst actually; yeah, I don't think she deliberately chose that.

D: Did anyone suggest that it was a hypnagogic hallucination? That you were falling asleep, and they were not really there. That it was just your imagination?

K: Yeah, that's how he explained it. You know, looking at it now, of course if somebody was trained in Freudian analysis, there would be really easy ways to explain that away to a child or ways to dismiss it. So I just found that confusing. I was like, "Well no, but I don't think it is. There's more to it than that." I mean it didn't leave a bad taste in my mouth, but I just

THE GIFT

thought, "Well, he just doesn't get it; he just doesn't understand." So I kind of kept it to myself, but things like that were pretty common as a kid.

My mother's side of the family and my mother were quite open, like they were curious about it. I had family members that were long dead before I came around, who read tea leaves or were healers in, you know, that kitchen kind of way. Some of my mom's family comes from the Appalachia region. So these would have been like granny healers or medicine people, mostly medicine women reading tea leaves and prescribing things. So there's some sort of precedent for this, and I guess lucky for me, my mom's side of the family, at least, took it sort of seriously. They didn't dismiss me as a child with an overactive imagination or a child that was making things up.

My mom would say "Well, you've probably got The Gift" or "You've got The Gift. I don't have it, but you must have it. You know, my grandmother had it, my great-grandmother had it, my aunt has it, but I don't have it."

And I'd be like, "Okay, well I don't know what The Gift is, but okay."

D: [Laughs] You know, that would be "The Shining" in the Stephen King book [*The Shining*]. Or as they say on *The Simpsons*, "The Shinning." "She's got the Shinning!" [said in the Scottish accent of the school janitor character] [Laughs].

K: [Smiles] It was good.

D: Because it didn't invalidate you, but it also ... Did you feel like it was good? That it seems like you're saying that it was good, because they didn't invalidate your experience, but did you think that that kind of language encouraged you?

K: Yes, I mean, I don't think so. I don't think that it was encouraged because they themselves are not particularly engaged with it. For my mom to say that it was almost like a passive statement, it wasn't all, "You've got this gift. So can you tell me the future ..."

D: Oh right.

K: Or, "Do you see anything?" It was just kind of said, accepted, and then left alone, you know, and I don't think they necessarily knew to or wanted to exploit or ask about it or anything like that. Which I find also a bit interesting, because my mom's still like, "Okay, you read cards for a living. That's cool. You have The Gift," but at no point does she ever say, "Well, can you read my cards?" Or, "Can you tell me what's going to happen?" or anything like that. So that's kind of interesting. I don't know why that is. So it doesn't seem taboo, but it also doesn't seem like something to be encouraged or like a gift to be cultivated or anything like that.

D: Okay. Interesting. So, this was the context, and you are going to this particular place [Ellicott City] because in a way ... Did you feel like it was its own entity and you were being drawn to it? Or was it more an unconscious thing? Like you thought, "This is kind of the place that I ought to be" ... or ...

K: It did feel very unconscious. It did have a hold on me. I'm not going to say it was good or bad, it just was. But towards that point when I was a teenager, like a late teenager, I had spent a lot of time there. I was basically there all the time. And I did have things like olfactory kind of things happening, smells and knowing what's going to happen before it happened. And I didn't really think too much about it. Like, I guess the social group I was in didn't really think it was weird. They were all pretty weird too.

Here we learn that Kat's mother was somewhat ambivalent about Kat's gift. While freely admitting that she had "The Gift" and letting Kat pursue her interests, her mother did not seek to actively cultivate her gift or take it seriously enough to ask for advice or have her cards read. We also learn about Kat's family history of women who also possessed "The Gift"—grandmother, great-grandmother, and great-aunt, for examples. These women were healers and medicine women and read cards or tea leaves as forms of divination. I found this intriguing, and it supports the folklore that psi abilities seem to run in families. This has led people like Dean Radin to investigate the possible genetic links related to psi abilities.[11]

In the following section, since Kat mentioned "knowing what's going to happen before it happened," I ask her specifically about her experiences with precognition.

D: Okay, right. Is there any kind of precognitive experience that sticks out in your mind? So, for example, I have a friend here who when he was younger used to have these weird déjà vu experiences like going into a bar and knowing everything that was going to happen in the next ten minutes. Like what a person was going to say, who was going to walk into the room, and he could tell people ahead of time right before it happened. It really freaked his friends out. Was there something like that that kind of sticks out in your mind?

K: Yeah. And it still happens. I sort of employ it a bit with card reading and stuff.

D: Yeah, it would be useful for that.

K: Yeah, it is. You know, not necessarily know what people are going to say, but I will think of somebody, and it could be the most random person, and I think I am going to hear from them today. And then I do. Or I know who's on the phone, you know, which is a little less relevant now that we have cell phones. But certainly when I had a landline. So, sometimes I knew who it was when the phone rang. Yeah. So that kind of thing or, you know, things would happen to friends, and I would know that they're going to get in an accident or something's wrong. You know, something's not right. Even if I couldn't place what that thing was, it's like, "Ah something's not right. There's a disturbance in the Force."

D: [Laughs] Right! Some Jedi powers. I get it.

K: You know that type of thing. And yeah, it was like a little bit unnerving but also a bit random. It wasn't something I could switch on or anything like that. And even reading cards now, it doesn't always happen. Like I will read people's cards, and I get a sense of what to say like, in addition to interpreting the cards, you know, something else will come through, and I'll say, "Well, this is going to happen." And I don't know where it comes from; it's not coming directly from the cards, I mean, certainly the cards put you in the environment, in the ballpark . . .

D: Right. It's like the context for the intuition to come through, or it's like a channel for the intuition or something like that.

K: Yes. But then something will come into my mind, and I'll just say something. Like, for example, I have a regular client. I hear from her probably every two weeks or so. And I've been talking to her for months about this guy that she's interested in. And we are reading her cards, and I say, "Well, this is going to happen. He's gonna take you out for dinner, probably on Saturday." And she always wants to know the timing of things. And it's my least favorite thing to do. But I said, "Well probably Saturday, maybe Friday at the earliest. He'll ask you out for dinner."

D: I see. What happened?

K: The last time I spoke to her she called in a couple of weeks and said, "Yes, you were right. He called and he asked me out for dinner on Saturday. Now what's going to happen?"

D: [Laughs] Right, right. Go on.

K: It's like, right? Well, you know, my personal belief about it is, it's not passive. You still have a choice in this matter.

D: Yes. I know what you mean.

K: Things don't have to happen, but the trajectory that they are on will lead to certain future events, you know? So, a couple of weeks ago, she said, "Well, we're seeing each other sort of, but he's not really committing."

I said, "Right. Well, let's see what will happen." I pulled the cards, and I was like, "Well, things still look good, but . . ." and I don't know where it came from, but I said, "He's going to ask you out for dinner again. And, at first, he's going to say, 'No, no. I don't want to commit,' or 'I don't want to be your boyfriend,' or whatever, you know, 'I don't want to be in a relationship.' But, if you get up and you walk out, he'll tell you that he's joking."

And she said, "Well, why would he do that?"

And I said, "I don't know." I don't know why I said that.

And she called me the other day. I think it was Monday, and she said, "Oh my God, you were right! We went out to dinner, and I asked him, 'What are we?' And I said I really liked him and asked him if he liked me." And I think she's in her fifties and she's pretty forward for a New Zealander. And he said, "No I don't like anyone." So, she got up to walk out of the dinner, and she gets to the door, and he comes after her and says, "No, no, no. Wait, wait, wait. I do want to be with you. I do want to be your partner. I do like you; I was joking."

D: Oh, wow! [Laughs]

K: And I said, "Oh, that's pretty cruel, but that makes sense." I don't know why he did that. I don't know why that came up for me.

D: Right, right.

K: But he was like, no, no, no, yes. So, I don't know where that came from. I don't know why. I'll say stuff. I don't know why I said that, but it's not an entity. It's not being possessed. It's not like Jane Roberts or anything, where I feel like I'm doing automatic writing, or automatic talking or channeling something. I don't know what it is. I call it clairsentience, but I don't know, I don't really know.

Here Kat provides some important insight into her abilities. Sometimes she just knows things or feels things. It happens randomly; sometimes it is about present things, and sometimes it is about future things. Also, the cards can facilitate this process. This is the "remote viewing" the CIA and U.S. Department of Defense studied. She calls it clairsentience, but it has also been called "claircognizance," the ability to know things through nonordinary means. I have also had this experience several times in my life (see chapter 8 for details), and like Kat it seems to happen randomly—information just enters the mind through some unknown mechanism.

In the following section, Kat talks about her hospitalizations, the effect of her medication on her psi abilities, and her battle to overcome the medicalization and pathologization of her gift.

D: So how did this all kind of climax, and you end up getting hospitalized when you're a teenager?

K: I should say at that time in my life, I was, you know, straight edge. I didn't drink, didn't smoke weed, didn't smoke cigarettes. I took no medication whatsoever. I was vegan. I was pretty clean living in the sense that I would not even take aspirin or Advil. I was a very, very strict vegan. And so, it couldn't be explained by substance abuse or anything like that; it was not side effects from medication either. There was none of that. I don't know. I had kind of a detachment from reality. I do think at this point, you know, a lot of it had to do with the environment. It just reminds me of some of those films or stories where the house's sentient and like kills people, or eats people, or people disappear.

D: [Laughs]

K: It was a little bit like that where you felt like you were in something else, and you felt like . . . I felt like the environment contributed a great deal to my emotional, mental, and spiritual state.

D: Mhm. I see what you mean.

K: And it would either embrace you or reject you. I would almost say even the city had a trickster element to it; that's how I would best describe it. As if it was almost like a trickster, you know. Spending so much time there I do feel like I broke from my otherwise normal kind of day-to-day trajectory. It felt like, I guess you could call it almost possession or being one with some sort of environment where I did start to get somewhat, you know, not erratic, but I changed. The "hallucinations" were more prevalent. I wasn't living with my parents at the time, but I would still see them quite often and . . .

D: Were you living alone when you were there?

K: No, at that time, I was living with a partner, and I wasn't living on the main street, but I was living a couple streets up.

D: I see. Please go on.

K: So still within the city, definitely still within a window's view of that main street called Main Street. I think it's called Main Street. But it almost felt like I very rarely left the area. I very rarely left those blocks of area. I would do all my shopping there. And I mean there wasn't really a grocery store but there are markets and things. I don't think I ever really left. I ended up just leaving my job and catching trains and all that kind of stuff. I became quite what I thought was liberated. But my parents and other people were very concerned because they were like, "What's going on with you?"

And I was just living within this. I don't know how to describe it. Just living within this town or this geographic area. And it was providing me with everything I needed. And I didn't need to be tethered to anything else. At least that's how I thought about it as a very young person. And that did get to a point where I went to go see my parents and they were concerned about me. They were like, "Well, you quit your job. What's going on?" And they even said, "Will you take us down there, so you can explain to us what it is about this place?"

D: I see. They were really concerned.

K: You know, like, "Take us there. We want to know if we feel it, too." You know, I can't quite articulate it. It was almost like its own person. I was *very* protective of it. I was like, "No, you wouldn't understand," Yeah, and this kind of culminated into them saying, "Okay. Get in the car and we will take you back home." And instead, they brought me to the hospital. Yeah, classic. I mean, I've forgiven them since, but at the time I was pissed.

D: Yeah. You would be.

K: Yeah. And I went to the hospital and got an assessment, and of course I was pretty wound up, and it was at that point, and I decided to tell them, basically, everything that I just said to you as well as you know, they said, "Well, do you have any other beliefs that maybe are different than a lot of other people's?" or something like that.

D: Aha.

K: Ha ha [laughs]. And that was the time that I decided was a good time to tell them about the moon hoax theory . . .

D: Oh, like the moon landings were faked?

K: Yeah. You know, it's not that big a deal. I just said the moon landing wasn't real. It was not . . .

D: Okay. Yeah, I see where this is going . . .

K: Yeah. So, pro tip: don't talk about that . . .

D: [Laughs] Yeah! Don't talk about that stuff!

K: [Laughs] Yeah. And I knew it too, like as soon as I said it, I was like, "Oh shit . . ."

D: Like, "Oh shit, I put my foot in it now!"

K: Yeah, and I did too. They were like, "Mmm, really, really . . ."

D: Yeah, they just nod and smile and write it all down in their notes. [Laughs]

K: So, you know, it's kind of funny now. I mean certainly I think if it were to happen now, I think that it probably would be handled differently than when it happened to me. I think people are *little bit* more sophisticated. I mean, I probably still would have ended up in the hospital, but I think there would have been maybe just a little bit more sophistication around the questions or the way that they kind of interpreted things.

D: Did they think that you were a danger to yourself or others? Because that's usually the criteria for being committed . . . You were involuntarily admitted?

K: Yes, involuntarily. Yeah. I mean, I wasn't a danger to others. I think they probably thought I was a danger to myself because I was pretty out there. I think I had a psychotic break is how they described it. So, you know, I was diagnosed with schizophrenia. And I resisted that a *great deal* because I said, "Look I'm not hearing voices!"

D: Yeah right. That's one of the main diagnostic features.

K: I mean at that point it was like, "I'm not hearing voices; nobody's telling me to do anything, so you guys got it wrong." Which again, that's seen as, you know, being oppositional.

D: Oppositional. Yeah. Of course. And so, they medicate you. Did they force you to take medication?

K: Yeah, yes, they did. I was on Haldol. Yeah, *for several years*, the old class 1 medications. So, you know, that put an end to everything, really. I mean I didn't really do too much after that. And was seeing a psychiatrist, and, you know, he was a nice guy, but absolutely atheistic in his way of viewing the world. And I was desperately trying to cling to what I had had. And he would say, "Well, you know, if you're on the medication and you're not getting your premonitions, or you don't smell anything anymore, then we can say that it was psychosis."

D: Yeah. Right. Not really. I mean it's like being chemically lobotomized. So, if you have any psi, it's not going to work, if you're taking like massive doses of Thorazine, or Haldol, or whatever other antipsychotic! [Laughs]

K: I know. That's it, and I said, "No, but it's taken everything away."

D: Yeah, right. It is like you are brain dead. How long did that go on for? How long did you take it?

K: All of my twenties.

D: Oh, okay.

K: I did go back to the hospital another time. Maybe like a year later. I didn't have a television, but I had been somewhere public where there was a television, you know, like a bar or restaurant or something like that. They had a TV, and I saw on the TV footage of an air accident, a plane accident. And I thought, "Oh, that's terrible." I was with my sister, and I said, "Did you see that? There has been a plane crash. Some midair explosion or something." And she said, "What are you talking about?"

And I said, "It was on the TV. There was just like a plane crash."

And she was like, "No, I don't think so."

You know and we didn't have smartphones, so we waited, and there was no other news of it. And of course, this was of *some* concern to her. So my sister, bless her, tattled and told my parents, "I think she's insane again."

And it was the next day, and I don't remember what, what event it was. I'd have to go look it up, but it was the next day. There was a plane crash. And I said, "See, I told you." I said, "I just knew it was going to happen; I just saw it before you all did."

And they were like, "Nah. No."

And I said, "No, it's true." I said, "I was sitting there watching. I watched the news before it happened. It just happened the next day," and I said, "It's the same thing. I knew there was going to be an air collision, air crash."

And that wasn't good enough. So, [laughing] back to the hospital, you know. And I really resented it; I really did at that point. I was like, "Fuck this." You know, I barely get anything anymore, and I know for certain that it was just something that came out. And here I am again getting stuffed with medication. And I hated that.

D: Were you off the medication when that happened, or were you still taking it?

K: No, I was still taking it, and it, it's like something slipped through. It was like something that I hadn't seen or felt in a while. So, you know, I kind of read it as real [precognition] because I wasn't expecting anything. But I realized the next day, "Oh okay. I just got that information before, before all of you did, you know? So that's cool. It is still there." But I was pretty certain that the medication was doing something to me. And it was taking something away from me.

D: Oh yeah. No, it makes sense that something could still break through, especially if it is something traumatic [like a plane crash]. But that's funny. It's funny to me how the circular logic works: people can't have precognitive visions; therefore, your experience was not a premonition; and therefore, you must be crazy.

K: Yeah.

D: It was like, oh, okay, that's perfectly airtight. [Laugh]

K: Yeah.

D: It's reasoning that is *faulty*. Because if people can have these experiences, then maybe . . . I am certain, you know, there are gifts or talents that some people have and other people don't have. You know, it's like, if you're in a country of blind people and you try to tell them what color looks like. No one's going to believe you. So, after that . . . you left. Was part of the reason why you left that area and went to Canada, was to start over, or kind of get away from the whole thing?

K: Yes, it was.

D: I totally get where you're coming from. Because in my twenties I had a drug-induced psychosis when I was in Sri Lanka from overdosing on this Ayurvedic medicine. I took a very, very large dose, orally ingested cannabis in a ghee paste, and then I flew all the way home for like thirty-six hours or so. By the time my plane landed in New York, I was totally out of it. And then was hospitalized and put on medication. And my mom had a psychotic break, her midlife crisis thing. And, and she was on medication for about ten years. She was . . . because my dad was an alcoholic, he enabled her drinking. So between the alcohol and the medication, she was chemically lobotomized for about a decade.

But for me, once I got back on my feet again, I moved away, and I never lived within a thousand miles of my family. And I think part of that was like, you know, family, this family dynamics, and you get typecasted, and they say, "You're the crazy brother" or "You're the crazy sister." And unless you can physically escape from that, then you're always going to be forced to play that role.

K: Yeah. Yeah, it did. I mean like I was on that medication for all of my twenties. And you know there was kind of a point where I just gave up. I was like, "Well, maybe I am crazy," or, I mean, my thoughts weren't right. I was, yeah, I was just kind of like the walking dead, really. It was like, I can't make anything out of anything, and I don't know. And, I stayed, I lived with my parents on and off for maybe months at a time. They were concerned. And they wouldn't . . . I didn't have a car; I would have to tell them where I was going. They really did truly think that I was schizophrenic, you know. And it didn't really help that the hospital would say "Oh well, you know, she's just going to be like this" or "You know, she's probably going to have multiple breaks in her life" or "You know, she'll probably end up homeless. Here's a big book of shelters. It'll get too much for you to deal with."

I mean I was never belligerent. Knowing friends now who are schizophrenic . . . Or I don't know. I actually question that. I know people who are diagnosed with schizophrenia and take medication for schizophrenia. You know, they are also as adults in their thirties, forties and fifties, still very heavily monitored by their family, or do not live independently, or their world is comparatively small compared to other people. It seems to be something that's recommended.

Like they took all of that kind of stuff out of my life. I didn't have much access to mystical texts, occult texts, magic, all that kind of stuff that I have read as a child or been interested in as an adult. You know that was like, "No you don't want to engage with that, because that'll just make you feel crazy."

So it was a pretty low point in my life. Eventually, I had either proven myself or convinced my family enough that I could go to university. I was like, "I'm going to leave the country." They didn't resist that. Which is good. I guess I had proved myself to them that maybe I was on the mend. You know, but in reality, I didn't want to take medication anymore. I did really feel that something had been taken away from me, like, quite profoundly.

I was still interested in the same old kind of stuff. You know, like I'll say occult stuff in general. So that never stopped, but it was a way to gain my sense of self back from otherwise well-meaning people who were trying to follow the doctor's orders. And now, when I talk about it with them, because I've not been on medication for years now, certainly not since I've been in New Zealand and before that.

Now they're like, "Oh well, we can see that we didn't handle this well. We should not have taken you to the hospital. There's nothing wrong with you." You know, as far as accepting that I'm a fortune teller by trade, that I have experiences. Or have had experiences where I live with some sort of gift, they accept that now. They've gone back to like, saying, "Well, that's real. That's true. We shouldn't have listened to the doctors" and it's like, yeah, "Thanks for that."

D: "Thanks, can I have the decade of my life back?"

K: Yeah, I guarantee you, my life would be a lot easier if I had not taken the meds. So I find that really sort of validating, not in that "I told you so kind of way," but it's like, "Okay, well cool that you accept this and acknowledge that you were just trying to do right maybe. And that at this point you feel like there's nothing wrong with me."

But I do think that the years of medication have changed or altered, whatever my gift is. You know, I think it *has* changed it. I think it's something that I had to actively work to regain. I don't think it is as strong as it probably would have been had I not been on class 1 antipsychotics. Things like that. So, I am sad about that, I guess. Not resentful, but . . .

D: Yeah.

K: I was a little, but I do think it had an effect on me. It like changed maybe my third eye, or it changed my openness towards things. And it narrowed it, and while it is still there, but it's not as easy as it used to be, or not as frequent as it used to be. So I've kind of let it go at this point. I accept it, you know, but it has changed. It's changed. *Everything*. It's just changed.

D: Oh yeah. I see that. And it makes me really sad.

K: You know, if I do any sort of spell work, or I'll just use the word "magic" in general to encompass all of those things. If I am doing those things, it's much more of a laborious process to get the results that I want, versus when I was younger, I could just think things and they would happen. I'm not as open as I used to be . . . So it's still there, but it's not free flowing anymore.

I was struck by the similarity in Kat's age and lifestyle to Rick's description of his young adulthood in the previous chapter. Both were in their late teens and followed a strict lifestyle of no meat, drugs, or alcohol. Also, both were spending much of their time with people living alternative lifestyles, in environments where unusual experiences seemed to happen with some frequency. Moreover, both experienced a spiritual crisis where they felt like their psychic sensitivities made them vulnerable to occult forces. Rick fortunately was able to practice his "reverse *sādhanā*" and find a way out of his frightening experiences. Unfortunately for Kat, she was involuntarily hospitalized, medicated, and misdiagnosed with schizophrenia. This pathologization of her gift led to a decade of medication and a restricted lifestyle. Through sheer determination, she was eventually able to break away from this stigmatization and medicalization and rediscover her latent psi abilities. Sadly, however, the medication she took for all those years seems to have permanently altered the strength and frequency of her psi.[12]

Summing Up

When reflecting on my conversations with Kat, a scene from the movie *Shrek* kept replaying in my mind where the cartoon ogre Shrek tells his companion Donkey, "Ogres are like onions. They have many layers." I found Kat to be an enigma defying any neat categorization, and in our short time talking together only a few of her many layers were revealed to me. I have no doubt in my mind that if she had lived in medieval Europe, she would have been burned at the stake as a witch. And I mean that as a compliment.[13]

Kat's descriptions of herself as a "weird," "strange," and "spooky" kid indicates to me that she always knew she was wired differently from most other people. This difference connected her to an unseen world, which exists for her as an ever-present reality that at times she can sense—feel, hear, smell, and see things others could not. Sometimes she just knows things about the present or future. Her family calls this "The Gift" and recognizes it as something that had been passed down the female line for generations. Kat's gift drew her to the magical, the occult, and the Catholic veneration of saints and relics from an early age. She was fascinated with human remains and not afraid of death. This fascination led to her work as a funeral director and eventually brought her to the Thai occult, a system that meshed seamlessly with her affinity to the deceased and her moral sensibilities, based as they are on the notions of karma.

But who is Kat really? A witch, a clairvoyant, a necromancer, a fortune teller, occult practitioner, worshipper of Death? In some sense, she is all these and more. For me, her life story provides a lens into the living presence of the paranormal and how it is deeply and inextricably woven into the social fabric of gender, class, culture, and the taboos and prejudices of the modern world.

SEVEN

Toward a Phenomenology of the Paranormal

THIS CHAPTER SERVES a dual function: it is a summary and conclusion to the current study and a prolegomenon for future study of the paranormal based on a phenomenological approach. Specifically, I propose phenomenology as a bridge between the humanistic and scientific study of the paranormal that avoids dogmatic belief whether religious or scientific. Moreover, since the paranormal is an integral part of human experience, such an approach has wider implications for not only the study of the paranormal but also for human inquiry in general and has the potential to break down artificial disciplinary boundaries and hierarchies within the academy.

Summary of Findings

Chapter 1 surveys some of the primary canonical and scholastic literature that addresses the paranormal in Indian Buddhist literature. In traditional Buddhist cosmologies, the multiverse is teeming with various nonhuman intelligent beings of all sorts, according to the doctrines of karma and rebirth. Also, from its earliest formation, through the Mahāyāna and up to the late tantric phase of Indian Buddhism, supernormal powers, psychic abilities, and magical powers have always been a part of Indian Buddhism. These features would continue to play an important role as Buddhism spread throughout the world. Everywhere Buddhism has traveled its cosmology and notions of the paranormal and psychic blended and adapted to local beliefs and practices. While canonical and scholastic accounts of the paranormal are useful systemizations of the most prominent understandings of these powers and abilities, most Buddhists throughout history likely learned about miraculous events and extraordinary powers from their daily family lives, their local folklore, and the various collections of popular Buddhist stories both orally transmitted and written down throughout the centuries.

Chapter 2 explores the institutions and individuals in "The West" who have systematically studied the paranormal over the last 140 years. Some of the most important of these have been the Society for Psychical Research, Charles Fort, J. B. Rhine and the Parapsychological Association, Charles Tart, Dean Radin, Ian Stevenson and the Division of Perceptual Studies (DOPS) at the University of Virginia, the U.S. intelligence agencies, and the U.S. Department of Defense. These enquiries attempted to investigate the paranormal "scientifically," or at least empirically. Individuals like Rhine, Tart, and Dean have studied psi in laboratory settings. Laboratory results based on meta-analysis demonstrate statistically significant results way above chance. This suggests that certain psychic abilities such as telepathy, precognition, clairvoyance, and micropsychokinesis are "real." While lab results have been significant but generally weak in favor of psi, certain rare individuals, "exceptional subjects," or psychic sensitives appear to possess exceptional psi abilities. Moreover, Dean Radin put forth some evidence to suggest that meditation may enhance these abilities, as is maintained by the Buddhist and Hindu traditions. "Anecdotal" studies into reincarnation, OBEs, NDEs, apparitions, and mediumship indicate that consciousness may possess nonlocal aspects that operate independently of the brain. This has led leading psi researchers such as those at DOPS to conclude that physicalism or metaphysical materialism (the mind is the brain) must be wrong.

Chapter 3 explores contemporary Buddhist stories about five psychic phenomena: clairvoyance, precognition, telepathy, retrocognition, and psychokinesis (PK). From the accounts in chapter 3, we see that psychic phenomena are alive and well for modern Buddhist practitioners. Whether someone finds these stories compelling accounts of actual ESP and psychokinesis depends on several factors, including someone's metaphysical presuppositions and philosophical commitments, whether they find the narrator a credible source, the amount of detailed evidence presented, and the subjective and intersubjective nature of the phenomena. The "human element," or interpersonal and intersubjective aspect, of psi is often a central feature of these stories. These phenomena are often connected with strong emotions, dreams, altered states of consciousness, and life-and-death situations. Sometimes the impact of these experiences is massive and changes the course of someone's life. The "real-world" effects of these anomalous events mean that it is vital to give them serious consideration when trying to comprehend the significance of narratives about the paranormal for contemporary Buddhists.

Chapter 4 investigates contemporary Buddhist stories of out-of-body experiences (OBEs), near-death experiences (NDEs), and encounters with animals, ghosts, spirits, deities, and holy beings. For each of these categories there were a range of responses, and often different phenomena would overlap. While some accounts appear to be no more than examples of random weirdness, others are clearly interpreted through a Buddhist lens and highlight themes specific to Buddhist thought and practice. These experiences ranged from simply sensing the presence of some being to full-blown waking visions of other entities. These events seem to erupt into daily life often spontaneously in waking consciousness and in dreams. Sometimes they are triggered by life-and-death situations and altered states induced through meditation, illness, or psychoactive substances. They often are profoundly personal and emotional, involving close family, friends, and teachers. They are deeply meaningful, sometimes changing the course of a person's life. And they are commonly interpreted through a Buddhist worldview within which karma, rebirth, and nonhuman intelligent entities play important roles.

Chapter 5 is about Rick Repetti. Rick grew up in a large Italian-American family in a low-income housing development in New York City. One day in 1973, when he was fifteen years old, Rick was thrown into a profound out-of-body experience during the final stages of a postural yoga class he was following on TV. This event precipitated an intense spiritual search involving deep states of meditation and an active involvement with a spiritual community led by Ram Dass, Hilda Charlton, and Joya Santayana. For the next several years, Rick had countless experiences of both psi and paranormal encounters. Some of his most profound experiences were precognitive dreams such as the one he shared with his cousin about being in an accident when Rick lost control of his oil truck. At the dissolution of his community, Rick's psychic sensitivities took a dark turn, so he consciously undertook what he calls "reverse *sādhanā*" by eating meat, drinking alcohol, and taking drugs as a way to dampen his psi abilities. Although somewhat successful, Rick was profoundly altered by these early life events and began the academic study of Buddhism and free will in an attempt to intellectually come to terms with them. Also, during the subsequent decades Rick's meditation practice shifted from very intense yogic concentration to more Buddhist-based meditations focused on mindfulness, insight, and compassion.

Chapter 6 is about Kat Smith. Kat was born and raised in the Washington, DC, area and grew up in the 1980s as a self-avowed "weird kid." From an early age, Kat had experiences of hearing and sensing things that put her in touch with an unseen world. Her early connection to the spirits of the deceased drew her from a young age to Catholicism and as a young adult inspired her to get a degree in mortuary science and work for several years as a funeral director. Growing up her parents told her she had "The Gift," her family's term for perceived psychic sensitivity, which could be traced back down the family's female line. However, as Kat grew into young adulthood her psychic sensitivities became pathologized, leading to forced hospitalizations and medication, which damped down her psi. She was eventually able to break free of this pathologization of her gift and move away. After living for a time in Montreal and France, Kat immigrated to New Zealand. In her thirties, Kat traveled to Thailand and discovered the Thai occult. Through the acquisition of amulets and other objects containing human remains, Kat now works to establish mutually beneficial relationships with the deceased spirits associated with these artifacts so as to aid the deceased in the acquisition of good karma for their future births. In addition to her Buddhist practices centered on the Thai occult, Kat also employs her psychic abilities as a full-time card reader.

In chapters 3–6, a wide range of experiences were described, from very brief accounts of somewhat unusual events to highly detailed stories about profound paranormal experiences. Statistical analysis of the survey results demonstrates that for the respondents the paranormal is alive and well. These results mirror the survey findings done in the United States on the belief in the paranormal and on the widely held acceptance of psi, magic, and encounters with nonhuman entities found throughout history within the Buddhist traditions. Some of the most detailed accounts given by participants in this study, such as those of Mei, Elma, Wystan, Angela Sumegi,

TOWARD A PHENOMENOLOGY OF THE PARANORMAL

Ayyā Mettikā, Karma Lekshe Tsomo, Ajahn Chandako, Rick Repetti, and Kat Smith, provide rich descriptions and context for these paranormal experiences. The participants in the survey and interviews covered a broad range of people, from those with some (minimal) experience with Buddhism or Buddhist practice to people who had ordained and were fully committed to the Buddhist path, such as Ayyā Mettikā, Karma Lekshe Tsomo, and Ajahn Chandako. Unsurprisingly, those highly committed to the Buddhist path tended to interpret their experiences in traditional Buddhist terms, employing Buddhist concepts like impermanence, karma, rebirth, and nonattachment. However, even those less committed often understood their experiences in terms of karma, suggesting that belief in karma, as a more generalized principle that the universe is governed by a moral order based on one's intentional actions, exceeds its strictly Buddhist (and Hindu) origins and has been embraced more widely by those engaged with Asian religions and meditative practices.

As contemporary tales, the stories recounted in this book function as a window into modern Buddhist folklore. The demographic who participated in this study are largely white Anglophone converts to Buddhism or practitioners of some Buddhist-based meditation. However, a significant portion of the participants were from non-Western and non-Anglophone countries. Also, from my interviews with Karma Lekshe and Ajahn Chandako, we heard contemporary stories of the paranormal from the Tibetan community in India and the international Thai Forest Tradition. Interestingly, even from the Western converts and practitioners, who are probably the most likely demographic to be influenced by scientific naturalism and physicalism, we learned of some profound experiences of psychic and paranormal phenomena. Thus, these stories suggest that paranormal experiences have not declined with the so-called disenchantment of the world through scientific materialism but may have moved underground. In other words, given the prestige of this scientific worldview and the taboo attached to the paranormal, Western converts typically only disclose their experiences to close friends and family for fear of social stigma and ridicule.

As stated from the beginning, I have avoided trying to "prove" the reality of the paranormal or the truth of these accounts. Instead, I have taken a phenomenological approach that has bracketed both the naïve realist view that an objective world exists out there independent of us and metaphysical commitments such as to physicalism or idealism. Specifically, I have chosen to look at stories. Stories are the way humans have always made sense of the lifeworld. And stories are always narrated by someone from a particular point of view for some real or imagined audience. Thus, these stories narrated herein have been co-created by the study's participants and myself for you—Dear Reader. Of course, for many of you reading this book, a fundamental question will remain: "Yes, but are these stories true?" Whether you believe these tales depends on your presuppositions and how dogmatically you adhere to them. Many who already believe will accept them (or a subset thereof) as real, while the skeptics (those that even bother to get past the title) can surely find many reasons to doubt. With regard to the reality of these paranormal tales, I am reminded of Jacque Vallée's words at the end of *Passport to Magonia*, his classic study on UFO phenomena: "We cannot be sure that we study something real, because we do not know what reality is; we can only be sure that our study will help us understand more, far more, about ourselves."[1] Likewise with the paranormal, since we have no sure grasp of what reality is, how can we thus categorize the events in these stories? But regardless of whether you believe them or not, they tell us something important about ourselves.

If pressed, however, about the veracity of these stories, I would say that for those who had these experiences, they are "real enough." By this I mean that the events described in these stories made a real impact on their narrators' lives. Some were profound enough to alter the entire course of someone's life. For example, recall Angela Sumegi's vision of Mahākāla or Rick Repetti's precognitive dream of his truck crash. Both Angela and Rick ended up pursuing academic careers in part to better understand these experiences. Thus, we see that these experiences and the stories about them have "real" effects—they can change a person's life. I believe that this alone makes them worth our attention and effort to better understand the phenomena they represent.

Toward a Phenomenology of the Paranormal and the Unification of Human Knowledge

In this study I have employed a Buddhist phenomenology to study contemporary Buddhist stories of the paranormal. I also contrast and contextualize this approach with the approaches found in canonical Indian Buddhist sources and modern scientific studies of the paranormal. My phenomenological approach was in part an attempt to steer a "middle path" between the canonical religious views and modern science. Doubtlessly the canonical sources present stylized accounts of psychic powers and encounters with nonhuman entities for rhetorical purposes such as to enhance the prestige of the Buddha and promulgate the teachings of the Dharma. Likewise, scientific study of the paranormal possesses its own limitations and assumptions. Is there a way to reconcile these different approaches and overcome their limitations? I believe that phenomenology, as a form of radical empiricism that takes into account perspective, context, and social embeddedness, could provide an overarching framework that could do this, and not just for Buddhism and the paranormal. More broadly, phenomenology has the potential to reconcile and synthesize different approaches to human knowledge found in the humanities, social sciences, and even the natural sciences.

The Dalai Lama famously once said, "If scientific analysis were conclusively to demonstrate certain claims in Buddhism to be false, then we must accept the findings of science and abandon those claims."[2] For some aspects of traditional Buddhism this is already the de facto case. Take cosmology, for example. I think a contemporary researcher would be hard pressed to find any educated Buddhists in the world today arguing for the traditional Buddhist view of Mount Meru as the center of our world surrounded by seven concentric mountain chains. This is because of the global dominance of modern science, which is backed by centuries of careful geological and astronomical observations with ever-more-sophisticated equipment such as telescopes that can now probe into the depths of the vast cosmic web of trillions of galaxies. Contrariwise, the traditional Buddhist view that the cosmos is teeming with other intelligent life forms seems much more probable from a contemporary scientific perspective, given the discovery of thousands of exoplanets in recent decades. However, whatever life is out there, it is not likely to correspond exactly with canonical descriptions. How far the Dalai Lama's assertion goes is an open question. Are there any Buddhist doctrines or values that are not on the table for possible revision? The Dalai Lama also has said, "My religion is very simple. My religion is kindness."[3] I think this provides us with a clue—certain Buddhist virtues such as loving-kindness, compassion, sympathetic joy, equanimity, and wisdom, if abandoned, would, I think, result in something other than Buddhism. But what of karma, rebirth, impermanence, no-self, suchness, nirvana, enlightenment, and emptiness?

Assuming that the Buddha was a good phenomenologist, many Buddhist claims would and could be subject to empirical verification or falsifications. Karma and rebirth are good examples. Although many think such notions are simply metaphysical doctrines, we have evidence from around the world in the form of testimonies from thousands of children who recall memories and possess associated physical characteristics that seem related to experiences in previous lives. These concepts can be empirically investigated using phenomenological analysis. In the same way, we may investigate the paranormal phenomenologically to better understand what the canonical texts and contemporary scientists can offer to our understanding. Future studies in Buddhism and the paranormal have a vast wealth of Buddhist stories, cultures, and historical periods to draw from. Future investigations, by providing thick descriptions of Buddhist experiences in the lifeworld, will add vital nuance to our understanding of these phenomena and their role within the Buddhist traditions. Likewise, phenomenology may be used to better understand the role of the paranormal in other traditions, societies, and cultures throughout human history.

Human knowledge is constantly subject to revision, and while worldviews often clash with one another, our human instinct to seek truth attempts to harmonize and synthesize existing knowledge into a coherent whole. However, currently within the academy there exists a regime of truth whereby the natural sciences are placed at the top of an epistemological hierarchy, followed by the "softer" disciplines of psychology and the social sciences, and finally at the bottom humanities. This compartmentalization and hierarchization of knowledge are reflected in patterns of funding for academic programs by governments and the private sector, as well as by differences in rates of pay for faculty members in academic institutions, student funding, etc. This system has been the reigning paradigm for too long. Not only does it downgrade disciplines vital to human self-understanding and promote the myth of objectivity, but it has also led to the stigmatization and denigration of subjects deemed either unscientific or pseudoscientific, such as the academic study of the paranormal. Moreover, this epistemological hierarchy is based on a presumed ontological hierarchy that positions physical objects and materiality as "more real" than human subjectivity, that is, our feelings, meaning making, thoughts, and ethics. The semantic similarities between expressions like (philosophical) objectivism and the "objectification of women" and (metaphysical) materialism and "materialistic" (as in greed for object acquisition) are not accidental. When a society valorizes the possession of things like sports cars over feelings such as love for one's mother, it is not surprising that global consumer capitalism and the ensuing destruction of the planet are the results.

In this regard, phenomenology can help. Although phenomenology is not a monolithic tradition, it does offer a set of basic principles that can aid us in this search for a unified field of human knowledge.[4] First, it does not assume that the lifeworld can be divided into strictly objective or subjective experience. All experience is always perspectival, and there is no view from nowhere. It recognizes that all knowledge is embedded in individuals, communities, and societies with histories. While eschewing metaphysical speculation and naïve realism, phenomenology seeks to develop an ontology based on a radical form of empirical investigation of the phenomena; it is radical in the sense that it attends to our conscious involvement with the "furniture" of the world and is continuously subject to revision. In this respect, there is an ontological leveling of physical objects and subjective or intersubjective phenomena—the world of physical things is not more "real" than peoples' nightly dreams, mystical visions, and inner thoughts and feelings. They are all part of the furniture of the lifeworld. And given that everyone spends a third of their lives asleep and that many psi and paranormal phenomena occur in the dream state, perhaps we should start paying more attention to this dimension of experience.

Consciousness and the first-person perspective are always intentional and entangled with the "facts." Our world, the "real world," is the intersubjective embodied lifeworld. No sharp divisions can be drawn between human meanings, interests, values, and interpretations and things in the world. From within this epistemological framework academic disciplines can each contribute to human knowledge in an interdisciplinary and nonhierarchical fashion. This includes the natural sciences. In this regard, the words of the philosopher Robert Crease are instructive:

> Phenomenology provides an excellent framework for a comprehensive understanding of the natural sciences. It treats inquiry first and foremost as a process of looking and discovering rather than assuming and deducing. In looking and discovering, an object always appears to a someone, either an individual or

community; and the ways an object appears and the state of the individual or community to which it appears are correlated....

Phenomenology of science treats discovery as an instrumentally mediated form of perception. When researchers detect the existence of a new particle or asteroid, it assumes these will appear in other ways in other circumstances—and this can be confirmed or disconfirmed only by looking, in some suitably broad sense....

Phenomenology looks at science from various "focal lengths." Close up, it looks at laboratory life; at attitudes, practices, and objects in the laboratory. It also pulls back the focus and looks at forms of mediation—how things like instruments, theories, laboratories, and various other practices mediate scientific perception. It can pull the focus back still further and look at how scientific research itself is contextualized, in an environment full of ethical and political motivations and power relations.[5]

Thus, phenomenology offers a way forward that avoids the relativism of social constructivism and the objectivism of scientific realism. Phenomenology's notion of intentionality implies that parts are only understood against the background of wholes and objects against the background of their horizons. Science seeks to discover objects that are invariants within their horizons. When viewed with a phenomenological frame, we also recognize our participation in this process as embodied consciousnesses to whom the objects appear. In this way scientific discovery can be contextualized within human history, culture, politics, ethics, and power relations. This in turn leads to a more democratic and holistic understanding of human knowledge wherein the various disciplines can each contribute their part and allows for previously occluded phenomena such as the paranormal to be reintroduced (without prejudice or stigma) into the whole field of human inquiry.

EIGHT

Autobiographical Postscript

IN THE FOLLOWING PAGES I recount some of my own stories concerning the paranormal from experiences I had at various stages of my life. I do this in part for the sake of full disclosure. Since I attempt to ground my methodology firmly within human subjectivity, it would be somewhat disingenuous if I withheld my own personal experiences involving psychic and paranormal phenomena. Needless to say, these experiences have biased my outlook toward such phenomena. As should be obvious at this point, I do "believe" in the paranormal in the sense that I think psi and encounters with nonhuman entities are experienced and have been experienced by people throughout human history. And I know this in part from my own experiences of it. That said, there are some strange events in my life that I am more convinced are true examples of the paranormal, while there are others that I strongly believe may have mundane explanations. Thus, I do not accept everything that I describe in what follows as true or real with the same degree of confidence. Some of these stories were written many years ago, and others I have written down here for the first time. A few I wrote originally as very loosely fictionalized versions of actual events. For example, in the "Black Magic Valentine" section, I am Logan. I have kept the narrative voice and style of each story as I originally wrote it. The earlier versions I am sure capture much more detail than I would be able to recall now, although some are not written as I would write them today (being older and hopefully a bit less arrogant than I was in my youth). But enough said: time to tell some tales . . .

Childhood Precognition

I was born on the winter solstice in 1967. My earliest childhood memory is of a blue ducky I used to play with in the bath when I was one year old, recalled through self-hypnosis (see preface). My earliest experiences of psi were forgotten by me, until I began research for this book a few years ago. Before my mother passed away in September 2021, I would speak to her regularly over videoconferencing software. When I mentioned to her my plans to write a book on Buddhism and the paranormal, the following conversation took place.

She said to me, "As a child, you used to know when things would happen before they happened."

"I did? I don't remember that."

"Yes, when you were a young boy, maybe seven or eight, sometimes you would tell me things that were going to happen, and then they would. Once you said to me, 'We are going to get a flat tire when we go out.' And sure enough, when we went out, I was driving around a corner, and a school bus came the other way. I panicked and I moved over too far to the right and hit a rock on the side of the road, puncturing the tire."

As soon as she told me this, I remembered the incident. Now my mother, bless her, was not a very good driver and often drove too close to the right side of the road. Redding, Connecticut (my hometown), is heavily wooded, and the woods are filled with rocks deposited from glaciers during the last ice age. The town is also hilly, so the country roads are winding, with many blind corners. The corner where we had our little accident was notoriously dangerous—the turn was sharp—almost ninety degrees—and blind, and the road narrow.

When all the factors are considered—the time of day when the school bus was usually at that section of road, my mother's habitual driving too far to the right, and the particular nasty turn, it makes sense that such an event would occur. But how I knew that this would happen that day in such a matter-of-fact manner, I have no idea. The thought simply appeared in my head, and I knew it was true, just like Kat's experience reading the cards when she just "knew" how her client's boyfriend would act on their date. The term sometimes used is claircognizance, the psi ability to know things through some nonordinary means; sometimes people just know stuff, as if the information were downloaded into their head from a mysterious source. I cannot recall any other childhood experiences like this, but this precognitive flash happened to me in my forties (see later discussion).

A Canine Connection

In 1992, after a transformative retreat at Godwin Samararatne's meditation center in Nilambe, I found myself back in Kandy, Sri Lanka. At that time, I was residing with the Jayatillekas, a well-to-do family living on one of the lush hills overlooking Kandy Lake. It was an idyllic and tranquil location, save for one rather intimidating presence—the family German shepherd named Zimba. As a newcomer to this household, I quickly learned to tread carefully around the guardian of the estate. Zimba was clearly the king of this castle. He would rush toward anyone at the bottom of the pecking order, barking menacingly and barring his teeth just to intimidate them. Even after I had stayed with the Jayatillekas for a week, he would still bark at me every morning when I came down from my little *kuti* (hut) to the main house. This was our daily morning ritual. He also enjoyed removing people's sandals from their feet with his teeth, which newcomers quickly learned was not optional.

One sunny morning, after a month at Nilambe, I returned to Kandy with a group of fellow meditators. After this intense period of practice my mind was very still, my senses alert, and my body relaxed. The van driver dropped me off at the Jayatilleka residence, and I began making my way up the winding path toward the family's front door. I was acutely aware of Zimba's presence. I could hear his low, deep growls beginning to increase in volume as he sensed my approach. He was poised to defend his territory, his eyes fixed on my figure, his bared white teeth gleaming in the morning sunlight.

I felt my stomach tense, but then I remembered the story of the Buddha and the intoxicated elephant (see chapter 4) and what Godwin had taught us about the power of *metta*, loving-kindness. Taking a deep breath, I continued up the steps while radiating feelings of love and goodwill toward

Zimba. Then something incredible happened. Zimba, who had been ready to pounce just moments ago, suddenly froze in his tracks. His menacing growls gave way to an uncertain silence, and his aggressive stance softened. Then he turned on his heels, returned to the doorway, and lay down, his once-intense stare now soft and contemplative. Before my very eyes, the fierce guardian of the gate had transformed into a docile lamb.

Psychedelic Psi: Telepathy and Precognition

As I recall, it was March 4, 1996, and I had recently returned from my first Goenka ten-day vipassana retreat. That by itself was an amazing experience filled with its own epiphanies, but that is a different story. I was living in Seattle at the time, and my girlfriend Sarah and I were pretty big into psychedelics. While I was away on my retreat, Sarah had gotten hold of some very high-quality LSD, so one Saturday afternoon we decided to stay indoors and trip, just the two of us.

The trip was very intense and truly amazing. All the meditation I was doing had really "cleaned out" and "opened up" my neurophysiology, subtle body, chakras, or whatever you want to call the energetic pattern of consciousness/mind/body I like to call "me." A lot happened on that trip—telepathy, visions of alternate versions of me, and such, but the most significant moment occurred when I went into the bathroom and looked in the mirror. The mirror was rectangular, stretched across the wall above the sink, and about four feet long by two feet high. As I was looking into it, suddenly I could "see" a giant translucent salamander (about a foot and a half long) positioned in the top-right corner of the mirror. I watched in amazement as this salamander walked across the mirror from the top-right to the lower-left corner, and then disappeared. Now, in all the many psychedelic experiences I have had, I very rarely have "visual hallucinations," and this salamander definitely takes first place for the most vivid and "real" experience I have ever had of such things.

Jumping ahead to May 9, Sarah and I decided to go on the First Thursday Art Walk in Pioneer Square, in downtown Seattle. This is actually the oldest art walk in the United States, dating back to 1981. The idea is that all the neighborhood art galleries are free to enter; there is wine and cheese and no pressure to buy. The public is invited just to explore recent works by local artists and have a good time. As Sarah and I entered the first gallery, I was drawn immediately to a large mural painting on the far wall, rectangular and painted in a single creamy pink tone of varying shades and contours. In the top left of this painting was an image of a wizard with a flowing beard, in the middle left was a young woman with flowing hair, and in the top right corner there was a giant salamander about a foot and a half long facing toward the bottom left corner.

As soon as I saw the salamander, chills came over my whole body. *This is the salamander I saw in the mirror while tripping two months ago!* There was no doubt in my mind whatsoever. *But if this is true*, I immediately realized, *I had seen something while tripping that was two months in the future!* Now, at this point in my life I had already begun my study of the Mahāyāna Buddhist scripture called *The Supreme Array* (Gaṇḍavyūha), and I knew that according to the scripture's worldview all time is one time and all space is one space. However, reading about this in an ancient Buddhist scripture is one thing, but experiencing it in your everyday life is something else entirely! From that day forward, I knew that my linear experience of time is only caused by my limited perspective and that the future in some sense "already exists." It also confirmed for me that the visions in *The Supreme Array* are much more than mere flights of religious fantasy—that they in fact are maps to higher-dimensional realities encoded in literary form.

Alice's Adventures in Kew Gardens: A Precognitive Dream

It all started with a dream. Early one Saturday morning in November 2002, after a late night of clubbing in Shoreditch, it came to me. I dreamed I was in Kew Gardens, with children playing everywhere. The Royal Botanical Gardens at Kew, located in southwestern London, covers over five hundred acres and is the largest repository of plant and mushroom species (both living and preserved in seed and spore banks) in the world. In my dream, on the ground around all the bushes, trees, plants, and flowers, were thousands of thousands of magic mushrooms. I thought, "How can I pick them and get them out of the gardens without anyone noticing?" A few seconds later I woke up. I was lying in our spare bed. Lola snored softly in the big bed. My head throbbed, but I knew one thing for sure—I had to go to Kew

Gardens, and I had to go that morning. My heart pounded with excitement. Something was going to happen today, something *big* . . .

Lola felt too hungover to come with me. Besides, she had to get ready for her big date that night. *What kind of life do I live?! Lola was getting ready for a date, while I went out to hunt magic mushies!* This was the alternative lifestyle we were living in the slums of East London while I was writing my PhD in religion at the University of London, School of Oriental and African Studies, and working part-time at the British Museum and British Library. *Curiouser and curiouser, as Alice would say . . .*

I left our flat in East London around eleven AM and headed north down Kingsland Road. I crossed Dalston Junction and walked another hundred yards or so to the Dalston-Kingsland Rail Station. After buying my return ticket to Kew Gardens, I descended the stairs to the westbound platform on the Silverlink. As I stood on the platform waiting for the next train, I scanned the wood-chip covered hillside that sloped up about twenty yards to a brick wall. Sometimes I could spot one of London's nearly cat-sized rats scurrying in the bushes. That morning my eye caught something much more exciting—a little baby-blue halo, *Psilocybe cyanescens*, one of the most powerful hallucinogenic mushrooms in the world. I walked over to it slowly in utter disbelief, feeling all the while a tingling feeling down the back of my neck. I picked it. It was only about an inch high. Its chestnut-brown cap had not yet become wavy with a thin blue rim but was only a little bead. Its snow-white stem showed no signs of the blueing common in the adults of the species. I held it tenderly between my thumb and first finger, lovingly admiring its beautiful coloring and delicate form.

I went over to the bunch of mushrooms and politely said to the old gentleman standing in front of them, "Excuse me, Sir. I collect mushrooms. Do you mind?" and gestured behind him. I had learned after a few years of living in England that it is always better to put things in the form of a question. ("Nice day, isn't it?"; "Do you think we should go?"; etc.—you get the idea!)

"Are you sure they are not poisonous?" The kind fellow looked genuinely concerned.

"Oh yes, I'm sure. I test them when I go home to make sure."

The man picked one and looked at it with suspicion but stood aside so I could snatch up the rest. My heart was pounding in my chest.

AUTOBIOGRAPHICAL POSTSCRIPT

The train ride to Kew seemed to last forever but was only about forty minutes. I was so nervous that I was going to miss my stop that I almost did. For some reason, I thought Kew was the last stop on the line, but there was one more—Richmond. When I got off the platform, I followed signs for the gardens. It was a beautiful day. It had been raining, but the sun was out now, beaming warmly upon the wet grass and fallen autumn leaves. I walked down a quiet street past what we Americans would call "quaint" little shops and cafes, while the excitement mounted. Already things started to seem less real. Already the magic was starting. *If these people only knew how close the other worlds are to this one . . .*

When I got to the main entrance of the gardens, I paid a student price and went in. Looking at my map, I saw that there were over five hundred acres of land within the gardens, surrounded by a high wall. In front of me, across a small pond, stood a massive green house. Paved paths wound themselves here and there in every direction. I had no real plan except to look for the wood-chip landscaping. I was nearly insane with anticipation. *Try to look normal!* I kept thinking to myself.

I was in a section mostly covered with green lawn. Interspersed within the grass were bushes and trees of various sorts. And there were lots and lots of wood chips. And lots and lots of mushrooms . . . but not the right kind! Keeping my head down, I found all sorts of edible, poisonous, and mildly hallucinogenic ones, but no blue halos. After about forty-five minutes of this, I was dying for a piss. It was now getting close to eleven in the morning. The weather was still absolutely gorgeous, and the air smelled fresh. Looking on my map, I saw that I was close to a handicapped toilet. Suddenly, I got an idea—*I would eat one of the mushrooms I had already found, and it would lead me to the others!*

By my second season hunting mushrooms in Seattle, I came to believe that eating mushies put one in an altered state of consciousness that made it easier to find them. I am sure this belief was influenced by Terence McKenna's book *Food of the Gods*. McKenna pushed this notion to its logical religious extreme: the idea that the mushrooms wanted you to eat them and would actually guide you to them—a belief consistent with what is widely known as shamanism. I believed this idea because I believed in the magic of the mushrooms and because it seemed the simplest explanation for how certain things happened to me. But probably more important than believing in the mushrooms is that, just maybe (you may think I am mad for this—and you may be right!), *they believe in me . . .*

So I had my slash in the loo, took out a single adult of the species, washed it off, and ate it. Fresh mushies are the strongest. A certain amount of the active chemicals always breaks down when you dry them out. Fresh, the mushrooms tasted very mildly metallic. I hated the taste of them dried. It had been almost two years since I had eaten them fresh, and I thoroughly enjoyed this one's soft crunchiness. I strolled out into the sunshine. Within fifteen minutes I was feeling the first effects. A warm tingling feeling came over me. I felt relaxed, extremely calm, and gently happy. Another fifteen minutes went by, as I wandered from tree to tree and bush to bush, looking at the wood chips around them. The next thing that happened, Dear Reader, you most likely will find hard to believe. I certainly would. It actually happened to me, and I still hardly believe it . . .

I came up to a large tree with great branches stretching out from it at least twenty feet in all directions. Wood chips and leaves covered the ground around it—and something else. Something light brown and wavy. I took a closer look and absolutely could not believe my eyes. I kneeled down on my knees, shivers of excitement and joy shot through me. *There they were! The mother lode!* Thousands and thousands and thousands of blue halos covered the ground around this tree. Enough to get fifty thousand people completely off their tits! It was Christmas in November.

As I kneeled there in utter disbelief and sheer religious awe, a young girl, about seven, with long blond hair and bangs stepped out from behind the tree and stood there smiling at me. *The dream! Just like in the dream!* I thought. She was way too real to be a hallucination (after all, I had eaten only one mushroom). But how could this *really* be happening? After about ten seconds (or was it a lifetime?) of smiling at each other, the girl's father came around the tree, gave me a suspicious look, took his daughter by the hand, and walked off.

I started picking. I was wearing a sporty rain jacket with lots of pockets and zippers. *Fuck!* I should have brought my backpack. But I remember reading at the Kew Gardens website a warning about not taking anything out of the gardens and was worried they would check my pack. Luckily, the jacket had a single wide front pocket to warm your hands in. I stuffed handfuls into the pockets, zipped them up, and sat down on a nearby bench to send a text message to Lola.

AUTOBIOGRAPHICAL POSTSCRIPT

I pulled out my mobile, my hand shaking with excitement, and keyed in, "FOUND THE MOTHER LODE!"

Less than a minute later, I got back, "You are kidding?!"

I was too excited to key in anything and really feeling trippy now, so I called and quickly told her the story.

Suddenly she sounded scared. "Be careful, Baby."

"I will," I reassured.

"I'm worried."

"Nothing bad is going to happen. Trust me." I replied.

"I'm getting a bad feeling about this . . ."

"It's gonna be fine, Lover. I am going to walk around for a little while and then come home. I should be home in a few hours."

"Okay. Be careful."

"I will."

"Love you."

"Love you too."

Little did I know how significant Lola's premonition would be. The day I found the mushrooms and she went on her first date with another guy was the beginning of the end of us.

Spontaneous Telepathy Event #1

Back in the summer of 2003, while I was living in East London, I had two experiences of what you could call spontaneous telepathy. Psychics might call what happened clairsentience; some charismatic Christians refer to such events as "Word of Knowledge" and see them as a gift of the Spirit. They came spontaneously to me, unasked for and without effort. The ability vanished as suddenly and mysteriously as it came. To this day, I don't know how or why I could do this. This is how the first one happened.

In the summer of 2003, Europe experienced one of the worst heat waves in recorded history; thousands died that summer from heat. In June of that year, my wife, Lola, and I had separated, and I had rented a room in a house just north of Finsbury Park. I distinctly remember meditating under a tree in the park in about hundred-degree heat. It felt like sitting in a furnace.

I was devastated by the breakup. We had been married four years earlier in New Hampshire. We had met two years before that in Seattle. In 2000, we had moved to London so I could finish my PhD at the University of London. Being a poor student and a social worker, we ended up living in some of the roughest neighborhoods in East London—Whitechapel, Hackney, and Dalston. We were living on the Kingsland Road in Dalston when we split. We both liked to party and prided ourselves on our alternative lifestyle. However, when Lola's mom had a stroke and nearly died and my dad was diagnosed with terminal cancer, we used partying to escape the pain. Our "friends" from our local pub, who considered substance use an extreme sport, were happy to enable our bad behavior. To make a long story short, to save my life and sanity I jumped off that runaway train long before she did.

Even though my dad was dying and my marriage was blown to pieces, I still had a job to do—I needed to finish my PhD. But before I could do that, I needed to get clean. So I got into a program and went cold turkey. I worked the program, went to meetings, and got honest with myself and others. It was brutal, and I was in agony. I meditated Zen-style every day for hours. It hurt so bad on the inside that I actually enjoyed the scorching heat—it was karmic penance for my sins. I ditched the old friends and neighborhood and moved to Finsbury. After six months of sobriety, I quit the program and went back to drinking but managed to stay off anything else for a while at least.

This was one of the lowest points of my life—I was alone in this huge monstrosity of a city, dirt poor, and emotionally an open wound. I had been so sure Lola was "the one" for me—my soulmate, my one true love. I contemplated suicide daily. I continued meditating with a discipline born of despair. At least by sitting still with the pain, I wasn't doing anything stupid, and I wasn't using.

Around November of that year, I couldn't take my self-imposed isolation any longer. I needed to go out and do something, talk to someone, be around other people; I needed something to distract me for a little while at least. Even though I had practically no money, I had a bus pass and a few pounds—enough for a pint somewhere. I took a bus down the Kingsland Road to Shoreditch, the old stomping ground, and found a club I didn't have to pay to get into. I bought my pint and sat down at a table along the back wall.

All around people were talking, laughing, dancing, and chilling to the house music. I went to the toilet to take a piss and brought my pint with me. I could see the residue of cocaine on the back lid of the toilet seat. Returning to my table, I moved my eyes across the room. The place was filled with hipsters all dressed in their party clothes. Everyone seemed fake, like plastic windup dolls, pretending to have fun when inside they seethed with anger, hatred, greed, lust, pain, and sorrow. Then my eye caught sight of a woman in her early thirties sitting at a table with her friends. She wasn't talking to anyone. She was somewhere else, and I recognized that place. I felt drawn to her and knew I had to talk to her.

I walked up to her, leaned down, and spoke close to her ear, so she could hear me over the music.

"You and I are alike, you know," I said.

She looked up somewhat cautiously with a glance that said, *I am not in the mood to be chatted up*, but indulged me anyway and replied, "Oh really? Why is that?"

"We are both here and not here," I answered.

"How do you mean?" I now had her attention.

"You have recently gone through a breakup, right?" I replied with another question.

"That's right."

"It was two or three months ago, wasn't it?"

"It was three."

"You broke up with him because he cheated on you."

"Yes . . ."

"You were together five or six years."

"Five years. How do you know all this?" She looked a little disconcerted.

Her friends had taken notice and were leaning in to listen, getting ready to give me the shove off should I upset their fragile friend.

"I don't know," I replied, honestly.

"Why are you telling me this?"

"I don't know . . . I saw you across the room and I just knew what you are going through. I broke up with my wife six months ago, and she was unfaithful to me. I know exactly how you are feeling." She looked like she was going to cry and was keeping back the tears. "You want to forgive him, but don't think you can. This is not the first time he has done this. You thought he was the love of your life, but now you are beginning to realize that it is not going to work, and you don't know if you are strong enough to get over it."

She sat listening with her head down. One of her girlfriends pulled her chair closer and leaned into hearing range. "Hey, mate, she's not really interested. We are having a girls' night out." It was said without malice but out of a misguided attempt to protect her friend from being hit on by some drunken stranger.

I knew my time was running out. "I'm sorry," I said. "I didn't mean to intrude." I looked back at my companion in sorrow. "I'm not trying to pick you up or anything. I just wanted to tell you that the pain does get less. You will get better. You will heal. And you will find someone else who you can trust and who will love you for you. I know it doesn't feel that way right now, but you are not alone. I get it." She kept her head down and quietly wiped away a tear in each eye. I stood up and gently put my hand on her shoulder and said, "It will be okay. You will get through this."

I walked away draining my beer as I waded through the crowd of plastic people headed for the exit. They no longer bothered me. I had done what I was supposed to do. There was no reason to be there anymore. Not looking back, I went out the door onto the street. I never saw her again.

Spontaneous Telepathy Event #2

About a week after my first experience of spontaneous telepathy in 2003, I had another very similar experience in East London. One evening I headed out to the Dalston area, eventually ending up in a trendy little club near Dalston Junction called the Jazz Bar. For several hours I had been hanging out with a group of four people, a male-female couple and two other women. They were all friends in their early to mid-thirties out for drinks on a Saturday night. We had met about three hours prior down the Kingsland Road at a different club, and I was tagging along. The vibe was interesting. They all seemed somewhat suspicious of me, but one of the women, Jenny, appeared mildly interested.

However, Jenny was sending me some rather mixed signals. She was somewhat flirtatious but also had an ironic sense of humor that at times hinted at sarcasm. The four were professionals who worked in the City, London's central business district, and made significantly more money than me, but they were dressed in that London hipster style iconic of the trendy yuppies of the gentrified East Side. These were not people with whom I would ordinarily socialize. However, I was lonely and had been isolated for many months, so some company on a Saturday night in my book was better than none. I felt a bit like a fifth wheel. there were plenty of inside jokes and stories; I had no idea what they were talking about, and no one felt the urge to fill me in. I considered getting up and going home, but something was compelling me to stay.

The night was getting on, and three of the four headed for home. Somewhat surprisingly, Jenny invited me back to her place for a cuppa. *I might get lucky tonight*, I thought. But I wasn't feeling any chemistry there. I didn't feel particularly attracted to Jenny, and I didn't sense she was attracted to me. She was not unattractive—she had a medium-sized, somewhat athletic body with small breasts, chin-length auburn hair, and an aesthetically pleasing face. But I sensed that there was something not right about her. She behaved in a very proper English upper-middle-class way; however, I felt something just under the surface lurking. She was a good conversationalist but was guarded and closed lipped about any personal details. Her general outlook on life seemed pessimistic, self-depreciating, and cynical.

The walk back to her place took about twenty minutes. Once inside, we sat in her lounge for our cup of tea. All the while, I kept getting these feelings about her. In retrospect, I learned that this is what some people call "clairsentience"—the ability to sense or feel things beyond the five senses. On a deep intuitive level, it felt like pieces of a puzzle were falling into place for me about her and her background. Things I felt were true but should have no way of logically knowing. How did I sense these things? Was I somehow "reading her mind?" Were her microexpressions or tone of voice giving me "tells" into her personality and personal history? Was I getting clues from what she didn't say as much as what she did say? To this day, I am unsure. I just knew that I knew.

After our tea and some more small talk there was a lull in the conversation. I looked at my watch—it was after one in the morning. I could feel she wanted me to go. *No getting lucky tonight*, I realized, without much disappointment. However, by this time I was pretty tired and wouldn't have minded a warm couch to sleep off the drink and weed.

"Well, I'm knackered," Jenny said with a suggestive sigh. "I need to get some sleep."

"Okay, no worries." But I felt I needed to find out if I was right about her before I left. "Before I go, can I ask you a question?"

"Yeah, sure." She appeared ready to repel any chat up lines or moves I might try to make on her to get her in bed.

"Did you break up with someone, say in the last few months?"

"Yes, my fiancé and I split up three months ago."

"You were going out for a long time, weren't you? Like six years?"

"Yes, we had been together about six and a half years," she replied.

"You broke up because you cheated on him."

"How do you know that?" She looked decidedly uncomfortable now.

"You cheated on him with a Mediterranean guy."

There was a long pause while she stared at me as if I walked in on her naked. "He was Italian." She said in a measured way and then, with an attempt at flippancy, added, "What, are you psychic or something?"

"No, I just had a feeling," I replied, honestly.

Awkward silence, then, "Okay, well it is time for you to go," she said rather abruptly.

"You know, you don't have to be like this," I said.

"Like what?" She replied defensively.

"You don't have to be so guarded and mistrusting of everyone. I know you were hurt in the past and vowed you would never be again. But you've closed yourself off from everyone to protect yourself. You don't think anyone will truly love you and be faithful, so you make sure you never get too close to anyone. You knew cheating on your fiancé would end the relationship, but you didn't want to marry him anyway. You had no true feelings for him and didn't for the Italian guy you had the fling with. You feel dead inside and use sex to forget, and as a way to keep people from getting too close to you."

"Okay, you really have to go now." She stood up and started walking toward the door.

I followed her and waited for her to open the front door. I stepped outside onto the entry way and turned to face her. "I'm sorry. I didn't mean to upset you. I just thought you should know. Know that you can change. Know that you can find real love with someone someday. But it is going to take some work."

Jenny's expression softened, and for a moment she looked more genuine, more real. The armor had come down, if only for a moment. "Thanks. It has been . . . interesting to meet you. You take care. Maybe I'll see you around."

I looked into her eyes. Her guard was back up, but I had gotten in and touched something. I had planted a seed that one day might bear fruit. As awkward and uncomfortable as it was, we had made a real connection. I had spoken to that little wounded girl inside her, and she had heard me. I couldn't sense anything else about her. The "gift" was gone. I had said what I was supposed to say.

I held her gaze for another two seconds and then said, "You won't see me again," turned, walked down the front steps onto the street, and began my long, late-night walk home. I never saw Jenny again.

Black Magic Valentine

In was six in the evening, and Logan sat on the floor of his room in a rundown six-bedroom house in London's Stoke Newington neighborhood, cutting out images of eyes and mouths from a stack of old porno mags. His other five housemates were drinking beers and smoking weed in the lounge on the other side of the kitchen. It was February 14, 2005, Valentine's Day.

Two hours earlier, he had said goodbye to his now ex-girlfriend Claire. That afternoon, Claire had helped him move into the house. He had been renting a room in a house with an old woman in a posh North London neighborhood before the move. It was not a good fit, and the landlady had asked him to move ten days ago. This was in part because of Claire, and her helping him move was her attempt to make amends. With her mission accomplished, she was ready to have "the chat" about their relationship.

It had never been much of a relationship, but for the last couple of weeks it had been pretty shit. Actually, if they were being honest, it had been kinda fucked from the get-go. For starters, Logan was Claire's lecturer in her Introduction to Philosophy course at the University of London's School of Oriental and African Studies (SOAS). Claire fancied him from the first lecture. She thought his American accent and voice were sexy. Also, he was young for a lecturer (in his mid-thirties), with a fit stocky body to go with his brains—another turn-on for Claire.

Logan had just finished his PhD from the university last summer and was on a .4 contract as a teaching fellow. In essence, he was the slave labor for the year while full-time staff worked to meet their research quotas. A year and a half earlier, he and his American wife had separated, and he was desperate to get out of London. But without any other job prospects, he was forced to take the fellowship.

AUTOBIOGRAPHICAL POSTSCRIPT

Claire was originally a Kiwi but had moved to London fifteen years before with her then husband. They had a little boy, but hubby turned out to be an abusive fuck, so she left him and had been a single mum for the last ten years. In her younger days, she had been quite the wild child. Motherhood had taken the edge off of that, but she did still like to party now and again. In her thirties with her son almost a teenager, she decided she would go to university and get her BA. Petite with olive skin, an athletic body, and bobbed brown hair, Claire had maintained her youthful looks with the added charm of her maturity.

She had taken a fancy to Logan back in September. By December she was on a mission. But how to approach him? She soon discovered that Logan liked to hang out with his postgrad friends and students down in the SOAS bar tucked into the basement of the main building. Back in the 2000s, students openly smoked weed in the bar. Since SOAS was Queen's Land, the police would only come on campus if invited by SOAS security. The unspoken rule was that unless people were dealing or selling hard drugs, the security looked the other way. After several weeks, Claire figured out when Logan was likely to be drinking in the bar. She began to stalk him like a predatory big cat. Finally, the day came when she walked past Logan holding court with his Indian Philosophy master's students and brushed her hand casually over his shoulder, tossing him a quick smile. *Trap set and bait taken.*

Logan had not been in a good way since he and his wife had split up in June 2003. A year after that, in April 2004, his dad had died of cancer. Somehow, he managed to finish his PhD in Asian philosophy and passed his oral exam two months after seeing his dad breathe his last. Once finished with his studies, he desperately wanted to leave London, but without a full-time job to go to, he did not even have enough money to move back to the States. After five years of living there, central London had become for him a colossal prison of seven and a half million inmates. He hated the grime, pollution, and crowds of the city. Desperately lonely, he tried dating six months after his breakup but was not emotionally equipped to engage in anything that was more than superficial. After his dad died, he had split with his girlfriend Ruth, who was a sweet gentle soul, because he couldn't be close enough to her to share his pain.

By some strange alchemy, his complete lack of emotional availability combined with his new academic status, American accent, Mediterranean good looks, and hipster style made him rather successful with the SOAS ladies. As a bookworm and study nerd his entire academic career, he found his sudden desirability surprising but not unwelcome. Casual sex was at least real human contact, and his string of superficial liaisons acted as a mild panacea to the vacuity and pain he felt on the inside.

Things with Claire started casually enough. They began going out to pubs and then clubs together. After hooking up a few nights, he started staying overnight and getting invited to dinners. Claire's younger brother Mikey had also moved to London. In his mid-twenties, he was a regular East London boy and was dating Stacy. Claire had spent a good part of her childhood parenting her younger brother, and now in London with her twelve-year-old son Stephen she continued the tradition acting as the family matriarch for her brother, brother's girlfriend, and her own son. Logan had been adopted into the family as something of a stray, a lost puppy in need of a home.

At university, Logan was the authority figure; however, once he crossed the threshold into Claire's low-rent apartment in central London their roles were reversed—she was boss. Logan didn't mind playing this game as long as the sex was good and the clubbing continued. Like him, Claire had a kinky side, so they even managed to make it to London's Torture Garden for a night of naughty fun like he used to with his ex-wife.

The peak of their steamy affair came one unexpected night when Logan was home sick with the flu. Claire came over and cooked him dinner. The lady of the house was unimpressed with what she judged to be Claire's lower-class status and manners. After dinner they retired to Logan's room, and it was clear Claire wanted payment for services rendered. Undoubtedly the landlady heard her cries of pleasure as Logan gave it to her hard. Shortly after this night their casual relationship took a decided and irreversible turn.

Logan was hanging out at Claire's place and had just climbed out of a hot bath. It was a cold January night, and the whole family, Mikey, Stacy, and Stephen were over, staying indoors to keep warm. Claire decided to order some fish and chips from the local shop and asked Logan to go get them. He refused. Up until this point, he had been given the royal treatment; however, in Claire's mind his grace period as guest was over and now he needed to start contributing as a member of the family. Logan's refusal was an unforgivable offense to her.

AUTOBIOGRAPHICAL POSTSCRIPT

A week after this, Logan's landlady asked him to move out, no doubt in some measure because of Claire's dinner/nooky run to his place. Logan felt no pain at leaving the place—he thought the woman was a stuck-up bitch. However, now he needed a new place to stay. Claire, always the woman in charge, found him a place and arranged a meet-up with the other tenants. The house in the Stoke Newington area of London's East Side was a dump and no doubt managed by some dodgy slumlord. Each week, one of the six tenants delivered a cash envelope to a petrol station twenty minutes' walk away to pay the rent. But the price was right, and the other housemates were young and liked to party like Logan, so things looked like they would work out. Logan gave them his deposit and got his key.

A few days later, Claire helped him move into his dingy ground-floor room. Afterward, they went for a coffee at a tiny greasy spoon down on the high street. Since the fish-and-chips incident, Claire had been decidedly cold to him. He knew he should have stepped up and gone out into the cold that night, but he honestly just was not invested enough to care. He didn't realize at the time that this had been a test. The message now was loud and clear—*You are either part of the team or not.* And with Claire it was her way or the highway. Logan had failed the test, and "Coach" had mentally cut him from the team that night. He knew this now and that the hatchet wasn't far away. He waited with quiet resignation. She remained polite but cold for way too long. *Just fuckin' do it already,* Logan thought. Too apathetic to do it himself, he resented her protracted cold-shoulder treatment.

Toward the bottom of their coffees there settled between them an awkward silence. Finally, Logan could stand it no longer, "We're over, aren't we?" he said in an expressionless tone.

"Yeah," was all she said.

"Yeah. No worries. It was fun while it lasted."

"Still friends?"

"Sure," Logan replied. "Thanks for helping me find a new place."

"No worries."

They made their way to the door. Logan gave Claire an awkward hug and said, "See you around?"

"Definitely."

They started to walk apart from each other. Logan stopped and said, "Hey Claire?" She turned back around. "Happy Valentine's Day."

Claire flashed him a weak smile, turned, and walked away.

When Logan got back into his new rental, he started to unpack, feeling numb all over. Everything felt far away to him. Then something began to grow deep inside him like a hot coal burning in his breast. Soon the indistinct feeling grew like a wildfire into a rage. *What a bitch! I hate her. I hate her. I hate her* became his mantra. He felt like smashing something. He needed to do something to channel these feelings. Ever since he was a young boy he had liked to draw. Sometimes drawing was the only thing he could do to keep his sanity. Deep in his gut he felt he needed to draw now.

Guided purely by instinct, he grabbed his art supplies and some of his old porn magazines and began cutting out eyes and mouths. Once he had about twenty of them, he glued them randomly onto a piece of A3 drawing paper. He made the eyes weep tears of blood and blood drip from the mouths. Then he wrote across the whole thing in red ink, "Happy Valentine's Day! I love you. Cross my heart hope to die, stick a needle in my eye!" Then he took a needle and stuck it into the middle eye, a sexy brown right eye of some large-breasted model. *Catharsis*. The rage subsided. It was like all the frustration, anger, and loss from the past two years had been channeled into that one piece of paper. Suddenly it was gone. He felt empty now. He climbed into bed and slept.

A week and a half later, he ran into Claire at the SOAS bar. The eyelid of her right eye was dark brown and swollen almost completely shut.

"What happened to you?" he asked, innocently enough.

"Oh that. I got some weird eye infection about a week ago. You should have seen it then—it was much worse."

About a month after this Logan started hanging out with Claire again, now just as friends. One night over beers, he told her about his "Valentine's Day Card." She laughed loudly, looked him straight in the eye, and said, "You're a dickhead."

Nothing was said about it after that, and they drank together fairly often for the next several months until Logan landed a full-time job in New Zealand and left London for good. They stayed in touch for years afterward.

Fifteen years later, Logan came across something written about Chaos Magick and discovered what is called the "cut-up technique." In this method, the chaos magician creates a collage of images to cast a spell. He smiled to himself and thought, *maybe there is something to this shit after all*. Researching further, he discovered that some of the seminal figures for the formation of

Chaos Magic back in the day were called the Stoke Newington Sorcerers.¹ *Part of a noble tradition, I guess*, he mused.

Mahāyāna Holy Beings

Sadly, only twice in my life have I had an encounter with a Mahāyāna holy being. Neither experience was dramatic or anywhere near the full-sensory visionary encounter Angela Sumegi had of Mahākāla. The first happened in a dream one night in East London, the second during a meditation retreat in New Zealand.

In 2001, Lola and I were living in Whitechapel in East London, at the time a heavily Bengali region of the city. We were living above a chip shop right on the A13 highway. The big lorries on the highway used to make our building shudder, and each morning around 5 AM we would feel the first train from the Underground shake our tiny one-bedroom flat. One night I had a very vivid dream. In it I was on a commercial flight to somewhere, and suddenly in the middle of the aisle appeared a being made of pure white light. Emanating from the blinding outline of this human figure were rainbow colors shooting off in all directions. In the dream, I knew that everyone on the plane would see this visitation differently, based on their own religious beliefs. The being radiated love and compassion, and I was filled with a profound sense of peace. When I woke, I was convinced the being who had visited me in the dream was Avalokiteśvara, the Bodhisattva of Compassion.

My next encounter happened several years later. In July 2005, I had left London and moved to Palmerston North, New Zealand, to begin my job as a lecturer in Massey University's religious studies program. Within a few months of being in Palmerston North, I met Beth, an English woman doing her master's degree in philosophy at Massey. We were soon dating and about six months later moved in together. Around this same time, I discovered the Amitabha Kadampa Buddhist Center in Palmerston North. The New Kadampa Tradition is a new religious movement, founded by a Gelukpa Geshe named Kelsang Gyatso, who broke away from mainstream Tibetan Buddhism. Popular among western Buddhists and controversial for their missionary zeal and devotion to Dorje Shugden, their protector deity, the New Kadampas have over 1,300 centers all over the world. In 2006, the head teacher at Amitabha was a lovely woman named Kelsang Demo. Initially Beth and I were quite taken in by Demo and the New Kadampas and became serious lay practitioners for about six to eight months.

During our serious engagement with the New Kadampas, Demo had organized a weekend retreat at an activity center called Sextus Lodge, in the foothills of the Ruahine Range located in the Manawatu district of New Zealand's North Island. During our retreat, we engaged in several hours of devotional practices and meditation and listened to Demo's long discourses on the Dharma. On the last day during our silent meditation following a *sādhanā* to Mañjuśrī, the Bodhisattva of Wisdom, I reached a profound sense of calm and stillness. Then from out of this silence I heard a very soft voice whisper into my right ear, "*There is only the ceaseless flow of empty phenomena.*"

I was both startled and confused by this. Was this just my imagination, or had I really heard something? Or was this Mañjuśrī imparting to me a powerful and pithy teaching on emptiness? I discussed it with Demo, who saw it as a good sign of my progress. In the heat of my devotion, I became convinced that it was Mañjuśrī. Now, I think *perhaps*. Having contemplated this event, I realized that if this teaching There is only the ceaseless flow of empty phenomena is correct, even the little voice that spoke in my ear is merely another empty phenomenon. But if this experience leads to my greater insight into emptiness, then what could possibly be its source if not the embodiment of Wisdom itself?

A Child Will Be Born:
A Case of Spontaneous Precognitive Claircognizance

In 2011, I once again had a powerful experience of spontaneous precognitive claircognizance. In February of that year, I was living alone in our four-bedroom country villa in the little village of Kimbolton, in the Manawatu district of New Zealand's North Island. Beth and I had separated in December 2010, and she had taken our seventeen-month-old son, Alex, up north to Cambridge, New Zealand. I was devastated to be parted from my son and desperately lonely, living in our empty house with only our two ridgebacks to keep me company. After placing an ad on an online dating site, I got a response from a woman living in Woodville, about fifty kilometers away.

Ann, who answered my ad, was a Kiwi primary school teacher of Chinese and Norwegian descent. She had traveled some in Thailand, lived in

Australia, and was athletic and into music and dancing. She seemed nice enough, and after some email correspondence we agreed to meet at an Irish pub in Palmerston North for a drink. I'll never forget when she walked into that pub and I first saw her. I immediately felt a very visceral sensation within me and just *knew* at that very instant that she was going to have my child. It was very specific this way—I did not sense she was the love of my life or that we would be together forever, only that she would have my child.

Over the course of the following six months Ann and I dated. Our relationship was tumultuous. During this time, I was driving up to Cambridge fortnightly to see Alex. Beth soon made it clear that she was interested in getting back together. I knew I wasn't over my feelings for Beth and therefore found it difficult to commit to being with Ann. While in the middle of trying to negotiate a more casual relationship with Ann, her mother suddenly died. In the midst of her grief, Ann found it difficult to deal with the uncertain nature of our relationship. Eventually, I sensed that she had a lot of unresolved issues and suppressed anger, which I was just not willing to deal with, so I ended our relationship.

A month passed, and during this time Beth offered to see a couple's counselor and work on our relationship. Then one fateful Saturday morning, she agreed to give us another try and move back to Kimbolton with Alex. I was very happy and excited about our second chance to be a family again. Then my mobile phone rang. I looked at the caller and saw that it was Ann. Immediately, I knew why she was calling. I felt this incredible sinking feeling and disassociation from my body; suddenly everything felt far away. I recalled the line from the movie *Fight Club* when the main character discovers Tyler Durden's true identity and his voiceover declares, "We have just lost cabin pressure." I answered the phone. She told me she was pregnant and was going to have our baby.

Disincarnate Guest

Back in 2014, I was living in an old country villa on three acres of land in Kimbolton, a little village up in the hills of mid-central North Island, New Zealand. It was July, midwinter in the Southern Hemisphere, and the weather was cold and wet, as was typical for that time of year. At that time, Eric, a good friend of mine, had become quite the magic mushroom hunter. Each autumn he would show up at my front door with a bag of fresh mushies to see if I wanted to engage in some shamanic activities. Despite my Mrs.'s disapproval, I was usually game. This is how the high strangeness began ...

One evening Eric came over, and we planned an experience around a little campfire in the back paddock. Well after dark on a cold night, with my wife and two young boys tucked up in bed, the dogs asleep in the lounge, and the horses dozing in the shelter of our stand of pine trees, Eric and I prepared for our ceremony. We went to the middle of the back paddock, set up a small circle of rocks, built the fire, divided our stash of mushrooms in half, and ate them. As the mushrooms came on, we stretched our muscles and did some martial arts moves to get the chi energy flowing. Once the initial wave had passed, we cracked a couple of beers, and Eric started talking about how his granddad had passed away that very day after a long illness. I expressed my condolences, and we both sat around the fire for several moments quietly contemplating the dance of the flames.

As we sat crossed-legged in a semi-trance-like state looking into the flames and feeling the waves of psilocybin ride over us, suddenly we both felt the presence of someone else with us.

"Bro, do you feel that?" I said, "Do you feel like someone is here with us?"

"Yes, I think it is my grandpa Bob."

I nodded as if it was completely normal for this to happen. Then I got up, made another seat at the fire, cracked open another beer, and poured some on the ground in front of the spot for Bob, inviting him to the party. After this we continued to feel a vague presence around us as the trip progressed. About three hours in, I remember peaking, with the sense of my ego dissolving into a pulsating geometric grid of multicolored lights. On the comedown, we moved the party inside, lit the wood burner in the lounge, and talked into the late hours. We went to bed around three AM, with Eric crashing on the couch and leaving early the next morning.

Eric and I didn't speak for some time after that, and I completely forgot about our "visit" from his granddad. About two weeks after our trip, my wife took our boys and moved out. This was the second time we had broken up. The earlier time, two years ago, she took our firstborn when he was one year old and moved three hours north to her parents' town. After a year apart, she wanted to give it another try. But despite our best intentions, we'd tried again and it had not worked out. Needless to say, I was gutted when she took my boys away, took her horses, and moved in with our friends living in the country about ten minutes from the village, leaving me alone in our four-bedroom house. Luckily, I still had our two ridgebacks to keep me company. Jasper and Kaiko were big gentle brothers who were fiercely loyal companions. Kaiko, the more sensitive of the two, used to come over and put his paw on me as I cried myself to sleep at night.

After I was home alone for about a week, the weirdness started. One night I woke with a start at two-thirty in the morning. The fire alarm in the hallway was beeping. But it was a strange beeping noise—not the noise for smoke or for the battery running low—but four distinct beeps, then it would stop, and start again—four beeps, stop, then four beeps. I went into the hall and looked at it for a while. We had twelve-foot-high ceilings in the house, and I really didn't want to go out to the barn to get the ladder and change the battery in the alarm. Then after about thirty seconds, it just stopped.

The next day, I changed the battery in the alarm and didn't think any more of it. The next night I woke up at 2:45 and couldn't fall back to sleep. Then I heard it, the hall alarm was going off again! I went out and looked up at it, and then after about a minute it stopped. *Weird*, I thought. *Can't be the battery.* There was not much I could do, so I went back to bed.

A couple of nights later it was two in the morning, and I couldn't sleep. Then I heard it, the damn beeping! But it sounded louder. I went out of my bedroom into the lounge, and this time it was the lounge fire alarm. *What the fuck!* Four beeps, then stop. Four beeps, stop. Four beeps, stop. Then it just stopped. I was up until about five, lying awake. *What is causing this? Something in the atmosphere?*

The next morning, I changed the batteries in all the fire alarms in the house. I had no idea what else I could do. I didn't want to take the batteries out in case I did actually have a fire. Three nights went by and there was nothing. *Okay, problem solved*, I thought. After another restless night, I finally fell asleep at about one. BEEP, BEEP, BEEP, BEEP pause BEEP, BEEP, BEEP, BEEP! I startled awake. It was four, and the fire alarm in my bedroom just six feet away from me was beeping! Chills ran all through my body. *Okay, someone or something is doing this.* It was then I remembered our visit in the paddock from Grandpa Bob. *Could this be Bob?* I thought.

Nothing like this ever happened to me before, and I am generally inclined to look for logical explanations for things. I have heard ghost stories and stories of poltergeists before and held an agnostic position about such things. *A lot of weird shit happens, so why not spirits?* was my view. Even though I still held on to the notion that there probably was a logical explanation for all this, I thought to myself just in case, *Hi Bob, you are welcome here if you want to hang out, but I really need to get to sleep, thanks.* The beeping stopped.

Several lonely days passed, and I was busy just trying to keep my shit together. Nearly overwhelmed with grief, I focused hard on doing a few hours of work each day (I was teaching Asian philosophies at the local university and working on my next book), keeping the house clean, eating three squares a day, feeding the dogs, and taking them for walks in the village. I was too distraught to think much about the fire alarms and began to forget the whole thing.

Three-thirty-one in the morning and I sat bolt upright. *What the hell is that noise!* Still half asleep I got up and followed the sound into the kitchen. Entering our little galley kitchen, I stared in disbelief as all the lights on the microwave flashed; the thing beeped over and over again like a pulsing heart. The flashing and beeping were coordinated so it was *FLASH/BEEP, FLASH/BEEP, FLASH/BEEP. What the fuck!* My heart was pounding in my chest like a jackhammer in rhythm with the possessed microwave. The power cord was behind the refrigerator, so I went to the dining area and grabbed a chair to stand on, so I could reach behind and switch it off at the wall. Once I got the chair against the fridge, the microwave stopped. I went back to bed and didn't sleep the rest of the night.

The next morning, I tested the microwave and it worked fine. *What's wrong with it, and why would it do that? Some kind of electrical fault? Is it Bob?* Although the stuff with the alarms and microwave was freaky, I didn't get the sense of a malevolent presence. From what Eric had told me that night we were tripping, Bob had been a good guy. A war vet who was fond of his beer, fishing, and hunting, but nobody to be worried about during life. I thought, *Okay, if you are here, Bob, you can hang, I've got lots of room for you now. Just be cool, and we will be fine.* I tried to get in touch with Eric to tell him what was happening, but he wasn't answering his phone.

These activities kept on for another week or so. Some nights nothing. Then between two and four in the morning, an alarm would go off for several sets of four beeps and then stop. Other nights, the microwave would do its thing. It only happened in the middle of the night. I would get up and look at the offending piece of electronic equipment as if to say, *Yes, I see you, I know you are here*; then it would just stop.

Days passed. My grief and sleep deprivation made everything seem somewhat surreal. The alarms and microwave just became one of those things that happened. Eat breakfast, do dishes, go for a walk, wake up at three and look at the fire alarm or microwave beeping, go back to bed, repeat. One afternoon when I was hanging out in the lounge with the dogs, I got a phone call. It was from Will and Jenn. My wife must have told them we had broken up, and they were checking in on me. I put on my brave face and told them I was fine. Then I said, "But some weird shit is happening here at night . . ."

I figured I could talk to them, because they were a couple of hippy vegans into spiritual stuff. In the middle of telling them about the fire alarms' and microwave's unusual behavior out of nowhere from the kitchen was a very loud *THUMP*, as if something had slammed one of the pots or pans onto the counter. I turned my head quickly but saw nothing there. The dogs looked toward the kitchen and put their tails between their legs. Chills ran all through me (I can even feel them now as I write this). I told Will and Jenn what had just happened, and Jenn whispered into the phone, "Okay, you are freaking me out." Me being me, I was like, "It's just my Disincarnate Guest, no big deal."

After that phone call and thump in the kitchen all the nighttime activity stopped. The alarms and microwave just went back to behaving as they are supposed to. A couple of weeks later I met Krystal, and we now live happily in a new home with our two daughters.

Experiments with Psychokinesis

In 2021, while reading Dean Radin's book *Supernormal* as research for this project (see chapter 2 for a discussion of the book), I became personally interested in psychokinesis (PK), also known as telekinesis. According to Radin, meta-analysis on research into "micro-PK," that is, studies to test if humans can influence systems like electronic random number generators, indicates statistically significant results above chance. In his discussion on PK on macroscales ("macro-PK") in inanimate systems, such as the ability to move objects like coins, pieces of paper, furniture, etc. with the mind, Radin states, "The bottom line about macro-PK is that the jury is out."[2] In other words, Radin does not consider the current evidence to be sufficient to demonstrate a real effect. However, there is quite a significant amount of anecdotal evidence for so-called spoon bending, something Uri Geller was (and still is) famous for. People have even organized "spoon bending" parties, where at times someone's metal spoon will suddenly become soft like putty and bend easily, only to regain its rigidity just as quickly. Since stage magicians can easily replicate these types of results using sleight of hand, debunkers have been quick to dismiss such experiences as evidence of real psi.

Curious to find out about PK myself, I purchased the book *Defy Your Limits: The Telekinesis Training Method* (2017) by Sean McNamara.[3] In this book, McNamara maps out a step-by-step procedure for training your mind to move a piece of tinfoil mounted on a pin under a glass jar. At the beginning stages of practice, one is instructed to use your hands around the foil. Once you can make the foil spin around easily, you place it under glass and attempt to move it while still placing your hands on the side of the glass bowl. Eventually, you move up to McNamara's "Level 4," where you can spin the foil without your hands on the sides, using only your mind to move it.

In August 2021, I began conducting my own experiments using McNamara's method with foil and with a "psi wheel" (a piece of paper folded with four points and eight sides) mounted on a pin. I then videoed some of these experiments and posted them on my YouTube channel (@DouglasOsto). I posted eleven videos, beginning with ones where I simply use my hands, then using my hands with the foil or wheel under glass, to my final video where I just used my "mind" to spin the foil for over six minutes.

It is clear to me that when my hands were placed next to the foil or wheel, some effect was causing it to spin around. It could have been heat from my hands or what in traditional Chinese martial arts and medicine they call *qi* (*chi*), that mysterious vital energy that permeates the universe and that the soft styles of martial arts are said to tap into. At this point, I had been doing Tiger-Crane Kung Fu for almost three years. Each day I would do a *qigong* exercise meant to move the *qi* into and between my two outstretched hands. I seemed to be able to get the foil or wheel under the glass to move, but the effect was a lot weaker, and I am unsure if it could have been caused by subtle vibrations or something else. For my last video, I was truly amazed to see the foil continue to spin for over six minutes in the direction I was trying to make it move with my mind. I noticed, when watching the video afterward, that the sun was shining on the foil, and I considered that the light might have been pushing the foil. This is called a "light mill" and has been constructed in laboratory settings, but there the mill is placed in a vacuum to remove the air friction. In my description of the video, I write:

> Sean McNamara's Level 4 = "Look, Mom, no hands!"
> No one is going to believe this . . . Hell, I don't even believe it myself. Looked at the foil, wanted it to turn, and it did for over six minutes . . . Normally the foil settles down after about 30 seconds and will only sway a little and not move from its general position for the rest of the day. This is after one week of practicing with Sean McNamara's book "Defy Your Limits: The Telekinesis Training Method," three years of Chi Kung (Qigong) and thirty-six years of meditation. I have no idea how or why this works. It is not a trick. Is it just the sunlight pushing the foil like a light mill? Let me know your thoughts.

I have not been able to replicate these results, but I also have not put any time or effort into further training my "abilities" since August 2021. So, at the end of the day, I agree with Dean Radin and think that the jury is still out on macro-PK. However, I think the topic is worthy of further investigation, especially the group phenomenon where people are spontaneously able to bend spoons.

The End of This Journey and the Beginning of What Comes Next

So, dear reader, this is the extent of my "paranormal" experiences thus far. They range from somewhat strange to the more truly anomalous. As with all the stories provided in this book, these were not presented in any way as "proof" of the paranormal but as significant experiences in my life that seem to defy ready explanation. My experiences of what appear to be precognition truly baffle me. However, a working hypothesis of mine is that time exists in multiple dimensions and that it appears there are rare events that occur either spontaneously, in some crisis, in meditation, in dreams or altered states of consciousness, whereby information from future events is transmitted back in linear time to the present. What this means for human free will, I cannot say.

I will say that I personally am convinced by my own and others' experiences that consciousness possesses nonlocal properties and that we are connected to one another in ways we do not fully understand. I think these properties can be investigated from a phenomenological perspective without assuming that consciousness functions as some type of metaphysical substrate to phenomena, as is maintained in certain forms of philosophical idealism. I also think, based on all the information we have on psychic and paranormal phenomena, that metaphysical materialism (physicalism) is false. My general position is that any metaphysical speculation is at best premature and likely doomed to failure, given the natural limits of human knowledge. Moreover, such speculation is dangerous because it forecloses the open-minded inquiry that is required to investigate the unknown.

In the final analysis, the term "paranormal" is far too crude of a tool for what is required of us to advance our knowledge. Hopefully, in the future it will be abandoned for a more precise vocabulary accounting for these phenomena, which currently reside at the very edge of our comprehension. We live in an exciting age of rapid technological development. It is my sincere hope that the angels of our better nature win over our capacities for greed, power, exploitation, and destruction. If so, we will be able to save our planet and allow our natural curiosity to lead us into a new age of exploration into the great unknown.

Notes

Preface

1. Alfred E. Johns, *Scientific Autosuggestion for Personality Adjustment and Development: Your Key to Mental and Physical Health* (Westport, CT: Associated Book Sellers, 1957).
2. Edward Conze, *Buddhist Scriptures* (London: Penguin, 1959), 131–32.
3. D. E. Osto, *Altered States: Buddhism and Psychedelic Spirituality in America* (New York: Columbia University Press, 2016), 219.
4. David E. Presti, ed., with Bruce Greyson, Edward F. Kelly, Emily Williams Kelly, and Jim B. Tucker, *Mind Beyond Brain: Buddhism, Science, and the Paranormal* (New York: Columbia University Press, 2018). For a review, see Douglas Osto, "Mind Beyond Brain: Buddhism, Science, and the Paranormal," *Religion* 50, no. 1 (2020): 178–82, https://doi.org/10.1080/0048721X.2019.1658173.

Introduction

1. And in even rarer cases, sometimes people get struck by lightning *and* experience the paranormal. See Elizabeth G. Krohn and Jeffrey J. Kripal, *Changed in a Flash: One Woman's Near-Death Experience and Why a Scholar Thinks It Empowers Us All* (Berkeley: North Atlantic, 2018), for an account of a woman who experienced a profound out-of-body experience from being struck by lightning and the subsequent psychic abilities she developed from this experience.
2. *Oxford English Dictionary Online*, s.v. "paranormal, adj. & n."

INTRODUCTION

3. J. Maxwell, Charles Richet, and Oliver Lodge, *Metapsychical Phenomena: Methods and Research*, trans. L. I. Finch (New York: G. P. Putnam's Sons, 1905).
4. Frederic Myers coined the term "telepathy." See Jeffrey J. Kripal, *Authors of the Impossible: The Paranormal and the Sacred* (Chicago: University of Chicago Press, 2010), 79.
5. Maurice Merleau-Ponty, *The Phenomenology of Perception* (1945), trans. Donald A. Landes (London: Routledge, 2012).
6. Kripal, *Authors of the Impossible*, 23.
7. Merleau-Ponty, *The Phenomenology of Perception*, lxxxiv.
8. Merleau-Ponty, *The Phenomenology of Perception*, lxxx–lxxxi.
9. Merleau-Ponty, *The Phenomenology of Perception*, lxxxiii–lxxxiv.
10. Bhikkhu Thanissaro, trans., "Cula-Malunkyovada Sutta: The Shorter Instructions to Malunkya," MN 63, Access to Insight, 1998, http://www.accesstoinsight.org/tipitaka/mn/mn.063.than.html.
11. Bhikkhu Thanissaro, trans., "*Rohitassa Sutta*: To Rohitassa," AN 4.45, Access to Insight, 1997, http://www.accesstoinsight.org/tipitaka/an/an04/an04.045.than.html.
12. Dan Lusthaus, *Buddhist Phenomenology: A Philosophical Investigation of Yogācāra Buddhism and the* Ch'emg Wei-shih lun (London: RoutledgeCurzon, 2002), 11–35.
13. Lusthaus, *Buddhist Phenomenology*, 35–36.
14. Lusthaus, *Buddhist Phenomenology*, 36.
15. Rick Repetti, "About Me," 2017, https://www.rickrepetti.com/about-me.

1. The Paranormal in the Indian Buddhist Tradition

1. Some works in the south Indian language of Tamil are also very ancient.
2. Angelika Malinar, "Yoga Powers in the Mahābhārata," in *Yoga Powers: Extraordinary Capacities Attained Through Meditation and Concentration*, ed. Knut A. Jacobsen (Leiden: Brill, 2012), 33, 43.
3. Malinar, "Yoga Powers in the Mahābhārata," 33.
4. Christopher Key Chapple, "*Siddhi*s in the Yogasūtra," in *Yoga Powers: Extraordinary Capacities Attained Through Meditation and Concentration*, ed. Knut A. Jacobsen (Leiden: Brill, 2012), 223–40.
5. Knut A. Jacobsen, "Introduction: Yoga Powers and Religious Traditions," in *Yoga Powers: Extraordinary Capacities Attained Through Meditation and Concentration*, ed. Knut A. Jacobsen (Leiden: Brill, 2012), 4.
6. Lloyd W. Pflueger, "Holding On and Letting Go: The In and Out of Powers in Classical Yoga," in *Yoga Powers: Extraordinary Capacities Attained Through Meditation and Concentration*, ed. Knut A. Jacobsen (Leiden: Brill, 2012), 245–46.
7. Lloyd W. Pflueger, "Holding On and Letting Go," 246.
8. Malinar, "Yoga Powers in the Mahābhārata," 58.
9. See Julie Gifford, "Insight Guide to Hell: Mahāmoggallāna and Theravāda Buddhist Cosmology," in *Constituting Communities: Theravada Buddhism and the Religious Cultures of South and Southeast Asia*, ed. John Clifford Holt, Jacob N.

1. THE PARANORMAL IN THE INDIAN BUDDHIST TRADITION

Kinnard, and Jonathan S. Walters (Albany: State University of New York Press, 2003), 71–84. An account of these powers is given in what follows.
10. Edward Conze, *Buddhism: Its Essence and Development* (1951; New York: Harper & Row Publishers, 1975), 49.
11. However, there are exceptions. In Pāli one does find something like a myth of origins in the text *Aggañña-sutta*. See Richard Gombrich, "The Buddha's Book of Genesis?," *Indo-Iranian Journal* 35, no. 2–3 (1992): 159–78; and Steve Collins, "The Discourse on What Is Primary (*Aggañña-sutta*): An Annotated Translation," *Journal of Indian Philosophy* 21 (1993): 301–93. Some Hindu *bhakti* traditions also developed a number of cosmogonic myths found in the Purāṇas.
12. T. W. Rhys Davids, and William Stede, *The Pali Text Society's Pali-English Dictionary* (Oxford: Pali Text Society, 1921–1925), 587.
13. See Rupert Gethin, *The Foundations of Buddhism* (Oxford: Oxford University Press, 1998), 144. The Indian philosopher Vasubandhu puts the total at 1,000,000,000. Gethin, *The Foundations of Buddhism*, 144.
14. Franklin Edgerton, *Buddhist Hybrid Sanskrit Grammar and Dictionary*, 2 vols. (Delhi: Motital Banarsidass Publishers Private Limited, 1953), 259.
15. For examples, see "The Great Trichiliocosm": Edward Conze, trans., *The Perfection of Wisdom in Eight Thousand Lines and Its Verse Summary* (San Francisco: Four Seasons Foundation, 1973), 323; "Three-thousandfold, multi-thousandfold world system": Luis Oscar Gómez, "The Bodhisattva as Wonder-Worker," in *Prajñāpāramitā and Related System: Studies in Honor of Edward Conze*, ed. Lewis Lancaster and Luis Oscar Gómez (Berkeley: Berkeley Buddhist Studies Series, 1977), 242; "world system of three thousand great thousand worlds": Gregory Schopen, "The Manuscript of the Vajracchedikā Found at Gilgit," in *Studies in the Literature of the Great Vehicle: Three Mahāyāna Buddhist Texts*, ed. Luis Gómez and Jonathan A. Silk (Ann Arbor: Center for South and Southeast Asian Studies, University of Michigan, 1989), 123; and "Trichiliomeghachiliocosm": Paul Harrison, trans., *The Samādhi of the Direct Encounter with the Buddhas of the Present: An Annotated English Translation of the Tibetan Version of the* Pratyutpanna-Buddha-Saṃmukhāvasthita-Samādhi-Sūtra (Tokyo: International Institute of Buddhist Studies, 1990), 13.
16. A description of this structure may be found in Gethin, *The Foundations of Buddhism*, 115–19. For diagrams of a single world realm, see Luis Oscar Gómez, trans., *Land of Bliss: The Paradise of the Buddha of Measureless Light: Sanskrit and Chinese Versions of the Sukhāvatī Sūtras* (Honolulu: University of Hawai'i Press, 1996), 257–58.
17. The Sanskrit term for these beings is *preta* ("deceased"). "Hungry ghost" seems to come from an English translation of a Chinese term for them. See William Edward Soothill and Lewis Hodous, *A Dictionary of Chinese Buddhist Terms with Sanskrit and English Equivalents and a Sanskrit-Pali Index* (1937; Delhi: Motital Banarsidass Publishers Private Limited, 1977), 454.
18. For a graphic description of these hells in a Mahāyāna *sūtra*, see Upasaka Tao-tsi Shin, trans., *The Sutra of Bodhisattva Ksitigarbha's Fundamental Vows* (New York: Sutra Translation Committee of the United States and Canada, n.d.). In the Indian Buddhist *Mahāvastu*, one of the Buddha's chief disciples, Maudgalyāyana

1. THE PARANORMAL IN THE INDIAN BUDDHIST TRADITION

(Pāli: Mahāmoggallāna), uses his psychic powers to travel to these hells. J. J., Jones, trans., *The Mahāvastu* (London: Pali Text Society, 1949), 1:6–21. This account and those of the hero Phra Malai's visits to hell are even more gruesome in the later vernacular stories of Theravāda Southeast Asia. See Gifford, "Insight Guide to Hell."

19. Gómez, *Land of Bliss*, 8.
20. Gethin, *Foundations of Buddhism*, 119.
21. See Gethin, *Foundations of Buddhism*, for a useful overview of Buddhist meditation.
22. The Theravāda classic meditation manual *Visuddhimagga* (vii.40–4, xiii.29–65) provides a description of these states. For details, see Bhikkhu Buddhaghosa, *The Path of Purification* (Visuddhimagga), trans. Bhikkhu Ñāṇamoli (Kandy: Buddhist Publication Society, 1991).
23. Bradley S. Clough, "The Higher Knowledges in the Pāli Nikāyas and Vinaya," *Journal of the International Association of Buddhist Studies* 33, no. 1–2 (2010): 409.
24. Clough, "The Higher Knowledges," 409. This section draws heavily on Clough, "The Higher Knowledges"; and Nathan Katz, *Buddhist Images of Human Perfection: The Arahant of the Sutta Piṭika Compared with the Bodhisattva and the Mahāsiddha* (Delhi: Motilal Banarsidass Publishers, 1982). Despite being written nearly thirty years before Clough's article, Katz's insightful account of the *abhiññā*s in his *Buddhist Images* appears to have been overlooked by Clough in his otherwise erudite treatment of the topic.
25. Katz, *Buddhist Images*, 99.
26. Katz, *Buddhist Images*, 100; Clough, "The Higher Knowledges," 410.
27. Clough, "The Higher Knowledges," 411.
28. Clough, "The Higher Knowledges," 411; Katz, *Buddhist Images*, 100.
29. Translation by Clough, "The Higher Knowledges," 416.
30. Clough, "The Higher Knowledges," 417.
31. Clough, "The Higher Knowledges," 417.
32. Translation by Katz, *Buddhist Images*, 107.
33. Katz, *Buddhist Images*, 110.
34. Katz, *Buddhist Images*, 110–11.
35. See Katz, *Buddhist Images*; Clough, "The Higher Knowledges"; and David. V. Fiordalis, "Miracles in Indian Buddhist Narratives and Doctrine," *Journal of the International Association of Buddhist Studies* 33, nos. 1–2 (2010): 381–408.
36. Katz, *Buddhist Images*, 102; Clough, "The Higher Knowledges," 418–19.
37. Clough, "The Higher Knowledges," 418.
38. Clough, "The Higher Knowledges," 421; Katz, *Buddhist Images*, 103.
39. Clough, "The Higher Knowledges," 423.
40. Clough, "The Higher Knowledges," 423. Clough, "The Higher Knowledges," 426, points out that in the *Majjhima Nikāya* the Buddha says he recalls his lifetimes back ninety-one eons, but elsewhere he says he can for "immeasurable" number of eons.
41. Katz, *Buddhist Images*, 104. My brackets.

1. THE PARANORMAL IN THE INDIAN BUDDHIST TRADITION

42. Clough, "The Higher Knowledges," 426n38, refers to a commentary on the *Sutta Nipāta* wherein an elder monk is said to remember a thousand past lives and a thousand future lives.
43. Translation by Clough, "The Higher Knowledges," 427.
44. Katz, *Buddhist Images*, 105.
45. Translation by Clough, "The Higher Knowledges," 429.
46. Clough, "The Higher Knowledges," 430.
47. Katz, *Buddhist Images*, 106.
48. The literature in this area is vast. For a recent look at the state of the field of early Mahāyāna, see Paul Harrison, ed., *Setting Out on the Great Way: Essays on Early Mahāyāna Buddhism* (Sheffield: Equinox, 2018).
49. Peter Harvey, *An Introduction to Buddhism: Teachings, History, and Practices* (Cambridge: Cambridge University Press, 1990), 89–90.
50. In *The Supreme Array Scripture*, "form bodies" (*rūpakāya*) are used in place of the 1 and 2.
51. For a discussion of the term, see Edgerton, *Buddhist Hybrid Sanskrit*, 401. As Edgerton points out, "*buddhakṣetra*" occurs often in the *Mahāvastu* and therefore cannot be considered a strictly Mahāyāna notion.
52. For a table of the different types of buddha lands, see Gómez, *Land of Bliss*, 262. For a discussion of the meaning and significance of jeweled buddha-fields in the Mahāyāna, see D. E. Osto, *Power, Wealth, and Women in Indian Mahayana Buddhism: The Gaṇḍavyūha-sūtra* (London: Routledge, 2008).
53. The most popular and detailed buddha land for Mahāyāna Buddhists throughout Asia seems to have been Amitābha's Happy Land (Sukhāvatī), described in the *Sukhāvatīvyūha sutras*. For an erudite study and translation, see Gómez, *Land of Bliss*.
54. See, for example, Jens Braarvig, trans., Akṣayamatinirdeśasūtra, vol. 2: *The Tradition of Imperishability in Buddhist Thought* (Oslo: Solum Forlag, 1993), 24–26; chapter 23 of *The Lotus Sutra* (for an English translation of the Sanskrit, see H. Kern, trans., *The Saddharma-Puṇḍarīka or The Lotus or the True Law* [1884; New York: Dover, 1963, 394ff.]; for the Sanskrit text, see P. L. Vaidya, ed., *Saddharmapuṇḍarīka* [Darbhanga: Mithila Institute, 1960], 244ff.); chapter 9 of the *Vimalakīrti-nirdeśa* (for English translation, see Robert A. F. Thurman, trans., *The Holy Teaching of Vimalakīrti: A Mahāyāna Scripture* [University Park: Pennsylvania State University Press, 1976], 79); and the beginning of *The Sutra on the Ten Stages* (for an English translation, see Thomas Cleary, trans., *The Flower Ornament Scripture: A Translation of the Avatamsaka Sutra* [Boston: Shambhala, 1993], 695; for the Sanskrit text, see P. L. Vaidya, ed., *Daśabhūmikasūtra* [Darbhanga: Mithila Institute, 1967], 67.
55. Important *sūtras* that express this idea are *The Samādhi of the Direct Encounter with the Buddhas of the Present* (for an English translation, see Paul Harrison, trans., *The Samādhi of the Direct Encounter with the Buddhas of the Present: An Annotated English Translation of the Tibetan Version of the* Pratyutpanna-Buddha-Saṃmukhāvasthita-Samādhi-Sūtra [Tokyo: International Institute of Buddhist Studies, 1990]), *The Flower Ornament Scripture* (*Avataṃsaka*) (for an

[283]

1. THE PARANORMAL IN THE INDIAN BUDDHIST TRADITION

English translation, see Cleary, *The Flower Ornament Scripture*), the *Saṃdhinirmocana-sūtra* (for an English translation, see John Powers, trans., *Wisdom of the Buddha: The Saṃdhinirmocana Sūtra* [Berkeley: Dharma, 1995]), and the *Laṅkāvatāra-sūtra* (for an English translation, see D. T. Suzuki, trans., *The Laṅkāvatāra Sūtra: A Mahāyāna Text* [London: Routledge and Kegan Paul, 1973]; for a Sanskrit edition, see P. L. Vaidya, ed., *Laṅkāvatārasūtra* [Darbhanga: Mithila Institute, 1963]). For a recent and detailed study of Yogācāra as a type of Buddhist phenomenology, see Dan Lusthaus, *Buddhist Phenomenology: A Philosophical Investigation of Yogācāra Buddhism and the* Ch'emg Wei-shih lun (London: RoutledgeCurzon, 2002).

56. Luis Oscar Gómez, "Selected Verses from the Gaṇḍavyūha: Text, Critical Apparatus, and Translation," PhD diss., Yale University, 1967, lxxvi. For example, from the *Laṅkāvatāra-sūtra* (P. L. Vaidya, *Laṅkāvatārasūtra*, 31), we read that "bodhisattvas ... hear the teaching of the Dharma that all phenomena are void of non-origination, decay, permanence and annihilation just like the state of illusions, dreams, appearances, reflections or the moon in water [*bodhisattvāś ... māyāsvapnapratibhāsapratibimbodakacandragatisamānutpāda-bhaṅgaśāśvatocchedarahitān sarvadharmān ... dharmadeśanāṃ śṛṇvanti*]."
57. Har Dayal, *The Bodhisattva Doctrine in Buddhist Sanskrit Literature* (London: Kegan Paul, Trench, Trubner & Co., Ltd., 1932), 168.
58. Dayal, *The Bodhisattva Doctrine*, 168.
59. For a description of tenth-stage bodhisattvas, see Gethin, *Foundations of Buddhism*, 231.
60. Donald S. Lopez Jr., *Buddhism: An Introduction and Guide* (London: Penguin, 2001), 84.
61. See Cleary, *The Flower Ornament Scripture*, 724–25. For the Sanskrit text, see Vaidya, *Daśabhūmikāsūtra*.
62. Dayal, *The Bodhisattva Doctrine*, 112–13.
63. Cleary, *The Flower Ornament Scripture*, 725.
64. Dayal, *The Bodhisattva Doctrine*, 106–34.
65. Florin Deleanu, "Bodhisattvabhūmi," in *Oxford Bibliographies Online in Buddhism* (Oxford: Oxford University Press, 2018), https://www.oxfordbibliographies.com/view/document/obo-9780195393521/obo-9780195393521-0254.xml.
66. Dayal's original text footnotes this sentence with a reference to a 1908 publication by R. Schmidt. Dayal, *The Bodhisattva Doctrine*, 347n114.
67. Dayal, *The Bodhisattva Doctrine*, 112–13.
68. I propose a similar hypothesis concerning the textual accounts of *samādhis* found in Mahāyāna sources, suggesting that they may find their basis in altered states of consciousness experienced by Indian Mahāyāna Buddhists. D. E. Osto, *Altered States: Buddhism and Psychedelic Spirituality in America* (New York: Columbia University Press, 2016); and Osto, "Altered States and the Origins of the Mahāyāna."
69. Dayal, *The Bodhisattva Doctrine*, 113; Luis Oscar Gómez, "The Bodhisattva as Wonder-Worker," in *Prajñāpāramitā and Related System: Studies in Honor of Edward Conze*, ed. Lewis Lancaster and Luis Gómez (Berkeley: Berkeley Buddhist Studies Series, 1977), 230.
70. The following list is adapted from Dayal, *The Bodhisattva Doctrine*, 113.

1. THE PARANORMAL IN THE INDIAN BUDDHIST TRADITION

71. Dayal, *The Bodhisattva Doctrine*, 114–15.
72. Dayal, *The Bodhisattva Doctrine*, 115.
73. Osto, *Power, Wealth, and Women*, 4.
74. Osto, *Power, Wealth and Women*, 24.
75. Osto, *Power, Wealth and Women*, 19.
76. For information about Borobudur, see Jan Fontein, *The Pilgrimage of Sudhana: A Study of Gaṇḍavyūha Illustrations in China, Japan, and Java* (The Hague: Mouton & Company, 1967); Jan Fontein, *Entering the Dharmadhātu: A Study of the Gandavyūha Reliefs of Borobudur* (Leiden: Brill, 2012); and Luis Oscar Gómez and Hiram W. Woodward Jr., eds., *Barabuḍur: History and Significance of a Buddhist Monument* (Berkeley: Berkeley Buddhist Series, 1981).
77. For another example of supernormal powers in the Mature Mahāyāna, see Fiordalis's illuminating discussion of the *Vimalakīrtinirdeśa* in David. V. Fiordalis, "The Wonderous Display of Superhuman Power in the Vimalakīrtinirdeśa: Miracle of Marvel?," in *Yoga Powers: Extraordinary Capacities Attained Through Meditation and Concentration*, ed. Knut A. Jacobsen (Leiden: Brill, 2012), 97–125.
78. Luis Oscar Gómez, "The Bodhisattva as Wonder-Worker"; and Luis Oscar Gómez, "On Buddhist Wonders and Wonder-Working," *Journal of the International Association of Buddhist Studies* 33, nos. 1–2 (2010): 513–54.
79. Gómez, "The Bodhisattva as Wonder-Worker," 231. Brackets mine.
80. Gómez, "The Bodhisattva as Wonder-Worker," 232. Brackets in the original.
81. Gómez, "The Bodhisattva as Wonder-Worker," 234.
82. The notion of *śūnyatā* may itself be related to the invention of the concept of zero in ancient Indian mathematics.
83. The Chinese Huayan masters understood this relationship between the two, describing the undivided Dharma Realm as "Principle" (*li*) and the divided Dharma Realm as "phenomena" (*shih*). According to Huayan, phenomena depend on Principle for their existence, but Principle also depends on phenomena. In other words, there is no ground without appearances. This view argues against the Dharma Realm or Dharma Body possessing any independent metaphysical status from the phenomena it contains; hence my interpretation of it as "groundless ground."
84. Gómez, "The Bodhisattva as Wonder-Worker," 234–35.
85. Gómez, "On Buddhist Wonders," 543.
86. For a useful introduction to Buddhist Tantra, see Paul Williams, Anthony Tribe, and Alexander Wynne, *Buddhist Thought: A Complete Introduction to the Indian Tradition*, 2nd ed. (London: Routledge, 2011), 143–85. See also David Snellgrove, *Indo-Tibetan Buddhism: Indian Buddhists and Their Tibetan Successors*, 2 vols. (Boston: Shambhala, 1987); and Ronald M. Davidson, *Indian Esoteric Buddhism: A Social History of the Tantric Movement* (New York: Columbia University Press, 2002).
87. Williams, Tribe, and Wynne, *Buddhist Thought*, 146.
88. See Dan Martin, "Illusion Web—Locating the *Guhyagarbha Tantra* in Buddhist Intellectual History," in *Silver on Lapis: Tibetan Literary Culture and History*, ed. Christopher I. Beckwith (Bloomington: Tibetan Society, 1987); Charles Orzech, "Mahāvairocana," in *The Encyclopedia of Religion* (New York: Macmillan, 1987);

1. THE PARANORMAL IN THE INDIAN BUDDHIST TRADITION

David McMahan, "Transpositions of Metaphor and Imagery in the *Gaṇḍavyūha* and Tantric Buddhist Practice," *Pacific World Journal*, 3rd series, no. 6 (Fall 2004): 181–94; Douglas Osto, " 'Proto-Tantric' Elements in the *Gaṇḍavyūha-sūtra*," *Journal of Religious History* 33, no. 2 (2009): 165–77; and Williams, Tribe, and Wynne, *Buddhist Thought*, 143–85.

89. See Osto, " 'Proto-Tantric' Elements in the *Gaṇḍavyūha-sūtra*"; McMahan, "Transpositions of Metaphor and Imagery."
90. Williams, Tribe, and Wynne, *Buddhist Thought*, 184–85.
91. Williams, Tribe, and Wynne, *Buddhist Thought*, 151–63.
92. Williams, Tribe, and Wynne, *Buddhist Thought*, 160.
93. David B. Gray, *The Cakrasamvara Tantra (The Discourse of Śrī Heruka): A Study and Annotated Translation* (New York: Columbia University Press, 2007).
94. Williams, Tribe, and Wynne, *Buddhist Thought*, 163; Katz, *Buddhist Images of Human Perfection*, 279–85.
95. For an English translation from the Tibetan, see James B. Robinson, trans., *The Buddha's Lions: The Lives of the Eighty-Four Siddhas* (Berkeley, CA: Dharma, 1979).
96. Ryan Richard Overbey, "On the Appearance of Siddhis in Chinese Buddhist Texts," in *Yoga Powers: Extraordinary Capacities Attained Through Meditation and Concentration*, ed. Knut A. Jacobsen (Leiden: Brill, 2012), 127–44.
97. Siddhas were apparently fond of doing this. Katz, *Buddhist Images of Human Perfection*, 110n51.
98. For a modern example of this siddhi, see Wim Hof, "The Wim Hof Method," https://www.wimhofmethod.com/.
99. See, for example, the "Six Dharmas of Naropa." Herbert V. Guenther, *The Life and Teaching of Naropa: Translated from the Original Tibetan with a Philosophical Commentary Based on the Oral Transmission* (Boston: Shambhala, 1995); and Chen Chi Chang, trans., *Esoteric Teachings of the Tibetan Tantra*, ed. C. A. Muses (York Beach: Samuel Weiser, 1982). One power favored by "sinister yogis" was the ability to possess another person's body. David Gordon White, *Sinister Yogis* (Chicago: University of Chicago Press, 2009), 122–66.
100. David B. Gray, "Tantra and the Tantric Traditions of Hinduism and Buddhism," in *Oxford Research Encyclopedias, Religion* (Oxford: Oxford University Press, 2016), 13.
101. Sam van Shaik, *Buddhist Magic: Divination, Healing, and Enchantment Through the Ages* (Boulder, CO: Shambhala, 2020).
102. Ronald M. Davidson, "Magicians, Sorcerers, and Witches: Considering Pretantric, Non-sectarian Sources of Tantric Practices," *Religions* 8 (2017): 188.
103. Fiordalis, "The Wonderous Display of Superhuman Power in the Vimalakīrtinirdeśa," 383.
104. Fiordalis, "The Wonderous Display of Superhuman Power in the Vimalakīrtinirdeśa," 384. For an English translation of this, see "The Miracle Sūtra" (*Prātihārya-sūtra*) from the *Divyāvadāna* (Andy Rotman, trans., *Divine Stories: Divyāvadāna, Part I* [Boston: Wisdom, 2008], 278).
105. Rotman, *Divine Stories*, 279–80.
106. Fiordalis, "The Wonderous Display of Superhuman Power in the Vimalakīrtinirdeśa," 386.
107. van Shaik, *Buddhist Magic*, 9–10.

108. On the Jātaka Stories, see Naomi Appleton, *Jātaka Stories in Theravāda Buddhism: Narrating the Bodhisatta Path* (Burlington: Ashgate, 2010); and E. B. Cowell, ed., *Jātaka: Or Stories of the Buddha's Former Births*, 2 vols. (Delhi: Cosmo, 1973). On the avadāna stories, see, for example, Rotman, *Divine Stories*; Andy Rotman, *Hungry Ghosts* (Boston: Wisdom, 2021); and Joel Tatelman, *The Glorious Deeds of Pūrṇa: A Translation and Study of the Pūrṇāvadāna* (Surrey: Curzon, 2000).
109. For two important studies on the Third Karmapa, see Ruth Gamble, *Reincarnation in Tibetan Buddhism: The Third Karmapa and the Invention of a Tradition* (New York: Oxford University Press, 2018); and Ruth Gamble, *The Third Karmapa Rangjung Dorje: Master of Mahāmudrā* (Boulder: Shambala, 2020). For an accessible English translation of Milarepa's life, see Lobsang P. Lhalungpa, trans., *The Life of Milarepa* (New York: Arkana, 1977).
110. On the early medieval period, see Donald E. Gjertson, "The Early Chinese Buddhist Miracle Tale: A Preliminary Survey," *Journal of the American Oriental Society* 101, no. 3 (1981): 287–301; and Robert Ford Company, *Signs from the Unseen Realm: Buddhist Miracle Tales from Early Medieval China* (Honolulu: University of Hawai'i Press, 2012). On thaumaturgy, see Alan J. Berkowitz, "Account of the Buddhist Thaumaturge Baozhi," in *Buddhism in Practice*, ed. Donald J. Lopez Jr. (Princeton, NJ: Princeton University Press, 1995), 578–85. On the *Lotus Sūtra*, see Daniel B. Stevenson, "Tales of the Lotus Sūtra," in *Buddhism in Practice*, ed. Donald J. Lopez Jr. (Princeton, NJ: Princeton University Press, 1995), 427–51. On Amitābha's Pure Land, see Daniel B. Stevenson, "Death-Bed Testimonials of the Pure Land Faithful," in *Buddhism in Practice*, ed. Donald J. Lopez Jr. (Princeton, NJ: Princeton University Press, 1995), 592–602.
111. On wizards from Burma, see Patrick Pranke, "On Becoming a Buddhist Wizard," in *Buddhism in Practice*, ed. Donald J. Lopez Jr. (Princeton, NJ: Princeton University Press, 1995), 343–58; and Patrick Pranke, "On Saints and Wizards—Ideals of Human Perfection and Power in Contemporary Burmese Buddhism," *Journal of the International Association of Buddhist Studies* 33, nos. 1–2 (2010): 453–88. On Thai masters, see Stanley Jeyaraja Tambiah, *The Buddhist Saints of the Forest and the Cult of Amulets: A Study in Charisma, Hagiography, Sectarianism, and Millennial Buddhism* (Cambridge: Cambridge University Press, 1984).

2. The Enchanted West: The Contemporary Scientific Study of the Paranormal

1. Jason A. Josephson-Storm, *The Myth of Disenchantment: Magic, Modernity, and the Birth of the Human Sciences* (Chicago: University of Chicago Press, 2017).
2. Josephson-Storm, *The Myth of Disenchantment*, 24; italics in original.
3. For a history of the Society for Psychical Research, see Zofia Weaver, "Our History," Society for Psychical Research, London, 2022, https://www.spr.ac.uk/about/our-history; and D. West, "Society for Psychical Research," *Psi Encyclopedia*, Society for Psychical Research, London, 2019, https://psi-encyclopedia.spr.ac.uk/articles/society-psychical-research.

2. THE ENCHANTED WEST

4. Weaver, "Our History."
5. George P. Hansen, *The Trickster and the Paranormal* (Bloomington: Xlibris, 2001), 176.
6. Jeffrey J. Kripal, *Authors of the Impossible: The Paranormal and the Sacred* (Chicago: University of Chicago Press, 2010), 55.
7. Weaver, "Our History."
8. For an account of Myers's life and work, see Kripal, *Authors of the Impossible*, 36–91.
9. American Society for Psychic Research, "About the Society," American Society for Psychic Research, New York, http://www.aspr.com/who.htm.
10. See Christopher Partridge, *Re-Enchantment of the West: Alternative Spiritualities, Sacralization, Popular Culture, and Occulture*, 2 vols. (London: T & T Clark, 2004–2005).
11. Kripal, *Authors of the Impossible*, 94–95.
12. Charles Fort, *The Book of the Damned* (1919; New York: Boni and Liveright, 2019).
13. Charles Fort, *New Lands* (1923; New York: Ace, 1968); Charles Forte, *Lo!* (1931; New York: Ace 1968); Charles Fort, *Wild Talents* (1932; New York: Ace, 1965).
14. Kripal, *Authors of the Impossible*, 97.
15. Kripal, *Authors of the Impossible*, 105.
16. Kripal, *Authors of the Impossible*, 105; M. Colborn, "Forteana," *Psi Encyclopaedia*, Society for Psychical Research, 2014, https://psi-encyclopedia.spr.ac.uk/articles/forteana.
17. Sally Rhine Feather and Barbara Ensrud, "JB Rhine," *Psi Encyclopedia*, Society for Psychical Research, 2023, https://psi-encyclopedia.spr.ac.uk/articles/jb-rhine.
18. J. B. Rhine, *Extra-Sensory Perception* (Boston: Bruce Humphries, 1934).
19. Rhine Feather and Ensrud, "JB Rhine."
20. J. B. Rhine, *New Frontiers of the Mind* (New York: Farrar and Rinehart, 1937).
21. J. B. Rhine, J. G. Pratt, C. E. Stuart, B. M. Smith, and J. A. Greenwood, *Extra-Sensory Perception After Sixty Years* (New York: Henry Holt, 1940).
22. Rhine Feather and Ensrud, "JB Rhine."
23. Rhine Feather and Ensrud, "JB Rhine."
24. K. M. Wehrstein, "Charles Tart," *Psi Encyclopedia*, Society for Psychical Research, 2022, https://psi-encyclopedia.spr.ac.uk/articles/charles-tart; California Institute of Integral Studies, "Charles Tart," 2022, https://www.ciis.edu/faculty-and-staff-directory/charles-tart.
25. Charles T. Tart, "CTT Brief Bio" 2022, https://blog.paradigm-sys.com/brief-bio/.
26. Tart, "CTT Brief Bio."
27. Charles T. Tart, *The Secret Science of the Soul: How Evidence of the Paranormal Is Bringing Science and Spirit Together* (Napa: Fearless Books, 2017), chap. 1.
28. Tart, *The Secret Science of the Soul*, chap. 5.
29. Tart, *The Secret Science of the Soul*, chap. 6.
30. Tart, *The Secret Science of the Soul*, chap. 6.
31. Tart, *The Secret Science of the Soul*, chap. 12.
32. Tart, *The Secret Science of the Soul*, chap. 13.

2. THE ENCHANTED WEST

33. Robert McLuhan and Michael Duggan, "Dean Radin," *Psi Encyclopedia*, Society for Psychical Research, 2023, https://psi-encyclopedia.spr.ac.uk/articles/dean-radin.
34. Institute of Noetic Science (IONS), "Dean Radin, MS, PhD: Chief Scientist," 2023, https://noetic.org/profile/dean-radin/.
35. McLuhan and Duggan, "Dean Radin."
36. McLuhan and Duggan, "Dean Radin"; Institute of Noetic Science (IONS), "Dean Radin."
37. Dean Radin, *Supernormal: Science, Yoga, and the Evidence for Extraordinary Psychic Ability* (New York: Deepak Chopra Books, 2013).
38. Radin, *Supernormal*, 3.
39. Radin, *Supernormal*, 5.
40. Radin, *Supernormal*, 5.
41. Radin, *Supernormal*, 70.
42. Radin, *Supernormal*, 89–90.
43. Radin, *Supernormal*, 122.
44. Radin, *Supernormal*, 134.
45. "Analysis of 770 free-response tests conducted at SRI resulted in odds against chance of over 300 million to 1. Another 445 tests conducted at SAIC resulted in odds against chance of 1.6 million to 1. At Princeton, a total of 653 sessions were conducted, resulting in odds against chance of 33 million to 1." Radin, *Supernormal*, 142.
46. Radin, *Supernormal*, 161.
47. Radin, *Supernormal*, 189. Radin follows his mention of this astounding result with a statement about newer fully automated studies that were conducted specifically "to overcome all known skeptical complaints about the previous studies," which also demonstrated telepathy, though with less impressive results but still significant odds against chance of 517 to 1. Radin, *Supernormal*, 189.
48. Radin, *Supernormal*, 207–9.
49. Radin, *Supernormal*, 222.
50. Radin, *Supernormal*, 230.
51. Roger Nelson, "Global Consciousness Project," 2020, https://noosphere.princeton.edu/index.html. Analysis of deviations from randomness during 9/11 are dramatic and began to appear several hours before the first Tower was struck. Roger Nelson, "Formal Analysis: September 11 2001," Global Consciousness Project, 2020, https://noosphere.princeton.edu/911formal.html.
52. Radin, *Supernormal*, 235.
53. Radin, *Supernormal*, 265.
54. Radin, *Supernormal*, 268, 279.
55. Radin, *Supernormal*, 297.
56. Radin, *Supernormal*, 300.
57. David E. Presti and Edward F. Kelly, "Prologue: Deepening the Dialogue," in *Mind Beyond Brain: Buddhism, Science, and the Paranormal*, ed. David E. Presti (New York: Columbia University Press, 2018), xvi–xvii.

2. THE ENCHANTED WEST

58. Ian Stevenson, *Twenty Cases Suggestive of Reincarnation* (1966; Charlottesville: University of Virginia, 1974).
59. David E. Presti, ed., with Bruce Greyson, Edward F. Kelly, Emily Williams Kelly, and Jim B. Tucker, *Mind Beyond Brain: Buddhism, Science, and the Paranormal* (New York: Columbia University Press, 2018).
60. Bruce Greyson, "Near-Death Experiences," in *Mind Beyond Brain: Buddhism, Science, and the Paranormal*, ed. David E. Presti (New York: Columbia University Press, 2018), 22–44.
61. Bruce Grayson, *After: A Doctor Explores What Near-Death Experiences Reveal About Life and Beyond* (New York: St. Martins Essentials, 2021).
62. Jim B. Tucker, "Reports of Past-Life Memories," in *Mind Beyond Brain: Buddhism, Science, and the Paranormal*, ed. David E. Presti (New York: Columbia University Press, 2018), 45–68.
63. Jim Tucker, *Return to Life: Extraordinary Cases of Children Who Remember Past Lives* (New York: St. Martin's Griffin, 2013); Jim Tucker, *Before: Children's Memories of Previous Lives* (New York: St. Martin's Essentials, 2021).
64. Leslie Kean, *Surviving Death: A Journalist Investigates Evidence for an Afterlife* (New York: Three Rivers, 2017).
65. Tucker, "Reports of Past-Life Memories," 68.
66. Emily Williams Kelly, "Mediums, Apparitions, and Deathbed Experiences," in *Mind Beyond Brain: Buddhism, Science, and the Paranormal*, ed. David E. Presti (New York: Columbia University Press, 2018), 69–91; Edward F. Kelly, "Paranormal Phenomena, the *Siddhis*, and an Emerging Path Toward Reconciliation of Science and Spirituality," in *Mind Beyond Brain: Buddhism, Science, and the Paranormal*, ed. David E. Presti (New York: Columbia University Press, 2018), 91–120.
67. Kelly, "Paranormal Phenomena," 100.
68. E. F. Kelly, E. W. Kelly, A. Crabtree, A. Gauld, M. Grosso, and B. Greyson, *Irreducible Mind: Toward a Psychology for the 21st Century* (Lanham, MD: Rowman & Littlefield, 2007).
69. Kelly, "Paranormal Phenomena," 112; italics in original.
70. E. F. Kelly, A. Crabtree, and P. Marshall, eds., *Beyond Physicalism: Toward Reconciliation of Science and Spirituality* (Lanham, MD: Rowman & Littlefield, 2015).
71. David E. Presti, "An Expanded Conception of Mind," in *Mind Beyond Brain: Buddhism, Science, and the Paranormal*, ed. David E. Presti (New York: Columbia University Press, 2018), 121–46.
72. For my review of this book, see Douglas Osto, "Mind Beyond Brain: Buddhism, Science, and the Paranormal," *Religion* 50, no. 1 (2020): 178–82.
73. Annie Jacobsen, *Phenomena: The Secret History of the U.S. Government's Investigation Into Extrasensory Perception and Psychokinesis* (New York: Little, Brown, 2017), 40–43, 119, 5.
74. Jacobsen, *Phenomena*, 127, 134, 136–37.
75. Jacobsen, *Phenomena*, 143–44.
76. Jacobsen, *Phenomena*, 6–7.
77. Jacobsen, *Phenomena*, 179, 181.
78. Jacobsen, *Phenomena*, 150.
79. Jacobsen, *Phenomena*, 159–60.

2. THE ENCHANTED WEST

80. For examples of Pat Price's abilities, see Tart, *The Secret Science*, chaps. 7, 11; Russell Targ, "Remote Viewing at Stanford Research Institute in the 1970s: A Memoir," *Journal of Scientific Exploration* 10, no. 1 (1996): 77–88; Jacobsen, *Phenomena*, 162–67.
81. Targ, "Remote Viewing"; Jacobsen *Phenomena*, 166–67.
82. Jacobsen, *Phenomena*, 181–83.
83. Targ, "Remote Viewing," 88, 78.
84. Jacobsen, *Phenomena*, 370.
85. Hansen, *The Trickster and the Paranormal*.
86. Jacobsen, *Phenomena*, 380.
87. D. W. Pasulka, *American Cosmic: UFOs, Religion, Technology* (Oxford: Oxford University Press, 2019), 14.
88. Jacques Vallée, *Passport to Magonia: From Folklore to Flying Saucers* (1969; Daily Grail, 2014); Charles Fort, *The Book of the Damned*, 287.
89. For some of the evidence, see Robert Hastings, *UFOs and Nukes: Extraordinary Encounters at Nuclear Weapons Sites*, 2nd ed. (Robert Hastings, 2017); Vallée, *Passport to Magonia*; and Leslie Kean, *UFOs: Generals, Pilots, and Government Officials Go on Record* (New York: Harmony, 2010).
90. Kean, *UFOs*, 9–10.
91. Helene Cooper, Ralph Blumenthal, and Leslie Kean, "Glowing Auras and 'Black Money': The Pentagon's Mysterious U.F.O. Program," *New York Times*, December 16, 2017.
92. Many copies of these videos are on the internet. For one example on YouTube, see "Pentagon Officially Releases 'UFO' Videos," *Guardian*, YouTube video, April 28, 2020, https://www.youtube.com/watch?v=auITEKd4sjA.
93. "Navy Pilots Describe Encounters with UFOs," *60 Minutes*, YouTube video, May 17, 2021, https://www.youtube.com/watch?v=ZBtMbBPzqHY.
94. Office of the Director of National Intelligence, "Preliminary Assessment: Unidentified Aerial Phenomena," June 25, 2021, 1.
95. Office of the Director of National Intelligence, "Preliminary Assessment," 4–5.
96. See Leslie Kean and Ralph Blumenthal, "Intelligence Officials Say U.S. Has Retrieved Craft of Non-human Origin," *The Debrief*, June 5, 2023, https://thedebrief.org/intelligence-officials-say-u-s-has-retrieved-non-human-craft/; and Dutch UAP Disclosure, "We Are Not Alone | News Nation | Full Interview | Ross Coulthart with Dave Grusch, 11-06-2023," Dutch UAP Disclosure, YouTube video, June 15, 2023, https://www.youtube.com/watch?v=V6JxUHkyDuY.
97. "We Are Not Alone."
98. "House Holds Hearing on UFOs, Government Transparency," *CBS News*, YouTube video, July 27, 2023, https://www.youtube.com/watch?v=SNgoul4vyDM.
99. Chris Eberhart, "Pentagon Denies Secret UFO Retrieval Program After Whistleblower Bombshell," *Fox News*, June 7, 2023, https://www.foxnews.com/us/pentagon-denies-secret-ufo-retrieval-program-after-whistleblower-bombshell.
100. For a recent example, see James T. Lacatski, Colm A. Kelleher, and George Knapp, *Inside the U.S. Government Covert UFO Program: Initial Revelations* (Henderson, NV: RTMA, LLC, 2023), 43, where the authors state: "Thus, paranormal phenomena

and psychic effects are closely related to the UAP phenomena and they cannot be dismissed. The relationship is unavoidable."
101. Vallée, *Passport to Magonia*, 21, 7, 25, 9, 25.
102. Pasulka, *American Cosmic*, 35, 29, 35, 52, 75.
103. Kripal, *Authors of the Impossible*, 146.
104. Hansen, *The Trickster and the Paranormal*, 192.
105. John A. Keel, *The Mothman Prophecies: The True Story of the Alien Who Terrorized an American City* (1975; London: New English Library, 2002). A movie was made based on this book. See Mark Pellington, dir., *The Mothman Prophecies* (New York and Culver City, CA: Screen Gems and Sony Pictures, 2002).
106. Keel, *The Mothman Prophecies*; Hansen, *The Trickster and the Paranormal*, 195; Vallée, *Passport to Magonia*, 78.
107. *The Secret of Skinwalker Ranch*, television series, History Channel, https://www.history.com/shows/the-secret-of-skinwalker-ranch.
108. Colm Kelleher and George Knapp, *Hunt for the Skinwalker: Science Confronts the Unexplained at a Remote Utah Ranch* (New York: Paraview Pocket Books, 2005).
109. James T. Lacatski, Colm Kelleher, and George Knapp, *Skinwalkers at the Pentagon: An Insider's Account of the Government's Secret UFO Program* (Henderson, NV: RTMA, LLC, 2021), introduction.
110. Lacatski, Kelleher, and Knapp, *Skinwalkers at the Pentagon*, introduction.
111. Lacatski, Kelleher, and Knapp, *Skinwalkers at the Pentagon*, 81–82.
112. Lacatski, Kelleher, and Knapp, *Skinwalkers at the Pentagon*, 81.
113. Lacatski, Kelleher, and Knapp, *Skinwalkers at the Pentagon*, 82, 136–37.
114. Jacobsen writes: "Gallup polls and Pew Research Center studies reveal that a majority of Americans alive today harbor paranormal beliefs: 73 percent say they have had a supernatural or paranormal experience, and 55 percent believe in psychic or spiritual healing. Many Americans also believe in extrasensory perception or telepathy (41 percent); believe that extraterrestrials have visited Earth (29 percent); or say they've seen a ghost (18 percent). A minority 27 percent do not believe in anything supernatural." Jacobsen, *Phenomena*, 7. For example, a 2011 Associated Press–GfK poll shows that 77 percent of adults believe angels are real. "Poll: Nearly 8 in 10 Americans Believe in Angels," *CBS News*, December 23, 2011, https://www.cbsnews.com/news/poll-nearly-8-in-10-americans-believe-in-angels/. These believers include many non-Christian members who likely consider themselves "spiritual, but not religious."
115. Hanson, *The Trickster and the Paranormal*.
116. The British UFO researcher Jenny Randles coined this term. Lacatski, Kelleher, and Knapp, *Skinwalkers at the Pentagon*, 137.

3. Tales of Psychic Phenomena

1. Three respondents reported they were seventeen, so their responses were discarded, as they were under the minimum age for the survey.

3. TALES OF PSYCHIC PHENOMENA

2. D. E. Osto, *Altered States: Buddhism and Psychedelic Spirituality in American* (New York: Columbia University Press, 2016).
3. Charles Prebish, "The Academic Study of Buddhism in America: A Silent Sangha," in *American Buddhism: Methods and Findings in Recent Scholarship*, ed. Duncan Williams and Christopher Queen (Richmond: Curzon, 1999), 183–214.
4. For example, see Rick Fields, *How the Swans Came to the Lake: A Narrative History of Buddhism in America*, 3rd. rev. and updated ed. (Boston: Shambala, 1992); Stephen Batchelor, *The Awakening of the West; The Encounter of Buddhism and Western Culture: 543 BCE –1992* (London: Aquarian, 1994); Charles S. Prebish and Kenneth K. Tanaka, eds., *The Faces of Buddhism in America* (Los Angeles: University of California Press, 1998); Richard Hughes Seager, *Buddhism in America* (New York: Columbia University Press, 1999); Duncan Ryūken Williams and Christopher S. Queen, eds., *American Buddhism: Methods and Findings in Recent Scholarship* (Richmond: Curzon, 1999); Charles Prebish, *Luminous Passage: The Practice and Study of Buddhism in America* (Berkeley: University of California Press, 1999); James William Coleman, *The New Buddhism: The Western Transformation of an Ancient Tradition* (Oxford: Oxford University Press, 2001); Charles Prebish, *Buddhism: The American Experience* (Journal of Buddhist Ethics Online Books, 2003); and David L. McMahan, *The Making of Modern Buddhism* (Oxford: Oxford University Press, 2008).
5. See Jan Nattier, "Who Is a Buddhist? Charting the Landscape of Buddhist America," in *The Faces of Buddhism in America*, ed. Charles S. Prebish and Kenneth K. Tanaka (Los Angeles: University of California Press, 1998), 183–95.
6. One of my interviewees had a number of intense mystical experiences but none that were overtly paranormal as I define it in this study. Therefore, data from this interview has not been included here.
7. See Stanley Jeyaraja Tambiah, *The Buddhist Saints of the Forest and the Cult of Amulets: A Study in Charisma, Hagiography, Sectarianism, and Millennial Buddhism* (Cambridge: Cambridge University Press, 1984).
8. Oxford English Dictionary, s.v. "clairvoyance, n.," *OED Oxford English Dictionary Online*, July 2023.
9. There are numerous accounts of modern Thai masters from the Forest Tradition possessing psychic powers. For a detailed study, see Tambiah, *The Buddhist Saints of the Forest and the Cult of Amulets*.
10. There appears to have been some debate within the U.S. government agencies as to whether remote viewers were "born" or "made." See Annie Jacobsen, *Phenomena: The Secret History of the U.S. Government's Investigation into Extrasensory Perception and Psychokinesis* (New York: Little, Brown, 2017) 296–308.
11. "Buddhist Nun Recommends Calming the Mind to Cope with Pandemic," *The World*, April 10, 2020, https://theworld.org/stories/2020-04-10/buddhist-nun-recommends-calming-mind-cope-pandemic.
12. This last one states that the "metanormal" is normal in Buddhism, raising the issue of applying the term "paranormal" to certain Buddhist experiences. I return to this issue is chapter 7.
13. *Oxford English Dictionary Online*, s.v. "precognition, n."

3. TALES OF PSYCHIC PHENOMENA

14. Rick Repetti, *Buddhism, Meditation, and Free Will: A Theory of Mental Freedom* (New York: Routledge, 2019).
15. Although the survey was anonymous, for a number of the participants I was able to discern their identities from the information they supplied. However, to protect their privacy, I have changed their names and names of other people and places mentioned in their responses.
16. The name given here is a pseudonym. "Ayyā" is a title in Pāli meaning "noble one." I am assuming, since the survey was anonymous and the Ayyā requested that I not use the actual names of places mentioned, that she felt that it was not an infraction of monastic rules to relate this story. The name of the city has also been changed.
17. Repetti, *Buddhism, Meditation, and Free Will*.
18. This precognitive visual image of a piece of artwork shares some similarities with a precognitive vision I had of a work of art induced through an altered state of consciousness in my twenties. See my autobiographical postscript for details.
19. Place names have been changed to protect Elma's anonymity.
20. Elma informed me (personal communication, October 4, 2023): "In reality there was a petrol station in the exact same place as the 'garage' in the dream. The petrol station was in close vicinity to the consulting rooms, at least a few houses or so away and on the same side of the avenue."
21. Elma informed me (personal communication October 4, 2023): "In the dream the woman had given me two paintings. When I went to frame Priya's painting, I took the backing off and there underneath the original was another painting or part thereof. It had been discarded and used as a backing sheet."
22. For the most dramatic case of a precognitive dream in this study, see Rick Repetti's account in chapter 5.
23. *Oxford English Dictionary Online*, s.v. "telepathy, n."
24. Liz Wilson, *Charming Cadavers: Horrific Figurations of the Feminine in Indian Buddhist Hagiographic Literature* (Chicago: University of Chicago Press, 1996).
25. Wilson, *Charming Cadavers*, 73.
26. Ñāṇamoli, trans., *The Path of Purification* (Visuddhimagga) by Bhadantācariya Buddhaghosa, 5th ed. (Kandy: Buddhist Publication Society, 1991), 173–90.
27. Tambiah, *The Buddhist Saints of the Forest and the Cult of Amulets*.
28. *Oxford English Dictionary Online*, s.v. "retrocognition, n."
29. Bhikkhu Anālayo, *Rebirth in Early Buddhism and Current Research* (Somerville, MA: Wisdom Publications, 2018).
30. Anālayo, *Rebirth in Early Buddhism*, 137.
31. Anālayo, *Rebirth in Early Buddhism*, 138–39.
32. For some samples of Dhammaruwan's chanting, see SuttaCentral, "Dhammaruwan—Chanting—1970's," https://discourse.suttacentral.net/t/dhammaruwan-chanting-1970s/8279; see also Lankaramaya Dubai, "Dhammachakka Sutta Dhammaruwan," YouTube video, May 12, 2018, https://www.youtube.com/watch?v=QOB2c9QVa_M.
33. Anālayo, *Rebirth in Early Buddhism*, 137.
34. Anālayo, *Rebirth in Early Buddhism*, 140.

35. Anālayo, *Rebirth in Early Buddhism*, 176, 189.
36. For more on Rick, see chapter 5.
37. See Ananda K. Coomaraswamy, "*Saṃvega*, 'Aesthetic Shock,'" *Harvard Journal of Asiatic Studies* 7, no. 3 (1943): 174–79.
38. Anālayo, *Rebirth in Early Buddhism*, 99.

4. Tales of OBEs, NDEs, and Close Encounters

1. John Crow, "Taming the Astral Body: The Theosophical Society's Ongoing Problem of Emotion and Control," *Journal of the American Academy of Religion* 80, no. 3 (September 2012): 691–717.
2. Carleton University, "Religion Faculty: Angela Sumegi," https://carleton.ca/religion/people/angela-sumegi/.
3. Angela Sumegi, *Dream Worlds of Shamanism and Tibetan Buddhism: The Third Place* (Albany: State University of New York Press, 2008); Angela Sumegi, *Understanding Death: Identity and the Afterlife in World Religions* (Malden, MA: Wiley-Blackwell, 2014).
4. When Angela mentioned this "loud roaring sound" in our interview, I pointed out the similarity of this experience to one described by the contemporary Nondual Śaiva master Swami Lakshmanjoo that occurs when one enters the "junction" between wakefulness and sleep while maintaining awareness. According to the swami, this is the start of the *turya*, the fourth state of pure consciousness. Compare this passage to Angela's statement: "And when that giddiness becomes stabler and remains for a longer period, then the aspirant falls asleep at once. Yet at this point he does not enter into the dreaming state; rather, he enters the gap, that junction. This junction is known to be the start of *turya*. In entering this junction, the aspirant enters into another world. It is not wakefulness, nor is it the dreaming state, nor is it sound sleep, but a fourth world. . . . *At that moment, the aspirant hears hideous sounds and sees furious forms*. Those aspirants who are frightened by these things try at once to come out from this state and, after exerting great effort, they come out and are again in the waking state." See John Hughes, ed., *Kashmir Shaivism: The Secret Supreme Revealed by Swami Lakshmanjoo* (1985), rev. ed. (Universal Shaiva Fellowship, 2007), 109; my italics.
5. For some useful accounts of dream yoga, see Tenzin Rinpoche Wangyal, *The Tibetan Yogas of Dream and Sleep* (New York: Snow Lion, 1998); Evan Thompson, *Waking, Dreaming, Being: Self and Consciousness in Neuroscience, Meditation, and Philosophy* (New York: Columbia University Press, 2015); and Andrew Holecek, *Dream Yoga: Illuminating Your Life Through Lucid Dreaming and the Tibetan Yogas of Sleep* (Boulder, CO: Sounds True, 2016).
6. Recall Ajahn Chandako's comments about the dangers of getting too attached to astral projection, given the extremely pleasant feeling of being outside of the physical body.
7. See Sumegi, *Dream Worlds of Shamanism and Tibetan Buddhism*, 80–81; Thompson, *Waking, Dreaming, Being*, 177; Holecek, *Dream Yoga*, 176.

4. TALES OF OBES, NDES, AND CLOSE ENCOUNTERS

8. Sumegi, *Dream Worlds of Shamanism and Tibetan Buddhism*, 81.
9. Thich Thanh Tu, "What to Think About at Death," *Tricycle: The Buddhist Review*, Winter 2012, https://tricycle.org/magazine/what-think-about-death/; Mahasi Sayadaw, "Basic Buddhism: The Theory of Karma," Buddhadharma Education Association & Buddhanet, 2022, https://www.buddhanet.net/e-learning/karma.htm.
10. For examples from medieval Japan, see Jacqueline I. Stone, *Right Thoughts at the Last Moment: Buddhism and Deathbed Practices in Early Medieval Japan* (Honolulu: University of Hawai'i Press, 2016).
11. See Stone, *Right Thoughts at the Last Moment*; and Daniel P. Stevenson, "Death-Bed Testimonials of the Pure Land Faithful," in *Buddhism in Practice*, abridged ed., ed. Donald J. Lopez Jr. (Princeton, NJ: Princeton University Press, 2015), 447–58.
12. See Philip Kapleau, *The Wheel of Death Writings from Zen Buddhist and Other Sources* (London: Routledge, 1972), 63–75; and Francis V. Tiso, *Rainbow Body and Resurrection: Spiritual Attainment, the Dissolution of the Material Body, and the Case of Khenpo a Chö* (Berkeley, CA: North Atlantic, 2016).
13. See Charles Keyes, "Death of Two Buddhist Saints in Thailand," in *Charisma and Sacred Biography*, ed. Michael Williams (Chico, CA: Scholars Press, 1981), 149–80.
14. See Gyurme Dorje, trans., *The Tibetan Book of the Dead: First Complete Translation*, ed. Graham Coleman and Thupten Jinpa (London: Viking, 2006).
15. For a historical outline of research, see M. Duggan, "Animals in Psi Research," *Psi Encyclopedia*, Society for Psychical Research, 2022, https://psi-encyclopedia.spr.ac.uk/articles/animals-psi-research.
16. Thanissaro Bhikkhu, trans., *Muccalinda Sutta: About Muccalinda (Ud 2.1)*, Access to Insight (BCBS Edition), August 30, 2012, http://www.accesstoinsight.org/tipitaka/kn/ud/ud.2.01.than.html. Nāgas are semidivine serpent-like beings.
17. Mingun Sayadaw, trans., "Part 4—The Story of Devadatta," in *The Great Chronicle of Buddhas*, Wisdom Library, 1990, https://www.wisdomlib.org/buddhism/book/the-great-chronicle-of-buddhas/d/doc364624.html.
18. I had an experience with a dog in Sri Lanka that reminded me of this story (see chapter 8).
19. See Andy Rotman, *Hungry Ghosts* (Boston: Wisdom, 2021).
20. For a recent discussion, see Leslie Kean, *Surviving Death: A Journalist Investigates Evidence for an Afterlife* (New York: Three Rivers, 2017).
21. For a detailed study of the origins, history, and character of psychedelic Buddhism in the United States, see D. E. Osto, *Altered States: Buddhism and Psychedelic Spirituality in America* (New York: Columbia University Press, 2016).
22. Christopher Partridge, *Re-Enchantment of the West: Alternative Spiritualities, Sacralization, Popular Culture, and Occulture*, 2 vols. (London: T & T Clark International, 2004–2005).
23. Yu Xue, "Merit Transfer and Life After Death in Buddhism," *Ching Feng* 4, no. 1 (2003): 29–50.
24. See Paul Harrison, trans., *The Samādhi of the Direct Encounter with the Buddhas of the Present: An Annotated English Translation of the Tibetan Version of the*

4. TALES OF OBES, NDES, AND CLOSE ENCOUNTERS

Pratyutpanna-Buddha-Saṃmukhāvasthita-Samādhi-Sūtra (Tokyo: International Institute of Buddhist Studies, 1990); and Douglas Osto, "Altered States and the Origins of the Mahāyāna," in *Setting Out on the Great Way: Essays on Early Mahāyāna Buddhism*, ed. Paul Harrison (Sheffield: Equinox, 2018), 177–205.

25. For example, see Ruth Gamble, *The Third Karmapa Rangjung Dorje: Master of Mahāmudrā* (Boulder, CO: Shambhala, 2020).
26. J. Vogel, *Indian Serpent Lore, or The Nāgas In Hindu Legend And Art* (London: Arthur Probsthain, 1926).
27. "Naga," *Encyclopedia Britannica*, https://www.britannica.com/topic/naga-Hindu-mythology.
28. Vogel, *Indian Serpent Lore*, 93–165.
29. D. S. Lopez, "Nagarjuna," *Encyclopedia Britannica*, August 23, 2017, https://www.britannica.com/biography/Nagarjuna.
30. See Paul Harrison, "Searching for the Origins of the Mahāyāna: What Are We Looking For?," *Eastern Buddhist* 28 (Spring 1995): 48–69; Harrison, *The Samādhi of the Direct Encounter with the Buddhas of the Present*; and Osto, "Altered States and the Origins of the Mahāyāna."
31. Richard Payne, "Firmly Rooted: On Fudō Myōō's Origins," *Pacific World: Journal of the Institute of Buddhist Studies* 4 (1988): 6–14.
32. See Richard Payne, "Standing Fast: Fudō Myōō in Japanese Literature," *Pacific World: Journal of the Institute of Buddhist Studies* 3 (1987): 53–58; and Sampa Biswas, *Fudō Myō-ō: (Acalanātha Vidyārāja) in Art and Iconography of Japan* (Delhi: DK Printworld, 2011).
33. David Leeming, "Benzaiten," in *The Oxford Companion to World Mythology* (Oxford: Oxford University Press, 2006); "Benten," *Encyclopedia Britannica*, February 16, 2018, https://www.britannica.com/topic/Benten.
34. "Jurōjin," *Encyclopedia Britannica*, December 27, 2021, https://www.britannica.com/topic/Jurojin.
35. In a personal communication (email on October 6, 2023), Wystan provided the full verse:

    Your mind, nondually aware and empty, is the embodiment of truth.
    So if you leave things in their natural, unfabricated state, clarity will arise on its own.
    Only by doing nothing at all will you do what is to be done.
    Letting everything remain in naked, empty awareness, chant the six-beat mantra.

36. In a personal communication (email on October 6, 2023), Wystan elaborated on the experience: "I walked outside, rather bowled over, everything vivid, empty, radiant, yada yada, and Avalokiteshvara's face appeared in/as the expanse of the sky, like a rainbow in mist, and wordlessly he communicated that he, as well as everything, 'my' apparent identity, was the self-display of nondual empty awareness."
37. In a personal communication (email on October 6, 2023), Wystan provided me with an update on his practice: "These days I'm now practicing deity yoga

4. TALES OF OBES, NDES, AND CLOSE ENCOUNTERS

(principally Vajravarahi) and Dzogchen trekcho and togal as my main practices under the guidance of a lama. 'Visions aren't the point.' Direct quote. Nice signs and gateways, though. I don't believe in supernatural miracles, but based on my own past and ongoing experiences I've no doubts regarding the phenomenological veracity of visionary literature."
38. For an example of a contemporary scholar who does not dismiss these "supernatural" elements as fictions, see Gamble, *The Third Karmapa Rangjung Dorje*.
39. Paul Churchland, *Matter and Consciousness*, 3rd ed. (Cambridge, MA: MIT Press, 2013). For a discussion in relation to altered states of consciousness, see Osto, *Altered States*.

5. The Yogin

1. Rick Repetti, *Buddhism, Meditation, and Free Will: A Buddhist Theory of Mental Freedom* (New York: Routledge, 2019), xiii.
2. Rick Repetti, "About Me," 2017, https://www.rickrepetti.com/about-me.
3. Richard Hittleman (1927–1991) was an American yoga teacher and author who popularized yoga through several books and one of the first yoga television series, *Yoga for Health*. Jack LaLanne (1914–2011) was an American fitness and nutrition guru and motivational speaker who popularized fitness in America through his television shows, health clubs, and books.
4. Ram Dass, *Be Here Now* (San Cristobal: Lama Foundation, 1971). This book has been reprinted many times.
5. All information in this paragraph was obtained from Golden Quest, "About: Hilda Charlton," https://www.hildacharlton.com/about-hilda-charlton. Golden Quest is an organization dedicated to the promulgation of Charlton's teachings and published works.
6. F. X. Charet, "Ram Dass: The Vicissitudes of Devotion and Ferocity of Grace," in *Homegrown Gurus: From Hinduism in America to American Hinduism*, ed. A. Gleig and L. Williams (Albany: State University of New York Press, 2013), 15–40.
7. See D. Lattin, *The Harvard Psychedelic Club: How Timothy Leary, Ram Dass, Huston Smith, and Andrew Weil Killed the Fifties and Ushered in a New Age for America* (New York: HarperOne, 2010); and D. E. Osto, *Altered States: Buddhism and Psychedelic Spirituality in America* (New York: Columbia University Press, 2016).
8. Love Serve Remember, "About: Richard Alpert / Ram Dass: Biography," https://www.ramdass.org/about-ram-dass/.
9. Colette Dowling, "Confessions of an American Guru," *New York Times*, December 4, 1977.
10. Dowling, "Confessions of an American Guru."
11. As cited in Dowling, "Confessions of an American Guru."
12. See Francis V. Tiso, *Rainbow Body and Resurrection: Spiritual Attainment, the Dissolution of the Material Body, and the Case of Khenpo a Chö* (Berkeley, CA: North Atlantic, 2016).

13. Taylor Hackford, dir., *Devil's Advocate*, October 17, 1997 (Burbank, CA: Warner Brothers, 2005).
14. However, new revelations about Rick's dream continue to this day. After our interviews, Rick contacted me by email (July 20, 2021) to tell me about a new connection he had uncovered between the two churches in his dream. He writes: "I was just reading an article by one of the contributors to my forthcoming book (*The Routledge Handbook on the Philosophy of Meditation*), Christian Coseru, critiquing Evan Thompson's new book, *Why I Am Not a Buddhist*, which compares why Christian is unlike Evan, the latter who grew up in a spiritual community, Lindisfarne, founded by his father [William Thompson], which I had read about vaguely once. In the footnote, Coseru mentions that the community was at one time located at the 'Church of the Holy Communion and Buildings in Manhattan, the Lindisfarne Association (1972–2012),' so I looked that up, because, if you recall, I remember learning at some point that the Limelight Disco of my precognitive nightmares was somehow connected with Lindesfarne, though I don't recall how I learned that.... Turns out Lindisfarne was housed in the Limelight right around the time I was having those precognitive dreams, and also headquartered in St. John the Divine (where Hilda had her weekly meditation meetings, recall), neither detail of which I knew back when I had the dreams. Recall that in those dreams, I was coming out of St. John's along with everyone else after a Hilda meeting, and many of us walked down the street, and were walking into another, smaller church, which turned out to be the Limelight years later, where a mystical/paranormal something-or-other was going on, with Gregorian chanting, but which turned into a supernatural bar with blood red wine, a demonic leader, etc. These two new bits of info, that not only was there a connection between Lindisfarne and the Limelight, but that they were actually housed there as well as at St. John's, is mind-blowing to me." Thus, we see that Rick's dream was both precognitive and clairvoyant in that it presaged the transformation of the church into the Limelight and his meeting with the bowtie man, and it intuited a connection between the two churches through the Lindisfarne organization. This group possessed a strong theosophical and esoteric orientation, and Rick suspects the mysterious man's mention of a group meeting at the church Thursday evenings was in fact Lindisfarne.
15. Francis Lawrence, dir., *Constantine*, February 17, 2005 (Burbank, CA: Warner Brothers, 2005).

6. The Gift

1. The language from the transcriptions has been tidied up and redacted for more conciseness, but I have tried at all times to stick to the original meaning and intention of the speaker.
2. Stanley Tambiah, *The Buddhist Saints of the Forest and the Cult of Amulets: A Study in Charisma, Hagiography, Sectarianism, and Millennial Buddhism* (Cambridge: Cambridge University Press, 1984).

3. *Prai* is a Thai word meaning an item that possesses part of a corpse or has absorbed the essence of the body after death. See Jenx, *The Thai Occult* (Timeless Editions of France, 2020), 3.
4. *Luk krok* is Thai for the spirit of a stillborn child, which is used for a strong form of protection. Jenx, *The Thai Occult*, 3.
5. *Kata* is Thai for a chant from the Buddhist scripture. Jenx, *The Thai Occult*, 3. In Pāli, the word is *gāthā*.
6. A botanica is a small shop that sells herbal remedies, charms, incense, candles, and other items used for religious or spiritual purposes.
7. In our third interview, Kat revealed that her parents were more ambivalent about her gift. Although generally accepting of it, sometimes they questioned her mental health. This questioning eventually led to a crisis in her early adulthood.
8. A first-degree relic is the body part of a saint, such as a bone.
9. Peter Brown, *The Cult of the Saints: Its Rise and Function in Latin Christianity* (Chicago: University of Chicago Press, 1981); Tambiah, *The Buddhist Saints of the Forest and the Cult of Amulets*.
10. For an account, see D. E. Osto, *Altered States: Buddhism and Psychedelic Spirituality in American* (New York: Columbia University Press, 2016), 229.
11. See Helané Wahbeh, Dean Radin, Garret Yount, Michael A. Woodley of Menie, Matthew A. Sarraf, and Marcela V. Karpuj, "Genetics of Psychic Ability: A Pilot Case-Control Exome Sequencing Study," *Explore* 18, no. 3 (2022): 264–71.
12. Some of this decrease in strength and frequency (if Rick's life is indeed similar) could be attributable to age or change in lifestyle, but it also makes sense that taking such powerful antipsychotic medications would inhibit one's natural psychic potential.
13. She recently revealed to me in a Facebook private message (October 2023) that she self-identifies as a witch.

7. Toward a Phenomenology of the Paranormal

1. Jacques Vallée, *Passport to Magonia: From Folklore to Flying Saucers* (1969; Daily Grail Publishing, 2014), 157.
2. Linda Heuman, "Under One Umbrella: Can Tradition and Science Both Fit? An Interview with Thupten Jinpa Langri," *Tricycle*, Summer 2014.
3. "My religion is very simple. My religion is kindness.—Dalai Lama," *Quotespedia*, 2022, https://www.quotespedia.org/authors/d/dalai-lama/my-religion-is-very-simple-my-religion-is-kindness-dalai-lama/.
4. For an excellent introduction to phenomenology, see Dan Zahavi, *Phenomenology: The Basics* (London: Routledge, 2019).
5. Robert Crease, "Phenomenology and Natural Science," *Internet Encyclopedia of Philosophy*, https://iep.utm.edu/phenomsc/#H7. Robert Crease is one of the foremost contemporary scholars of phenomenology in relation to the natural

sciences. See "Robert Crease: Department Chair, Professor," Stony Brook University, 2023, https://www.stonybrook.edu/commcms/philosophy/people/_faculty/crease.php.

8. Autobiographical Postscript

1. See Peter J. Carroll, "Charlie Brewster," *Specularium* (blog), June 5, 2015, https://www.specularium.org/blog/item/176-charlie-brewster.
2. Dean Radin, *Supernormal: Science, Yoga, and the Evidence for Extraordinary Psychic Ability* (New York: Deepak Chopra Books, 2013), 222.
3. Sean McNamara, *Defy Your Limits: The Telekinesis Training Method* (Mind Possible, 2017).

Bibliography

Anālayo, Bhikkhu. *Rebirth in Early Buddhism and Current Research*. Somerville, MA: Wisdom Publications, 2018.
Appleton, Naomi. *Jātaka Stories in Theravāda Buddhism: Narrating the Bodhisatta Path*. Burlington, VT: Ashgate, 2010.
Batchelor, Stephen. *The Awakening of the West: The Encounter of Buddhism and Western Culture, 543 BCE –1992*. London: Aquarian, 1994.
Berkowitz, Alan J. "Account of the Buddhist Thaumaturge Baozhi." In *Buddhism in Practice*, ed. Donald J. Lopez Jr., 578–85. Princeton, NJ: Princeton University Press, 1995.
Biswas, Sampa. *Fudō Myō-ō: (Acalanātha Vidyārāja) in Art and Iconography of Japan*. Delhi: DK Printworld, 2011.
Braarvig, Jens, trans. *Akṣayamatinirdeśasūtra*. Vol. 2: *The Tradition of Imperishability in Buddhist Thought*. Oslo: Solum Forlag, 1993.
Brown, Peter. *The Cult of the Saints: Its Rise and Function in Latin Christianity*. Chicago: University of Chicago Press, 1981.
Buddhaghosa, Bhikkhu. *The Path of Purification* (*Visuddhimagga*). Trans. Bhikkhu Ñāṇamoli. Kandy: Buddhist Publication Society, 1991.
Campany, Robert Ford. *Signs from the Unseen Realm: Buddhist Miracle Tales from Early Medieval China*. Honolulu: University of Hawai'i Press, 2012.
Carroll, Peter J. "Charlie Brewster." *Specularium* (blog). June 5, 2015. https://www.specularium.org/blog/item/176-charlie-brewster.
CBS News. "House Holds Hearing on UFOs, Government Transparency | Full Video." *CBS News*, YouTube video, July 27, 2023. https://www.youtube.com/watch?v=SNgoul4vyDM.
——. "Poll: Nearly 8 in 10 Americans Believe in Angels." *CBS News*, December 23, 2011, https://www.cbsnews.com/news/poll-nearly-8-in-10-americans-believe-in-angels/.

BIBLIOGRAPHY

Chang, Chen Chi, trans. *Esoteric Teachings of the Tibetan Tantra*, ed. C. A. Muses. York Beach, ME: Samuel Weiser, 1982.

Chang, Garma. *The Buddhist Teaching of Totality: The Philosophy of Hwa Yen Buddhism*, University Park: Pennsylvania State University Press, 1983.

Chapple, Christopher Key. "Siddhis in the Yogasūtra." In *Yoga Powers: Extraordinary Capacities Attained Through Meditation and Concentration*, ed. Knut A. Jacobsen, 223–40. Leiden: Brill, 2012.

Charet, F. X. "Ram Dass: The Vicissitudes of Devotion and Ferocity of Grace." In *Homegrown Gurus: From Hinduism in America to American Hinduism*, ed. A. Gleig and L. Williams, 15–40. Albany: State University of New York Press, 2013.

Churchland, Paul. *Matter and Consciousness*. 3rd ed. Cambridge, MA: MIT Press, 2013.

Cleary, Thomas. *Entry Into the Inconceivable: An Introduction to Hua-yen Buddhism*. Honolulu: University of Hawai'i Press, 1983.

Cleary, Thomas, trans. *The Flower Ornament Scripture: A Translation of the Avatamsaka Sutra*. Boston: Shambhala, 1993.

Clough, Bradley S. "The Higher Knowledges in the Pāli Nikāyas and Vinaya." *Journal of the International Association of Buddhist Studies* 33, nos. 1–2 (2010): 409–34.

Colborn, M. "Forteana." In *Psi Encyclopaedia*. London: Society for Psychical Research, 2014. https://psi-encyclopedia.spr.ac.uk/articles/forteana.

Coleman, James William. *The New Buddhism: The Western Transformation of an Ancient Tradition*. Oxford: Oxford University Press, 2001.

Collins, Steve. "The Discourse on What Is Primary (*Agañña-sutta*): An Annotated Translation." *Journal of Indian Philosophy* 21 (1993): 301–93.

Conze, Edward. *Buddhism: Its Essence and Development*. 1975. New York: Harper & Row, 1951.

———. *Buddhist Scriptures*. London: Penguin, 1959.

———, trans. *The Perfection of Wisdom in Eight Thousand Lines and Its Verse Summary*. San Francisco: Four Seasons Foundation, 1973.

Cook, Francis. *Hua-yen Buddhism: The Jewel Net of Indra*. University Park: Pennsylvania State University Press, 1991.

Coomaraswamy Ananda K. "Saṃvega, 'Aesthetic Shock.'" *Harvard Journal of Asiatic Studies* 7, no. 3 (1943): 174–79.

Cowell, E. B., ed. *Jātaka: Or Stories of the Buddha's Former Births*. 2 vols. Delhi: Cosmo, 1973.

Crow, John. "Taming the Astral Body: The Theosophical Society's Ongoing Problem of Emotion and Control." *Journal of the American Academy of Religion* 80, no. 3 (September 2012): 691–717.

Dass, Ram. *Be Here Now*. San Cristobal: Lama Foundation, 1971.

Davids, T. W. Rhys, and William Stede. *The Pali Text Society's Pali-English Dictionary*. Oxford: Pali Text Society, 1921–1925.

Davidson, Ronald M. *Indian Esoteric Buddhism: A Social History of the Tantric Movement*. New York: Columbia University Press, 2002.

———. "Magicians, Sorcerers, and Witches: Considering Pretantric, Non-sectarian Sources of Tantric Practices." *Religions* 8 (2017): 188.

Dayal, Har. *The Bodhisattva Doctrine in Buddhist Sanskrit Literature*. London: Kegan Paul, Trench, Trubner & Co., Ltd., 1932.

BIBLIOGRAPHY

Deleanu, Florin. "Bodhisattvabhūmi." In *Oxford Bibliographies Online*. Oxford: Oxford University Press, 2018. https://www.oxfordbibliographies.com/view/document/obo-9780195393521/obo-9780195393521-0254.xml.

Dorje, Gyurme, trans. *The Tibetan Book of the Dead: First Complete Translation*. Ed. Graham Coleman and Thupten Jinpa. London: Viking, 2006.

Duggan, M. "Animals in Psi Research." In *Psi Encyclopedia*. London: Society for Psychical Research, 2022. https://psi-encyclopedia.spr.ac.uk/articles/animals-psi-research.

Dutch UAP Disclosure. "We Are Not Alone | News Nation | Full Interview | Ross Coulthart with Dave Grusch, 11–06–2023." YouTube video, June 15, 2023. https://www.youtube.com/watch?v=V6JxUHkyDuY.

Edgerton, Franklin. *Buddhist Hybrid Sanskrit Grammar and Dictionary*. 2 vols. Delhi: Motital Banarsidass Publishers Private Limited, 1953.

Fields, Rick. *How the Swans Came to the Lake: A Narrative History of Buddhism in America*. 3rd. rev. and updated ed. Boston: Shambhala, 1992.

Fiordalis, David. V. "Miracles in Indian Buddhist Narratives and Doctrine." *Journal of the International Association of Buddhist Studies* 33, no. 1–2 (2010): 381–408.

———. "The Wondrous Display of Superhuman Power in the Vimalakīrtinirdeśa: Miracle of Marvel?" In *Yoga Powers: Extraordinary Capacities Attained Through Meditation and Concentration*, ed. Knut A. Jacobsen, 97–125. Leiden: Brill, 2012.

Fontein, Jan. *Entering the Dharmadhātu: A Study of the Gaṇḍavyūha Reliefs of Borobudur*. Leiden and Boston: Brill, 2012.

———. *The Pilgrimage of Sudhana: A Study of Gaṇḍavyūha Illustrations in China, Japan, and Java*. The Hague: Mouton & Co., 1967.

Fort, Charles. *The Book of the Damned*. 1919. New York: Boni and Liveright, 2019.

———. *Lo!* 1931. New York: Ace Books, 1968.

———. *New Lands*. 1923. New York: Ace Books, 1968.

———. *Wild Talents*. 1932. New York: Ace Books, 1965.

Gamble, Ruth. *Reincarnation in Tibetan Buddhism: The Third Karmapa and the Invention of a Tradition*. New York: Oxford University Press, 2018.

———. *The Third Karmapa Rangjung Dorje: Master of Mahāmudrā*. Boulder, CO: Shambhala, 2020.

Gethin, Rupert. *The Foundations of Buddhism*. Oxford: Oxford University Press, 1998.

Gifford, Julie. "Insight Guide to Hell: Mahāmoggallāna and Theravāda Buddhist Cosmology." In *Constituting Communities: Theravada Buddhism and the Religious Cultures of South and Southeast Asia*, ed. John Clifford Holt, Jacob N. Kinnard, and Jonathan S. Walters, 71–84. Albany: State University of New York Press, 2003.

Gjertson, Donald E. "The Early Chinese Buddhist Miracle Tale: A Preliminary Survey." *Journal of the American Oriental Society* 101, no. 3 (1981): 287–301.

Gombrich, Richard. "The Buddha's Book of Genesis?' *Indo-Iranian Journal* 35, no. 2–3 (1992): 159–78.

Gómez, Luis Oscar. "The Bodhisattva as Wonder-Worker." In *Prajñāpāramitā and Related System: Studies in Honor of Edward Conze*, ed. Lewis Lancaster and Luis Gómez, 221–61. Berkeley, CA: Berkeley Buddhist Studies Series, 1977.

———, trans. *Land of Bliss: The Paradise of the Buddha of Measureless Light: Sanskrit and Chinese Versions of the Sukhāvatī Sūtras*. Honolulu: University of Hawai'i Press, 1996.

———. "On Buddhist Wonders and Wonder-Working." *Journal of the International Association of Buddhist Studies* 33, nos. 1–2 (2010): 513–54.
———. "Selected Verses from the Gaṇḍavyūha: Text, Critical Apparatus, and Translation." PhD diss., Yale University, 1967.
Gómez, Luis Oscar, and Hiram W. Woodward Jr., eds. *Barabuḍur: History and Significance of a Buddhist Monument*. Berkeley, CA: Buddhist Studies Series, 1981.
Gray, David. B. *The Cakrasamvara Tantra (The Discourse of Śrī Heruka): A Study and Annotated Translation*. New York: Columbia University Press, 2007.
———. "Tantra and the Tantric Traditions of Hinduism and Buddhism." In *Oxford Research Encyclopedias, Religion*. Oxford: Oxford University Press, 2016.
Grayson, Bruce. *After: A Doctor Explores What Near-Death Experiences Reveal About Life and Beyond*. New York: St. Martins Essentials, 2021.
———. "Near-Death Experiences." In *Mind Beyond Brain: Buddhism, Science, and the Paranormal*, ed. David E. Presti, 22–44. New York: Columbia University Press, 2018.
Guenther, Herbert V. *The Life and Teaching of Naropa: Translated from the Original Tibetan with a Philosophical Commentary Based on the Oral Transmission*. Boston: Shambhala, 1995.
Hansen, George P. *The Trickster and the Paranormal*. Bloomington: Xlibris, 2001.
Harrison, Paul, trans. *The Samādhi of the Direct Encounter with the Buddhas of the Present: An Annotated English Translation of the Tibetan Version of the* Pratyutpanna-Buddha-Saṃmukhāvasthita-Samādhi-Sūtra. Tokyo: International Institute of Buddhist Studies, 1990.
———. "Searching for the Origins of the Mahāyāna: What Are We Looking For?" *Eastern Buddhist* 28 (Spring 1995):48–69.
———, ed. *Setting Out on the Great Way: Essays on Early Mahāyāna Buddhism*. Sheffield: Equinox, 2018.
Harvey, Peter. *An Introduction to Buddhism: Teachings, History and Practices*. Cambridge: Cambridge University Press, 1990.
Hastings, Robert. *UFOs and Nukes: Extraordinary Encounters at Nuclear Weapons Sites*. 2nd ed. Robert Hastings, 2017.
Heuman, Linda. "Under One Umbrella: Can Tradition and Science Both Fit? An Interview with Thupten Jinpa Langri." *Tricycle*, Summer 2014.
History Channel. *The Secret of Skinwalker Ranch*. Television series. https://www.history.com/shows/the-secret-of-skinwalker-ranch.
Hof, Wim. "The Wim Hof Method." https://www.wimhofmethod.com/.
Holecek, Andrew. *Dream Yoga: Illuminating Your Life Through Lucid Dreaming and the Tibetan Yogas of Sleep*. Boulder, CO: Sounds True, 2016.
Hughes, John, ed. *Kashmir Shaivism: The Secret Supreme Revealed by Swami Lakshmanjoo*. Rev. ed. 1985. Universal Shaiva Fellowship, 2007.
Institute of Noetic Science (IONS). "Dean Radin, MS, PhD: Chief Scientist." 2023. https://noetic.org/profile/dean-radin/.
Jacobsen, Annie. *Phenomena: The Secret History of the U.S. Government's Investigation Into Extrasensory Perception and Psychokinesis*. New York: Little, Brown, 2017.
Jacobsen, Knut A. "Introduction: Yoga Powers and Religious Traditions." In *Yoga Powers: Extraordinary Capacities Attained Through Meditation and Concentration*, ed. Knut A. Jacobsen, 1–31. Leiden: Brill, 2012.

Jenx. *The Thai Occult*. Timeless Editions of France, 2020.
Johns, Alfred E. 1957. *Scientific Autosuggestion for Personality Adjustment and Development: Your Key to Mental and Physical Health*. Westport, CT: Associated Book Sellers, 1957.
Jones, J. J., trans. *The Mahāvastu*. Vol. 1. London: Pali Text Society, 1949.
Josephson-Storm, Jason A. *The Myth of Disenchantment: Magic, Modernity, and the Birth of the Human Sciences*. Chicago: University of Chicago Press, 2017.
Kapleau, Philip. *The Wheel of Death Writings from Zen Buddhist and Other Sources*. London: Routledge, 1972.
Katz, Nathan. *Buddhist Images of Human Perfection: The Arahant of the Sutta Piṭika Compared with the Bodhisattva and the Mahāsiddha*. Delhi: Motilal Banarsidass, 1982.
Kean, Leslie. *Surviving Death: A Journalist Investigates Evidence for an Afterlife*. New York: Three Rivers, 2017.
——. *UFOs: Generals, Pilots, and Government Officials Go on Record*. New York: Harmony Books, 2010.
Kean, Leslie, and Ralph Blumenthal. "Intelligence Officials Say U.S. Has Retrieved Craft of Non-Human Origin." *Debrief*, June 5, 2023. https://thedebrief.org/intelligence-officials-say-u-s-has-retrieved-non-human-craft/.
Keel, John A. *The Mothman Prophecies: The True Story of the Alien Who Terrorized an American City*. 1975. London: New English Library, 2002.
Kelleher, Colm, and George Knapp. *Hunt for the Skinwalker: Science Confronts the Unexplained at a Remote Utah Ranch*. New York: Paraview Pocket Books, 2005.
Kelly, Edward F. "Paranormal Phenomena, the *Siddhis*, and an Emerging Path Toward Reconciliation of Science and Spirituality." In *Mind Beyond Brain: Buddhism, Science, and the Paranormal*, ed. David E. Presti, 91–120. New York, Columbia University Press, 2018.
Kelly, E. F., A. Crabtree, and P. Marshall, eds. *Beyond Physicalism: Toward Reconciliation of Science and Spirituality*. Lanham, MD: Rowman & Littlefield, 2015.
Kelly, E. F., E. W. Kelly, A. Crabtree, A. Gauld, M. Grosso, and B. Greyson. *Irreducible Mind: Toward a Psychology for the 21st Century*. Lanham, MD: Rowan & Littlefield, 2007.
Kelly, Emily Williams. "Mediums, Apparitions, and Deathbed Experiences." In *Mind Beyond Brain: Buddhism, Science, and the Paranormal*, ed. David E. Presti, 69–91. New York: Columbia University Press, 2018.
Kern, H., trans. *The Saddharma-Puṇḍarīka, or The Lotus or the True Law*. 1884; New York: Dover, 1963.
Keyes, Charles. "Death of Two Buddhist Saints in Thailand." In *Charisma and Sacred Biography*, ed. Michael Williams, 149–80. Chico, CA: Scholars Press, 1981.
Kripal, Jeffrey J. *Authors of the Impossible: The Paranormal and the Sacred*. Chicago: University of Chicago Press, 2010.
Krohn, Elizabeth G., and Jeffrey J. Kripal. *Changed in a Flash: One Woman's Near-Death Experience and Why a Scholar Thinks It Empowers Us All*. Berkeley: North Atlantic, 2018.
Lacatski, James T., Colm A. Kelleher, and George Knapp. *Inside the U.S. Government Covert UFO Program: Initial Revelations*. Henderson, NV: RTMA, LLC, 2023.

———. *Skinwalkers at the Pentagon: An Insiders' Account of the Government's Secret UFO Program*. Henderson, NV: RTMA, LLC, 2021.

Lankaramaya Dubai. "Dhammachakka Sutta Dhammaruwan." YouTube video, May 12, 2018. https://www.youtube.com/watch?v=QOB2c9QVa_M.

Lattin, D. *The Harvard Psychedelic Club: How Timothy Leary, Ram Dass, Huston Smith, and Andrew Weil Killed the Fifties and Ushered in a New Age for America*. New York: HarperOne, 2010.

Leeming, David. "Benzaiten." In *The Oxford Companion to World Mythology*. Oxford: Oxford University Press, 2006.

Lhalungpa, Lobsang P., trans. *The Life of Milarepa*. New York: Arkana, 1977.

Lopez Jr., Donald S. *Buddhism: An Introduction and Guide*. London: Penguin, 2001.

———. "Nagarjuna." In *Encyclopedia Britannica*, August 23, 2017. https://www.britannica.com/biography/Nagarjuna.

Love Serve Remember. "About: Richard Alpert / Ram Dass: Biography." https://www.ramdass.org/about-ram-dass/.

Lusthaus, Dan. *Buddhist Phenomenology: A Philosophical Investigation of Yogācāra Buddhism and the Ch'emg Wei-shih lun*. London: RoutledgeCurzon, 2002.

Malinar, Angelika. "Yoga Powers in the Mahābhārata." In *Yoga Powers: Extraordinary Capacities Attained Through Meditation and Concentration*, ed. Knut A. Jacobsen, 33–60. Leiden: Brill, 2012.

Martin, Dan. "Illusion Web —Locating the *Guhyagarbha Tantra* in Buddhist Intellectual History." In *Silver on Lapis: Tibetan Literary Culture and History*, ed. Christopher I. Beckwith. Bloomington: Tibetan Society, 1987.

Maxwell, J., Charles Richet, and Oliver Lodge. *Metapsychical Phenomena: Methods and Research*, trans. L. I. Finch. New York: G. P. Putnam's Sons, 1905.

McLuhan, Robert, and Michael Duggan. "Dean Radin." In *Psi Encyclopedia*. London: Society for Psychical Research, 2023. https://psi-encyclopedia.spr.ac.uk/articles/dean-radin.

McMahan, David L. *The Making of Modern Buddhism*. Oxford: Oxford University Press, 2008.

———. "Transpositions of Metaphor and Imagery in the *Gaṇḍavyūha* and Tantric Buddhist Practice." *Pacific World Journal*, 3rd ser., no. 6 (Fall 2004): 181–94.

McNamara, Sean. *Defy Your Limits: The Telekinesis Training Method*. Mind Possible, 2017.

Merleau-Ponty, Maurice. *The Phenomenology of Perception*. 1945. Trans. Donald A. Landes. London: Routledge, 2012.

Ñāṇamoli, trans. 1991. *The Path of Purification* (Visuddhimagga) *by Bhadantācariya Buddhaghosa*. 5th ed. Kandy: Buddhist Publication Society.

Nattier, Jan. "Who Is a Buddhist? Charting the Landscape of Buddhist America." In *The Faces of Buddhism in America*, ed. Charles S. Prebish and Kenneth K. Tanaka, 183–95. Los Angeles: University of California Press, 1998.

Nelson, Roger. "Formal Analysis: September 11 2001." Global Consciousness Project, 2020. https://noosphere.princeton.edu/911formal.html.

———. "Global Consciousness Project." Global Consciousness Project, 2020. https://noosphere.princeton.edu/index.html.

Office of the Director of National Intelligence. "Preliminary Assessment: Unidentified Aerial Phenomena." June 25, 2021.
Orzech, Charles. "Mahāvairocana." In *The Encyclopedia of Religion*. New York: Macmillan, 1987.
Osto, D. E. *Altered States: Buddhism and Psychedelic Spirituality in American*. New York: Columbia University Press, 2016.
———. "Altered States and the Origins of the Mahāyāna." In *Setting Out on the Great Way: Essays on Early Mahāyāna Buddhism*, ed. Paul Harrison, 177–205. Sheffield: Equinox, 2018.
———. "Mind Beyond Brain: Buddhism, Science and the Paranormal," *Religion* 50, no. 1 (2020): 178–82.
———. *An Indian Tantric Tradition and its Modern Global Revival: Contemporary Nondual Śaivism*. London: Routledge, 2020.
———. *Power, Wealth and Women in Indian Mahayana Buddhism: The Gaṇḍavyūha-sūtra*. London: Routledge, 2008.
———. " 'Proto-Tantric' Elements in the *Gaṇḍavyūha-sūtra*." *Journal of Religious History* 33 no. 2 (2009): 165–77.
Overbey, Ryan Richard. "On the Appearance of Siddhis in Chinese Buddhist Texts." In *Yoga Powers: Extraordinary Capacities Attained Through Meditation and Concentration*, ed. Knut A. Jacobsen, 127–44. Leiden: Brill, 2012.
Partridge, Christopher. *Re-Enchantment of the West: Alternative Spiritualities, Sacralization, Popular Culture, and Occulture*. 2 vols. London: T & T Clark International, 2004–2005.
Pasulka, D.W. *American Cosmic: UFOs, Religion, Technology*. Oxford: Oxford University Press, 2019.
Payne, Richard. "Firmly Rooted: On Fudō Myōō's Origins." *Pacific World: Journal of the Institute of Buddhist Studies* 4 (1988): 6–14.
———. "Standing Fast: Fudō Myōō in Japanese Literature." *Pacific World: Journal of the Institute of Buddhist Studies* 3 (1987): 53–58.
Pellington, Mark, dir. *The Mothman Prophecies*, January 25, 2002. Screen Gems and Sony Pictures, 2002.
Pflueger, Lloyd W. "Holding On and Letting Go: The In and Out of Powers in Classical Yoga." In *Yoga Powers: Extraordinary Capacities Attained Through Meditation and Concentration*, ed. Knut A. Jacobsen, 241–63. Leiden: Brill, 2012.
Prebish, Charles. *Buddhism: The American Experience*. Journal of Buddhist Ethics Online Books, 2003.
———. "The Academic Study of Buddhism in America: A Silent Sangha." In *American Buddhism: Methods and Findings in Recent Scholarship*, ed. Duncan Williams and Christopher Queen, 183–214. Richmond: Curzon, 1999.
———. *Luminous Passage: The Practice and Study of Buddhism in America*. Berkeley: University of California Press, 1999.
Prebish, Charles S., and Kenneth K. Tanaka, ed. *The Faces of Buddhism in America*. Los Angeles: University of California Press, 1998.
Presti, David E. "An Expanded Conception of Mind." In *Mind Beyond Brain: Buddhism, Science, and the Paranormal*, ed. David E. Presti, 121–46. New York, Columbia University Press, 2018.

Presti, David E., ed., with Bruce Greyson, Edward F. Kelly, Emily Williams Kelly, and Jim B. Tucker. *Mind Beyond Brain: Buddhism, Science, and the Paranormal.* New York: Columbia University Press, 2018.

Presti, David E., and Edward F. Kelly. "Prologue: Deepening the Dialogue." In *Mind Beyond Brain: Buddhism, Science, and the Paranormal,* ed. David E. Presti, xiii–xxii. New York: Columbia University Press, 2018.

Powers, John, trans. *Wisdom of the Buddha: The Saṃdhinirmocana Sūtra.* Berkeley, CA: Dharma, 1995.

Pranke, Patrick. "On Becoming a Buddhist Wizard." In *Buddhism in Practice,* ed. Donald J. Lopez Jr., 343–58. Princeton, NJ: Princeton University Press, 1995.

——. "On Saints and Wizards—Ideals of Human Perfection and Power in Contemporary Burmese Buddhism." *Journal of the International Association of Buddhist Studies* 33, nos. 1–2 (2010): 453–88.

Repetti, Rick. *Buddhism, Meditation, and Free Will: A Theory of Mental Freedom.* New York: Routledge, 2019.

Radin, Dean. *Supernormal: Science, Yoga, and the Evidence for Extraordinary Psychic Ability.* New York: Deepak Chopra Books, 2013.

Rhine, J. B. *Extra-Sensory Perception.* Boston: Bruce Humphries, 1934.

——. *New Frontiers of the Mind.* New York: Farrar and Rinehart, 1937.

Rhine, J. B., J. G. Pratt, C. E. Stuart, B. M. Smith, and J. A. Greenwood. *Extra-Sensory Perception After Sixty Years.* New York: Henry Holt, 1940.

Rhine Feather, S., and B. Ensrud. "JB Rhine." In *Psi Encyclopedia.* London: Society for Psychical Research, 2023. https://psi-encyclopedia.spr.ac.uk/articles/jb-rhine.

Robinson, James B., trans. *The Buddha's Lions: The Lives of the Eighty-four Siddhas.* Berkeley, CA: Dharma, 1979.

Rotman, Andy, trans. *Divine Stories: Divyāvadāna, Part I.* Boston: Wisdom, 2008.

——. *Hungry Ghosts.* Boston: Wisdom, 2021.

Sayadaw, Mahasi. "Basic Buddhism: The Theory of Karma." Buddhadharma Education Association & Buddhanet, 2022. https://www.buddhanet.net/e-learning/karma.htm.

Sayadaw, Mingun, trans. "Part 4—The Story of Devadatta" In *The Great Chronicle of Buddhas.* Wisdom Library, 1990. https://www.wisdomlib.org/buddhism/book/the-great-chronicle-of-buddhas/d/doc364624.html.

Schopen, Gregory. "The Manuscript of the Vajracchedikā Found at Gilgit." In *Studies in the Literature of the Great Vehicle: Three Mahāyāna Buddhist Texts,* ed. Luis Gómez and Jonathan A. Silk, 89–140. Ann Arbor: Center for South and Southeast Asian Studies, University of Michigan, 1989.

Seager, Richard Hughes. *Buddhism in America.* New York: Columbia University Press, 1999.

Shin, Upasaka Tao-tsi, trans. *The Sutra of Bodhisattva Ksitigarbha's Fundamental Vows.* New York: Sutra Translation Committee of the United States and Canada, n.d.

Snellgrove, David. *Indo-Tibetan Buddhism: Indian Buddhists and Their Tibetan Successors.* 2 vols. Boston: Shambhala, 1987.

Soothill, William Edward, and Lewis Hodous. *A Dictionary of Chinese Buddhist Terms with Sanskrit and English Equivalents and a Sanskrit-Pali Index.* 1937. Delhi: Motilal Banarsidass Publishers Private Limited, 1977.

Stevenson, Daniel B. "Tales of the Lotus Sūtra." In *Buddhism in Practice*, ed. Donald J. Lopez Jr., 427–51. Princeton, NJ: Princeton University Press, 1995.

Stevenson, Daniel B. "Death-Bed Testimonials of the Pure Land Faithful." In *Buddhism in Practice*, ed. Donald J. Lopez Jr., 592–602. Princeton. NJ: Princeton University Press, 1995.

———. "Death-Bed Testimonials of the Pure Land Faithful." In *Buddhism in Practice*, abridged ed., ed. Donald J. Lopez Jr., 447–58. Princeton, NJ: Princeton University Press, 2015.

Stevenson, Ian. *Twenty Cases Suggestive of Reincarnation*. 1966. Charlottesville: University of Virginia, 1974.

Stone, Jacqueline I. *Right Thoughts at the Last Moment: Buddhism and Deathbed Practices in Early Medieval Japan*. Honolulu: University of Hawai'i Press, 2016.

Sumegi, Angela. *Dream Worlds of Shamanism and Tibetan Buddhism: The Third Place*. New York: State University of New York Press, 2008.

Sumegi, Angela. *Understanding Death: Identity and the Afterlife in World Religions*. Malden, MA: Wiley-Blackwell, 2014.

SuttaCentral. "Dhammaruwan—Chanting—1970's." https://discourse.suttacentral.net/t/dhammaruwan-chanting-1970s/8279.

Tambiah, Stanley Jeyaraja. *The Buddhist Saints of the Forest and the Cult of Amulets: A Study in Charisma, Hagiography, Sectarianism, and Millennial Buddhism*. Cambridge: Cambridge University Press, 1984.

Targ, Russell. "Remote Viewing at Stanford Research Institute in the 1970s: A Memoir." *Journal of Scientific Exploration* 10, no. 1 (1996): 77–88.

Tart, Charles T. *The Secret Science of the Soul: How Evidence of the Paranormal Is Bringing Science and Spirit Together*. Fearless Books, 2017.

Tart, Charles T. "CTT Brief Bio." 2022. https://blog.paradigm-sys.com/brief-bio/.

Tatelman, Joel. *The Glorious Deeds of Pūrṇa: A Translation and Study of the Pūrṇāvadāna*. Surrey: Curzon, 2000.

Thanh Tu, Thich. "What to Think About at Death." *Tricycle: The Buddhist Review*, Winter 2012. https://tricycle.org/magazine/what-think-about-death/.

Thanissaro Bhikkhu, trans. "Cula-Malunkyovada Sutta: The Shorter Instructions to Malunkya." MN 63. Access to Insight, 1998, http://www.accesstoinsight.org/tipitaka/mn/mn.063.than.html.

———, trans. "Muccalinda Sutta: About Muccalinda." Ud 2.1. Access to Insight, 2012, http://www.accesstoinsight.org/tipitaka/kn/ud/ud.2.01.than.html.

———, trans. "Rohitassa Sutta: To Rohitassa." AN 4.45. Access to Insight, 1997, http://www.accesstoinsight.org/tipitaka/an/an04/an04.045.than.html.

Thompson, Evan. *Waking, Dreaming, Being: Self and Consciousness in Neuroscience, Meditation, and Philosophy*. New York: Columbia University Press, 2015.

Tiso, Francis V. *Rainbow Body and Resurrection: Spiritual Attainment, the Dissolution of the Material Body, and the Case of Khenpo a Chö*. Berkeley, CA: North Atlantic, 2016.

Tucker, Jim B. *Return to Life: Extraordinary Cases of Children who Remember Past Lives*. New York: St. Martin's Griffin, 2013.

Vaidya, P. L., ed. *Daśabhūmikasūtra*. Darbhanga: Mithila Institute, 1967.

———, ed. *Laṅkāvatārasūtra*. Darbhanga: Mithila Institute, 1963.

———, ed. *Saddharmapuṇḍarīka*. Darbhanga: Mithila Institute, 1960.

Vallée, Jacques. *Passport to Magonia: From Folklore to Flying Saucers*. 1969. Daily Grail, 2014.
van Shaik, Sam. *Buddhist Magic: Divination, Healing and Enchantment Through the Ages*. Boulder, CO: Shambhala, 2020.
Vogel, J. *Indian Serpent Lore, or The Nāgas In Hindu Legend And Art*. London: Arthur Probsthain, 1926.
Wahbeh, Helané, Dean Radin, Garret Yount, Michael A. Woodley of Menie, Matthew A. Sarraf, and Marcela V. Karpuj. "Genetics of Psychic Ability: A Pilot Case-Control Exome Sequencing Study." *Explore* 18, no. 3 (2022): 264–71.
Wangyal, Tenzin Rinpoche. 1998. *The Tibetan Yogas of Dream and Sleep*. New York: Snow Lion, 1998.
Weaver, Zofia. "Our History." Society for Psychical Research, 2022. https://www.spr.ac.uk/about/our-history.
Wehrstein, K. M. "Charles Tart." In *Psi Encyclopedia*. London: Society for Psychical Research, 2022. https://psi-encyclopedia.spr.ac.uk/articles/charles-tart .
West, D. 2019. "Society for Psychical Research." In *Psi Encyclopedia*. London: Society for Psychical Research, 2019. https://psi-encyclopedia.spr.ac.uk/articles/society-psychical-research.
White, David Gordon. *Sinister Yogis*. Chicago: University of Chicago Press, 2009.
Williams, Duncan Ryūken, and Christopher S. Queen, ed. *American Buddhism: Methods and Findings in Recent Scholarship*. Richmond: Curzon, 1999.
Williams, Paul, Anthony Tribe, and Alexander Wynne. *Buddhist Thought: A Complete Introduction to the Indian Tradition*. 2nd ed. London: Routledge, 2011.
Wilson, Liz. *Charming Cadavers: Horrific Figurations of the Feminine in Indian Buddhist Hagiographic Literature*. Chicago: University of Chicago Press, 1996.
Xue, Yu. "Merit Transfer and Life After Death in Buddhism." *Ching Feng* 4 no. 1 (2003): 29–50.
Zahavi, Dan. *Phenomenology: The Basics*. London: Routledge, 2019.

Index

abhiññā/abhijñā, 17, 20–23
altered states (of consciousness), xvi, 11, 12, 47, 51, 62, 83, 101, 123, 148, 157, 242, 277, 284n68, 298n39
Amitābha. *See* Buddha
astral body, 22, 126, 127, 129, 161, 177,
astral projection, 22, 64, 126, 127, 128, 129, 183, 295n6
Avalokiteśvara, 27, 150–52, 154, 269

bodhisattva, xvi, 25, 26–35, 36, 80, 136, 144, 148, 149–51, 154, 157, 174, 269–70; ideal, 25; path, 27–29; perfections, 27–28; stages, 28; vow, 26, 115
Buddha, 6–7, 9, 14, 20, 22–26, 30, 37, 39–40, 51, 87, 101, 104, 105, 110, 119, 122, 137, 138, 144, 145, 214, 246, 247, 252, 281n11, 282n40; Akṣobhya, 26, 37; Amitābha, 26, 27, 134, 148–49; Maitreya, 26, 90, 91; Padmasambhava, xvi, 149; Vairocana, 37, 149. *See also* Padmasambhava
Buddhism, xiv–xvii, 5–10, 39–41, 58, 71–73, 75, 84, 88, 91, 101, 120, 130, 134, 136, 144, 159, 189, 195, 204, 205, 211, 221, 240–41, 243, 244, 246–47; convert, 76; early, 14–15, 110, 116;

Indian, 1, 14–15, 16–20, 108; Japanese, 149–50; Mahāyāna, 4, 7, 8, 25–36, 115, 131; mainstream, 21–24; Pure Land, 134, 204; tantric, 36–39; Thai, 13, 104, 107–10, 143, 193, 199, 202–3, 215–16; Theravāda, 73, 103, 106, 107–10, 193, 196, 199, 215–18; Tibetan, 73, 77, 82, 106, 116–17, 131, 133, 134, 145, 152–56, 269. *See also* Zen

calm meditation, 19–21. *See also samatha/śamatha*
chaos magic, 13, 268–69
claircognizance, 194, 231, 252, 270–71
clairvoyance, 2, 3, 10, 11, 13, 15, 23, 40, 43, 44, 46, 47, 48–50, 52, 55, 59, 68–71, 77, 83, 85, 88, 129, 178, 191, 216, 241; definition, 76–77
concentration, 15, 16, 19, 21, 24, 35, 40, 77, 97, 98, 103, 106, 110, 117–18, 122, 123, 148, 182, 183–84, 189, 216, 243
Conze, Edward, xiv, 281n15, 284n69

Dass, Ram, 13, 162, 163, 165, 166–67, 175, 177, 242
Dee, John, 3

[313]

INDEX

demons, 2, 3, 15, 18, 40, 65, 136, 149, 176, 178–79, 189, 191, 299n14
determinism, 55, 88, 157, 159
deva, 90–91, 103, 129, 143, 144, 146–47, 200
dhyāna, 19, 28
Division of Perceptual Studies (DOPS), xvi, 56–58, 68, 110, 241
dream(s), xxi, 12, 27, 44, 47, 68, 85, 123, 135, 140–42, 148, 154, 155, 157, 167, 190, 207, 208–9, 217, 242, 248, 277; clairvoyant, 82–84; flying, 90, 128–29, 132; OBE, 126, 128–34; past life, 113–18; precognitive, 84, 88–95, 97–101, 128, 168–70, 176, 179–82, 184–86, 187–89, 191, 245, 254–58; telepathic, 101–3; world as, 27, 33–35; visitation, 140–41, 148, 176–77, 269; yoga, 39, 88, 131

emptiness, 7–8, 25, 27, 29, 34–35, 145, 156, 190, 247, 270,
extrasensory perception (ESP), 46, 57–60, 76, 83, 85, 90, 102, 123, 184, 241

Fort, Charles, 10, 44–46, 62, 68, 139–40, 241,
free will, 23, 55, 87, 88, 91, 101, 159–60, 184, 189, 243, 277
Fudō Myōō, 149–50

Gaṇḍavyūha-sūtra, 9, 31–36, 254. See also Supreme Array Scripture
ghosts, 3, 10, 12, 13, 18, 43, 45, 70, 103, 125, 136, 137, 140–44, 157, 193, 195, 197–201, 209, 214–16, 218–20, 223, 224, 226, 242, 273, 281n17, 292n114; hungry (preta), 18, 19, 24, 30, 41, 143; "whispering," 218
gods/goddesses, xvi, 2, 3, 12, 15, 18, 22, 30, 33, 78, 91, 128, 129, 136, 144, 147, 148–50, 157, 214, 215. See also deva
Guru Rinpoche. See Padmasambhava

hallucinations, 43, 133, 154, 158, 175, 190, 225, 231, 253, 257; hypnogogic, 96, 154, 226

Harvard, xv, 166, 195, 298n7
hypnosis, xi–xiii, xiv, 43–44, 47, 251

iddhi, 3, 17, 20–21, 38
imagination, xi–xii, 11, 18, 30, 36, 45, 69, 93, 101, 110, 142, 148, 226, 227, 270

jhāna, 19, 21, 24, 28, 116, 122. See also dhyāna

karate, xiv
karma, 8, 10, 12, 14–19, 23, 24, 27, 40, 70, 82–83, 86, 88, 91, 101, 104, 110, 116, 118, 123, 133, 140, 142, 144, 149, 155–57, 164, 165, 174, 177, 190, 193–95, 198, 199–201, 203, 204, 209, 210, 212, 224, 239, 240–43, 244, 247, 259; "death-approximate," 134
Kripal, Jeffrey, 4, 44, 45, 65, 279n1

Lindisfarne, 299n14
Lusthaus, Dan, 8, 34

Madhyamaka (Buddhism) 7–9, 27, 32
Mahākāla, 12, 153–55, 245, 269
Maitreya. See Buddha
Mañjuśrī, xvi, 27, 152, 270
meditation, xiv–xv, 10, 12, 13, 14–22, 24, 28, 35, 36, 41, 51–52, 55, 68, 69, 71, 74, 76, 77, 82, 83, 84, 85, 88, 90, 96–97, 101, 102, 108–10, 113–19, 121–23, 126, 128, 139, 145, 147–48, 151, 152, 154, 157, 159–65, 168–73, 182–84, 191, 195, 197, 199, 221, 241–44, 252–53, 269–70, 277; masters, 85–87, 104, 106–8, 119, 121, 127, 138, 143, 146. See also calm meditation; concentration; samādhi; samatha/śamatha; vipassana; zazen
Merleau-Ponty, Maurice, 4–5, 8–9

nāga, 18, 137–38, 144–47
Nāgārjuna, 7–9, 145
near-death experience (NDE), xvi, 1, 3, 49, 56–57, 69–70, 82, 125,

INDEX

126, 127, 134–35, 157, 161, 242, 279n1
nirvana, 7, 14, 20–26, 28, 29, 91, 214, 218, 247

out-of-body experience (OBE), 1, 3, 47, 49, 56, 70, 82, 94, 125–34, 157, 159, 161–62, 167, 183, 242, 279n1

Padmasambhava, xvi, 12, 133, 149
paranormal, xv–xvii, 1, 4–5, 9–13, 17, 41, 46, 47–48, 51–52, 56–58, 60, 62, 64–69, 70–72, 75–76, 78, 85, 87, 91, 93, 96, 101, 106, 110, 123, 125, 127, 129, 134–37, 140, 142, 156–58, 160–61, 163–65, 167, 173, 177–78, 180, 182, 184, 189, 191–92, 194–96, 220–25, 239, 240–49, 250–51, 277–78; definition, 2–3; as "normal," 146–47
parapsychology, 44–47, 50, 53, 59, 68, 241
past life memories. *See* retrocognition
phenomenology, 4–6, 8–9, 13, 34, 120, 177, 240, 245–49
precognition, 2, 3, 10, 11, 13, 16, 23, 44, 46, 47–49, 52, 55–57, 64, 68, 70, 71, 77, 83, 84–101, 128–29, 155, 159, 167, 169–70, 176, 182, 184–86, 187–89, 191, 194, 206, 208, 216, 217–18, 228–31, 235, 241–42, 245, 251, 252, 253–58, 270–71, 277, 294n18, 299n14; definition, 85
Presti, David, 58, 71
psi (psychic), 2, 3, 10, 11, 24, 25, 47–52, 56, 91, 96, 103, 113, 123, 124, 140, 165, 178, 193, 194, 209, 216, 217, 242, 243, 248, 250, 251, 276; abilities 10, 13, 49–50, 52, 55, 59, 68–69, 85, 87, 103, 120, 123, 137–39, 177, 194, 217, 228, 231, 234, 238, 241, 243, 252–53; phenomena, 3, 11, 30, 48, 51, 52, 55, 57–60, 62, 65, 91, 96, 113, 137, 225; research, 11, 24, 46–55, 57–62, 68, 241
psychic abilities, 10, 11, 15, 17, 20–23, 27, 38–40, 45, 48–51, 55, 57, 59–61, 64, 68, 77, 87, 101, 103–6, 108–10, 118, 119–23, 138–39, 158, 183, 189, 194, 216, 240–41, 243, 246, 279n1. *See also* psi
psychokinesis (PK), 13, 44, 45, 46–48, 50, 52–55, 58–60, 64, 70, 118, 120, 123, 241, 275–77. *See also* telekinesis
psychology, xiv, xv, 18, 27, 46, 47, 50, 53, 57, 247. *See also* parapsychology

Radin, Dean, 10, 50–56, 58, 68, 85, 94, 101–2, 228, 241, 275, 277
ṛddhi. *See* iddhi
rebirth, 7, 12, 14, 15–19, 21, 23–24, 58, 70, 110–18, 131, 134, 143–44, 149, 157, 198, 201, 203, 212, 240, 242, 244, 247. *See also* reincarnation
regression (hypnotic), xiii, xv; past life, 113
reincarnation, 10, 49, 56–57, 68, 241. *See also* rebirth
retrocognition, 3, 11, 70, 110–18, 177–78, 241; definition, 110
Rhine, J. B., 10, 46–47, 58, 68, 101, 241

sādhanā, xvi, 74, 172, 182, 184, 189, 190, 238, 243, 270
samādhi, 16, 26, 77, 103–6, 122, 139, 147, 166, 167. *See also* concentration
samatha/śamatha, 19, 21, 24, 74, 122,
School of Oriental and African Studies (SOAS), xv–xvi, 255, 264
Shingon, 73, 149,
siddhi, 3, 16, 17, 38, 50, 52–53, 216–1
spirits, 3, 10, 12, 13, 15, 18, 40, 42, 70, 125, 136, 137, 140, 144, 146, 148, 157, 193–94, 198, 200–201, 206, 209–12, 217–18, 242, 243, 273. *See also* ghosts
Stevenson, Ian, xvi, 10, 56–57, 68, 110, 111, 241
suchness, 7, 247
Supreme Array Scripture, 9, 31–37, 254,

Tart, Charles, 10, 47–50, 58, 68, 101, 241
telekinesis, 2, 16, 57, 120, 275. *See also* psychokinesis

[315]

telepathy, 3, 10, 11, 13, 14, 16, 23, 43, 44–49, 52–56, 58–59, 64, 68–70, 71, 101–2, 107, 109, 119, 129, 136, 167, 171, 178, 184–85, 191, 216–17, 241, 253, 258–64, 289n47, 292n114; definition, 101
Tendai, 73, 149,
transcendental meditation (TM), xiv

UAP. *See* UFOs
UFOs, 10, 44, 45, 62–66

Vallée, Jacques, 10, 62, 64, 65, 68, 245
Vairocana. *See* Buddha
vipassana, xv, 19, 74, 183, 253

yoga, 3, 12, 13, 15–16, 37–38, 50–52, 128, 135, 159, 160–64, 171, 182–83, 242; deity, 74; dream, 38, 88, 128, 131; guru, 74; sexual, 36–38
Yogācāra (Buddhism), 8–9, 27, 29, 32, 33, 34,

zazen, 74, 128, 134, 162, 204, 259, 296n12,
Zen (Buddhism), xiv, xv, 33, 73, 84, 86, 104, 109, 204
zen meditation, xiv, xv, 84, 85, 96. *See also* zazen

GPSR Authorized Representative: Easy Access System Europe, Mustamäe tee
50, 10621 Tallinn, Estonia, gpsr.requests@easproject.com

www.ingramcontent.com/pod-product-compliance
Lightning Source LLC
Chambersburg PA
CBHW022031290426
44109CB00014B/820